W9-CEA-109

The SOUL of Popular Culture

The SOUL of Popular Culture

Looking at Contemporary Heroes, Myths, and Monsters

Edited by Mary Lynn Kittelson

OPEN COURT
Chicago and La Salle, Illinois

The image used on the front cover is from the *anime* movie, *The Wings of Honneamise,* © 1987, 1995 Bandai Vis.

Open Court Publishing Company is a division of Carus Publishing Company.

Copyright © 1998 by Carus Publishing Company

First printing 1998

All rights reserved. No part of this publication may be reproduced, stored in a retrieval system, or transmitted, in any form or by any means, electronic, mechanical, photocopying, recording, or otherwise, without the prior written permission of the publisher, Open Court Publishing Company, 315 Fifth Street, P.O. Box 300, Peru, Illinois 61354-0300.

Printed and bound in the United States of America.

Library of Congress Cataloging-in-Publication Data

The soul of popular culture : looking at contemporary heroes, myths,
    and monsters / edited by Mary Lynn Kittelson.
        p.   cm.
    Includes bibliographical references and index.
    ISBN 0-8126-9363-9 (pbk : alk. paper)
    1. Psychoanalysis and culture. 2. Jungian psychology.   3. Popular
culture—Psychological aspects.   I. Kittelson, Mary Lynn, 1946–   .
BF175.4.C84S68   1998
306—dc21   97-31982
                                                               CIP

Contents

Part III
The Mirror of Culture: Finding
Ourselves Within

Acknowledgments

The original impetus for this collection of essays was a series of talks delivered in St. Paul, Minnesota, in the fall of 1994 by the Minnesota Region Jungian analysts and I-RSJA (Inter-Regional Society of Jungian Analysts) training candidates. That symposium, entitled "Psyche in America," centered on the mythical image of the beautiful Psyche, a mortal woman whose name means "soul." As in the myth of Eros and Psyche, we imagined the psyche or soul of America wandering lost, undergoing trial after trial, abandoned, frustrated, and even tortured.

Louise Mahdi, who attended the talks, provided the spark for publishing a book of essays incorporating some of the presentations delivered in St. Paul, but as we thought about the possible volume and discussed the possibilities with Open Court editors, we came to see the need to focus on contemporary popular culture as expressing the soul of the American culture, and we then began to work with essays from other sources too.

Kerri Mommer of Open Court guided this collection through the rocky shoals of all its many stages. I am grateful for her editorial acuity, her steady hand, and her many fruitful suggestions.

As it turned out, ideas for topics, writers, and the overall format came from many scattered and serendipitous sources. It has been a fascinating and delightful process. Among the many people who have helped, I particularly wish to thank Lyn Cowan, Marita Digney, John Beebe, Ted Tollefson, the Minnesota Jung Association, as well as David Ramsay Steele and the other people at Open Court.

The authors of these essays, which had to be crafted to fit the aims of this collection, really deserve the most gratitude. They endured the challenges of writing for this book in good and resolute spirit. This project demanded a great deal of time and energy, involving, in complex ways, the mind, the heart, and, last but not least, the ego! I am grateful for the heartfelt energy and high quality of the work of each of the contributors.

About the Authors

GARY D. ASTRACHAN, Ph.D., is a clinical psychologist and Jungian analyst in private practice in Portland, Maine. He was a docent at the C.G. Jung Institute in Zurich, Switzerland, during the 1980s, is now a faculty member of the C.G. Jung Institute in Boston, and regularly lectures and gives workshops throughout North America and Europe. He is the author of numerous scholarly articles, particularly on the relationship between analytical psychology and Greek mythology, and is currently working on a book on the Greek god Dionysos.

JOHN BEEBE is a Jungian analyst in practice in San Francisco. He lectures frequently on films that reflect the American psyche and can be seen discussing American movies in the 1989 documentary film, *The Wisdom of the Dream*. Editor of *The San Francisco Jung Institute Library Journal,* he is the author of *Integrity in Depth* (1992) and the editor of C.G. Jung's *Aspects of the Masculine* (1997).

DOLORES E. BRIEN has a Ph.D. in American Civilization from Brown University at Providence, Rhode Island. She is the editor of *The Round Table Review*, a journal of contemporary contributions to Jungian psychology (http://www.cgjung.com/rtreview.html) and also contributes regularly to the website C.G. Jung, Analytical Psychology and Culture (http://www.cgjung.com) on such topics as the impact of technology on American life. In addition, she is a co-sponsor with Donald Williams of the ongoing discussion program, Jung-Book-Talks. Her e-mail address is RTReview@aol.com.

LYN COWAN, Ph.D., is a Jungian analyst in private practice in St. Paul, Minnesota, former Director of Training for the Inter-Regional Society of Jungian Analysts (a national Jungian training institute) and Professor of Psychology at the Minnesota School of Professional Psychology. She has essays in several anthologies, two photographs in *When I Am An Old Woman I Shall Wear Purple* (Papier-Mâché Press, 1987), and is the author of *Masochism: A Jungian View* (Spring Publications, 1982).

JOHN DESTEIAN, J.D., is a Jungian analyst in private practice in St. Paul, Minnesota. He is author of *Coming Together, Coming Apart* (Sigo, 1990) and Adjunct Professor of Analytical Psychology at the Minnesota School of Professional Psychology.

MARITA DIGNEY, D.Min., is a Jungian analyst and licensed psychologist in private practice in Philadelphia. She worked for many years as a counselor with adolescents. Following her own individuation path to California, she earned additional degrees in theology and ministry at the Graduate Theological Union at Berkeley. She is founder of the C.G. Jung Society of West Jersey, teaches at the Philadelphia Jung Institute, and has given workshops and retreats on feminine spirituality, initiation, and healing.

NANCY DOUGHERTY is a Jungian analyst in private practice in Birmingham, Michigan, and a member of the Chicago Society of Jungian Analysts. She has done numerous presentations on vampires from a variety of perspectives. She is currently working on a book about the archetypal roots of psychopathology with Jungian analyst Jacqueline West.

CLARISSA PINKOLA ESTÉS, Ph.D., is an internationally acclaimed poet, scholar, Jungian psychoanalyst, and *cantadora*, keeper of the old stories in the Latina tradition. She is the former Executive Director of the C.G. Jung Center for Education and Research, and has been in private practice for 26 years. Recipient of the Joseph Campbell "Keeper of the Lore" award, and the *Las Primeras* Award from the Mexican-American Women's Foundation, her prize-winning audio works are broadcast by community and National Public Radio networks across North America. Published books: *The Gift of Story*; *The Faithful Gardener*; and *Women Who Run With the Wolves*. She is a lifelong member of *La Sociedad de Guadalupe*.

KEVIN JONES is a licensed psychologist in private practice in the Twin Cities, Minnesota. He is an assistant professor at Saint Mary's University, teaching in the Graduate Counselling and Psychological Services Department and the Human Development Program. His enduring interests include archetypal psychology, phenomenological philosophy, and the *Star Trek* video collection in his basement (350 and counting . . .).

MARY LYNN KITTELSON is a Jungian analyst in private practice in the Twin Cities, Minnesota. She lectures, teaches, and leads workshops on animals, sound, shadow, dreams, image work, and other Jungian-related topics, and writes and edits professionally. She has published articles in a professional anthology and two journals and is author of *Sounding the Soul: The Art of Listening* (Daimon Verlag, 1996).

LYDIA S. LENNIHAN is a writer, painter, mythologist, and Jungian psychotherapist in Denver, Colorado. She has a master's degree in mythology and depth psychology from Pacifica Graduate Institute. Her primary field of research is the analysis of film as contemporary mythology, which incorporates Jungian theory, image, cultural identity, and memory.

ANTONIA LEVI is a writer and college admissions consultant in Portland, Oregon. Her Ph.D. is in history, and she has taught at the University of Southern California and Loyola Marymount University in Los Angeles, California State University in Long Beach, Amherst/Mt. Holyoke College in Massachusetts, and Whitman College in Washington State. She has published numerous articles on animation and Japan, as well as *Samurai from Outer Space: Understanding Japanese Animation* (Open Court, 1996). She writes a regular column for *Animeco*, a magazine about Japanese animation.

JAMES W. MAERTENS is a writer and Adjunct Professor of Humanities at Lakeland Medical-Dental Academy in Minneapolis, Minnesota, where he teaches a course in science, medicine, and culture. His Ph.D. is in English and he also writes fiction. He is associate editor of *Mythos Journal*, a publication of Mythos Institute, Minneapolis, Minnesota.

ELIZABETH MASIÉE has a background in humanities. She has directed two art galleries, written, edited, and designed books, and published essays and articles on creativity and the arts, with special interest in encouraging people to watch television as actively as they read books. She has also produced documentaries, videotaped dramatizations shown in universities, and filmed "Leonardo: To Know How to See." Currently, she is finishing the third of a trilogy of biographies of women artists and scripting another documentary for next year. And she is teaching multi-media, which incorporates all the arts—as do those Muses.

MARY ANN MATTOON, Ph.D., is a Jungian analyst in private practice in Minneapolis, Minnesota. She is a Professor of Clinical Psychology at the University of Minnesota and has taught and lectured widely. She is author of *Understanding Dreams, Jungian Psychology in Perspective* (a college textbook), and *Jungian Psychology after Jung*. Her interest in politics is longstanding.

MARY ANN MILLER, M.S.W., is a Jungian analyst in private practice in the Twin Cities, Minnesota. She also holds master's degrees in Library Science and Children's Literature. She teaches and lectures on Jungian topics, with a special interest in story, both in the traditional form of fairy tales and in the work of contemporary storytellers like Garrison Keillor.

ALMIRA F. POUDRIER is currently pursuing her doctorate in classics and ancient history at the State University of New York, Buffalo. She has had an abiding interest in *Star Trek* since she was secretary of the Beloit Science Fiction and Fantasy Association, and her interest in Jung developed while she was working as a teaching assistant in mythology.

JUDITH SAVAGE is a Jungian analyst in private practice in the Twin Cities, Minnesota, a licensed independent clinical social worker and a licensed marriage and family therapist. She is a frequent teacher and lecturer and is active in analytic training. She is author of *Mourning Unlived Lives: A Psychological Study of Childbearing Losses* (Chiron, 1989).

JANE ALEXANDER STEWART, Ph.D., is a clinical psychologist working and living in Los Angeles. In addition to a twenty-year private practice, she lectures and writes, especially on the topic of films as contemporary carriers and activators of cultural mythology. She has focused on diverse topics, including such subjects as the emerging feminine hero, the myth of time, and patriarchy with heart. She prepared a film series presentation at the L.A. County Museum of Art entitled "Tracking the Edge of the American Dream."

TED E. TOLLEFSON is a community-based minister affiliated with the Unitarian Universalist Association centered in Boston, Massachusetts, co-founder of Mythos Institute in the Twin Cities and Frontenac, Minnesota, and editor of *Mythos Journal,* an occasional quarterly celebrating the symbolic life in myth, dreams, rituals, folklore, and emergent mythologies (e-mail: mythos@mr.net). He teaches comparative religion at United Theological Seminary in New Brighton, Minnesota, and psychology at Metro State University in Minneapolis, Minnesota.

DONALD WILLIAMS has been a Jungian analyst in private practice in Boulder, Colorado, since 1976. His background was originally literature, and he has an active interest in film and in psychological reflections on psychoanalysis and culture. He has published a book, *Border Crossings* (Inner City Books, 1981) and numerous articles, mostly in film and Jungian journals. He is editor of the website, C.G. Jung, Analytical Psychology, and Culture (www.cgjung.com).

Editor's Introduction

The news, the media, the Internet, the global marketplace—it has never been clearer that in our times, we are players in a theater of dynamic social forces. As individuals and as citizens, we are interdependent, our lives linked up and bound together in ways that we cannot really fathom. Our world is complex, exciting, sensational, fast-paced, and often worrisome, as we move past the marker of the third millennium A.D. The cries of apocalypse accompanying this special turning of the calendar express our already-strong desire for more soul in our lives. We want to uncover some essential meaning in our culture. We want to know who we are and where we are going.

Without a doubt, the search for soulfulness, for our own values as a culture, is a major preoccupation of ours. Whether we couch it in terms that are religious or spiritual, philosophical or educational, political or scientific, the questions remain: Where do the deepest values lie in our culture? What directions and interconnections can we glimpse, what patterns are operating in our lives? Are there deeper or larger energies guiding us?

Where do we go to find answers to such questions of meaning—or for that matter, where do we go to find even the right questions? Collected here are the voices of some bringers of meaning. Many writers in this collection call themselves Jungians, and all are interested in bringing to light the way the soul lives in contemporary life. They have turned their attention to our liveliest energies as a society, that is, our social issues and obsessions, and especially our popular culture, whose life and color, and some would say superficiality, have in fact spread across the globe.

On this cultural level, just like on the individual level, there is a great deal more going on than we pick up consciously. *Our thesis is that in the popular culture and in the issues that engage us, we can discover information, patterns, and propensities that express the psyche, the soul, the deep places of meaning in the culture.* At its deepest level, the contributors to this book address the culture's crucial struggle with accusations of soullessness and meaninglessness during this millennial transition, with its inescapable imperative to change.

These subliminal layers, these less conscious levels of meaning and energy, are central to the way that the culture perceives and acts. The very fact that a great number of us participate widely in popular culture and in social issues and events means that the energy they carry is vital, not only expressing, but also influencing and even guiding our lives. In order to see these forces in the culture, we need to shift our gaze to what is moving

1

beneath the surface and what is hovering in the periphery of our focused gaze. We need to include the symbolic and archetypal levels as we seek for the "unconscious" of the cultural soul.

The Cultural Unconscious

Until recently, there has been relatively little Jungian writing which directly addresses societal issues, barring a few writers, among them, James Hillman, Andrew Samuels, and Arnold Mindell. Add to them the resonant voices of Joseph Campbell, Clarissa Pinkola Estés, and Thomas Moore, who have also won the ear of the culture. But like many schools of psychology, Jungians have concentrated on the individual; most Jungian work has shown a preference for introversion, and for seeking wholeness *from within oneself.* The core of Jungian thought concerns itself with the limits of "one-sidedness" and the necessity of "holding the tensions," an approach which complicates taking a stand on many societal and political decisions.

However, it is also central to Jungian theory that the psyche, the soul, operates not only on the individual level, but also on collective levels: families, communities, nations, global communities. And on the broadest level, it lives in the collective unconscious, that vast repository of images, structured by the archetypes, which provides the framework for the psyche of all humans.

In these essays, writers exercise a well-practiced ability to attend to the myths and symbols of the culture. They offer an eye and ear trained to the images and archetypes of our lives. Using psychological x-ray vision, the contributors, each in his or her own way, attempt to "see through" to the deep structures behind our cultural life. They discuss the figures and stories that are central to our lives, ones which reveal the stuff of our own souls, explaining how they structure and influence our cultural values, thoughts, and feelings. They illuminate and interpret our basic cultural fantasies and dreams.

Granted, it cannot be assumed that the "psychology of a culture" is like the psychology of an individual person. A culture is a highly complex organism, subject to a web of economic, societal, historical, and political forces. However, we do think of a country or culture as having a personality of sorts, and acting certain ways, such as "belligerent," "peace-loving," or "arrogant"; and we speak of countries as having "consumer confidence" or going through a "depression" or an "inflation," or indeed, exhibiting the "irrational exuberance" of the American Stock Exchange, as Mr. Greenspan, Chair of the Federal Reserve Board, has put it. It is not such a large leap to discuss cultural events as having a psychological side, as having to do with the mental health of a culture. And especially when issues are thematic or recurrent, it is only a small step farther to consider the possibility that cultures, like individuals, might have psychological "complexes," that is, certain typical patterns of attitude and behavior.

In the language of depth psychology, cultures have unconscious layers too. In Western society, we assume as citizens of "developed countries" that we are conscious and rational beings, rarely questioning the accuracy of this idea, much less its value as an ideal. Depth psychology questions both. It tells us that becoming more exclusively conscious or rational does not mean becoming wise or fully complete. On the contrary, it might well mean that we become more limited or one-sided in our outlook, more separated from the flow of the many kinds of energy in the world we inhabit, even though, all the while, we feel ourselves to be "on top of it."

We cannot really control things—in the larger world or in our own lives. The growing interest in Field Theory and Chaos Theory may indicate that we are finally getting over our infatuation stage with rationality, where applying linear logic is all that we can think of. In the intricate discussion on the state of the world in the film *Mind Walk*, the phrase "a crisis of perception" runs through like a leitmotiv, suggesting it is not so much the world, but our perception of it that is changing. Culturally as well as personally, we are awakening to a fuller reality than our current one, which has placed our own conscious and "controlled" selves as the center of the universe. Our shift in perception is as profound as when, in the sixteenth and seventeenth centuries, Western culture was struggling mightily to accept the Copernican theory that the Sun, and not our Earth, was the center of our system of planets.

The Images of the Culture

From a Jungian perspective, the way that the cultural psyche or soul reveals itself is through its images and dreams, wherever they occur. The most widespread and often the most vivid societal images are found in the society's popular culture; and thus to get a sense of the fullness and richness of this cultural soul, we need to explore its images. These images do not always have to be profound in an obvious way, for neither are many of our most interesting and revealing personal dreams that we may interpret and analyze. It is often beyond their surface meaning that these cultural images reveal us to ourselves. They show us vital aspects of what is in our heads and on our minds. Images flash before us in the shadows and light of our movies and on our TV screens. They live in all of the stories we read and watch and listen to on TV, radio, video, the Internet, and in the newspaper.

We have never before had this kind of access to our own images, or indeed, been so bombarded by them. TV is now the "hearth," the new center, of the culture, with current news reports stating that the average American watches an average of seven hours per day. Reports on local, national, and global events run nonstop in our homes. Increasing numbers of children and adults are glued to the tube, netted in the Web. In our consumer culture, marketing images are "in our face."

Yet for all the ubiquity of news and marketing images, it is the movies which most clearly portray our cultural dreams, and the main topic in twelve of the essays in this book. In a striking way, movies are like the collective culture dreaming: we assemble in darkened spaces, experiencing together an intense world of images. More directly than any other cultural phenomenon, the movies invite us to experience and ponder our lives and culture. But movies are also the culture dreaming while partially awake and indeed, the culture dreaming itself awake. Whether their quality is good or poor, movies are playing out the various levels of consciousness before our very eyes, offering us insight as we step into another world and then back out to our own lives. These flickering images of light and dark are bringing something necessary for our psychic[1] health. They make us think and feel, in great cultural waves, in a way that nothing else can.

Movies, like good television, show us how commonly that important issues show up in our everyday lives. On the black-and-white movie screens of the 1940s and 1950s, we discovered again and again, probably with some shock, that evil lurks in the simplest of neighborhoods. In our times, the dominant culture is assumed to have a great deal of bad or evil. In America, what we used to call evil is just part of doing business, just part of the landscape. It is good movies like *Pulp Fiction*, *Thelma and Louise*, and *The Silence of the Lambs* that help us see and understand our problems, often from a new angle.

While movies are an obvious source of cultural soul, our symbols and motifs also live in vivid ways in the media, in our public policies, our political events and issues, in our nonstop parade of ads and fads, and in all our cultural obsessions. Our assumptions, that is, the stories we are living in, are also clearly revealed in our budget allocations, our education policies, the Gulf War, and the craze for large-screen TVs, Beanie Babies, or Barbie dolls. Any of these are valid topics for "analyzing" the psychic life of the culture. Such dreams and themes of our culture arise with a seeming spontaneity, playing themselves out in the contemporary cultural scene. In this atmosphere of extraversion and attention to the outer world only, we do not get the chance to attend carefully to the imagination of the culture. We miss the chance to be audience to this theater of the soul of contemporary culture, with all of its play of themes and images.

The Unconscious Matters

The unconscious energies of our lives have a purpose, say depth psychologists. There is a kind of conversation going on between what we are conscious of in the moment, and our less conscious or unconscious attitudes, which nonetheless exert energy and power in our lives. Indeed, if these less conscious elements are too much ignored or exploited, they rise up in frustrated, inferior, maladapted forms, and with an especially strong force

---

[1] In common usage, "psychic" means beyond sensory perception, as in "ESP." In this psychological usage however, "psychic" simply means "having to do with the psyche or the mind."

which often feels inexplicable. Then as a culture, we swing from one pole to the other, without a sense of center or security. Caught in the grip of unconscious forces, we become prone to cultural obsessions, fads, and rages, official or condoned scapegoating of certain groups, "mad" political decisions, or even more serious, collective delusions, like a cultural psychosis.

In reaching toward our "cultural unconscious," we come into contact with our own dark and unknown sides, our own shadows. They are not far away, confronting us as they do in the guise of the "other," the "enemy," the "alien," which we then denigrate or reject. If we can notice and engage with the images and "dreams" of the culture, pleasant and unpleasant, we can learn a great deal more about ourselves.

Granted, this depth view of reality is complicated. It operates not by linear logic or rationality, but according to emotional and psychic patterns set by the needs of psychic life, by archetypal energies; in parallel fashion, our physical needs for food, safety, and reproduction are set by instinctual patterns. An approach that associative and imaginative is the best way to understand the reality of the psyche and its images. Rationality is, after all, a foreigner in the unconscious. Meaning occurs by means of metaphor, juxtaposition, multiple layers of thought or feeling; synchronicity matters. If we can be in contact with this deeper level of cultural knowledge, with this deeper wisdom, in a grounded way, we will be enriched. We will be able to connect better to our past and to the "other," to those of different persuasions, all around us. A depth view is necessary to our psychic health as a culture.

If we pay some attention to the less conscious aspects of cultural life, we may also get a better sense of where we are going. A discussion of cultural images not only helps us sort out the past and present, but it also helps us move into the future. In the less conscious stories and images of our culture, in the behind-the-scenes images and myths they suggest, may well lie the clearest indications of what is happening. As a matter of fact, this perception of potentiality, of what might be "trying" to come into being (at a largely unconscious level), is a particular forte of Jungian psychology, with its attention to *finality*—the direction something is headed toward—as well as *causality*—what it came or resulted from, which is the main focus of Freudian psychology. In watching for what is only just taking shape, we can be in an ongoing relationship with the next step.

Imagination is "Real"

Jungian thought offers the paradoxical yet wise idea that things become real through being in contact with the imagination. In our culture, we tend to treat imagination as only fluff or play. The authors of these essays describe, in many different contexts, just how "real" imagination is, that is, just how *psychically* real it is. This is to say that imagination guides our very sense of what *is* real. These essays elucidate some of the powerful ways the different underlying "myths" of our lives create our sense of meaning. Only when we see the hidden dreams and images that shape us can we get closer to a sense of what is real. Only then can we trust that our perceptions have validity in more than our own small world, that our lives have dimension and depth.

In our high-power efforts to develop consciousness and rationality, we have forgotten a central truth of our psyches: that *we have to dream,* and that *we are dreaming,* at some level, all the time. An accurate sense of reality requires an interplay of dreaming, fantasy, some play of an imaginative field, to be reliable. Our world is not a fixed world of true/false, but a world of subjectivities and probabilities, at best. Indeed, it is full of upsets and surprises, and contrary to our popular notion, these are not necessarily related to a failure of our rationality or to an insufficient data base. In the psyche's overlapping layers of energy, whether in the personal or cultural sphere, many events seem to occur spontaneously. There occurs an impish persistence of unscheduled events, far beyond our efforts at rationality or "happiness" control. Witness how rarely we can will ourselves out of over-eating, depression, or addiction. On a political level, witness the fall of the Berlin Wall!

Clearly, imagination *happens.* Its ties are with the unconscious, and as Jung was fond of saying, the unconscious is *unconscious!* Wherever cultural fantasy shows itself, that is, in the media and the arts, in fads, in regional and national events, we discover surprises, delights, and sometimes shocks. We are reminded that our culture is really, in its essence, a complicated and mysterious entity.

Heroes, Myths, and Monsters

The Soul of Popular Culture addresses many themes, from abortion and false memory syndrome to the Miss America Pageant. This collection cannot claim to cover all of the important areas in contemporary culture, but it does present a lively discussion of some of the most important topics. Many contributors discuss cultural themes by focusing on a movie, television show, media event, or some figure in contemporary culture, like the vampire, Garrison Keillor, Elvis Presley, or O.J. Simpson. Others address societal issues like violence, AIDS, gender roles, or abortion, attending to the meaning in their images, ear to the ground for the archetypal energies, for the voices of the "gods and goddesses" who are silently, invisibly informing these conflicts.

As Joseph Campbell has explained so well, when we say "myths," we do not mean "untrue stories," but rather, our essential storylines, recurrent ones which run deep in the psyche of the culture. These mythic themes, which express our deepest goals and values, give dramatic credence to our everyday lives in the shape of their settings, characters, and plots. They operate like our own individual dreams do, through the power of imagination, as they work on and play with issues in our inner and outer lives. With their archetypal background invisibly informing them, these cultural images and imaginings allow us to try out different modes, different roles. They play out challenges and problems, ones we may not be quite conscious of, pulling us deeper into one angle, trying out this scenario or that.

Myths show us basic patterns having to do with vital aspects of our lives: how to relate and love, how to come into mature femininity or masculinity, how to deal with change (win a new kingdom), how to deal with god or fate, how to deal with wounds. All myths have heroes in the sense of protagonists or main characters. But in our language here, the term "hero myths" refers to the kind of stories that teach us about dealing with obstacles, and sometimes learning from them, those that we encounter in the world, also those that lie within us, in our own attitudes.

For example, during the earliest years of the settlement of North America by Europeans, hero myths about Paul Bunyan or Johnny Appleseed sprang up, as did mythical tales based on real-life characters such as Daniel Boone and Davy Crockett. These myths told of the tenacity, strength, and toughness necessary to strike out and settle the "wilderness," to wrestle it into the shape of a Europeanlike civilization. In the inner world, hero myths tell the story of how people gain control and mastery over their own wilderness of energies, gaining practical and rational understanding of how to achieve defined purposes.

But myths change with the demands of the times, in response to new requirements. Nowadays, some knowledge of the Native American societies that were already present has permeated the society, and a certain proportion of us recognizes the great value of the native cultures that our forebears overran. Consciousness has changed, even to the extent that some leaders are looking to these formerly conquered peoples for guidance and balance. However, in settlement times, Paul Bunyan and Davy Crockett defined and inspired our way. Since then, heroic figures, whether totally or partially fictive, have stridden through the arena of our popular culture and the media, entertaining, challenging, and inspiring us in their specific ways. They include figures like Horatio Alger, Buck Rogers, Rosie the Riveter, the Lone Ranger, Martin Luther King, Luke Skywalker, and Xena, Warrior Princess, to name just a few.

In such examples, we see different ways that heroes show us "the right way" to act and think. There have always been different kinds of heroes for different kinds of tasks, all the way from the immensely powerful Hercules of Greek myth, whose strength is still legendary, to the unimposing Dummling in fairy tales, who saves the kingdom by listening to the neglected, the undervalued, the "odd" side of the issue. In mythology and folktales, it is the particular task of "the hero" to deal with evil. In this book, the cultural image of hero is addressed from many angles, sometimes as main theme and sometimes as a secondary subject. In our culture, our heroes have tended to be portrayed as strong, conquering, all-good, and always-winning. One theme in this collection, which different essays develop in different ways, is that this cultural hero figure seems to be shifting, or at the least, showing more faces.

Our usual kind of hero is one who fights evil as "other." He or she thus remains youthful—*too* strong, in a way—naive about himself or herself. But nowadays we seem to be seeing a more soulful kind of hero, whose concerns are not only winning in the world, but more importantly, leading a life of depth, walking a path of spiritual wisdom. This is a figure who can navigate what Jungians call "the second half of life," or undertake a journey of soul. Here, you do not only, or always, overcome evil. This kind of hero must know enough of evil in her or his inner self and also in the outside world. Naive purity and muscles do not suffice. Neither does mere cleverness. Humility matters, and a sense of perspective. In dealing with this deeper "quest," our new hero must allow in a confusing totality, a mix and flow of good and bad, weakness and strength, as shamans do. As you will read, so do Jules in *Pulp Fiction* (chapters 10 and 11) and Clarice Starling in *The Silence of the Lambs* (chapter 2), in their different ways, and so do the heroes in now-popular Japanese animation.

The theme of monsters, on the other hand, touches on all that is monstrous in us, all that is dark, inferior, undeveloped, evil. "Without the integration of evil," says Jung, "there is no totality" (par. 232). The essays in Part I deal with this dark side of ourselves as a central theme, most directly in Maertens's essay on the Jurassic Park "dragons" (chapter 13) and Dougherty's on vampires (chapter 12). But, like the theme of heroes, this monster theme runs throughout. In fact, heroes and monsters form natural opposites in a great many myths, with the monster trying to devour the hero, and the hero trying to overcome or kill the monster. But as in all confrontations, there are hidden aspects, ones important to know about, especially in the long run. For these heroes, often representing consciousness or ego, can be too one-sided in their goals, and blind to the big picture; and these monsters, with their primordial and unconscious force, can sometimes offer the energies we need most—in fact, those very ones we have neglected and rejected and thus see before us in their neglected, maligned, and malformed shapes.

Indeed, for a Jungian, it is as common to champion monsters as to conquer them, for it is a basic tenet that the dark side and the unconscious can offer necessary and balancing energies, ones which are full of creative potential. Coming into a right relationship with the monster, with the monstrousness in our own lives, involves a combination of confrontation and yet some basic respect. And such a process can sometimes transform its threatening aspects into spiritual gifts.

The Essays

Part I, entitled "Heroes and Myths: The Deep Structure of Ourselves," has as its central theme a seeing through to the gods and goddesses whose myths, that is, whose energies and patterns, underlie cultural events and societal issues. The gods and figures of myth move through our cultural landscape in many of these essays in this collection; but in this section, heroes, monsters, and myths in general are our central focus.

The wise and strong voice of CLARISSA PINKOLA ESTÉS begins the book, with her essay, entitled "Elvis Presley: *Fáma* and the *Cultus* of the Dying God" (chapter 1). Weaving personal reminiscence, her experience as a practicing Jungian psychoanalyst, and her own research, Dr. Estés, with quiet yet hair-raising eloquence, tells us of the unconscious blood sacrifice in our own culture of Elvis "The King," and others too of godlike fame, who have died untimely deaths. In connecting to this pattern of the dying god, a deeply mythic one, we can see the heart-breaking consequences of a starved culture filling its deepest needs. The reality and appetite of these cultural hungers Estés reveals to us in Estés's inimitable style of clarity and depth, which speaks to both mind and heart.

JANE ALEXANDER STEWART's "The Feminine Hero of *The Silence of the Lambs*" (chapter 2), with its stunning introduction, is a beautifully descriptive and acutely analytic look at the heroic journey of the feminine. Clarice Starling, a young FBI agent-in-training, enters into a deep and terrifying encounter with the cannibal psychopath, Hannibal Lecter. The way that she holds to the feminine values of relatedness and emotional honesty, the way she maintains an equilibrium with—instead of attempting a full-scale vanquishing of—the darkest evil are the expression of feminine values. Such a role, says Stewart, is quietly and profoundly radical, and a further step toward equal partnership between masculine and feminine energies.

ANTONIA LEVI returns to the theme of a redefinition of the hero in her sharply informative look (chapter 3) at the American hunger for a new kind of hero, one made from a more widely human mold, exemplified in Japanese cartoons. The considerable popularity in this country of *anime* (Japanese animation) and *manga* (Japanese comic books), says Levi, indicates our interest in and our need for a new definition of hero, one who has failures and flaws. This kind of hero, only recently appreciated in Western popular culture, can sometimes make mistakes or lose the battle, and can even be on the wrong side, as long as he or she has loyalty and "heart."

Next, MARITA DIGNEY (chapter 4) discusses our national obsession with one of our current heroes, or one of our many fallen heroes, O.J. Simpson. She compares his situation with that of Hercules, discovering in the process many broad and some minor but stunning similarities. The Hercules Complex, asserts Digney, is a central problem and has to do with the rampant violence, rage, and domestic abuse in our culture. She suggests that the myth of Hercules is helpful in clarifying the characteristics and origins of this complex, and could perhaps help us deal with it better.

The all-American concept of the hero figure also plays a central role in my essay, "Coming Home: Hyper-Images of the Hero and Child in America" (chapter 5). Working with my intense experience of culture shock upon returning to America, I discuss my nightmarish encounter with this dominating, rational, overambitious, materialistic/concretist brand of heroic energy. The ascendency of this kind of hero energy means that societally, we split off from, devalue, misuse, and even "abuse" especially one figure opposite to the hero: the child. And this child figure carries the qualities of imagination, openness, and play, ever scarcer qualities in our lives. They are however the qualities we need to return us to redreaming and redeeming our sense of ourselves and our "American dream."

In his essay "Cinemyths: Contemporary Films as Gender Myth" (chapter 6), TED E. TOLLEFSON has selected twelve American films that show a pattern of shifting gender roles. He discusses the relationship of woman to man as moving among back and forth among these themes: of woman as helpmeet or as subversive competitor, woman as equal and woman as teacher of men, and finally, "just around the bend," a new kind of woman embodying a wide range of capacities, among them, leadership, independence from men, and the ability to love other women fully and also erotically.

Part I ends on a humorous note, with ELIZABETH MASIÉE's highly entertaining frolic through the mythic parallels in two British comedies, *Butterflies* and *Fawlty Towers*. Compared to the Olympian gods, life on the mundane contemporary level looks pretty scruffy, and we must laugh at the same time as we bemoan our contemporary foibles and follies. In this essay, the gods are not dead; however, they are very much reduced, at least as they are mirrored in our lives. Chronos, Zeus, Demeter, Neptune, and the Muses, all live on among us in the most commonly absurd and foolish ways, providing a wry background against which to show up our inadequacies and eternal frustrations. As Masiée makes clear, we do indeed partake in a divine contemporary comedy.

Part II of this collection begins with the basics, the *prima materia* of the life process: "Shadows and Shades: Dealing with the Dark." When we deal with the evil, the weak, the rejected side of life, we need reminding that this experience, which comes upon us with the reliability of death and taxes, may just be worth all of the trouble. The dark side gives dimension and depth to the picture, and shows us that we can not only survive a negative experience, but perhaps glean some wisdom and strength from it.

So we continue our trek through the soulscape of the culture in Mist County, USA, in our nation's favorite mythical small town, Lake Wobegon, Minnesota. In her essay on Garrison Keillor as an archetypal storyteller (chapter 8), MARY ANN MILLER shows us, point by point, how deeply we need our American stories, how slyly and shyly Keillor's tales teach us about our places of shadow and redemption. In her own evocative and moving storyteller's voice, she tells us how Keillor's work gently mirrors us, in our sometimes narrow and middle-class souls, back to ourselves.

Next comes LYN COWAN's masterful essay, "Taking the Dark with Open Eyes: Hidden Dimensions of a Psychology of Abortion" (chapter 9). Artemis, she informs us, is the goddess who presides over the questions surrounding this difficult national debate. Our society has violated the highest values of this great goddess, those of protecting the young and valuing women. We desperately need the wisdom and ministrations of Artemis, says Cowan, as we deal in an ongoing way with this cultural wound that never seems to heal.

We have two essays on one of the most important films of our time, *Pulp Fiction*. The first, by JOHN BEEBE, is entitled "Deconstructing the American Shadow: A Review of *Pulp Fiction*" (chapter 10). Beebe's language and ideas move us, in as snappy and complicated a way as the film itself, through this aggressive movie with its "intuitive, visionary" drive. In an all-American climate where crime and violence are "business as usual," this film, says Beebe, offers several kinds of heroes, including the "coolly slack" Vincent and the "can-do" and "crafty" Coolidge. But it is in the totally original character of Jules that we see the main hope for any redemption. In a basically religious move, says Beebe, Jules takes the chance he is offered by a "miracle" to reappraise his own part in this culture of violence. As this movie makes so brilliantly clear, this reevaluation is a cultural task that also awaits us.

LYDIA S. LENNIHAN in her essay, "*Pulp Fiction*: From Shadowland to Heartland" (chapter 11), offers agreement and counterpoint to the Beebe essay. She elucidates Jules's call to self-examination in the light of the Jungian themes of shadow work, the coming together of opposites to produce a new solution, and alchemical imagery especially around the gold briefcase. In the language and visual images of this provocative and popular film, says Lennihan, we see how these dark energies, in a classical and yet unique way, bring Jules to the beginning of a spiritual awakening.

As already mentioned, the theme of monsters, or monstrousness, raises its head in many ways throughout this book. In her tastefully shocking essay entitled "Vampires, Eroticism, and the Lure of the Unconscious" (chapter 12) NANCY DOUGHERTY discusses the deepest, darkest "undead" forces, now in another resurgence in our culture. They are forces that can seduce us into desiring death over life, addiction over creativity, and consumerism over spirituality. Learning to mediate our own instinctual energies in our social lives and in our national and international policies is vital, she says. And she goes on to warn us in no uncertain terms: a better acquaintance with the predatory vampire is necessary, and brings with it the awareness that, as potential and as actual "victims," we must awaken from the passive, drowsy, and often erotic grip of destructive forces, within and without.

The essay that centers most directly on the theme of monsters is JAMES W. MAERTENS's "The Dragon and the Man-Machine: Reflecting on *Jurassic Park* and *Frankenstein*" (chapter 13). Human-made beings like the dinosaurs and Frankenstein's monster have to do with the ever-increasing power we humans wield. As Maertens clearly shows, this is a mythological theme we have always had to deal with, that of having godlike power. Yet in our times, as machines, genotechnology, and science in general have offered us more and more power, we have not been provided with an accompanying wisdom. It lies at the center of the human experiment, says Maertens, to learn not to use our power in such wrong-headed, wrong-hearted ways, ones which turn our creative and cultural products, as well as ourselves, into monstrous beings.

The AIDS virus functions rather like a modern monster, ravaging the land, and indeed, the globe. As JUDITH SAVAGE states in her essay, "Ain't No Angel: AIDS and the Abandoned Soul" (chapter 14), we have been sadly ineffectual and cold-hearted in our inability to deal with the suffering of AIDS victims, as well as with our own grief and loss. We have abandoned AIDS sufferers, she says, at the same time that we have kept out the god in sexuality. In this profoundly moving essay on our relationship to this first postmodern pandemic, Savage places AIDS within the history of epidemics and elucidates how this global tragedy touches and challenges us to the very depth and breadth of our souls.

And last in this section, we have GARY D. ASTRACHAN's essay "Looking through the Keyhole: Recollecting and Reflecting America's Soul in *Paris, Texas*" (chapter 15). This evocative piece gives us a peek into one of the sex industry's shadowy dives, where, as in the mythic journey of Orpheus, the profundity of human encounter between a man and woman reaches its darkest intensity and depth. It is only here, he explains, in the wasteland of culture, relationship, and sexuality, that our deepest wounds and longings can be encountered and, in part, healed.

Part III, "The Mirror of Culture: Finding Ourselves Within," consists of five essays which hold up central cultural images and issues for us to look into and reflect upon.

DONALD WILLIAMS's essay, entitled "*The Piano:* From Constriction to Connection" (chapter 16) moves us through the often breathtaking images of this award-winning film, many of which have continued to live in the hearts and minds of viewers. From the eloquent image of the grand piano on the abandoned beach, and then to piano keys, fingers, clothes, holes, rain, ocean, and so on, Williams traces how it is that these dreamlike images pull us deeply into the themes of constriction, isolation, love, communication, eroticism, and finally, sacrifice, and redemption.

Co-dependency theory has swept us up in a collective misperception of what is normal in human relationships, argues JOHN DESTEIAN in his essay entitled "Another Look at Co-dependency" (chapter 17). There is an inherent tension in relating to another person, a tension between being attached and being separate, and it cannot be labeled or trained or shamed away, says Desteian. Rather, for all its dangers and frustrations, being "attached" in a secure enough way, being responsible enough ourselves for the wounds we bear, brings healing and further development to the soul, to our relationships, to our individual selves, and to the way our culture looks at relationship.

Next, MARY ANN MATTOON offers us a challenge in her essay, "Dirty Politics, Clean Voters?" (chapter 18). Her question is whether nonvoters who try to avoid "dirty" politics can remain "clean." While political participation can be difficult and even seem contrary sometimes to the demands of individual development, Mattoon posits that it is not only necessary in a practical sense to deal with political realities, but that political participation can lead to the twin goals of individual development and societal health.

In "False Memories, True Memory, and Maybes" (chapter 19) LYN COWAN explains how we have falsely reduced memory to a true-or-false quiz or a data memory bank. Her essay reminds us, with power and eloquence, of the profundity and centrality of memory, who is, after all, a goddess. The questions that arise about a case of abuse in the courtroom are completely different than those that arise in the consulting room, or in a healing process, and Cowan shows us and makes us feel the difference. Memory, she says, is a profound and powerful archetypal force who, with her daughters, the Muses, are the real energies in bringing meaning, beauty, and healing to our lives.

The tremendous attention paid to the Miss America Pageant and to the many sports contests on the media and in the sports arenas of the nation is MARITA DIGNEY's topic in her essay, "No One Wins: The Miss America Pageant and Sports Contests as Failed Initiations" (chapter 20). The ritual and rites of initiation function to pass along the wisdom and history of a culture, teaching its members to step into adulthood, to take on societal responsibilities. Our initiation rites are vestiges, empty, obsessive, shallow, and often wrong-headed, says Digney, and we are sadly failing our children and adolescents, with tragic consequences.

In Part IV, the contributors look into possibilities for our future, asking such questions as "Where are we going?" and "What are we moving toward?"

How could we discuss the culture, in the present or the imagined future, without discussing the Internet? For all of its capabilities, there has been amazingly little attention paid to the *effects* of the Internet on the quality and the essence of our lives. DOLORES E. BRIEN has performed the invaluable task of gathering together the core ideas of the debate, pro and con, on the value and effects of the Internet in her essay, "A Psychology for the Age of the Internet" (chapter 21). She sees the Internet as indeed helping to usher in a new age. As British Jungian analyst Andrew Samuels has defined it, we are moving from the idea of life as having one unifying center to the idea of multicentrism, or the plural psyche. In this new age, says Brien, the psyche and the Internet may be said to be mirroring each other, the psyche describing the inner world of the individual, and the Internet describing the outer world of the collective.

Space is "our final frontier," according to the introduction to TV's *Star Trek* series, and two of our essays address this fascinating, ongoing cultural phenomenon of modern space fiction. How to deal with technology and our ever-expanding world is the theme of ALMIRA F. POUDRIER's essay, "Its Continuing Mission: *Star Trek's* Machine Mythology and the Quest for Self" (chapter 22). She takes us through our evolving interaction with the "other" and particularly with machines and technological aspects of our lives. In discussing *Star Trek* in the context of several major science fiction movies, she uses the following headings: nonsentient machines, the human-machine interface, and sentient machines as antagonist and protagonist. How are we challenged in our relationship with machines and technology, Poudrier asks, in our most basic mission, to find out what it is to be human?

KEVIN JONES also centers his attention on the alien in his essay "*Star Trek* and the Intimate Alien" (chapter 23). He offers a Jungian look at the images of this popular series, describing *Star Trek's* rich and evolving history of taking in the alien, and integrating it into the life of the starship and the Federation. This process mirrors our need, on both an individual and cultural level, for realizing alien parts of ourselves and our human family, and learning to live, and live well, with them. Jones clearly and convincingly shows how the *Star Trek* series teaches us, step-by-step, the overall necessity, the necessary attitudes, and the rich rewards, of such a "continuing mission."

And last, as the final essay in Part IV, we have MARITA DIGNEY's "Holy Madness at Heaven's Gate" (chapter 24). The fascination the public and media have exhibited with the Heaven's Gate cult, their expressed rejection and even scorn of it, has revealed a familiar and long-standing resistance to the most extreme demands of the spiritual path, the same ones taught by several mainstream religions. The religious impulses of Heaven's Gate members were not new, Digney points out, but only the images they chose to carry those impulses, which expressed a certain spirit of our times: a religious quest in cyberspace, the passing of the Hale-Bopp comet, and believing in the spaceship of higher beings. The mistake, if there was any, says Digney, was the same one that our entire culture tends to make: to take the symbolic images, which carry psychic, inner meaning, and interpret them instead in their concrete form.

The search for meaning and soul in contemporary culture goes on. In our search, we do not need to know exactly where that meaning lies. Nor do we have to know exactly where things are leading. Unpopular as it is to admit in our times, the human state of not knowing is a longstanding and familiar fact of life. The larger, underlying patterns in our lives, whether viewed as individual, cultural, biological, ecological, or archetypal, have always been largely invisible to participants, and discoverable primarily with hindsight.

In these deconstructionist and postmodern times, at least this fact is clear: we live with the old structures cracking, breaking, and with new concerns, new "rules," stepping to the forefront. As some have warned us, it is indeed the end of the world, the world we have known, once again! We have to start imagining how to function when Chaos Theory runs the world. It is a profound readjustment. We do not know exactly how to live with these ideas of radical relativism, of a more random fate. And especially, in this new paradigm, how do we take care of our culture and its values? How do we relate?

We need curiosity, openness, and humility so that we can come into better contact with the larger forces, interpersonally, culturally, and even archetypally. It takes a curious kind of courage and faith. These essays help us in reconnecting to our images and myths in these shifting times, as the forces of our lives move us toward places we have only an inkling of. We rediscover our essence, we re-collect ourselves and our values, when we attend to the ongoing phenomena of our cultural imagination. There, in the diverse intermingling of people and ideas, objects and colors, sounds and movements, shadow and light, we encounter and interact with the soul of our culture.

BIBLIOGRAPHY

Jung, C.G. *Psychology and Religion: West and East. The Collected Works of C.G. Jung.* Vol. II. Eds., H. Read, M. Fordham, G. Adler, W. McGuire. Trans. R.F.C. Hull. Bollingen Series XX. Princeton, NJ: Princeton University Press, 1958 and 1969.

Part I

Heroes and Myths: The Deep Structure of Ourselves

1

Elvis Presley: *Fáma,* and the *Cultus* of the Dying God

CLARISSA PINKOLA ESTÉS

Beginning thirty years ago, in part, because of the controversial mythos of my own heritage, *mestiza* and *Mexicana*, and partly from having seen two gifted women, Marilyn Monroe and Judy Garland, meet untimely and too early deaths, I delved more and more into the phenomena and mythos of sacrifice, the sacrificial victim, and the rites of human sacrifice. I was interested in what correlations I might find between the rites of human sacrifice and the psychology of moderns. Through a long phenomenological inquiry into many anthropological texts and various mythological accounts, I developed a concise and lengthy catalog of the psychological conditions and steps required to lead a soul, symbolically or otherwise, into becoming the sacrificial victim at the center of what I came to term "the *cultus* of the dying God."

Part of the conspectus that resulted from my research into which factors contribute to the "seductive destruction of a soul" is given later in this paper. I have found that certain persons, such as film actors and actresses, statesmen, musicians, and other sociometric stars, both large and small, can easily be caught up in the psychological equivalent of the "sacrificial victim role,"[1] especially if they are young and/or naive, and have in some cases, grown too self-important without realizing it—until much later, or, in certain cases, until it is too late.

Here, I lay out a few informal and preliminary thoughts and opinions, and some of my theorems, and apply them to a man who became one of

---

[1] I use the word *victim* here in the etymological sense, one who is led into peril without full knowledge.

the great forces of culture—Elvis Presley. Some might ask, "Why Elvis?" My précis is that between his life choices, and the influences of close-in and mainstream cultures, he eventually descended into becoming a king who would be sacrificed. He was ultimately seduced into living the kind of life that led him into the center of a "*cultus* of the dying God," wherein the king is not meant to live a long life, but rather is meant to revivify the culture, and then be lost to an early demise.

Elvis is a soul whose life of spirit has barely been examined.[2] He was massively creative—one of a handful of people who were responsible for bringing great cross-winds of change into the culture of his time. His life was remarkable, given that poor people of Elvis's time lived in a whirlwind of thoughtless and often violent classism and racism. In a social environment that insisted on castes and outcasts, people from the "underclass" were easy to mock and ridicule. No one gave a second thought to anyone who did so. Except as domestic and working class "help," poor "whites" were routinely ostracized from mainstream and so-called "highbrow" opportunities and culture. They were not considered worthy as contributors to culture, nor as subjects of literature, nor serious academic inquiry—with the exception of their folktales, their "folklife," and their music, which were often recorded and published by persons outside their own communities.

However, it is my hope that there has been much evolution in the greater culture since that time, and that we can now consider a person from a heritage like Elvis Presley's in a far more thoughtful light. Growing up in the woods myself, and having many insights into a more rustic culture, I find that many observations derived from my own eye-witness accounts enrich and enhance my psychoanalytic viewpoint, in ways that simply "reading about people" from afar, cannot.

In the 1950s, when I was a young girl, the evocative hero worship of rock 'n' roll singers passed me by. I was not drawn into the hysteria surrounding the earthy Elvis, nor that of the peripatetic Beatles. Perhaps this was because there were literally hundreds of good-looking young men in the back-country where I grew up; *vatos* with soft chiseled lips, strong chins, long, dark eyelashes, and fine sideburns. Most wore their T-shirt sleeves rolled up over their shoulders to show off their curvaceous, hard muscles. Their consecrated scapulars and their medallions of the Sacred Heart swung against their chests whenever they lifted, hauled, danced, or played a pick-up game of ball. There was enough swooning to be done locally, let alone globally.

---

[2] One notable exception, (there are others), is the biography *Last Train to Memphis: The Rise of Elvis Presley*, by Peter Guralnick.

Still, I deeply loved the sonorous backbeat of rock 'n' roll, and thought Elvis was a good man who paid proper homage to his mother. In the backwoods, we were not apprised of a then popular notion that a man must break from his mother in order to become a real man. In the back-country, a real man was a fierce protector of all familial women, brothers, cousins, elders and all little children, but, especially his mother. If anyone cared to challenge this backwoods sensibility, they[3] did so at risk—inside our boots were often sewn hidden sheaths that held adamantine-stone honed blades. Even so, and nevertheless, though highly aware of the beauty nearby, my life in spirit was often turned to additional matters, including the passions of poetry-making, and toward the great Souls I most longed for from a distance—The Lord, and *mi Guadalupe*, Our Blessed Mother. Definitely pre-rock 'n' roll.

It has now been more than four decades since Elvis first rose up on the waves of a constrained post-war culture that was just ripe for a public moistening. In a similar manner to that of Athena who was said to have been born from the head of Zeus, Elvis was also "birthed" by a man; the semi-Olympian Colonel Parker, Elvis's oracle, "handler," and business manager. It was all uphill, downhill, uphill, downhill, from there onward.

I recently watched one of Elvis's film clips on television. He sang (in back-country, we would say, "he romped and stomped . . . ") "Jailhouse Rock," as he slithered down a fire-house pole. Squinting at him now from an early crone's viewpoint, instead of from the sensibilities of a rustic young girl, I could see immediately that Elvis was far more than just a pretty-boy rock 'n' roll singer. He had come into the world with many gifts. In the film clip, one could see that he was a naturally gifted athlete, that he possessed an innate boon for the mastery of any dance-step, and that he had been granted an astonishing charism of voice. A charism of voice is far more than the ability to simply sing. By using the superior tones of such a voice—whether singing, speaking, teaching or preaching—one may evoke many levels of response in others.

He had another striking gift also: the boon of bodily presence, of being fully ensouled in the flesh. Elvis's spirit seemed very deeply fitted into his body. He was undeniably and unselfconsciously at ease in relation to his every limb, every digit, every pulse, every moment. This was in contrast to most other mainstream men, both young and old, who were swathed in cloth from their shoes up to their collars. Most women of the time pressed themselves into flesh-squishing girdles and other hydraulic underwear,

---

[3] To avoid use of the awkward, but grammatical, "him/ her," "himself/ herself," it is my custom to often use the more conversational anomaly of the personal "them" and "their," to match the singular subject.

with all skirt hems held at mid-calf and ankle. But more so, the customs of the times required that everything be held in, and held down—flesh, emotion, thoughts, longing, and especially, the joyous deportment of the body.

Jung, in his autobiography (1963), referred to the "number one" and the "number two" personalities, one being mundane, the other being more instinctual and uncanny. The latter seems to describe well the high spirit and the stunning physical lyricism of Elvis's performances. He seemed to have had pure habitation of that psychic space some call "flow," or "natural impulse"—that side of the individual that burgeons with innate grace—both mental and physical.

In situations requiring spontaneity and imagination, the mundane personality is understood to be ego-oriented and earth-bound; often embarrassingly self-conscious, hesitant to "just do it," preferring instead to spend much time thinking things through a thousand times before acting. The more fluid nature, however, contains the legendary attributes of charisma, grace, excellent insight, natural feel for optimum motion. It holds too, amongst other aspects, the natural abilities of timing, "attack," and follow-through that all coaches work to inspire in their athletes, that all Olympics trainers teach in order to develop their protégés. All these superior traits, both mindful and entrancing, seem to have been present in the young Elvis Presley, the seemingly otherwise ordinary boy from Tupelo.

That is, until *fáma* came sidling by. Indeed this young king achieved early on what the Latinate cultures called *fáma*, that is, *fame*. The word *fáma* means simply this: *to be talked about.* Certainly, Elvis became, and is still the subject of, no doubt by now, billions of conversations worldwide. This is no small phenomenon, and it is the typical outcome of *fáma* at work. But there is more to *fáma*, both deeper and darker. At its best, *fáma* is the passing back and forth of useful, effective, rousing or inspiring thoughts and information. But, at its worst, *fáma* is the petri dish of gossip, untruth, half-truth, falsified "truth,"—all of these being poisonous not only to those who generate them, but also potentially wounding to the subjects of them.

Aspects related to a *fáma* gone awry, I believe, greatly contributed to Elvis being inexorably drawn away from what might have been a fairly straightforward, rags-to-riches saga. But because the culture of his time was parched, the juicy Elvis was instead drawn into, what I would deem, the center of the *cultus* of the dying God—a drama in which a dried out culture requires the blood sacrifice of the king in order to atone, redeem, reverse, re-balance and/or rebuild itself.

Further, in *fáma* the subject is often massively projected upon and adulated at the same time. This has caused many potential kings and queens to lose their ways. For many years, I have studied dozens of well-known people whose lives were ended, or taken, very young, and too young. I have also interviewed well known persons in the fields of music, literature, theatre and film, sports and law. One sees that a ground-swell of *fáma* may evoke thousands, and even millions, of superficial speculations, long-shot projections, and verily ignorant assumptions by others about who a soul truly is from the ground upward. This may also create a falsified atmosphere in which the subject is invited to become drunken on public or private adulation. There are those who allow themselves to be lured by the illusory pleasures to be found there, and so strongly seductive can those pleasures be that they may forget all else and lose themselves forever in those perilous though alluring waters.

Thus far in my phenomenological study, it appears that the first steps to entering the *cultus* of the dying God, are to allow oneself to fall into a kind a darkness, wherein one begins to feel a repetitive "need" to forget, or to escape one's mundane life, or else to become "lost" in adulation, stimuli, or other emotive reactions to a *fáma* that pretends its subject is truly immortal. The person may find the falsified atmosphere seems to have effects similar to those of a pleasurable, but deadly and mind-numbing drug—one that drains while it creates pleasure. The person begins to crave such, again and again. They may feel an alternating grave anxiety and depression during the times when they are no longer being sung to by the mermaids.

Naiveté and seductibility are the necessary pre-requisites to being lured into taking the position of sacrificial victim. The inexperienced person marching into that dead zone almost never realizes that the particular mermaids one is seeking, through *fáma*, are definitely the harbingers of personal doom. It is better to be prepared and forewarned about facing the inevitable soul-stealing efforts that are the by-products of *fáma*. It is even better to have a guide, "one who has gone before."

In the myth of Odysseus, as he sailed for home, he was warned by his lover Circe, that while he could listen to the singing of the Sirens he would encounter, it would be his doom to enter Anthemoëssa, their island, to listen any further, or to try to live with them. The Sirens' island was a brilliant white color from all the skeletons of the many crazed mariners who had jumped from their ships and swum against the currents to shore just to further hear the sirens sing. The men of the sea had forgotten all home and hearth in the meantime, in order to ultimately waste away on the beaches whilst listening to a song that weakened them unto death.

So, following the advice of his lover, Odysseus filled his crewmen's ears with melted candle wax, and instructed them to bind him tightly to the great mast of the ship, and never to let him loose under any circumstances, no matter how insanely he might appeal to them. As the ship passed the Sirens' island, Odysseus could hear the intoxicating singing. The Sirens promised to reveal to him facts about his future, if he would only but come join them now. Though he cursed and struggled mightily to be let loose so that he could leap overboard and swim to the island, his crew bound him even more tightly to the mast. His men endured his rages and his pleadings, until their ship had safely passed the island, and the Sirens could be heard no more.

A soul who is isolated from experience, and exiled from wisdom, who has lost or devalues his home grounding, jumps overboard at the first sirenic note. Like Elvis, any soul on a heroic journey who responds to the call of the illusory by abandoning one's "earth-ship," so to speak, and who strives to be in a constant ecstasy, by so doing, becomes perilously isolated from real life, from home life, from earthly life. The mundane demands of a considered life, a rich but common-sensical life, more greatly shelters a gifted soul like Elvis. As it is said in *curanderismo*, "roots in earth; soul in flesh,"—remaining with one's roots in the earth prevents the soul from being separated from the flesh.

The effects of *fáma* can cause what some describe as a "soaring" sensation. This too, when faced without insight, can seduce one to death. The myth I find that ably represents this peril also, like the myth of Odysseus, carries a leitmotif of wax. The symbol of wax is understood in ancient alchemy as a substance from the flesh, that with wick lighted, can show the way. It is an apt metaphor for the solidity, yet the evanescence, of life.

Daedalus was an inventor and master craftsman, and he loved his son Ikaros so. They were imprisoned, but managed to escape with wings that Daedalus had fashioned from feathers and wax. The father warned his dear son not to fly too low, for the sea spray might wet his wings and cause him to falter: He also warned Ikaros not to fly too high, for the sun might melt the wax holding his feathers together. Ikaros, giddy from this astonishing ability to suddenly fly, forgot the warning, and soared so high over the Aegean sea that the heat of the sun melted the wax and caused the feathers to fall from his wings. Poor Ikaros fell from the sky to his death.

When the projections produced by *fáma* are not only great, but also remain unexamined by the subject of them; if in fact the subject is overly-titillated or enamored by the projective resonances of others; if the subject of the projections is unable to grasp them as a form of non-sustainable love; then the subject may lose their shape, their wits—and wings—utterly.

According to my study, once one enters the *cultus* of the dying God, a deterioration of one's creativity and "realness" begins to take place. This may occur, in part, because gradually, over the time of his reign, the king has been drained of vitality by many who suckle themselves at the nourishment his gifts provide to them in one way or another. Thusly drained, he may move more and more into formulaic and rote patterns that are devoid of his original rushes of inspiration. He may fear losing his appeal, and so try to "fake it" instead. All these represent loss of vitality, loss of creativity, and leakage of one's *élan vital*.

Because many elements leading up to the actual human sacrifice are pleasurable, at least at first, we can understand the allure of being invited to enter the *cultus* of pleasure. We can certainly understand the means by which a soul is hounded or lured into such. Did Elvis agree to become a blood sacrifice? I think, no. I think this is seldom the case with any soul who becomes enraptured. Instead, I think Elvis, and others like him, were inexorably seduced into the *fabula* over a long period of time, and without consciousness.

The inexperienced and over-eager may wish to forget that Ikaros let his soaring literally run away with him, and that the Sirens sing the loudest when a person with a true heart is nearest to them. Many persons, when confronted with the pleasurable sensations of *fáma,* wish to disbelieve its dangers. How can anything that feels so pleasurable, or that perhaps has been awaited so long, be so hazardous? Yet, a life that is moderated and mindful as much as possible, seems to better allow the one immersed in all aspects of *fáma,* to resist the temptation to don Daedelus's fabled wings just to see how high one can soar.

The naiveté of the victim is one of the pre-requisites for becoming a sacrificial victim. As with the buildings constructed on the former Azteca lake Tenochtitlán, no one realized they were being constructed on ground undermined by water. The buildings sank down more and more over time, at first imperceptibly. But, by the time it was realized that the beauty of those buildings was about to be destroyed, the under-structures and foundations of the work had been grossly compromised. It is not impossible, but it is costly to shore up structures that have suffered damage to the fundament. In the lives of those both illumined and stricken by *fáma,* better to strive toward conscious, and a dialog between conscious and unconscious, sooner rather than later.

A daily re-alignment with reality is essential. So too, a complete knowledge of one's own seductibilities, and an understanding of one's own "back door" hungers. Self-knowledge is fundamental to resisting "the sacrificial role." One must be able to carefully choose from what is offered. All must be thoroughly considered, rather than just taking "whatever is offered," no matter its pleasure quotient or its detrimental effect.

Also, amongst the original family and the pre-fame close-in friends there will be those who are less likely to fully engage in the fantasy-land of *fáma.* Some of them will act as the anchors when their loved ones' lives become vulnerable to a "soaring" inflation. It was the European Jungian psychoanalyst, Dr. Guggenbühl-Craig who strongly advised in his excellent work, *Power In The Helping Professions,* that one ought to cleave to one's stable friends and family members in order to mediate a potential jack-rabbit run toward a power inflation.

The roles of stable pre-fame friends and loved ones appear to be inestimable, even though there may be some inevitable fallout of those who might feel deeply envious or covetous, those who become intrusive, often without realizing it, and those who become self-important and inflated themselves. Regardless, the stable and wise family, the great-hearted friends remain the central bulwarks against being swept away. In my native Nahua mythos, *cenotes* are very deep sacred reservoirs into which it is said, many "exiled" sacrificial victims were thrown to their deaths by very enthusiastic celebrants during sacrificial rites. It is the more balanced family and primary friends, who, out of love and desire to remain heart-connected with their loved one, will call them back from the edges of the *cenotes*—if necessary, tearing them out of the arms of those who are happily bearing the soul to its death.

As I studied many anthropological accounts and mythos of sacrifice and propitiation, such as those found in Budge's Egyptian mythos, Boas's work, as well as sixteenth-century diaries, such as those of Bernal Diaz, I found several repetitive aspects which I have named:

"Sacrificial Victim Conditions Scale:
The Conditions Required To Lull, or Press
an Individual Into Becoming A Sacrificial Victim"[5]

Because of the constraints of space here, I cannot list, nor elaborate all. But, here are thirty of the recurring elements of sacrificial ritual that seem ultimately to assist or cause the debilitation and surrender of an individual's deepest life principle. Not all thirty are required for a person to slide into the auras of "sacrificial victim," perhaps only five or more. Some concern the pre-victim's disposition, some concern the underlying motives and modes that entrap and torment, leading the person to the final sacrifice. I believe Elvis Presley's life, as well as those of many famous others, finds close correspondence with many of the following:

1. Being psychically wounded disposes a person to agree to be "chosen" as a sacrificial victim. The larger culture claims it is a great honor to be "chosen" or "called" to be sacrificed. This may appeal in direct proportion to whatever degree of narcissism, wounding, hyper-inferiority, or superiority the candidate possesses. The person may mistakenly equate the idea of being "chosen" with being "specially protected" in various ways.

2. The subject often has a heightened ability to "fit" the projections of others, to be "a pleasing person," "a beautiful person," or one who has many gifts to give.

3. The subject is not easily roused to hatred or intense revulsion. Often kind, and accommodating, they may not resist, but rather go along, not realizing the planned culmination—loss of life.

4. Manifest destiny may be involved: One may believe this is meant to be so. It is claimed that the order of the world will be horrifically disrupted if the sacrificee resists his or her "destiny."
5. It is selfish to not cooperate. Others may lose their lives unless one agrees to die. It is said that important ritualistic positions, the status quo of many others, as well as material goods, or a once in a lifetime opportunity, will be lost forever if the sacrificial victim does not cooperate.
6. It is really God who favors this, or asks for this. If the subjects resist (or not), they are often laden with exorbitant gifts, or promises, and often pledged that they will, in return for their loyalty and their very lives, receive very special favor—a lifting up, or initiation via God, the Gods, Heaven, or from the powers that be.
7. Shame is used as a lever. If they resist, they may be told that they are dishonorable, and that great shame will descend upon them, and their families.
8. Threats of dishonor are made. The candidate may be threatened with removal of various civil rights and/or withholding of spiritual rites, or with actual imprisonment.
9. Threats of spiritual and civil harm or exile are made. The subject may be told they will be excommunicated and/or shunned by their community.
10. Threats of abject menace are made. They may be told they must submit, or else, they will be propitiously murdered.
11. Efforts are made to mesmerize and to anesthetize the candidate against reality. Like the "chosen one," the family of the designated sacrificee, may be given so much money, or so many gifts, or so much promise to maintain, or else raise, their status or caste: They may be offered so much protection and favor, or so much praise for "doing the right thing," or threatened with so much loss of face by going against their own best impulses, that they too become mesmerized and anesthetized psychologically, therefore finding it difficult to refuse to give one of their own over to destruction.
12. Isolation and/or exile occurs, especially from those who would give good counsel and/or protect. The subject may, in isolation from wise counsel, have become convinced his own counsel, even though skewed, is best. The "chosen one," who does not cooperate may suddenly be seized, tortured, exiled from sources of protection, and thus further debilitated, be thence led toward sacrifice without further discussion.
13. The candidate is given a new identity with the idea that the old self and one's old sins are expiated thusly. The subject is led to believe that they can be "re-virginated" in this way, and by so doing, have become more pleasing to the prevailing powers. The subject who cooperates

is often renamed, (a new name replacing one's less prestigious name) or given a special ritualistic name, such as Lord of the Flowers, or King of all Creation, or Primal Warrior, etc.

14. There may be an appeal to the subject's desire not to fail his or her captors, family, or culture. The subject is literally and figuratively drugged in various ways. They may be told that it is through their sacrifice, through their endurance in the face of cruelty, that they will become immortal and be remembered forever.

15. Alternately, there are adoration rituals: Figurative drugging is accomplished through extravagant and evocative rituals played out with the sacrificee as the central focus.

16. Cognitive understanding of the deleterious outcome is greatly delayed in the subject. The naive person does not realize, most often until much later, that he has been chosen not only as someone "special," but as one who is about to be maimed, or else to lose all of his life.

17. Drugs and alcohol are often added to the equation. But, by then the subject is often debilitated with substances and conditioning. No longer able to think clearly, or in some cases, semi-comatose, he is unable to act in his own behalf.

18. The subject is further adulated. The narcissistic aspects of the subject, their immaturity, and/or sense of privilege and/or grandiosity, makes them vulnerable to accepting further adulation. The subject's sense of their own a priori woundings or deficits, is attended to and soothed with words, consolations and compensatory gifts. He has been brought into position to be sacrificed by being lauded, perhaps by appealing to his sense of vanity, his desire for power and immortality, his desire to fulfill what is held out to him as a great honor, sometimes by his desire to overcome his sense of inferiority, that is, to be seen as "good," or his wish to be thought of as superior and/or heroic over all other men.

19. A symbiotic relationship is engendered. He is further drugged by having his every basic need anticipated and tended to.

20. More drugging occurs that divides the mind and weakens the will. He is anesthetized with praise, and made drunken with words.

21. Additional instillations are made. His reactions are slowed and suppressed with mood-changing substances; music, chanting, light, or else darkness.

22. His sense of warriorship, of being a major helper, is appealed to. He is taught that he is a principal and redemptive player in the battle between good and evil, or in the war between the light and the dark.

23. His appetites are evoked. The sacrificial victim is promised to have a future of, or given to enjoy now, dancing men *con las cinturas de agua*, with waists like water, or else maidens bearing oils and idolizing words.

24. Power of association and the ordination of others: If there are persons tending sexually, or otherwise, to the one chosen for sacrifice, those persons believe that they too are made holy through having sex, or other interactions, with a soul whose light is not only about to be offered up for the common good, but whose luminescence is supposed to shine through *them,* by association, and forever.
25. The final moment arrives. Right before the subject is led to his own death, rather than appearing beautiful and in heightened awareness, the sacrificee may look pompous, arrogant, completely wrapped up in self, out of touch—or else not in their right mind, debased, bedraggled, worn down, confused, babbling, pitifully staggering about, led like a beast, or else dragged to the killing floor.
26. The final moment often occurs amidst the deafening cries and huzzahs of the community.
27. Some plead for his life, but they are rebuffed. In the end, the result is this: The crowd mourns deeply and sincerely, for: the king is dead.
28. The same crowd also cheers and feels freshly energized. Though sadly having been given a tragic new hero to ritualize or memorialize, the throng continues toward the future feeling their lives have been deepened, and that they are newly engaged.
29. The slain corpus of the "chosen one" is left behind: Long live the king.
30. "The return of the slain God" is now greatly anticipated and awaited.

The "Sacrificial Victim Conditions Scale," may give insight into areas needing consciousness in both culture, as well as in individuals who are at risk. However, for our purposes here, this phenomenological list gives a good preliminary insight into why a person caught in the tangle of *fáma,* or desirous of such, might well be spirited away in the middle of the night, plied with pleasures, and without realizing that they will lose spirit and soul, and potentially, the life of the body as well. The loss of ability to assess and evaluate critical life offerings begins in this kind of milieu. The cost to Elvis of his early beatification and deification, of being the perfect blank screen for other people's projections, was that he did not mature into realizing that being vigilant would greatly assist in protecting himself against the complete theft or loss of personhood.

Here is some of the data I have been gathering about how one loses the self, and the Self:

- The subject is treated inhumanely, through exploitation, hidden *invidia,* envy and resentment, unreasonable demands that the subject fulfill their infantile desires for money, status, or other.
- Inadequate rest and sleep.
- Junk nourishment.
- Often solely ministered to by those who seem hungry ghosts themselves.

- Urged to perform in spite of badly needing rest.
- Offered drugs and excitement, instead of rest and attention to health and real relationships.
- Does whatever it takes to stay on one's feet, instead of allowing the long reposes a charismatic performer must have from time to time.
- Naively allows oneself to be mistreated, thinking others don't really realize or mean to be careless or cruel.
- Mistakenly believes that "offerings" of "excitement" are offerings of sustained nurturant love.
- Does not listen to voices of reason.
- Has no mentor who knows the way.
- Declines to, or is afraid to say no.
- Afraid to be righteous and set boundaries.
- Desires to be loved, more than desires to thrive.

I would turn now to speak to item #1 on the "Sacrificial Victim Conditions Scale," . . . "Being psychically wounded disposes a person to agree to be 'chosen' as a sacrificial victim." Some hope that early wounding will find its healing in *fáma* and other various pleasurable seductions. In mythos and ancient rite, the dying king, or the beautiful virgin chosen for blood sacrifice, are often fed flowers and made drunken with fermented matter, given adornments and praise, essentially drugged—all in preparation for their throats to be slit.

Preparation for sacrifice through the undercutting of the tender self may have begun in Elvis's life at an earlier age than previously suspected. He was taken by *fáma* and the *dying God cultus*, very young, certainly before the age of twenty.

Like Judy Garland, Janis Joplin, and others, Elvis received worship early in his career, likely before he was mature enough, experienced enough, vehement enough to sort it all through, before he was able to assess, and able to discard most, and to decide to keep only a little. He was captured before he could sink his roots into a completely down-to-earth and stable adult soil. In developmental psychology, we might say that *fáma* caused a major disturbance of the profound synthesizing stage that is supposed to take place at the junctures of adolescence and young adulthood.

Elvis's wounds and losses also began very early, the very first perhaps, being that Elvis's little twin brother died near term. In clinical practice we find that the loss of one's twin sometimes causes a life-long sorrow. The surviving twin might feel guilty, even though they had absolutely no responsibility whatsoever with regard to the loss of their twin. A soul who is a surviving twin often tells me they yearn for, long for that sibling. They feel they remember their twin, that they truly somehow knew them before they died, and that they feel sometimes a mild but enduring melancholy, normally associated with the death of someone one knew long and well. This is completely understandable given the high psychic sensitivities between twins.

I would charge that the next wounds to Elvis were those of classism and racism. Elvis, like the quixotic Janis Joplin, was ostracized as a child and as a young adult. He was considered, by certain segments of the culture, "just a hillbilly," a harsh, pejorative phrase, which, in the cultural discourse of that time, or lack of it, led to another pejorative: "white trash."[4] These both imply "sub-human," and "not worthy of human concern or decency." Additionally, in Elvis's early and later years, the abject demonization of African-Americans was complete and opaque. The suffering of blacks was profound. Elvis's soft Southern accent was criticized as sounding like a black man's. His mother's racial purity was questioned by the cultural ghouls of the time. Some said that Elvis was only an exploitative white boy trying to make like a talented black boy. Racial lines were drawn and insistence about "knowing one's place" were aimed at him from literally all directions

Additionally wounding was another slander directed toward Elvis: This young boy who was actually quite religious was said to be Satan himself. Elvis was demonized by many prominent adults of the time, as "the boy who is going to lead all the teenagers and young adults of the United States straight to Hades with no looking back." Many scurrilous, cruel, and untrue assertions were written and said about him before he was yet twenty years old. It would be quite a challenge for a person so young to survive such slashes to their sensibilities and intentions, without being deeply wounded. The aphorism, "If you can't stand the heat, get out of the kitchen," overlooks the very serious archetypal aspects of ritual sacrifice that coalesce to begin to wear down a gifted person, pushing them toward a future loss of life.

Elvis lost his mother when he was twenty-one years old. He had a great love for her, and she for him. She had suffered greatly, and so had he. They had an empathic relationship, and were of greatest support to one another. Although some have superficially looked at this relationship and emerged with knowing looks and leers, this relationship was one that is common and normal amongst poor families, wherein each family member is needed by the others both for love's sake and for survival's sake as well.

---

[4] Certain persons have held that "poor whites" are not really Caucasians of Euro-American origin, but that they are "other," that they are "stone snow," as it was said in our neck of the woods, meaning "dirty or sullied white." The phenomenon of demeaning backwoods and hill people continues in segments of culture today. Recently, the city of Cincinnati responded to the issue by passing an equal rights ordinance forbidding harrassment and discrimination against Appalachian-Americans.

The list of losses goes on: Elvis lost his first love when it became impossible to remain near enough to hold her attention. He lost whatever was left of his sense of "family" security when, horrifyingly, his life was threatened by the Ku Klux Klan for doing what was also horrifyingly called "nigger gyrations." For a young adult, all these constituted a tremendous amount of suffering. *Fáma*, success, and money, are never a compensation or consolation for sorrow and fear. Many persons grieve in many different ways; by trying sometimes to make others into "belongings," sometimes by trying to find something invincible to belong to. Enter, the brotherhood.

The wounds and blows that fall upon the heart and spirit during adolescence and young adulthood, are often struggled with and mediated over a lifetime. Many young men are wounded thusly by life, or by the loss of a great love early on. If unhealed, they often tend to fill their emptiness and longing by becoming lone wolves, or else by making bonds, not with women, but with other men who have had similar experiences, or who have similar outlooks regarding women.

Many dive into the milieu of a protective brotherhood. Elvis surrounded himself with men, some of them later forming a clique jocularly called the "Memphis Mafia." In a brotherhood, at its most organic, one man acts as another one's "blood brother." Different kinds of brotherhoods exist in all cultures worldwide. Some of the most ubiquitous are the brotherhood of the military, the brotherhood of soldiers, the brotherhood of bodyguards, the brotherhood of policeman, the brotherhood of the priesthood; all these belonging, in some way, to the archetype of the heavenly warrior, the one who saves, heals, and is an admired hero.

After Elvis's mother died—a huge psychic blow for him—one that cannot be underestimated, would not be underestimated by anyone who has lost a beloved mother young, Elvis seemed to have moved almost all his most sensitive feelings, that is, his ability to love, to his bodyguards, to policemen, to the *cultus* of Karate, to the huge audiences that prevailed around him.

But a critical error may have been made. The life chosen by Elvis was not related to eros, to relationship, but rather to duress. Quetzalcóatl, Osiris, El Cristo, all the dying Gods were all warriors also; warriors of light, spirit, and ecstasy, but with one important exception: they remained deeply related to the principles of nurturance, life, and rebirth.

Wanting to become a divine warrior may mean being safe, and providing for the safety of others. Elvis strove hard to become a literal warrior. One of the most astonishing documents existent is a letter from Elvis to Richard Nixon, asking if he could please work for the Central Intelligence Agency of the federal government. He said he was disturbed by all the drugging he found in the rock 'n' roll scene, and wanted to go undercover and root them out. His friends in rock 'n' roll, no doubt, would have been astonished at his request. But psychologically, this matter was more likely an outgrowth of Elvis's deep desire to be close to other warriors, or those he perceived as such. Once in the milieu of the CIA, or other similar conclave, one could expect to be brothered, fathered, and "mothered," all. In an archetypal mythos, the divine one always has not only close-in apostles, but also, a coterie, a nurturant circle of protectors.

One might think that human sacrifice has vanished from "civilized" cultures. I would say, no. It still exists—and in highly stylized forms. Its milieu may have changed, and it is more subtly applied. But the methods and processes used to form and deform others seem to remain similar to patterns found in the ancient rites of human sacrifice.

The definition of the word *cultus* derives from the Latin (in English, *cult*) meaning *worship*.[5] It is also derived from *colere*, meaning, to attend to, to cultivate, to respect. Some in "pop culture" use the word *cult* to designate an odd, offensive, unreasonable, or negative group at least by their sights. My grandmother Querida, a rustic anthropologist in her own right, used to say: "*Religion* is what a person calls their own devotion. A *cult* is what a person calls the devotions of others." Rather, the word *cultus* is a neutral term, also meaning to portray devotion, or an homage paid by a body of persons who have made professions of adherence to some agreed upon principle. The principle and adherence may be effective or not.

In a *cultus* of the dying God, the role of the subject is similar to that of the king in the ancient cult-dramas who was killed at the beginning of every new year. There was thought to be a method and reason to such. In that belief system, the once-young king's debilitation is speeded up. He must become old before his time and fall unto death. This must occur, in part, because it is thought that new life, new talent, new ideas, and new blood will flow into the kingdom in his place. So, the king is dethroned in one way or another, and dies, even though he has only served for a year, or for a few years.

Though the reigning king could renew himself, take on a new form of beauty, be beautiful and wise in many new ways, the "beauty of youth" is no longer upon him. Too often, in order to try to please his audience, or to maintain his coffers, or to support an enormous retinue, the king's

---

[5] The word *cultus* in this article is to be understood etymologically—a form of worship, a reverential homage rendered to what or whomever is perceived as a divine being or beings. *Cultus* may also be understood as a particular form or system of religious worship, especially in reference to its external rites and ceremonies.

energic qualities become rote instead of inspired. He "goes through the paces," instead of inventing new ones. He can no longer represent the surrounding culture's desire to be fed by spontaneous and unvanquished youth, by a vibrant energy that ignites all that it touches. He may not realize that the remedy lies not in more flailing about, but in rest, and refueling, and in cutting away those clinging and parasitic associations and endeavors that so constantly drain him.

Who might be vulnerable to these psychological pressures and seductions that creep out when one is drawn into the drama of *fáma*?

- Anyone who receives adulation.
- Any who receive and seek prizes.
- Those who receive awards and appointments or become credited with accomplishments of a kingly nature; including
- presidents, politicians, statesmen, movie stars, leaders, athletes, artists, mothers, fathers, religious, or
- any person having sought, or having been catapulted into a heroic undertaking, or into a position of power.

In addition to a naive high-profile person touched by *fáma* who may slide into these patterns unwittingly, this combination of elements may also affect others who are living ordinary lives, such as in cases of forced psychological enslavement, or when one torments another soul into obeisance, or when one compels another into fearful surrender of any kind.

It is also of interest to me, that more than half the aspects of the "Sacrificial Victim Conditions Scale" are applicable matches for processes followed when a soul is placed in jeopardy, this having little to do with *fáma*, such as:

- Any person struggling to individuate while inhabiting a constraining and/or punitive collective. Several of my analysands from the mideast, whose evolving psychological separations and maturities cause them to question their natal collectives, are, as a result of their new insights, placed in perils of many kinds.
- A person involved in social change or social justice work.
- Those who follow an undeveloped and/or malignant *senex*, a "sacrificer of the young." Examples are often found in current events: the old guard keeps mum about the hazards of chemicals; the drift of radioactivity is falsified; asserting that tainted water is safe; telling falsehoods and half-truths to the young, pressuring them to surrender hope, their children, their callings; taking something from someone without telling them the cost of losing it; and one of the most deadly dreams of the malignant *senex*, the debased elder—that of molding young men and women into *los soldaderos*, soldiers, thereby sending all the beauty and potential of youth into the false excitement of war. All these

seem to me to also fall into the dead center of the sacrificial victim syndrome.

- Much of the scale applies as well to any soul oppressed or menaced by a group, or by an individual, as in battered women and men, abused children, displaced souls, refugees, victims of torture, and those falsely imprisoned.

- Many of the scale's aspects also appear to be synchronous with heavy-handed methods used to press a person into choices that are to their own detriment; such as, elderly people forced to surrender their independence under threats and duress, and any person deprived of their most basic rights, civil and personal, who is told that they are inadequate and unworthy, in order to insist on their compliance to unjust rule.

All of these point to the idea that the entrapment of an individual into becoming a sacrificial victim is not a rare occurrence, but often, one that is horrifically rampant.

Because of this syndrome's ubiquitousness, Elvis might have fallen into this pattern, regardless of the onslaught of *fáma*. Had he remained just a boy with a harpoon from Tupelo, Mississippi, he would not have met his demise in such a public way. But the culture of the time was waiting for someone like him, and with great appetite.

Even though many new economic opportunities came in the post-war years, the *Zeitgeist*, spirit of the times, during Elvis's young life was very dry indeed. The spirit of the culture was just beginning to try to return from the land of the dead, where it had been cut down, along with all the young soldiers and nurses, and the hearts of gold-star mothers and fathers, and kid sisters and brothers, and surviving buddies who had, and who would continue, to sorrow for their lost loved ones for the rest of their lives. Ironically, in old mythos, when the culture or kingdom dries out for any reason, including *too much* death, the king is sacrificed in order that his special blood moisten and renew the earth once again. The loss of so many lives in the war had in fact created an *enantiodromia*, a culture turned back on itself in agony, one that had become dry from much loss of blood.

Contrary to some who imagined the post-war culture as a very "open" one, the society of Elvis's time was arid with regard to the ecstasies, and with regard to praise for the beauty of the temple of each person's body. There were however, certain persons who seemed "natural born" matches for the archetypal slots left open in the culture for Beauty, for "juiciness," for portraying the ecstasy of the body. Only a few persons at a time were chosen to be the stellar constellations representing the magnificent life of the body. Elvis and others, such as Marilyn Monroe, James Dean, and Edith Piaf were, by virtue of birth, seeming physical and sensual personifications of the ecstatic Gods; beautiful, earthy, able to make women and men cry out in desire and pleasurable pain.

As in the mythos of old, the "stars" are chosen by the larger culture. They may be selected based on their unusual gifts, talents, or perhaps, by whatever seems most needed to balance a one-sided culture. As young adults, all the above "stars" were chosen by the masses to portray the ecstasies of the body that were forbidden to most "civilized" persons. Few in the greater culture felt gloriously free enough to display, in an integrated manner, both body and soul—not in public, nor in private worlds.

But Elvis did. He had a complete repertoire of ecstatic music and rapturous body motions. Early photographs of Elvis's performances show him kneeling, genuflecting, and even stretched out along the floor, wailing into his microphone. I was reminded of the early bona fide circuit-riding preachers. One preacher or another always seemed to be lying down on the altar/stage, spreading his legs and showing the congregation his pelvis. The preachers danced horizontal dances while crying out in deeply ecstatic voices, moaning and whisper-breathing into the heavily chromed mikes, both to and about, God.

I sense that the psyche contains a drive toward anointing the body as a full participant in the mystical aspects of life. From having examined many individuals' night dreams portraying multiple images and symbols of ecstatic dance, song and other embodied rituals, it would seem that the psyche has an immense drive, definitely not to despise, but rather, to sanctify the body. In some of the oldest rituals that bless the body before and after great events, such as the birthing of a child, renewing one's commitment to one's God, setting off on a journey "to the end of the earth," many of the participants seemed to have had an understanding about the ecstatic body's great potential for living in, and through the least spoken of the senses—the sense of Godliness.

Elvis could definitely be seen as a representation of bodily ecstasy. Perhaps at one time it was not such an astonishing idea that both the religious and the bodily could be held together as one continuous principle. Amongst many of the back-country people I knew, the bounties of body, sexuality, religion, praise-song, spiritual ecstasy, and *alegria,* joy, were not held away from one another in leak-proof containers. It seemed that only when these aspects were *not* authentically held together with at least a modicum of awe, that one or another of the aspects degenerated. Many people continue today, through their charismatic practices, to weave all these elements into a more complete psychic fabric. Like Elvis Presley, and the charismatic preachers, many innately understand that life can be credibly sexual and sensual, as well as credibly spiritual—all at once. It was Elvis's ability, at the beginning, to meld these three together—the sexual, the sensual and the spiritual—these became his first steps on the way to being crowned king.

But, before and during his coronation, throughout the culture from east to west, and from north to south, there was a broad-based and deep ambivalence about sexuality and the nature of the body. The temperature of the overt culture, having settled way down from the terrible heat and smoke of World War II, now seemed to want only production, roads made straight, and forever peace—not as in justice, but as in non-movement, as in no more fear, as in stilled evolution, as in time to repair. But, Elvis Presley arrived as *El Niño*, an enormous weather-changing pattern in a culture trying to avoid even the first hints of changing weather, trying hard to make every last leaf, every last ocean wave be invested with propriety and stand completely still, all the Beats and bohemians aside.

One could argue that there was good reason for at least a certain caution with regard to the appetites and powers of the body, given some pups' frenzied sexual efforts *and* abilities to wear all the fur off their bodies before they were yet old enough to vote. More to the point, in certain aspects of Christianity and Judaism, as well as in other religions, there has been, ad infinitum, an ongoing contretemps with, and about, the body. Throughout history, it appears that on a regular basis, great energic notions arise in certain of the populace from time to time—these causing the question to be posed (once again) about whether the body can, *or even ought to*, co-exist *with* soul.

In that particular kind of dialogue, the body is often demeaned and demoted from its Godly associations. It is often deemed undependable, a suspicious character at best. At worst, the body is imagined somewhat like a demonic bouquet of writhing snakes. Elvis was seen in exactly these lights early on—either greeted with suspicion, or else condemned as a kind of rock 'n' roll incubus.

The demeaning of the body was projected upon Elvis personally. I find many of the structural motifs of attacks on the body to be the same descriptives used to characterize Elvis, such as:

- The body was reckoned to be "dumb": Elvis was supposed to have been "backward," and "stupid."
- The body was imagined as a temptress who leads individuals in the wrong directions: Elvis was to be mightily understood as a handbasket just looking for passengers so as to speed them all straight to hell.
- The body ought to be demeaned, slandered, looked down upon, demoted from its high shining. So too, Elvis.

Regardless of the aspersions, Elvis refused to demean the exuberance of the flesh. Instead of acting like Origen, one of the earlier church fathers who is said to have castrated himself, thinking that this would be pleasing to God, Elvis became as "get down" with his body as possible. He displayed a showy public ecstasy of the body.

He appeared to disagree with the premise that denial of the sanctity of flesh is good. He apparently felt that sacrificing the passion and soulfulness of the beloved body in order to become "an eunuch for God," that pretending to be "without body" so as to somehow be more pleasing to God, did not resonate with his innate viewpoint. He seemed more to understand that the flesh God created was infused with Godliness, and *was good*. He disregarded Matthew 19:12, " . . . *there be eunuchs, which have made themselves eunuchs for the kingdom of heaven's sake. He that is able to receive it, let him receive it.*" Instead, Elvis seemed to cleave more so to 1 Corinthians 6:20, " . . . *glorify God in your body, and in your spirit, which are God's.*"

There are further contradictions about the body in references in Old Testament Judaic-Christian scripture which seem to constrain humans from ever becoming peaceable with the flesh. In Psalm 56:4, we hear that the flesh has been "undependable" again: " . . . *in God I have put my trust. I will not fear what flesh can do unto me . . .* " Yet, in contrast, we hear in the poetry of Psalm 63:1— that the very flesh of us is sentient enough to long for God: " . . . *my soul thirsteth for thee, my flesh longeth for thee in a dry and thirsty land, where no water is . . . .*"

Ambivalence about the body's abilities to feel and to translate ecstasy were central concerns to the mainstream culture of the time. Any ecstasy, sexual or otherwise, and any spiritual practices associated with mystical ecstasies—such as meditation, hands-on healing, ecstatic dance, and many others that were meant to be lived out with grace and validation—all these were supposed, instead, to create feelings that were deemed greatly hazardous. Unlike certain Vedic and Tantric traditions, which hold that the potential of the body to feel ecstasy is to be understood as one of the several pathways to God, many believed the body ought to be excluded from theological and psychological inquiry and dialogue, and not just for the moment, but forever. I remember as a young girl, a favorite black-winged teacher took one of my poems to a very famous poet. The poem came back to me with many kind annotations of praise. But also, in a section that spoke to a passionate sensation of the body, the poet had written, "the body and its emotions are not subjects for poetry." This attitude was considered the "proper" aegis of the times.[6]

I find in my work with analysands, that an ongoing conflict about the body may be illumined by a peculiar anecdotal evidence, a phenomenon noted by Jung, and often productive in uncovering the root of some distresses. It is this: If an analysand presents a spiritual problem, the unraveling of such may well point to a sexual problem as its basis. If an analysand presents a sexual problem, it may well be, that at its root, it is

---

[6] Of course Sexton, Wakoski, di Prima, Levertov, and Rich, and others were soon to rise up, dispatching fine poems about the taboo aspects of the flesh; menstrual blood, madness, and vulvas, changing the "propriety of poetry" forever.

really a spiritual problem of great importance. The sexual "right here in River City" problem of the times, *vis à vis* Elvis's effect on others, may indeed have been a great cultural spiritual issue instead of a precisely sexual one—such as, the imbalance caused by years of war, blood lust, and blood loss, wherein the body had no parity whatsoever, for regardless of nationality, the blessed body was the main currency, used as no more than firewood in the furnaces of slaughter.

Additionally, a culture that both resisted the joyous body, and yearned for it at the same time, created an opening ripe for a soul like Elvis to step through. He would act out the wishes of others, show the way, trail-blaze. He would comport himself in ways that millions of others hungered to act also, but were afraid to do so, afraid of being ridiculed, fearing exile, fearing—and justly so—danger.

A vacancy is created in a culture when any important archetypal pattern is quelled, debased, fragmented, or missing. Elvis Presley can easily be imagined as the one who filled a vital vacancy in the collective—one that stands open in any culture that has high ambivalence about the euphoric resonances of the body.

There was further impetus to place Elvis into position as king. Young people are often imprinted by the first images, fragrances, sounds and so forth, they experience upon awakening sexually. Newly awakening young people who yearned for the ecstatic life of the body, may have struck the primary chord that generated Elvis Presley's complete and early acceptance in an otherwise arid culture. His moistening effect on the dry and too one-sided psyches of many persons, in the critics' opinions of the mainstream culture at the time, was much needed.

A dry culture cannot help but create a vacancy for a moistening archetypal presence. When a culture is unable to heal the split between its concepts of "bad body," and "blessed body," it creates a vacancy for at least one soul to rise up and to act as a kind of avatar, a kind of magnetized rod that collects and broadcasts ideas and images about what has been lost. The person who fills this vacancy is imagined, or is hoped to somehow lead the culture out of its unconsciousness into clear awareness about what it has lost, forgotten, reviled, or only secretly admired from afar. And such a great soul may, in fact, do so. But, according to errors made by countless heroes recorded in mythology, they must proceed carefully.

Once the vacancy is filled, then the gates to sacrificial ground may swing open. *Fáma* can almost always be depended upon to put out its enticements. In the mythos of the successful hero, one who may suffer, but who ultimately masters his destiny, and who wills out at the end, a castle of repose and honor is often set aside for him. However, in the mythos of the dying God, when the avatar has completed the transformation of individuals and/or culture, it is then time for them to be deposed, or else, to die from neglect or excess, or both.

Those who physically resemble major artistic representations of the Gods, appear to be almost pre-selected to fill the culture's God-like projections. The physical appearance of the young Elvis Presley is a *Doppelgänger* for the artistic representations of many of the beautiful deities, Krishna included. Attend to a painting of Krishna, as artists have imagined him described in the scriptures, and then look at the young Elvis Presley's photographs. They have many numinous features in common, the slender body, the luxurious hair, the beautiful clear visage, the completely sensual features.

Marilyn Monroe could easily have been the model for the Ephesian Artemis, or for Aphrodite *Natura*, born and borne fully-formed and naked on the sparkling sea foam. She matched the ancient archetypal representation of Beauty physically, and so it was easy to project upon her all elements of beauty, from the most debased, to the most highly held, for that reason alone.

But, there is more to "the shine" than beauty alone, and this was also true of Elvis Presley. To many people, there is almost nothing more compelling than a mingling of the opposites of angel and devil in a single person. Much of Elvis's, and Miss Monroe's, personalities wove together pure angel/devil opposites; not bad devils, but angelics who are just enough devilish at the same time. The archetypal patterns of angel/devil when augmented by beauty, often compel other women and men to be vitally lured. Additionally, there is almost no more astonishingly effective "bait" for the inexperienced than that of beauty mixed with trouble; either some degree of beautiful angst, or else some degree of highly stylized danger.

Also, those celebrities, heroes and heroines carry more than just simple charisma. Some say that a person can have only one way of being and behaving. But, in my twenty-seven years of clinical observation, people can become larger than life, at will. The psyche justly possesses two integrative aspects within a single personality; one ordinary aspect, and one extra-ordinary aspect.

In my process of studying the lives of people who became well known icons, the forms of divinity that have been projected onto them, as well as the archetypes surrounding them, I was reminded of a story an acquaintance told me about Marilyn Monroe. In the 1950s, he and she were walking along a Hollywood boulevard. Miss Monroe was incognito, wearing a headscarf and sunglasses, a long coat and flat heeled shoes. A group of strangers came out of a restaurant and walked down the sidewalk toward them.

Her friend cajoled her. "Do Marilyn!" he said.

She threw off her coat, tore off her babushka, left her sunglasses on, and did the walk, the breathy talk, and all the other nuances that created the very real "Marilyn." Instantly she was transformed from a quiescent person into an astonishing one—not only a vamp, but also seeming like a goddess. Everything, the tone of her voice, her eyes, even the loft and shine of her hair seemed to change, becoming augmented. The strangers were dazzled. After autographs all around, Miss Monroe and her friend walked on. By then she had returned to her first personality, all her extraordinary electricity withdrawn.

Was either demonstration of her natures false? No. The spectrum within her psyche contained both. They were authentic representations in the process of being integrated within one psyche. The conscious deportment of an ordinary self in tandem with an extra-ordinary self, I believe, is called "being gifted."

This dual aspect of the psyche is different than the *persona* which acts as a mask to cover all or most of the full personality. The extra-ordinary personality may be cohesive or not, dystonic, developed, under-developed; it may be immature or maturing. When souls are in the process of maturing and integrating the ordinary and extra-ordinary aspects of psyche, they often bounce from one to the other until they gain control of each. Eventually both are woven together. The person is no longer confused by either one, no longer questioning if only one is real and the other not. A time comes when one arrives at a strong and peaceful kinship relationship with both.

The extra-ordinary aspect of the psyche has the capacity to canalize sensations of awe, exhilaration and numinosity in self, and in others. Miss Monroe and Elvis Presley, both, had the ability to suddenly blaze with energy, to become a conduit for an archetype—*a divine archetype* is not too large a description.

The phenomenon of revealing the extra-ordinary self often causes others to react in very deep ways that they themselves can hardly explain. People sometimes ask why women (and men) screamed so at Elvis's appearances, that is, the "screamers" who were not shills. This is hard to explain in cognitive psychological terms. We might imagine that it is the result of a deep evocation. Sighing, screaming, and fainting may occur as a result of experience emanating from the psychoid unconscious, from that layer of psyche Jung calls ineffable, that which can only be represented indirectly, through symbols, images, poetics—or perhaps only by much humming, murmuring, or crying out. I only know that the explanation of what one understands in the gut is often difficult to convey in words alone. Once when one of our friends married a French construction worker, her men friends in particular, and a few of her woman friends also, wondered why an educated woman would marry an "uneducated" man? We, *las cacareas*, the old cacklers, just smiled and rocked in our chairs. "First of all, she loves him," we cawed. "Secondly, 'French construction worker,'" we crooned in unison, "with emphasis on the word *French*, and with emphasis on the words, *construction worker*." To elaborate this additionally as much as I believe possible here: ecstasy begets ecstasy.

"Crying out" by participants during mystical ritual is part of the ecstatic literature by many reports. It was noted that many screamed in ecstasy when they were present at Elvis's concerts. But their ecstasies seem to me to be striving, not toward Elvis exactly, but *through* him, toward a more divine goal. I find the film clips of screaming teens closer to the kinds of spiritual ecstasy found in entourages of snake handlers, or during the high crises of the drumming at the Hopi snake dances on the ancient Arizona mesas, or amongst various groups of people who enact ecstatic religious ritual, that is far more than just an odd meaningless phenomenon. The screaming does not seem to me so much directly sexual, as it seems to be a phenomenon of heightened and unleashed spirit. The latter *is* found in sexual arousal, but it also is found in religious excitement.

Why do people scream in ecstasy? Similar to the sensations produced by Tantric disciplines, hero- and heroine-based ecstasy ordained by the multitudes, contains all the psychic phenomena that occur when it is felt that a certain human being carries great luminosity. Luminescence seems to many, Godly. It is not only Moses who fainted and raved when, what he perceived as the shadow of God, passed over him.

Elvis seemed to easily become that rare creature, "the animus man," the one who acts out the unrealized soulfulness of others, while trying to appear to be only that which others most desired. This is one more variation on the beautiful sacrificial victim.

In a culture that so seeks the multiple comforts a woman can provide, there are more "anima women" than "animus men." In classical Jungian psychology *anima* and *animus* are terms that refer to the *contrasexual* component in each individual. Because the "anima woman" is more prevalent, and may therefore be more easily recognized by the reader, I will briefly describe her here. Her predilections and wounds are nearly identical to those of "the animus man." The anima woman can be understood, for instance, as one who has the ability to seem as though she can fit into any lover's fantasy of the perfect woman. She seems able to immediately transpose herself, to translate herself into anything a mate, or potential lover, employer or any other agent could dream up.

If a lover desires a woman who is interested in race cars, quite suddenly she studies and learns all she can about race cars; she is willing to clink down into the pit; she will arrange to get grease on her face in what she imagines to be the most darling manner. If a lover desires the anima woman to also be a ballroom dancer, all of a sudden she appears in Fortuny-pleated gowns hemmed with ostrich feathers. If the mate desires a high intellectual, she arranges to be caught reading Proust and Plato. If the mate wishes a stay-at-home wife, she suddenly loves babies and cannot have enough of standing at the cooker. Painfully, she loses herself entirely, and becomes what anyone wants her to be. She does not realize she is creating an act she cannot follow. Though she may seem a predator, she is not. She is prey—a prey who dances toward the predator without realizing the engagement she is making.

Like the anima woman, the animus man often feels that he is in great power when he fulfills another's fantasies. In fact, during those times, he is losing power. The former psychic sensation is the result of seduction. It is a cruel trick, for the power one feels is only an exhilaration, rather than a true mastery or prowess.

Why would a soul proceed straight into a box canyon? It is not because the anima woman or animus man is a simpleton. Quite the contrary, they are likely to have many gifts, but their understanding of the nature, reach, and use of their gifts may be disturbed, often by the possession of a serious, overt or covert, inferiority complex—the result of many wounds to a young or sensitive psyche. Via seductive behaviors, the sacrificial victim has learned to keep others alive, and lively, while they themselves, slowly and inexorably, starve to death. In return for admiring glances, long, and even hot, pursuits of various kinds, the sacrificial victim gives up their very flesh. None of what they evoke or receive can truly feed the soul and spirit—the dual magnetos of the psyche. The sacrificee's ego, which may have become used to junk nourishment and shallow infatuations—although a mighty thin gruel—these too often seem better than nothing.

Because of the response of others, the prey imagines that they are in fact the tracker, that is, the one in charge, when in fact it is quite the opposite. Something happens to certain men and some women in the presence of an anima woman or animus man. An unconscious person loses himself or herself, goes "ga-ga," as it is said, and acts as though they may have lost all their senses. Sliding into a fantasy world, "the admirer" regresses to an infantile state. They psychically resemble nothing so much more than a baby. They see the object of their affections as a kind of suckling nurse.

To be able to nurture others is a kind of power. But in the inexperienced person who becomes possessed by trying to be what others project onto them, this often entails doing too much for too many, for too long, for too little. This can lead to an early dying off of the person's interior life, the one that contains good instincts, early warnings, and open eyes. Elvis, as animus male, certainly, over time, became much like the mythic mother pelican who feeds her babes. But, when she has no more food to give, she plucks out her feathers and gives the hungry ones to drink from the blood of her own breast. The symbol of the seabird or songbird who feeds her babes her own blood, has long personified the God who willingly sacrifices himself or herself, so that others might be redeemed. It is quite one thing for a divine soul to attempt such, but for a soul who is fully human, it is a catastrophe, actually cutting short their ability to nurture anyone or anything over a long period of time.

Elvis was an apt candidate for taking on the role of the dying God. Although Elvis was very human, and certainly a person who not only inspired, but who earned much devotion, his phenomenon follows the same mythic pattern as other dying gods and mythical figures, including Osiris and Quetzalcóatl. The pattern of the dying God in mythos is this:

- The God who is destined to die young, (or over and over again) comes to earth, or is often born in an unusual manner. For instance, Quetzalcóatl, an Aztec deity is born with pale white skin. Elvis's birth anomaly could be seen as his being the twin who survived.
- The young God is sent by or sent for, with the idea of doing great good, of giving great warmth, helping to lift the people up, to heal, to shed holy light.
- But, ultimately the young God is exiled, dismembered and/or crucified by some means, most often before middle age is reached.
- And yet, after the God dies, he is revivified, comes back to life in some way, and at the same time, remaining completely beloved.
- He is often remembered as though he is still alive, and will soon return to earth, and to his people.
- In the thematic motifs of slain redeemers, after the king, high priest or God dies, or is killed,
  a. their followers are persecuted somehow,
  b. the God finds a way to rise up amongst his or her followers, further infusing them with strength,
  c. and in this way the slain God remains alive in memory,
  d. and in ritualistic vigil.
  e. the God continues to live, but *sine corpore*, without body.
  f. many who are in some way anointed will see him after death.

Elvis Presley's life definitely follows such a mythic pattern. He is seen as a divine force, and thusly enters the running for the role of the dying God. Long after his death, many claim "Elvis lives." He is seen by many as what might be called a *tremendum*, a great force emanating from the divine.

The decline of Elvis may have occurred in this way. He can be seen as one who, in large part, over a long period of time,

- unwittingly became an "animus man,"
- easily seemed like, looked like, whatever any person, in particular, craved a man to look like,
- became the one who had the ability to fill in the fantasy of almost any burgeoning soul who came along,
- thusly descended into the role of the sacrificee.

Elvis was definitely able to fulfill projections. If a person projected, "He is sexy," well, he *was* indeed sexy. If someone projected, "He is a good gospel boy, a good religious boy," well, he *was* exactly that. If one projected, "He is a man who loves his mother, yet a man who wears black leather and is kind of wild," he could be any and all of these: His career swayed forward on all the benevolent fantasies anyone could imagine about a man. He fulfilled these easily because he himself was filled to the brim.

As the *cultus* of the dying God has religious aspects, many elements of the post-Elvis culture follow religious archetypal patterns too. As with the saints and deities whose images have infused hearts and souls throughout all the ages in all religions, Elvis was, and is, surrounded by many rites and sacraments, or sacred moments:

- There is a vast system of relics; for instance, pieces and parts of his clothing, and blades of grass from his home.
- The house he lived in during his lifetime, Graceland, is his shrine.
- There are churches and congregations, these being fan clubs, and gatherings in commemoration of Elvis.
- There are prayers, which, in his case, are his many songs.
- There are many vigils and pilgrimages.
- Similar to the *imitatio Christi*, there are those who take on Elvis's life in imitation.
- There are claims of healing and transformations from people who feel strongly, that by hearing Elvis's live recorded voice, or by having seen him live in performance, or in a film, they have been changed.
- Some feel that even though he is now deceased, he remains responsible for curing various maladies.
- He is prayed to by some for intercession.
- Some believe his body to be incorrupt.

How to evaluate all this today? Is any of this "bad for people"? I am inclined to let this to be weighed by those who have love for Elvis, to decide for themselves. But if pressed I would respond that if such an interest causes one's life to become deeper, larger, more useful for the psyche, or assists the creative, spiritual and/or relational life of the person, then if so, little societal or psychological concern is needed.

It is more so the life of the gifted person that one ought be concerned about. Many have been destroyed by being caught in the headlights of a sullen or hungry culture. In the end, Elvis Presley trod the same tragic pathway as Judy Garland, Sara Teasdale, Janis Joplin, Sylvia Plath, Anne Sexton, Frances Farmer, Simone Weil, Jimi Hendrix, and many other generations of massively artistic souls. They all were captured in the headlights of the culture which longed for the archetype most desired at the moment,

most especially the dreaming about, and the yearning for, a messiah, a savior, a healer, a *saman*[7]—the understandable desire for experiences that
would place them in an ecstasy and draw close a sense of Godliness.

He, like others before him, became an energy source for others. Janis,
Judy, Marilyn, and Elvis—all became the fuel for the swooning, the kind
of rapture that flew the masses to the moon. Elvis himself was not the vehicle; but through his singing, dancing, posing, and posturing, he created the
massive energy that drove such. Elvis's audiences used their energy to
encourage him to use his energy, in their behalf. Like the *samanic* rituals
of yore, singer and circle both, were lifted to heaven together, the *saman's*
extra-ordinary ability to energize the numinous in others, at the core.

Samans ride their magical drums to the heavens, or to the depths of
the earth, or to under the sea, in order to propitiate or supplicate the deity.
The masses encouraged Elvis's production and ascension, or descent,
through their applause and appreciation. The culture of "soldiers" reinforced it. Remembering that the word *religion* comes from *relagáre*: meaning to bind all disparate sheaves together into one bundle, in other words,
a striving toward inherent Godly wholeness, the audience's desire "to
return to heaven without first dying," derived from each individual's own
deepest religious desires.

Elvis was urged on, and tried valiantly, even though exhausted.
Performers may be seduced into trying to please when an audience
encourages them to burn up their own energies past their own comfort levels or endurances, past the point of what is good for them healthwise or
soulwise. When Janis Joplin "chugged" a fifth of Southern Comfort on-
stage during performances, many screamed and applauded; they
whooped, they stomped, they encouraged her, to her own detriment. In
some out-of-balance Bacchanalia, she appeared to slug it down all the
faster. One might say she was no longer a *self*, but a *saman* in a culture
which had only broken shards of memory and knowledge about how to
regard and protect the one who gives up the Self so that others may live
fully alive. It may be said that we live in a culture so unconscious that its
own *samans* often accidentally die.

The *saman* is not supposed to *lose* shape or center, but rather aug-
ments or changes it. The dying God, in contrast, further loses consciousness, as though becoming stuck in a low gear, but at the same time going
very fast with high revolutions per minute that guarantee to wear out the
engine in a short space of time. In the film *The Rose*, the singer-heroine,
after her rock 'n' roll performances, returned to her room, weeping with
loneliness. "Coming down" from being projected upon by an enormous
ecstatic audience, and thence returning to mundane reality with a heavy
thud, is very difficult and takes the mastery of a well-centered person, one
who knows the way. Afterward, nothing of porkchops nor oatmeal can

---

[7] *Saman:* Magyar, for shaman.

equal an ecstatic union with Godliness. But one can learn a graceful detachment.

After performances, unless the person has close-in loved ones who mean something to them, as well as practices that center them back into a home reality, then the hero or heroine may feel so abandoned and so completely alone that they feel as though they have to do *something!* take drugs, have sex, with anyone, anywhere! Quick! do another performance! do something! anything! just please let that ecstasy mountain be ascended once again.

Idealization ought not be considered any form of nutrition either. It occurs independently of the subject's response or actions. Whether one attempts to remain a darkened screen, so that supposedly no one might easily make projections, or whether one attempts to become whatever one imagines the others want and need; either way, a one-sided idealization may take root very easily, especially in those who have a heightened capacity to love in many ways, and deeply.

However, an idealization with a person one admires but does not know, is different than a close relationship with one's teacher, elder or mentor. Having a good role model, or mentor, or an elder, is quite a different matter altogether. The latter are based on reciprocal relationship, on heartfelt, and earthly exchanges, ones based on support, succor, mutual respect, teaching and learning on both sides, a parity of needs. This often resembles a deep kinship relationship based on love, loyalty, and a good deal of admiration as well. A person who mistakes idealization for sustaining association takes a fatal mis-step, and will soon be bones and ashes.

Other negligences and omissions lead the dying God to his death. Alcohol and drugs are often "over-prescribed" in order to turn "non-effective" behavior into "profitable behavior," almost insuring that pure talent turns into a blood sacrifice. The photographs and film clips of Elvis performing in Las Vegas near the end of his life, reveal a man who is so clearly ill, so very physically sick, and seeming so very soul sick. The media reported that he had gained much weight, but that seemed the least of it. Anyone with a modicum of sense, any mother looking at such a son, would know immediately that he was sick unto death, and that something had gone terribly wrong.

In the cult of the dying God, the followers cannot save their hero from the sacrifice. I suspect that many of his fans began writing to him, trying to warn him, wanting to know what was wrong, and could they help? I would imagine too, with all the protective and pre-emptive walls around him, that he may never have seen the letters.

Before a dying God can be led to slaughter, they must be debilitated. What seemed to have occurred at the end of Elvis's life is similar to what happened at the end of Janis Joplin's and Judy Garland's life. Each became perilously swollen, both in physical body, as well as with hangers-on. Each became obviously and excruciatingly ill. Each kept trying to go on, to make appearances, to act as though nothing were really wrong, when in fact so much was wrong, so terribly wrong. Neither may have had anyone near whom they could let in, or who they would allow to talk sense into them—physical, psychological, or spiritual. All these great performers continued to be soulful, certainly, but also continued in life anesthetized, with crushed spirits, feeling duty-bound, as well as both more and more bereft and bewildered, and therefore likely more and more, angry and despairing.

There is a special cage for the dying God from which the chosen one is not allowed to escape. When one reads trustworthy and balanced biographies of personalities, one sees that many became captured in the projections that were placed upon them, as clearly as though the bars of a cage were lowered down upon them. Many could not break free. Jail-breaks did not occur when needed, in part, because pleasures of all kinds were mainlined right through the gilded cage, thus often keeping the captive in dreamland for life.[8] The cage, rather than the real life, became the place where one was fed, where one was admired, adulated and groomed to die. No one designated to be the dying God will, or can, agree to be sacrificed unless seduced by sustained pleasure sensations, unless given massive compensations that somehow appear a fair trade-off for one's very life.

The one who enters the *cultus* of the dying God may have, at first, been only truly hungry for the divine, the ineffable. A long held premise of mine in a cultural context, has been that some souls who drink and/or drug, are not out to become debased, but are actually, albeit, often unconsciously, seeking union with the living God. Psyches so deeply desire this, that some persons will take any means, no matter how fast, how dangerous or how debilitating, to try to reach what they intuitively realize the psyche longs for—wholeness. Though people might seek to deaden themselves to the mundane world, they may, in fact at the same time, be attempting to silence the din in order to be better able to hear, or to be nearer the Greater Voice.

The audiences and Elvis were after the same thing. One can long toward God without full awareness that this is what one is really longing for—even though one may have no name for it, no articulation, nor an informed sense of what it is they truly seek. "Blind, blindly, I stumble forward, following the fragrance of that which I cannot see."[9]

More individuation, more time spent maturing, more guidance of the effective kind, would have been needed for Elvis to repulse the "chosen one" role. With enough time, most humans have the opportunity to mature

---

[8] See chapter on *feral woman,* a phrase I coined to speak about the psyche, which, in famine, becomes excessive in appetite when finally released, and accidentally destroys self. *Women Who Run With the Wolves* by C.P. Estés © 1992, Ballantine/Random House.

[9] Excerpt from poem *"La Palabra es Sancta,"* © 1970 C.P. Estés.

into a more firm consciousness, and are able to seek and take much more support for soul and spirit. With more time, Elvis, Janis, Judy, or Marilyn would likely have come to agonize far less about saying no to many evocations, "deals," and orders. But since an essential consciousness and synthesis was stripped away, and in some cases, denied to them when young, they were offered, and, without realizing it, accepted too many poisons. A conscious person will not continue to injure themselves or allow injury, nor repeat where they erred before, while still expecting a different result. The latter is the definition of compulsive or unconscious behavior. This debilitates one's ability to act in one's own best interests, and it is most poignant in sacrifices.

For years, Elvis was at ease being an ecstasy maker, and this became the center of his life. He was captured so young, I am uncertain he ever realized what a private life ought to be. This, in my opinion is what contributed to his early death, truly. He was worthy of laudation, of love, of devotion, of awe, for he was massively talented. Though he may never have believed his publicists' hyperbole, he also did not realize that even those whom some imagine to be gods, need repose, reflection, quietude—something in addition to, or different from, "Las Vegas love."

The image of Elvis and other sacrificees as well, will continue to rouse as long as the culture is not whole. Elvis's (and Marilyn's and Judy's and Janis's, and Jimi's . . .) images continue to blaze long after their deaths. This is an expected response to the long numinous shadow cast by each. To remember them continues to serve a great collective need, a great projective need, a longing for spirit and soul that goes far beyond ego-longing. In a culture so alienated from the meaningful and the moist, "the very absence of God," as my old country grandmother Katerín, who survived four horrendous wars, says, "points us toward God." Likewise, the very absence of the ecstasies of God's creation of the body, point us toward the ecstasies of God's creation of the body. In fact, at its root, we all likely have a deep longing for a synthesis of the body and the *espiritu* of The Great, to be found in God's grace. And we would like to achieve such, without having to die for it.

Elvis was both nominated, and self-nominated, to be the moistener of the culture. The cultural *contra naturam*, that is, the "against nature" demotion of the body, caused Elvis, an endlessly fascinating person with great gifts, to appear somewhat like the singing, dancing *Kokopelli*, the engaging soul whom the Hopis celebrate as the moistener of women. He also represents the fertilizing force, the one who brings renewed vigor and life to souls after a long, dry, hard winter.

Elvis still lives for many, for there is a need for his effect on culture. In phenomenology, instead of asking "Why does this phenomenon exist?" we ask, "Why might people believe or agree, or hold open a place for this phenomenon?" The fact that it is claimed by some that "Elvis lives," continues to intrigue the culture at large. Most cultures, for instance, have many numinous, incorrupt saints and holy people. A culture keeps openings for whichever psychic resonances are most needed. For a great soul to somehow remain "alive" after death, is an insistent archetypal habitation in mythos. It meets in some part, a great longing, a great desire by many of the populace for a spiritual king, one that is grace himself, one that can lead the way to Godly ecstasy. It can be speculated that as long as the cultural discourse and fundament remain essentially secular, there will be a vast opening in the culture for the divine.

More than twenty years after Elvis's death, many still seek his lovely moistening effects. Certain idealizations and idolizations remain. Some wait for him to reappear. And no wonder. He was the king; he revivified the desiccated, and was present at the creation of the newest and freshest layer of the culture—the hardworking and hopeful young adults of his time. Why is there so much interest in Elvis long after his death? In addition to his talents, he, and others, who have taken up similar vacancies in the culture, those who have brought precipitation to the desert so to speak—he, and others like him will remain "alive" as long as the culture is parched and unresponsive with regard to the body—as long as the beloved body and the life surrounding it are seen as meritoriously sacrificable in war, as long as the bodies of those who are poor or ill are not considered as precious as any one else's, as long as little children's bodies are allowed to be used like sacrificial lambs, as long as the divine ecstasies of the body are mis-labeled as demonic—as long as an arid culture dreams hard for a blessed rain.

BIBLIOGRAPHY

Estés, C.P. "Sacrificial Victim Conditions Scale: Fifty Conditions Leading to Death." Private research paper, 1990.

Estés, C.P. *Women Who Run With the Wolves.* New York: Random House, 1992.

Guralnick, Peter. *Last Train to Memphis: The Rise of Elvis Presley.* Boston: Little, Brown, 1994.

Jung, C.G. *Memories, Dreams, Reflections.* Ed. Aniela Jaffé. Trans. R. and C. Winston. Rev. ed. New York: Alfred A. Knopf, 1963.

2
The Feminine Hero of
The Silence of the Lambs

JANE ALEXANDER STEWART

She emerges almost as if out of the earth and pulls herself up a steep incline, out of the abyss of a dark morning fog. As she reaches the top of the hill, she hesitates for a moment to get her bearings. The wings of a bird shudder and flutter. She starts to run. Alone in the woods, her footfalls echo in dead leaves crackling over hard ground. She picks up momentum, running slowly at first and then more rapidly, speeding through the deserted forest. Her eyes dart from side to side and she pushes herself to run faster with the resolve of a woman being chased, as if she fears some shadowy pursuer. Her breathing gets heavier. She scales a webbed fence three times her height and falls to the ground on the other side. Is there a sound of someone pushing his way through the bushes behind her? She breathes so loudly now that she would fail to hear the approach of any intruder and if he's there, she certainly doesn't see him. A man steps out behind her and calls out: "Starling!" [1] *She breaks from the obstacle course and, by the look in her eye, it's clear she works to be strong enough to compete with any man, that she won't be defeated by her size, her vulnerability, her sex. "Jack Crawford wants to see you in his office."*

In this very first scene, Jonathan Demme's terror-filled film *The Silence of the Lambs* from Ted Tally's Oscar-winning screenplay sets the audience in position to identify with a new heroic journey of the feminine. When Jodie Foster makes her appearance, an FBI agent-in-training alone in the forest, we feel the context of danger that is the familiar hallmark of a

The original version of this essay appeared in Vol. 14, No. 3, 1995, of the San Francisco Jung Institute Library Journal, *which has kindly granted permission for it to be reprinted here in slightly modified form.*

[1] This speech and those following were transcribed by the author from the video of *Lambs*.

woman's life. "She's not safe," the red light flashes in our brains. Any woman alone, anywhere, puts us on signal alert. Watching *Lambs* terrifies us because we, especially we as women, know the danger so well. We know a woman isn't safe living alone in her own apartment; and she tempts the fates when she chooses to run by herself through a park. Though classical mythology likens the female spirit to a nymph, at one with nature, invisible killers haunt the contemporary American landscape and women live with the fear that attack can come from out of nowhere. Not only do they fear men's attacks on their bodies but also they face denigrating social systems that reinforce a second class status and devalue what it means to live through a feminine point of view.

The character Clarice Starling represents an emerging model of a new female heroine. She embarks on a journey of confrontation with this hidden and pervasive annihilating force against the feminine in American society. Instead of following the precedent of most action/adventure films starring women, *The Silence of the Lambs* does not focus on the way in which women have to function from the masculine in order to get the job done. In Clarice, we see an action/adventure character who is full of feelings from beginning to end, one who never doubts that feelings are an asset, a source of power. We watch her balance her intuitive clarity with a skillful maneuvering of frank and intimate conversation. She has an uncanny ease with emotionally piercing scrutiny from her male bosses, peers, and even the male killers. Close examination of her most private thoughts does not rattle her. If anything, she becomes more focused. She is responsive, not passive, in the face of male betrayals and holds a mirror for the transgressors to look at themselves. And, against all warnings, she continues to place importance on establishing real interpersonal trust with Hannibal "the Cannibal" Lecter.

Clarice begins her story where classic stories of the heroine's journey end; at the return to ordinary life after the descent. Whether or not the filmmakers are aware, the first image of *Lambs* shows Starling pulling herself up from a metaphorical feminine center like Inanna (the Sumerian goddess), a vision that suggests a heroine making her return from the deep process of self-examination and affirmation. She lifts herself out of the abyss, stands at the top of the hill ready to go forward, to forge a career for herself guided by the strength she discovered on the inner journey. When Clarice Starling succeeds, she succeeds as a heroine who carries a set of feminine ethics. She goes beyond self-growth or professional accomplishment. She manages to achieve a far greater victory: she establishes the strength of the feminine up against unmitigated evil and creates hope for the safety of a feminine presence in our society. Clarice Starling is a larger-than-life heroine, one who leads us on a newly unfolding quest to transform *fear* of the feminine and for the feminine into a *triumph* of the feminine.

To imagine that a woman is safe—safer—because she adheres to her feminine values sharply contradicts our thinking. Conventional male-oriented rules for survival are symbolized in *The Silence of the Lambs* by the

FBI training that Clarice Starling receives: be strong, handle a gun properly, cover your back. By inference, this schooling suggests she must suppress her feminine qualities, qualities that are regarded both as provocation for attack and as explanation for women's helplessness. While the intention behind that training may come from the well-meaning desire to help women, schooling women to perform like men in order to achieve safety shows a refusal to trust or rely upon what the feminine has to offer.

The terror of *The Silence of the Lambs* is built upon our subliminal acceptance that a woman is, by her very nature, an invitation to irrational aggression from men. Before she receives her assignment, Starling has a moment alone in Crawford's office where she reacts to the pictures of serial killer Buffalo Bill's victims posted on Crawford's office walls. We know from the tensing in her face that this photographic vision of mutilation of the feminine affects Clarice in a more personal way than it ever could affect one of her male colleagues. Here is the first of many examples of this theme: women experience things differently from men.

At this early point in the film, we simply feel the fear behind that difference. We imagine the worst: unlike male trainees, Clarice could become a victim of an attack like this herself. We feel doubly frightened when we see the emotional way in which photos of the victims of Buffalo Bill affect Clarice because we *expect* those feelings to render her a helpless victim. We anticipate that, because she reacts emotionally, she will be unable to shield herself from that terrible, lurking violent force we have all come to accept as a part of the fabric of our daily lives.

Because we in the audience have worked so hard to numb ourselves in our own lives, our judgment of Clarice is unconsciously guided by the expectations of societally learned prejudices against the feminine. We hope that Agent Starling will submerge her natural inclinations to be emotional, that she will inhibit her true self; that if she insists on trying to become an FBI agent, she will at least be smart enough to realize that this is man's work and must be approached as if she were a man, performing the job the same way he would. We hope that she will emulate the male role model. And that hope is our Achilles' heel. We are afraid to identify with Starling, to choose her inclusion of emotionality as a path of honor and nobility. Her lack of regard for the rules heightens our fear even further as she ignores what we have been taught makes a woman safe.

"Do you spook easily?" Crawford asks Clarice just after he enters the office. On the surface, Jack Crawford appears to be the perfect father-figure and mentor, tough but interested in helping Starling's advancement within the FBI. He evaluates her outstanding record as if she were any one of his trainees, and our inclination is to interpret his treating her without special attention to gender as proof of his open-minded professionalism. But, this indifference speaks to a subliminal prejudice. Pretending to ignore Clarice's sexuality reinforces the belief system that says we should discourage the feminine approach in this arena where crimes must be solved and killers brought to justice. This is the Department of Behavioral Science, a world where agents must be trained to deal with serial killers who skin their victims. And Clarice is about to encounter a man who eats people alive, so terrifying that he can't even be trusted behind normal lock and key. An almost morbid curiosity is set in the minds of the audience: if men fear Hannibal Lecter so greatly, what spectacle will we observe when a woman encounters him?

We hesitate embracing Clarice Starling as an authentic hero for this story. The majority of stories told in our culture feature boys or men as protagonists and present human dilemmas through the masculine ethic. Using Joseph Campbell's outline, the hero's journey begins with the "call to adventure." The assignment—such as Luke Skywalker accepting the challenge to rescue Princess Leia—will be of the highest order and promises to put the hero to the ultimate test, helping him to learn what unique gifts he has to offer the world. The key to any heroic adventure is in the central character recognizing himself as in some way unique and outstanding. The mentor Obi Wan Kenobe teaches Luke that the Force is within him, that he must discover his inner power.

The stories of our culture, in the film arts as well as in literature, support a man's adventure to discover his outstanding qualities but inner feminine principles are not viewed as heroic. "'Cries very easily,'" writes Susan Brownmiller in the chapter "Emotion" from her book entitled *Femininity*, "was rated by a group of professional psychologists as a highly feminine trait" (207). The goal of the study, she goes on to remind us, is to elucidate the way in which "stereotypic femininity was a grossly negative assessment of the female sex and, furthermore, that many so-called feminine traits ran counter to clinical descriptions of maturity and mental health." In a letter to the *Los Angeles Times*, a female probation officer took offense at Jodie Foster's Academy Award night acceptance speech in which she called her character in *The Silence of the Lambs* a feminist hero. "The only way," this woman wrote, that Clarice Starling "got any pertinent information from Hannibal was to use her femininity (read 'vulnerability'), not through any superior analytical investigative skills." In other words, the only method of heroic behavior many women in positions of power know how to embrace is that which can be identified with the masculine: find out the facts, crash down the door, shove the gun out in front, throw the perpetrator on the floor, force his arms behind him and clap on the handcuffs.

Suspense builds as Starling makes herself an exception to these masculine rules of survival. She acts in a spontaneous and natural manner, following a compelling instinct to establish a relationship with Lecter. In her book *Psychotherapy Grounded in the Feminine Principle*, Barbara Stevens Sullivan writes the following:

> Masculine consciousness depends on splitting the world into opposites, on separating elements from their union with each other. . . . Masculine

consciousness separates the individual from his dark inner labyrinth: instead, the individual reaches in and pulls something out to be examined in the clear light of day, in the process of differentiation. . . . The central value of the dynamic feminine principle is Eros: the connections between individuals, the relationships that encircle our lives. . . . We call this feminine consciousness "wisdom." It is the intelligence of the heart, even of the stomach, it is the wisdom of feeling. (17–27)

In what might be described as the metaphorical inner labyrinth of our country's soul, Clarice makes a connection with what the masculine-oriented world hides away and dismisses as an enemy. Throughout the film, Clarice reaches out to intermingle with the "opposite," regarding the darkest areas of human nature as something she can learn from instead of categorizing them as monstrous and abhorrent. Her success lies in her wisdom of feeling. Through the power of her relationship with Lecter, she is able to draw him out and gain critical insights.

"Just do your job," Crawford commands Clarice. His advice is clear: feelings will work to her disadvantage. In a man's story, the strong and rational Crawford would be an appropriate mentor. In Clarice's story, he fails to see the force within her. "You're to tell him nothing personal, Starling. . . . And never forget what he is." True to the cultural prejudice against women, Crawford's message to Clarice says she must learn to be someone other than who *she* is. Her inner forces (for example, trusting in intuition, in revealing herself and interacting on the level of intimacy) are seen as her worst enemies, perhaps greater enemies than even the outer threat of an adversary like Hannibal Lecter.

This figure who in a classic hero's story would prove to be a mentor turns out to be a symbol of patriarchal disregard for the feminine in the *Lambs* heroine's story. In a hero's story, Jack Crawford would send his trainee to see Lecter as if he were going off to slay his dragon. In giving Clarice her assignment, Crawford downplays its importance (he calls it more of an "interesting errand" than a true assignment and assures her he expects little or no results). A few scenes into *The Silence of the Lambs* and it has already been established that Agent Starling has to depend on skills her FBI training does not provide. Crawford's half-hearted deception/offer hardly resembles a hero's call to action but something in his presentation arouses the heroine's attention. "What's the urgency?" Clarice wants to know. Intuition tells Clarice that she is onto something important. She senses Crawford's dishonesty. She refuses Crawford's attempt to gain obedience by frightening her with his simplistic description of evil. She shifts from intuition to another feminine trait we see her use often, the depth-searching question. "What is [Lecter] *exactly?*" Clarice wants to know.

"He's a monster," the chief psychologist Dr. Chilton answers in an elliptical film cut to the maximum security asylum. "Crawford's very clever, isn't he, using . . . a pretty young woman to turn [Lecter] on." Now we learn

that Crawford deliberately misled her, hoping her innocence would be dis-
arming to a menacing killer he knows might have information regarding the
Buffalo Bill case. Crawford dismissed her ability to be effective if she knew
the seriousness of her task. Crawford not only fails to acknowledge Starling's
value, he feigns a protective attitude as a cover to exploit her femininity, as
a lure to engage her cooperation without revealing his motive.

Where Crawford veiled his sexism, Dr. Chilton can't seem to contain a
leering misogyny: "We get a lot of detectives here but I must say I can't
ever remember one quite as attractive," he says upon meeting Starling.
From the moment she leaves the training ground, in the very first
encounter of her very first case, Clarice endures an open verbal assault on
her sexuality. Chilton alternately insults her and then flirts with her, refusing to accept her lack of interest and her professional manner. She holds
her ground as Chilton reveals he has no respect for Starling, not because
she is a trainee, but because she is a woman; he amplifies his disdain when
she refuses his advances. Again, the experience of the heroic journey
changes because Agent Starling is a woman. She can't rely on the patriarchal system to nurture or respect her talents.

As they travel down into the cellars of the building, below the ground,
towards the gallows where the state keeps its most demonic criminals, Dr.
Chilton coldly briefs her on the rules regarding conversations with
Hannibal Lecter. His prelude would frighten even the strong at heart.
Clarice surprises us. She stops and asks to proceed alone. While Clarice's
request might be interpreted as an effort to take control and assume a certain masculine bravado, her agenda remains hidden: she wants to
approach Lecter on her own terms. She knows everyone has failed in trying to gain cooperation from Lecter and maneuvers an opportunity to be
alone with him, using feminine wiles for the first time in order to gain
advantage. She finesses her rejection of Chilton by flattering him as someone with a power that Lecter reviles. Going alone to the interview with
Lecter, Clarice will be able to test and challenge herself, to plumb the
depths of her personal strength. Like a true heroine, she furthers her own
spiritual search as she pursues the information necessary to solving the
Buffalo Bill case.

If the opening scene of the movie hinted at the way in which we fear
for a woman's ability to protect herself, Clarice's slow approach to
Hannibal Lecter's cell vividly reminds us that locks and keys are not adequate reassurance. Even the following written description of this scene
from Ted Tally's screenplay sends chills:

INTERIOR. DR. LECTER'S CORRIDOR. MOVING SHOT—with Clarice, as her
footsteps echo. High to her right, surveillance cameras. On her left, cells. Some
are padded, with narrow observation slits, others are normal, barred. . . .
Shadowy occupants pacing, muttering. Suddenly, a dark figure in the next-to-
last cell hurtles towards her, his face mashing grotesquely against the bars as
he hisses: "I can smell your cunt!" (8–9)

Clarice's dress surely does not project an invitation to seduction in this scene but nevertheless she draws out sexual advances from hidden places by her sheer physical presence. The whispered obscenity by Miggs, a prisoner occupying a cell in the same basement with Lecter, burns like a hot coal, reminding us of Clarice's inherent vulnerability. She has entered into America's underground, the place we hide away the worst imaginable sociopaths, the physical representations of our greatest fears; and the object of their aggression is female sexuality. This symbolic underbelly of society holds a dark male secret, a lust for and hatred against the mysterious power of the feminine. From emotional fragility all the way through to the flash of a leg out of a slit-backed skirt, woman is seen as target in our culture. And because Clarice goes alone, we as the audience get our first view of what sustains the female heroine and helps her hold steadfast while being tested and degraded.

The confrontations between Agent Starling and Hannibal Lecter take us into new territory where we can begin to see the advantage of a woman at work with the demonic. Her method is receptive and responsive from the outset: she avoids a power struggle with the supernaturally charismatic doctor and instead defers to his authority. "I'm here to learn from you," she offers, reaching out to Lecter with an odd respect. He tests her sincerity immediately, asking what Miggs said to her, wanting to see how capable she is of emotional honesty; and she meets his challenge without reservation. Everything Clarice has been taught and told, from the most subliminal messages of systemic sexism to the direct warnings she's received from Crawford and Chilton, urges her not to allow Lecter even the most minimal insight into her feelings. Still, within moments of their first interaction, this heroine appears almost reckless in her willingness to engage Lecter.

That orientation towards personal connection affects Lecter more than even he might suspect. Where Crawford approached Clarice's gender with indifference, and everyone from the respected psychiatrists of the world (Chilton) to the deranged deviants (Miggs) respond to her sexuality with varying degrees of uninvited arousal, Hannibal Lecter acknowledges Clarice as unique. He finds himself fascinated, not titillated, by her character. In their first meeting, Jack Crawford read Starling's resume. Lecter reads her soul: who are you, where do you come from, what have you run from, and where do you want to go?

Her individuality intrigues him. She reveals herself and makes it clear that she is more than an FBI agent. She is a person, and, even more important, a woman. Later in the film, when the mother of the latest Buffalo Bill captive makes a televised plea for her child's life, Clarice remarks on how smart it is to make the killer aware of the girl as a feeling human being. "If he sees her as a person," Clarice says, "it's harder to tear her up." By giving Lecter a sense of who she is, Clarice has affected his desire to destroy her.

In their first meeting, Lecter does dismiss Clarice in an angry fit over her bold assertion that he use his high-powered perception to evaluate himself, but when, on her retreat from Lecter's cell, Miggs defiles Clarice by flinging his animal-semen at her face, Lecter is highly agitated. Witnessing this degrading attack on Clarice's sexuality spurs Lecter into a frenzy, and he offers her a proper call to adventure. He calls Clarice back and awards her with information directly related to the Buffalo Bill case.

Though the audience audibly gasps each time Clarice violates the rules and ignores the warning to remain impersonal, the underground demon surfaces now as Clarice's mentor. The true call to heroine action, the call to rise above ego, comes from the dark side. "Go deep within yourself," Lecter says echoing Obi Wan Kenobe, and he gives her a real life and death assignment that will lead to her finding Buffalo Bill. Her interpersonal treatment of Lecter elicits his feelings of empathy for her and prompts him to give her what she wants most: "advancement."

There is no doubt that on the surface he means to say he offers her advancement within the FBI system. However, the advancement he offers holds symbolic meaning as well and refers to her heroine's journey. Starling's "job" involves more than just catching a criminal. This story focuses on a woman who, while in training to develop her masculine side, discovers her exceptional nature lies in her ability to utilize feminine powers. She confronts an almost mythic demon who demands an emotional exchange whereby she must yield her softest innards in order to gain his cooperation. She opens herself up to Lecter and trusts—not in him—but in her own feminine capabilities as weapons in her fight for life and safety.

In translating Thomas Harris's novel into screenplay form, the filmmakers changed the name of the storage facility from "Split City Mini-Storage" to "Yourself Storage," heightening the metaphor of the heroine's journey, sending Starling literally deep within herself. And what does it mean that Demme photographed the scene to feel as though it were underwater? Here is a quotation excerpted from *The Woman's Encyclopedia of Myths and Secrets*:

> Students in mythology find that when the feminine principle is subjected to sustained attack, it often quietly submerges. Under the water (where organic life began) it swims through the subconscious of the dominant male society, occasionally bobbing to the surface to offer a glimpse of the rejected harmony. (Walker 1066)

In fact, the filmmakers continually photographed Clarice's voyage to feel as though it occurs in the underwater and the underground, the arenas of feminine exploration, emphasizing the closeness to the ebb and flow of nature and darkness that a woman experiences. She then resurfaces to resume her FBI training where her methods contrast with and test masculine rules for success.

"I don't know how to *feel* about this, sir," Clarice says when Crawford tells her that Lecter induced Miggs's suicide, presumably on her behalf. "You don't have to feel any way about it," he responds. This is a key scene regarding the delineation between the masculine and the feminine principle. Crawford thinks answers lie in the facts of what Lecter says while Clarice searches for meaning from the way his actions make her feel. Again from Sullivan's book:

> Masculine knowing seeks laser-like clarity that fosters perfection, analyzing life from a rational perspective, breaking it down into component parts, examining each piece, judging it in a directed, disciplined logical way. . . . Feminine knowing orients toward a state of wholeness that includes imperfection and that blurs edges and differentiations, a consciousness which exists within close proximity to the unconscious. (17–27)

The masculine approach disregards feelings and exalts factual information. The heroine works through feelings in order to make sense of factual information. Clarice has a "feeling" that Lecter is speaking metaphorically when he gives her the assignment to check out his former patient, Hester Mofet. Clarice evaluates the message in context of Lecter's character and decides he couldn't have been sincere about telling her to "look deep within yourself," that there must be some hidden message behind the phrase. Nothing in the facts of what we see would lead us to deduce, logically, that Hester Mofet was an anagram or that Lecter wants Clarice to discover a "Yourself Storage Facility." She uncovers those details through some unexplained intuitive understanding of Lecter's mind and, because of that ability, finds herself pulling back the American flag, deep within "Yourself," from the coffin-like hearse that holds the first clue connecting Lecter to the Buffalo Bill case.

This American flag Clarice pulls back is the first in a long list of references *Lambs* makes to American society. A close viewing reveals that when Clarice finally kills Buffalo Bill, a stray bullet breaks open a window and a small, tattered flag finally sees the light of day. The American flag also hovers above Buffalo Bill's sewing machine and he abducts his wonderbread-fed, size-fourteen girl-next-door victims from the very heartland of the country. When we meet the U.S. Senator's frizzy-haired blonde daughter, Katherine, just before she becomes Buffalo Bill's next captive, she's belting out this Tom Petty lyric, singing along with her car radio:

"After all it was a great big world, with lots of places to run to. Yeah and if she had to die trying, that one little promise she was going to keep. Oh, yes, take it easy, baby. Make it last all night. She was an American girl." (Used by permission)

The filmmakers clearly wanted *The Silence of the Lambs* to be more than a horror film; this is intended to be a culturally meaningful story about the patterns of our society that lead to this unacceptable victimization of women. What dynamics of the feminine do killers exploit? What societally suppressed powers of the feminine need to be re-emphasized in order to change the cycle of brutality? How is it that our mothers, sisters, and girlfriends find themselves cowering in the back of a van, trapped by a serial killer?

Haven't all women, at one time or another, walked from their cars, maybe even carrying groceries, and found some stranger or neighbor in need of a hand? The threat of danger usually overrides the natural inclination to offer assistance to someone in need; but every now and then, hasn't everyone just decided to put those groceries down and help push that car up the driveway or grab the end of that heavy couch? In her book, *In A Different Voice*, Carol Gilligan writes:

> The moral imperative that emerges repeatedly in interviews with women is an injunction to care, a responsibility to discern and alleviate "the real and recognizable trouble" of the world. For men, the moral imperative appears rather as an injunction to respect the rights of others and thus to protect from interference the rights to life and self-fulfillment. (100)

Women like to help. It's part of their desire to make connections, open up possibilities, to give and receive from each other. The violent serial killer, like Buffalo Bill, appeals to that desire and then exploits it. He draws upon a woman's generosity and then attacks her; and (the male-oriented) society turns the event around, blaming the woman for engaging in the interaction in the first place.

Blaming the victim distorts and undercuts a woman's ability to protect herself. American culture socializes women away from their natural means of defense. The character Katherine hesitates when the stranger asks her to step into his van and carry the couch all the way back where she'll be unable to escape if he is indeed Buffalo Bill. Her intuition tells her she should switch off her helping mode and stay out of the van, but she does as she's told and steps into danger anyway. She doesn't back away, retreat. Why? Like Katherine, American girls are taught from childhood to be the "good girl," to be agreeable and compliant, to promote an amiable emotional environment, to nurture even when it goes against innermost intuitive feelings of danger. In 1848, pioneer feminist Elizabeth Cady Stanton made the following, capitalized declaration to reporters: SELF-DEVELOPMENT IS A HIGHER DUTY THAN SELF-SACRIFICE (Gilligan 129).

Whether its message is directed toward a woman who follows the traditional goal to "stand by her man" or toward one, like Clarice, whose professional training suggests the importance of being like a man, patriarchal society teaches women to serve its goals at the expense of their own, less linear values.

The breakthrough aspect of *Lambs* is that the closer Clarice comes to accepting her true feminine self, the closer she gets to solving the crime; and the closer she gets to solving the crime, the more she has to grapple with who she is as a person. In their first meeting, Lecter chides Clarice for trying to cover up her hinterland roots. She surfaces from their tense confrontation in tears and has a comforting vision, from her provincial childhood, of her father returning home. Contrary to the negative assessment of what it means to cry easily, here we see a woman's inner, private life appearing to nurture her and help her work through the fear she has just been courageous enough to confront. When Crawford pulls her out of class and steps up her participation in the Buffalo Bill case, Clarice ironically has to go back to Virginia, the unsophisticated "state" from where she came. Both *Lambs* and Clarice Starling take Elizabeth Cady Stanton's advice by taking the next step. Clarice's self-development overcomes her fears of inadequacy and leads her to an even higher duty of asserting her feminine presence in the world. Self-acceptance leads to self-expression.

With her penchant for matter of fact confrontation of authority figures and her reliance on feeling, Clarice exhibits a growing confidence in her feminine complexity after she returns from her mission into the "self"-storage facility to meet with Lecter for the second time. Anything but the good girl, Clarice sits on the floor, wet from her submersion into the unconscious state of exploration and discovery, and she thoughtfully exposes her exhilaration at finding the beheaded former client of Dr. Lecter. As her emotional bravery becomes more visible, we are impressed and tentatively begin to look for Clarice Starling to be the one who will find the killer through her privileged conversations with this demon. We begin to trust in what initially we feared the most and are prepared to follow her on the heroine's journey that could transform our constrictive beliefs about the feminine.

Our first inclinations lead us to fear that Lecter has the upper hand, that he feeds Starling information in a way that will further endanger her. Because she reveals herself, maybe she isn't "watching her back," and ultimately Lecter will make his offer of collusion in an effort to do her in. Somewhere, somehow, he has a master plan to get out and kill everyone; and Clarice must be playing directly into his hands. Though resistance to taking the path of heroism through feminine principles is difficult to overcome, the audience enters wholeheartedly into this heroine's quest; we want Starling to succeed in her unorthodox method not just for her but for ourselves as well. We begin to trust Clarice not because she is capable and resilient but because she has exceptional talents suited to this particular battle.

Clarice's ability to set the boundaries between revealing herself and allowing exploitation defines both the level and the complexity of her heroic interactive skills: it puts her on par with Lecter's analytic prowess. Though she tacitly gives Lecter permission to probe her with personal questions, when he uses that privilege to focus on Jack Crawford's sexual interest in her, she stops him cold, refusing to dignify his verbal fantasy of Crawford's special interest in her with an answer. "Frankly, doctor, that doesn't interest me," she asserts, "It's the kind of thing Miggs would say." That emotional sophistication protects her from both her fear of Lecter and from our own subliminally accepted sexism out in the audience. The ability to differentiate emotional rapport from exploitation is one of the distinctive, heroic capacities of feminine instinct. Acting upon it enhances Clarice's status and establishes a boundary with Lecter: Lecter cannot take her as a fool. From this point on, Clarice's subtle, unspoken pride in her inner power must be honored. This is not to suggest that Lecter stops testing her or that he divulges his secrets to Agent Starling easily. As always, the demon/mentor has more in mind than helping Clarice solve the Buffalo Bill case. Clarice has established for herself a relationship that parallels the Obi Wan Kenobe/Luke Skywalker model: as she presses for answers that will help her complete her outer pursuit, Lecter holds out in order to teach her about her inner quest.

"All good things to those who wait," is Lecter's tutelary, snake-like response to Clarice's demand to know who killed his former patient. This adage, especially suited to the heroine's journey, speaks to the importance of the feminine ideal of immersion and contemplation, to let one's growth process "happen," so as to avoid blocking a discovery that is trying to surface in its own way.

Throughout this testing of her patience, Clarice is learning to accept and rely upon her unique self, now, in *all* its facets. Confronted by the grisly reality and heinous condition of the killer's latest victim in an autopsy scene, she drops any countenance of urbanity. Now, both her gender and her provenance work in her favor. Her understanding of the specificities of the habits of a "girl from the city" (versus one from the town) leads her to uncover things about the victim (the way her nails are painted means she is more likely to come from a particular area) that no other examiner can see. She is coming to a fuller awareness of the significance of self-respect or, in other words, she is learning the importance of cherishing and not disqualifying for any reason one's personal background experiences as valuable and relevant to the task at hand.

More important, we see Clarice consistently return to her inner gifts in order to further her double goal in the outer world, which is to solve the case while gaining recognition for feminine principles. This dual agenda emerged in an earlier scene, when Crawford resorts to a sexist ploy to win over the local sheriff. The FBI is being met with a cold reception for intruding into the community grief at the funeral of a hometown girl. Under the pretense of protecting Starling's delicate ears from hearing the description of the condition of the skinned girl, Crawford seeks—and obtains—a private conversation with the sheriff. Far from shielding Clarice, the exclusion draws attention to her sex from a roomful of male deputies, all of whom are already hostile to the FBI's intrusion into their investigation. Crawford leaves her standing alone to withstand the probing social gaze of these local policemen whose attention he has focused on her alleged inadequacy. Once again, we get a chance to see this action/adventure heroine plunge down inward. Without an ally to protect her from the invasive stares, she withdraws from a scene as uncomfortable as any of the film's more graphically malevolent moments by entering into the room of mourners and recalling a fantasy memory of her father's funeral.

Clarice's recurrent retreats into childhood memory imply that feeling images, even sad ones, have restorative power. Clarice's feminine strength helps her gain control of her emotions. She "resurfaces" from this immersion into self and handles the deputies with a heroic feminine gesture. Choosing not to assert her authority as an FBI agent to dismiss the deputies' participation in the autopsy, Clarice speaks up and assures the men that she understands their concerns. She asserts her control by taking their feelings seriously, deftly circumventing the power struggle in an unexpected way. Later, in the car, Crawford acknowledges his mistreatment of her. He tries to seek her approval, and she holds her ground to make what appears to be a small point, illuminating the higher value of the act. "Cops look at you to see how to act. It matters," she reprimands. Her point is taken: as a man in a position of authority, his devaluing of her leads to a greater acceptance of sexism. This is a subtle representation of what is the larger and most important issue that the film addresses. It is not sufficient to make a place for a woman on the job: what is needed is a place for the feminine to be expressed. Those men who hold positions of authority must break old habits of sexism and interact with the values and perspective of the women close to them.

The feminine hero wants male respect both for her ability to hold down a traditionally male job and to assert her own way of being in that job. She wants to enter and wield power in traditionally male institutions but with her soul intact, perhaps even doubly committed to feminine values. She may lack development in the male skills, be symbolically "in-training" like Clarice, but she is also making demands on her colleagues and superiors to accept the intrinsic value of a feminine orientation, one that has developed as a consequence of experiencing life as a female. Just as Clarice's goal involves more than finding the killer, the new heroine's goal reaches beyond any desire to overthrow the patriarchy: it strives instead for a transformation of what has become heartless in patriarchy, seeking above all, a societal rebalancing.

"What did you mean by transformation, doctor?" Clarice asks Lecter after she has revealed her worst memory of childhood and earned her turn to question him. *Quid pro quo*—a fair exchange: that is the ethic of Clarice and Lecter's confrontations with each other. The startling realization that these two could share an ethic suggests a symbolic basis for healing the imbalance in masculine and feminine principles that creates such frightening aggression in our culture. "Billy wasn't born a criminal, Clarice. He was made one through years of systematic abuse," answers Lecter. "Billy hates his own identity, you see, and thinks that makes him a transsexual. But his pathology is a thousand times more savage, more terrifying."

Buffalo Bill's character suffers from a severe detachment from his feminine, a theme which touches on us all, regardless of gender. This is a killer so out of touch with what it means to be feminine that he thinks he can achieve womanhood through stitching together a costume made from the hide of the outermost definition of what it means to be feminine. This is a sinister aggressive new strategy by the masculine to take an unmerciful hold on the feminine by appropriating its persona. Risking a homophobic interpretation, Demme presents the psychological disarray of Buffalo Bill (a character who disappointed many viewers, in contrast to the texture found in Starling and Lecter) as a masculine dementia driven to the point of pathological persecution and destruction of the female in the outer world. It is noteworthy that the pathological behavior of coveting what is coveted (in this case, a woman's appearance—her outer skin) finds credence as a desperate attempt on the part of a male killer for some remnant of self-esteem. This is an even darker thread of the evil wrought by the schism between masculine and feminine: a man trying to reverse self-hatred by killing and then clothing himself in a superficial representation of what he lacks within.

Resistance to using a feminine orientation as an inner authority is particularly intense because claiming authority as Clarice does means confronting that which male authority often fears the most: its unknown territory, its darkness. Masculine-oriented storytelling builds the hope that we can dominate life, that we can exclude darkness. Stories in which the good-hearted hero defeats the evil villain carry on the fiction of possibility that we can live happily ever after. This masculine ethic of transcendence through domination reinforces a defense of institutionalized aggressive behavior. The familiar result, socially, is to live in a false state of security, a world run by the masculine principle of protection from harm where killers lurk behind every tree. In such a world, women aren't safe to offer the counterbalance that includes respect for the dark side, an embracing of the side of humanity where solutions are not clear and problems of the shadow persist to the point that evil is a fact of life that must be continually confronted.

While Clarice does manage to fulfill the audience's expectations for heroic action by killing Buffalo Bill, the rescue sequence in the murderer's house is a parade of the heroine's powerlessness against controlling the evil underworld rather than the usual heralding of an FBI agent's ability to save the day. It is hard to recall a film in which the triumphing hero seems more vulnerable. As in her submersion into "Yourself Storage," or her descent to visit Lecter's gallows, Clarice almost swims through the depths of Buffalo Bill's subaqueous maze while he toys with his power to reach out and touch her in the darkness. What would in the usual detective film be the hero's victory in battle against the antagonist feels instead like a narrow escape from victimization; only in a flash of frightened intuition does Agent Starling manage to fire her gun in the right direction and save herself from the very fate of the kind of girl she has set out to liberate. This thin victory leaves the audience feeling unsettled because the threat of victimization continues: we don't feel secure about the defeat of the villain.

The masculine journey, to which we have become so inured, resolves through conquering and winning, (Lucas made it work by tapping into the joy of his boy-hero in *Star Wars*) but this feminine journey fails to wrap itself up so neatly. When in a masculine hero's journey, our knight slays the dragon, the new equilibrium is one of safety and the townspeople shower gifts upon their savior. Solving the Buffalo Bill case, on the other hand, gives Starling little more than an official commendation, and leaves the largest relationship of *The Silence of the Lambs* unresolved: we know that Lecter has escaped and remains at large. Even as she graduates with honors, with the always reticent Crawford adding his supposedly supreme compliments, a dry assurance that her father would be proud, Clarice gets a phone call from Hannibal Lecter. Crawford's awkward and indirect praise is contrasted with Lecter's presumptuously easy style and pointed congratulations, which imply that he hasn't forgotten their negotiation for a fair exchange. We respond to his insinuation uneasily: does she still owe him something? Even though we allow that their connection is strong and Clarice has proven herself a worthy adversary, we slip back into identifying with a woman who has violated all the rules, revealed herself and told too much. It's clearly not over. "I'll not be coming after you." Lecter's words are so unexpected that they ring out even as he speaks them in soft tones. "The world's a more interesting place with you in it," he explains. What has moved Lecter, the symbol of pure evil, to set this boundary of safety for Clarice? Why does the demon choose to let the heroine live? Is it possible that vulnerability has developed a safe passage instead of invited disaster? Could empathy and intimacy have protective power? We are left with questions.

Symbolically, this is Clarice's greatest triumph: she has achieved a new state of equilibrium with the darkest level where feminine values can not only withstand but *co-exist* with the hidden and terrifying consequences of an extreme masculine emphasis on control of objectionable elements. When Lecter asks Starling for reciprocity, for his liberty from her pursuit, she defines her power through empathetic language, "*You know* I can't do that," and here again she appeals, with confidence, to the connection between them. She doesn't say *I* can't do that, as if she were now separate and apart from him. She does not abandon the feminine orientation but keeps it as a basis for action. Her honesty is part of the balance, part of the give-and-take that is key to the bargain that the *Lambs* characters have established as a precedent for collaboration. Above all other imposed responsibilities, codes of honor or magnanimous pacts of exchange, it is Clarice Starling's prerogative to affect the world through asserting her principles and she takes it as her duty to do so. On a literal level, she can't let Lecter go because he is a criminal and she is an FBI agent; more profoundly, she can't let aggression that breeds on detachment live freely without offering the opposition of intimacy as a balance. In symbolic terms, the masculine and feminine opposites are not independent of each other: one force simply cannot prevail without influence from the other. *The Silence of the Lambs* ultimately suggests that the feminine hero's goal lies not in destroying the demon that masculinity has become under patriarchy but by creating a relationship with him, to affirm feminine value in a hostile world that has forgotten how desperately it needs her.

The Silence of the Lambs is an unusual story of a woman who, even in the face of all the pressure to behave like a man in order to remain safe and achieve success, confronts her fear, and in turn challenges our fear that to be feminine means you are a vulnerable target and a deserving victim. A symbol of the modern woman who no longer finds herself in the role of looking solely for personal approval or acceptance in a professional position, Clarice is neither demanding nor rebellious. She asserts her values with a self-possessed presence and a matter of fact manner of expression. She is able to gain crucial information from the most renowned serial killer alive as well as to learn from him. She succeeds where men have failed. By the time the movie ends, the hero has done the usual. She has saved the girl, destroyed the bad guy and graduated with honors; but something does not feel usual, ordinary. This hero won the day not by being an expert, male-identified FBI agent, but by breaking away and asserting herself as a woman who could rely on her feminine self to provide her with the special or "super" strength she needed. In this breakthrough film, as Jodie Foster recognized, the filmmakers vaunt a new type of heroine, one whose *feminine* capabilities make her exceptional.

BIBLIOGRAPHY

Brownmiller, Susan. *Femininity.* New York: Fawcett Columbine, 1984.

Gilligan, Carol. *In a Different Voice.* Cambridge: Harvard University Press, 1982.

Petty, Tom. "American Girl." © 1979 Almo Music Corp. (ASCAP) All rights administered by Almo Music Corp. (ASCAP) For the World. All rights reserved. International © Secured.

The Silence of the Lambs. A Jonathan Demme Picture. Videocassette. Orion Home Video, 1991.

The Silence of the Lambs. Unpublished version of the screenplay, with notes. 28 July 1989.

Sullivan, Barbara Stevens. *Psychotherapy Grounded in the Feminine Principle*. Wilmette, Illinois: Chiron Publications, 1989.

Tally, Ted. *The Silence of the Lambs*, Screenplay based on the novel by Thomas Harris, 1989.

Walker, Barbara G. *The Woman's Encyclopedia of Myths and Secrets*. San Francisco: Harper and Row, 1983.

3
The New American Hero: Made in Japan

ANTONIA LEVI

The lament for America's lost heroes is almost a national tradition. It begins whenever an athlete, actor, or politician turns out to be dishonest, promiscuous, or given to substance abuse. It ends only after all possible culprits have been carefully examined: the celebrity for having failed some unspoken test, society for its failure to maintain moral standards of yesteryear, even the media for having mentioned the whole sordid business in the first place.

An unspoken assumption behind such laments is a definition of the hero as someone, usually male, who is without flaw, spiritually or physically. It is a heroic ideal that could only come from a Judeo-Christian culture with its omniscient, omnipotent god. In Europe, that ideal is tempered by a pagan past, but America is a young nation and its heroic tradition expects nothing less than life-long perfection. Real-life American heroes, being merely human, inevitably disappoint their followers sooner or later.

The same is less explicably true for America's mythic heroes, those larger-than-life figures who embody the culture's most valued traits in human form. America is a young nation and only just in the process of creating its own myths. As a result, most of its heroes are still derivative and simplistic. Many are found in a genre traditionally viewed as light entertainment: in comic books, cartoons, and occasionally in sword-and-sorcery fiction.

Most of America's new mythic heroes are derived from European pagan traditions. Some, like *Conan the Barbarian* or *Hercules*, are easily identified with their originals. Others, like *Superman* or *Batman,* are more changed although they still fall clearly into god and demigod types. However, they share two major features. First, whatever ambiguities and imperfections may have been present in the original characters, they have been simplified into a "good guy" stereotype by America's puritanical version of the Judeo-Christian tradition as embodied in comic book and television codes. And second, these new heroes are overwhelmingly male; even the few female superheroes who have emerged, like *Wonder Woman* or, more recently, *Xena*, are simply female versions of a male heroic model.

Small wonder that most comic book, cartoon, and sword-and-sorcery heroes remain one-dimensional figures confined to the realm of light entertainment. Such heroes are without flaw and also without depth. They lack the humanity that would lend them interest as fictional characters and allow their audience to identify with them. Many cartoonists get around the problem of retaining interest in the fictional character by providing their superhero with a secret identity, usually a nerdish alter-ego that is never publicly associated with the heroic persona. This allows for greater plot complexity, but it still impedes identification since the division between the character's humanity and his heroism remains. Indeed, the greatest fear of most of America's superheroes seems to be the public exposure of that secret identity, of their humanity.

That became very evident in *Superman II* when the Man of Steel was literally forced to choose between crime-fighting and a normal life. He chose the crime-fighting. Later, the television series *Lois and Clark* managed to introduce some humanity into Clark Kent, but only at the cost of distancing him still further from his heroic alter-ego. Clark is becoming increasingly human, while Superman develops new, even less human powers having to do with cyberspace.

Small wonder, then, that the American hero is forever getting lost. As role models, such mythic heroes present a standard of behavior that is both unattainable and undesirable. As fictional characters, they are predictable and, except when in action, dull. And as mythic archetypes, they lack the depth and humanity that would allow ordinary people to identify with them. What America needs is a more approachable, realistic, and diverse image of what a hero truly is.

America has found that new image in a most unlikely place, in the sudden popularity of Japanese *manga* (comic books) and *anime* (animation), particularly those in the science fiction and fantasy genres. *Anime* and *manga* have their own definition of the hero, one which is based on Japanese mythology and warrior traditions. This is not surprising. What is surprising is that this uniquely Japanese definition of the heroic is finding a growing army of fans in America. Dubbed and subtitled *anime*, in particular, are entering mainstream American popular culture. Both as themselves and in the influence they have already had on American artists and writers, they are changing the American definition of the heroic.

It is a definition that places at least as much emphasis on motivation as it does on action. For the Japanese hero, the righteousness of the cause is less important than the purity of his or her commitment to it; a *kamikaze* pilot, for example, remains a hero even though the author concedes the evil of the empire he fights for. Success or failure is also unimportant;

indeed, failure is sometimes preferred since dying for a hopeless cause offers additional proof of the hero's absolute altruism. That emphasis on motivation means that the hero's personality must be presented realistically and in some depth. That kind of examination inevitably reveals some flaws, and most *manga* and *anime* heroes are flawed, some of them quite seriously.

Many of them are also female. That comes as a surprise to many Americans who assume that Japanese cartoons will reflect the low status of women. In fact, Japanese women face about the same degree of inequality as American women, but the nature of that inequality is very different. Their image, reflected in the popular media, reveals some shocking (to Americans) assumptions about women's "weaknesses," but it also reveals some surprising assumptions about women's "strengths."

Manga and *anime*'s flawed and/or female heroes are a needed addition to America's limited store of mythic heroes. That is why, despite the cultural and linguistic problems present in even the best translations, their popularity with Americans continues to grow.

The *Manga/Anime* Tradition

In Japan, *manga* and *anime* dominate popular culture far more profoundly than comic books and cartoons do in America. Although some are designed for children, most *manga* and *anime* are intended for a highly literate, adult audience. The best of them feature complex plots, multifaceted characters, and a wealth of allusions to a wide variety of literary, historical, and cultural sources. Most begin as serialized comic strips in cheaply printed monthly *manga* magazines. A popular series may run for years, and will usually be republished in paperback volumes. If it is popular enough to justify the expense, it may be animated as a television series or an OVA.[1]

In a general sense, *manga* can trace their ancestry back to the illustrated scrolls of the seventh century. However, the present form of *manga* and *anime* goes back no further than the 1950s. The universally acknowledged creator of *manga* and *anime* is Tezuka Osamu (1928–1989), an eccentric doctor turned cartoonist. Tezuka was influenced by both American animation and the animated propaganda produced in Japan during World War II, but in his own work, he deliberately departed from his models to create a new art form. Among the many legacies Tezuka left to subsequent *manga* and *anime* artists was a new definition of the modern hero.

Tezuka's World War II experience led him to become a life-long pacifist and also to distrust all claims to "purity": racial, cultural, ideological, or heroic. None of Tezuka's heroes are ever "pure" heroes; they are complex

---

[1] OVAs, or original video animations, are episodes which are released directly into the retail market rather than first being shown on television.

characters and complexity means that they are all, in some way, flawed. Blackjack, one of Tezuka's most popular heroes, embodies that principle in his physical appearance. His face is half black and half white, the result of a skin graft. Moreover, since the black part of the skin graft represents a life-saving donation from a black friend, making easy assumptions about which side represents good and which evil is a mistake. The same is true of Blackjack's character. He is a brilliant but mercenary surgeon, capable of great kindness as well as brutal cruelty.

That complexity and moral ambiguity is at the heart of Tezuka's definition of the hero and, therefore, at the heart of the new types of heroes coming from Japan today. Whether or not Americans would care for the original model is unknown. Little of Tezuka's work has yet been translated. His two most popular children's series, *Astro Boy* and *Kimba the White Lion*, enjoyed some success on American television in the 1960s, but only after American editors had edited out some of the more pronounced moral ambiguities. In 1996, Yuji Oniki began translating one of Tezuka's adult *manga, Adolf ni tsugu*, rendered into English simply as *Adolf*.

Adolf, a five-volume saga about World War II, presents Tezuka's heroic model in undiluted form. It actually has no heroes. *Adolf* concerns the lives of two boys, Adolf Kamil, a Jewish refugee growing up in exile in Japan, and his best friend, Adolf Kaufmann, the son of a German diplomat and his Japanese wife. Both boys must come to terms with not belonging; Kamil has no nationality and Kaufmann is half Japanese in a world where racial purity is all-important. Sent to Germany for indoctrination, Kaufmann ultimately becomes a raging anti-Semite, a loyal Nazi, and later on, a member of the PLO and the Black September group. Kamil does a bit better, but eventually he too succumbs to the murderous impulses of nationalism and war. As an Israeli soldier, he eventually kills his one-time friend, Adolf Kaufmann.

There are no flawless heroes in *Adolf*. There are also no total villains. That is because making moral judgments is impossible in a world where war is the villain. In one episode, for example, a Japanese journalist avenges his brother's death by raping the Nazi woman who betrayed him. Although the journalist is a sympathetic character overall, the rape is portrayed as a brutal act of hatred, and one that returns to haunt him. Nor is his victim necessarily sympathetic; she is a self-righteous racist, and even when she commits suicide, there is a strong suggestion that what really drove her to it was not simply being raped, but being raped by a man she considers racially subhuman. Neither the rapist nor his victim are easily defined as sympathetic or hateful. The reader is not permitted the luxury of knowing exactly what to think or how to feel.

It is still too soon to tell whether or not *Adolf* will prove popular with American readers. It may prove too alien. Yet, Americans have already embraced Japan's flawed heroes in many softer renditions produced by later Japanese cartoonists.

The Flawed Hero

Later cartoonists often subscribed to Tezuka's dictum to avoid heroes that were too easily identifiable as good or evil, but few remained quite as aloof from judgment. Most *manga* and *anime* heroes are more clearly identifiable albeit in a different way from America's flawless heroes. Heroism in most *manga* and *anime* is internal: heroes must be sincere and they must be selfless, at least at the moment of heroism. It is not necessary for a *manga* or *anime* hero to be an saint, to fight for the right side, or even to be successful. Anyone who sincerely gives his or her best efforts to almost any task can be a hero.

That definition of heroism did not begin with *manga* and *anime*. Japan has a long history of flawed heroes who go to their deaths in a futile defense of a hopeless cause. Indeed, the fact that the cause is hopeless is the ultimate proof of the hero's sincerity and selflessness. Noted Japanologist Ivan Morris called it "the nobility of failure," (Morris, *passim*) and compiled a collection of flawed, failed heroes dating from Japan's prehistory to the *kamikaze* pilots of World War II.

The Japanese definition of what it means to be a hero is one factor that helped the nation deal with its defeat in World War II. World War II remains a popular venue for heroism in *manga* and *anime*. Indeed, *Star Blazers*, one of the first *anime* to succeed on American television, is a space opera in which Earth defeats a technologically superior foe by building a spaceship around the ruins of the sunken battleship *Yamato*. The *Yamato* was a real ship which went down with all hands, and is now a sunken tomb rather like the U.S.S. *Arizona*. The reason the fictional spaceship *Yamato* wins against all odds is because it carries the heroic spirit of the original *Yamato*. Contrary to the fears of many Americans, such references do not mean that most Japanese still subscribe to the ideology of Imperial Japan or dream of an eventual victory over the United States. It simply means that the Japanese concept of heroism exists apart from ideology or victory.

That is an idea that appeals to many Americans, particularly Generation X. This generation of twenty-somethings has to deal with parents who fought in the Vietnam War, friends who fought in the Gulf War, and the possibility of children who will fight in even murkier battles in the post-Cold War era. The American heroic ideal often leaves them with a choice between denouncing the actions of those they love or finding a rationalization for causes they may find more than slightly questionable. Japan's flawed warrior-heroes offer them an alternative to that choice.

For example, *Captain Harlock*, a series and a character created by Leiji Matsumoto in the late 1970s, provides a classically flawed hero whose main claim to heroism lies only in the purity of his own heart. Harlock is a space pirate and, like Tezuka's Blackjack, his physical appearance reveals his ambiguous character. Gaunt, dressed in red and black with a skull and crossbones as his only ornamentation, featuring an eye patch on one side of his face and a disfiguring scar across the other, Harlock is a fairly terri-fying figure even in the diluted version that ran on Japanese television in 1978–1979 and on American television in 1985 (Ledoux 31–32). Later in a full-length movie, *My Youth in Arcadia*, Matsumoto provided more infor-mation about his character, making him more complex and more ambiva-lent than ever.

The unimportance of ideology and/or victory is spelled out fairly explicitly in an early scene in *My Youth in Arcadia* when a flashback sequence reveals how Harlock and his friend Ōshima Toshiro met in an earlier life, on a European battleground during World War II. At that time, the two men acknowledged the futility of the war in general and their side (the Axis powers) in particular. In the end, Harlock ferried Toshiro to safety in Switzerland so that he could live to pursue his dream of conquering space rather than killing other human beings. Harlock, however, returned to face the advancing enemy, remaining loyal unto death to a cause he did not believe in. That behavior contrasts sharply with the decision he makes 1,000 years later when Earth is occupied by imperialistic aliens. When Earth's cowardly governors decide to collaborate by helping the invaders in their imperialistic designs, Harlock chooses to obey the spirit rather than the letter of his oath of loyalty to the planet, and becomes an outlaw.

The World War II version of Captain Harlock is no more or less a hero than his later incarnation. He may be a little wiser the next time around, but his heart is still the same. He is brave, loyal to his friends, and willing to die before betraying his own feelings about what is right. He is no more successful than his German self was 1,000 years before. As a space rebel, Harlock has three major aims: to save the planet Tokarga from destruction, to save the life of the woman he loves, and to awaken the spirit of resis-tance among his fellow Earthmen. By the end of the movie, despite Harlock's best efforts, Tokarga has been annihilated, Maya is dead, and the majority of Earthmen remain cowardly collaborators. Harlock and his crew find the final expression of their heroism in the purity of their intentions and the vastness of space.

That heroic ideal is not confined to the battleground. Not all *manga* and *anime* heroes are warriors. Many are ordinary people who become heroes simply by remaining true to themselves. That too poses an inter-esting alternative for Generation X. Living in an uncertain economic cli-mate in which their defining characteristic is that they are the first generation of Americans who will not do better than their parents, Americans in their twenties are also attracted by an ideal that stresses the importance of effort and commitment over the prestige, importance or suc-cess of the task. For a college graduate who has just discovered that the best job she can get is a sales position at The Gap, that definition of hero-ism can be a useful survival skill.

It is no accident that one of the most popular *anime* heroes in America today is Shiro Lhadatt of *Wings of Honneamise*. Where Harlock and his world had obvious ties to World War II, Shiro is a hero designed for the *shin jinrui*,[2] Japan's version of Generation X. Shiro is a young man living on an Earthlike planet at the beginning of its space age. Shiro shows no outward sign of his internal struggles. His appearance is ordinary, neither ugly nor handsome, perhaps a bit stupid and loutish. He holds a variety of meaningless jobs and finally winds up in the Royal Space Corps, a despised unit of losers whose main feature is that they are expendable and available for flights in underfunded, undertested spacecraft. When he meets Riquinni, a female missionary with a message of universal love and peace, Shiro is fascinated. The reason for his interest is not so much sex or the nature of Riquinni's religious beliefs, but simply her ability to believe so utterly in anything.

Eventually Shiro ruins his relationship with Riquinni by getting drunk and trying to rape her. By that time, however, he has learned from her that heroism exists in the heart and not in external circumstances. He learns that lesson just in time, immediately before he is loaded into a poorly made space capsule that will very likely burn up on re-entry. As he begins his orbit, he looks down to see fires indicating that another pointless war has broken out. At the end of *Wings of Honneamise*, Shiro finds the true meaning of heroism in much the same place as Captain Harlock, in the sincerity of his own heart and the austere purity of space itself. Unlike Harlock, who at least had his crew and a powerful ship at his command, Shiro is alone in a capsule over which he has almost no control. In the Japanese scheme of things, that makes him more rather than less heroic.

Shiro's flaws are many, but except for his attempted rape of Riquinni, which is pretty half-hearted and easily thwarted, he is not dangerous. That is not true of all *anime* heroes. Perhaps one of the most flawed *anime* heroes popular with Americans today is Gally (called Alita in the translated *manga*), the hero of *Battle Angel*. Gally is a cyborg with amnesia. Found on a garbage heap and rebuilt by an eccentric scientist, she cannot remember her original programming. However, when her benefactor is attacked, she displays the lightning reflexes and instincts of a trained assassin. She soon finds work as a bounty hunter, tracking down criminals in a society that has no real police, but Gally does not find her heroism in her career. Her heroism lies in her determination to find humanity and love in a world that has little of either.

The *anime* version of *Battle Angel* chronicles Gally's first attempt to find love. Yugo, the young man she loves, is driven by his desire to buy his way out of the slums in which he and Gally live. He yearns for a better life in the floating city of the elites. To that end, he resorts to murder, killing his fellow slum dwellers for their organs, which he sells on the

---

[2] Literally translated, *shin jinrui* means new human being. It carries the connotation that they are a whole new species, quite separate from their hard-working elders.

black market. Gally, who is still too recently rebuilt to have much moral sense, decides to help him. Her assassin's skills are an asset and result in a series of grisly killings. Gally becomes a walking horror show of kicking, slashing, and ripping gore, but her intentions are pure. She wants only to buy her beloved Yugo his dream. She fails. In the end, with Yugo dead, Gally achieves heroism simply by surviving with her own dream of love intact.

With heroes like Gally, it sometimes becomes difficult to tell the hero from the villain. Indeed, some of *anime* and *manga*'s most seriously flawed heroes are its villains. The first of these to reach America was Leader Desslok (Dessler in the Japanese original), the handsome, blue-skinned commander of the invading alien force in *Star Blazers,* which aired in 1979–1980 (Ledoux 21–22). His behavior caused some real problems for the censors who edited the series for an American audience. Such editing was necessary partly because of different cultural standards, but also because American television insisted upon regarding all animation as children's fare. In fact, the Japanese version of *Star Blazers, Uchū Senkan Yamato* (*Space Cruiser Yamato*), was designed for an audience of teenagers and young adults, and included a fair amount of violence and sexual themes.

Even so, the censorship of scenes surrounding Desslok went beyond what was required to satisfy American television codes or a younger audience. The American editors were particularly troubled by Desslok's tendency to execute his subordinates for minor failings. These scenes were not only cut, but the death of the subordinate was often disguised; he simply disappeared from the story without explanation. For a villain, Desslok's behavior should have been acceptable even if the graphic depiction of it might be too much for children. The reason it troubled the American editors was that Desslok was not villainous enough. He had too many heroic attributes. Despite his arrogance, his brutality, and his love of luxury, he was brave, intelligent, and sincerely committed to doing what he felt was best for his doomed planet and his people; unfortunately, that happened to involve the destruction of humanity. At the same time that the censors eliminated much of Desslok's brutality, they tried to undermine his heroic stature by giving him a syrupy, almost effeminate voice that was nothing like the deep bass of his Japanese persona.

Desslok was, in fact, not so much a villain as a flawed hero fighting on the wrong side, an enemy-hero. Such enemy-heroes are at least as common as villains in *manga* and *anime,* and often replace the villain altogether. Enemy-heroes usually embody the same flaws as the central character but in a more extreme form. This was certainly the case with Desslok, who set off the character of Derek Wildstar (Kodai Susumu in the original), the central hero of *Star Blazers.* Like Desslok, Wildstar's flaws were those of youth. He was often overconfident, judgmental, and impulsive. He never shot anyone on his own team, but in times of stress, he often lashed out with words at whoever was nearby. Since *Star Blazers* was a long-running series (seventy-seven television episodes and five movies), he had plenty of time to mature. So did Desslok. In the end, he and Wildstar admitted their admiration for each other; Desslok then committed suicide and Wildstar followed him soon after.

Desslok was not an isolated instance. *Manga* and *anime* include many enemy-heroes who behave much worse than Desslok without sacrificing an ounce of their popularity. One such is Char Aznable, the enemy-hero of *Gundam*. Like Desslok, Char is brave and intelligent, but his sincerity is in doubt from the start. Char is the disguised son of a murdered ruler who infiltrates the government of the usurpers to avenge his murdered father. Such vengeance is an acceptable goal, possibly even a laudable one, but it does involve the betrayal of a ruler to whom Char has vowed loyalty. The situation becomes worse when Char shifts his allegiance, to the creation of a new, improved race of people with telepathic powers. It gets worse whenever Char shifts his allegiance which is all too often. He is usually sincere enough about whatever commands his allegiance at any given moment, but he is overly complex, given to ornate masquerades and Machiavellian schemes. Ultimately, these undermine his sincerity and therefore his heroism. He dies only just in time before the self-hatred generated by too many betrayals changes him from an enemy-hero to a villain with a few good qualities. Or maybe he dies too late for that. Fans disagree.

Despite the moral ambiguity that surrounds Char Aznable, or maybe because of it, *Gundam*'s popularity has been phenomenal in both Japan and America. In Japan, the series actually caused riots when model kits went on sale (Schodt 93). Its popularity in America is less dramatic, but still surprisingly strong given that *Gundam* is not actually available in English translation. *Gundam* fans who are not fluent in Japanese must make do with illegal fan-subs[3] or the synopses available on the Internet or through *anime* clubs.

American popular culture is only slowly beginning to realize the value of the enemy-hero. Aside from the fact that having a worthy foe sets off the exploits of the hero, the enemy-hero allows for greater emotional complexity of response. The audience can never totally rejoice in his or her downfall. They must recognize that for every victory, someone else must suffer a defeat. Such mixed feelings may take some getting used to, but most Americans seem to find them more fulfilling than those evoked by a simple struggle between clearly defined good and evil. In time, it may even affect the way Americans look at their domestic and international policies

---

[3] Fans sometimes edit their own subtitles onto Japanese tapes. The results are then copied and exchanged between *anime* clubs. This violates American and Japanese copyright laws.

The Female Hero

Given the prominence of American women in the feminist movement, there are surprisingly few women among America's mythic heroes, and none who embody a specifically female model of the heroic. *Manga* and *anime*, on the other hand, feature at least as many women as men in heroic roles. In some cases, these women play roles that are little different from their male counterparts. In others, however, the fact that they are women is part and parcel of their unique type of heroism.

The sheer number of female heroes in *manga* and *anime* does not, in itself, reflect any feminist agenda. *Manga*'s defining feature is its preference for the outrageous, the titillating, and the satirical. Strong female characters are often introduced precisely because strength combined with femininity is considered outrageous and titillating. Such works are often intended as satires or soft porn.

Even in those that are not, female heroes who are simply female versions of the male heroic model do not necessarily send a positive message about women. Often, they are flawed because of their gender. This is the case with Remy Shimada, the female hero of *GoShogun:The Time Étranger*. In this metaphysical fantasy, Remy, the only female member of a giant robot fighting team, battles Death itself. She shows all the attributes of the traditional flawed hero. She is brave, intelligent, persistent, loyal to her comrades, and able to joke in the face of terror. Her flaw, however, is her gender, and the physical weakness that it is presumed to entail. Although her martial arts skills carry her through most of the time, there are occasions when she cannot run quite fast enough, or jump quite far enough, or, in the final battle, completely control the huge gun she insists on using. That does not completely negate her heroism. Even gender-flawed heroes like Remy Shimada stand taller and prouder than almost any American female mythic hero with the possible exception of *Xena, Warrior Princess*.

However, *manga* and *anime* do have female heroes for whom gender is not a flaw, for whom it is actually the source of their heroism. These come in two basic forms, both drawn from Japanese tradition: the warrior's woman and the *miko*, the Shinto priestess.

Japanese tradition has always celebrated the warrior's woman: the seemingly frail, obedient creature whose outward subservience hides a core of pure steel. *Manga* and *anime* have continued that tradition, particularly *manga* and *anime* that are aimed at a male audience. Maya, Captain Harlock's lover, is eulogized as a woman who, despite her physical weakness, stood by her man and her beliefs to the bitter end. Her particular virtue is that she had sufficient strength not to tie her man down, hold him back, or require his support when greater events urged him on.

Margo, the beloved of Seno Hiro in *The Venus Wars* presents a more up-to-date version of that ideal. At the beginning of *The Venus Wars*, Margo is simply a cute girl with, seemingly, no real idea of what the coming war means to her life. She is Hiro's "girlfriend," but he actually shows little real interest in her until he is seriously wounded and crawls to her for help. She is shocked, but she copes. Later, as the war progresses, Margo reveals further coping skills. Hiro finally realizes the full intensity of his love for her at the end of *The Venus Wars* when he finds her calmly organizing the evacuation of her family. As a cute little girl who longed for his support, she rated amused affection at best. As a woman capable of caring for others, she merits the true love of her warrior.

American women are unlikely to become enamored of the Japanese warrior's woman style of heroism with its emphasis on self-sacrifice. Japanese women are no longer terribly enthralled with it either, and such women usually play secondary roles in *manga* and *anime* designed for men. Even so, the Japanese warrior's woman is an improvement over the American warrior's woman, whose seemingly frail exterior often hides an equally frail interior.

Perhaps the most dramatic role women play in *manga* and *anime* is based on the *miko*, the Shinto priestess. In ancient times these female shamans were sometimes rulers, often empresses. Even after they were displaced by other forms of government, they continued to serve as mediums, oracles, and exorcists until they were banned in 1873 by the Meiji government as part of the effort to create a new, nationalistic form of Shinto. Since 1945, they have made a modest comeback and can often be seen assisting priests or even dancing at Shinto festivals in their distinctive red and white (occasionally just red or white) costumes. A few have even justified the formation of new shrines and sects claiming spirit possession or powers of divination (Blacker 127 and Reader 65–70). That real-life comeback is nothing, however, compared to their resurgence in the fantasy world of *anime*. There, in the hearts and minds of modern Japanese, the *miko* rule again. One suspects they never really left.

Despite their ancient antecedents, *miko* often appear in contemporary or futuristic *manga* and *anime* stories. They are easily identified, even when translations do not preserve their actual title. Most live in Shrines and wear the traditional red divided skirts (*hakama*) with a white top; a few dress entirely in white, the Shinto color of purity. Some *anime miko* have also adopted some of the paraphernalia of Western witches such as pentagrams and black cats. Unlike Western witches, however, *miko* have never had a reputation for evil, although they can be a bit spooky. Aside from those who identify themselves as *miko*, *manga* and *anime* also contain a plethora of mediums, magical girls, and transformative women, all of whom are based on the *miko* tradition.

The source of a *miko*'s power is her ability to communicate with, control, and sometimes become part of, the supernatural world. That power is usually hereditary and passed down through the female line. In addition, the young *miko* is generally trained by a female relative. This is the case with Mai, the hero of the *manga, Psychic Girl Mai*. She is actually a little behind in her development, since she was brought up by her father. When danger threatens, however, her mother returns from the dead to instruct her daughter in her hereditary duties. Mai's mother does not come alone. She is accompanied by a long line of *miko* who appear in the *manga* as a tableau of bare-breasted women, Mai's ancestors, stretching back in time. When Mai ultimately faces down the international forces of war and destruction, she too goes into battle bare-breasted.

Most *miko* seem to wind up naked, at least from the waist up, when they go into battle. It is easy to dismiss this simply as titillation, and that is one reason for it. However, a more basic reason is that the *miko*'s powers are intimately connected with gender. There are no male *miko*, and in the few cases where a man demonstrates *miko*-like powers, he is usually portrayed as effeminate and sometimes as homosexual. Thus, when a *miko* like Mai bares her breasts in the climactic moment, she is showing the proof of her womanhood and the source of her power.[4] She is not stripping for sex, but for battle.

Sex can, however, be part of a *miko*'s supernatural arsenal. Keiko, the *miko* hero of *Doomed Megalopolis*, certainly uses it in this way. Keiko is not an obvious sexpot; when not in her red *hakama*, she dresses in traditional kimono. Yet, she uses her charms to marry into the family that guards the shrine where she knows the demon she has vowed to fight will manifest. And when she finally confronts the demon, she does so naked. Indeed, her exorcism technique is one of seduction. She offers the demon the one thing his evil cannot resist: absolute, unconditional, and unplatonic love.

Sex and gender also affect the powers of many female heroes who do not identify themselves as *miko*. The most prolific of these are the transformative women who are as basic to *manga* and *anime* as costumed superheroes are to American comics. These women are usually teenagers who, often because of heredity, acquire superpowers when they reach puberty. That can cause confusion when presented to an American audience.

In an early episode of *Sailor Moon*, a recent *anime* success on American television, the thirteen-year-old heroes discuss one another's breast development. When the series aired on American television, censors wondered whether or not they should cut these "irrelevant" sexual references. A wider acquaintance with this particular genre would soon have revealed that such references are far from irrelevant. They are a signal that these heroes are about to reach full power, that the girls are becoming women. *Sailor Moon* presents a rather subtle variation on this theme. *Blue Sonnet*, which has not made it to American television although it is available on videocassette, offers some more obvious links between puberty

---

[4] Editor's Note: For a fascinating and detailed followup on this theme, read Jane Alexander Stewart's essay in the present volume, "The Feminine Hero in *The Silence of the Lambs.*"

and power. In the opening episode, Lan Matsuzaki collapses on the high school tennis courts with "stomach cramps." Her friend takes her into the locker room and the next frame shows a thin trickle of blood flowing down the shower drain. Shortly thereafter, things are flying off the walls and Lan is revealed as a new telekinetic hero: the Red Fang.

Such references to puberty do not necessarily mean that the new hero is about to become sexually active. Quite the reverse. Most transformative women are explicitly virginal. This is not a question of prudery, but of power. Series about transformative women draw on *miko* traditions and folk beliefs in their unspoken assumption that since women's power develops with puberty, it can be destroyed by sexual experience, especially if that experience is traumatic or too early in life. This is what happens to Yukari in *Doomed Megalopolis*. As a young girl, Yukari shows signs of power; she is actually the first to see the demon who has invaded Tokyo. However, Yukari is also the victim of incestuous rape, a circumstance that distorts her powers, leaving her uniquely vulnerable to demonic possession.

Of course, Yukari is an extreme case but she is not atypical. In *Devil Hunter Yohko*, Yohko's mother lacks the demon-fighting abilities of her clan because she became sexually active too soon, before those powers were fully developed. Yohko's grandmother is determined to prevent that from happening to Yohko, and on one occasion crashes her motorcycle into a hotel just in time to drag the embarrassed, naked girl out from under her high school boyfriend. Granny is not anti-sex; quite the reverse, but she wants Yohko to realize her own powers first. If self-esteem is substituted for demon-hunting powers, most American psychologists would probably agree with Yohko's granny.

The *miko* and her offshoots are long overdue in American popular culture. The American women's movement has opened unprecedented opportunities for women, but young women often lack the confidence to take advantage of them. According to a report released by the AAUW in 1991, most young American women lose their self-confidence in their early teens, just about the time when *manga* and *anime* women power up (AAUW, *passim*). Japan's *miko* and transformative women tradition with its positive attitude toward the physical changes that occur at this time of life may well have something to offer America's teens. Of course, the absence of strong female mythic heroes is the not the only reason for the AAUW results, but it is a contributing factor.

New American Heroes?

The popularity of *manga* and *anime* is a fairly recent development in America. It began as a campus cult phenomenon in the 1980s, but it has only begun to reach the mainstream in the past four or five years. At the moment, American fans seem content with translations of Japanese works. As translated *manga* and *anime* enter the American mainstream, however, they will begin to affect what Americans expect from their own comic books, cartoons, and other sources of mythic fantasy. They will certainly begin to expect more complex heroes. And American cartoonists will try to respond with a more American version of Japan's flawed, often female, heroes.

In fact, that has already begun. Most efforts are still closely tied to the Japanese *manga* and *anime* industry. For example, *Star Blazers* and *Robotech*, two *anime* series that succeeded on American television, have continued in comic book form; the new comic book series are written and drawn by Americans although they feature the same characters relatively unchanged. In one case, a cartoonist named Adam Warren has actually purchased the rights to a *manga* series, *Dirty Pair*, and produced his own series featuring the same female heroes; Warren's version, however, tends to emphasize the titillating aspects of the series over its action and comedy components. Another cartoonist, Ben Dunn, created his own series based on the comedic *manga* style; the result, *Ninja High School*, is effective as a satire on American superheroes, but offers little in the way of creating its own heroic types. Stan Sakai combined the American cartoon tradition of anthropomorphizing animals with Japanese themes to produce *Usagi Yojimbo*, a Samurai rabbit who strives to retain his honor in a war-torn world; sometimes he succeeds, sometimes he doesn't.

Manga and *anime* have also begun to make themselves felt more indirectly in more mainstream comics and cartoons. The new, darker version of *Batman*, for example, seems to be trying to redraw this classic American superhero in a more ambiguous light. *Batman*'s creators have explained this new "dark side" as a reversion to the feel of the prewar series. That explanation does not ring true. The prewar series was darker in feel, but that darkness related more to its portrayal of the villains, not the hero. The prewar Batman may have been more brutal than he later became, but he was always identifiably a "good guy." He still is; the new Batman's flaws are minor, no more than an occasional lapse of confidence or a temporary round of vampirism. However, the villains have become a bit more sympathetic, thus throwing the few flaws of the hero into greater prominence. The animated version of *Batman* also reveals some stylistic traits of *anime* such as the attention to shading, the use of stills for dramatic effect, and the stylized portrayals of water, smoke, and fire.

The same is true of other superhero comic books and cartoon series such as *X-Men, Wild C.A.T.S.,* and *Exosquad*. Although still embarrassingly simplistic when compared to Japanese efforts, these new superheroes are more deeply defined as characters, less perfect and more inclined to self-doubt and self-recrimination than ever before. If that trend continues, American cartoonists may yet produce a genuinely American mythology with a new pantheon of indigenous mythic heroes.

Unfortunately, they will still be overwhelmingly male. Although the new series do feature a few female superheroes, these all fall into the realm of a woman playing a male heroic role. This is partly due to the fact that there are few women in decision-making positions in the industry. There are also remarkably few female cartoonists anywhere in the mainstream comic book and cartoon industry.[5] That will undoubtedly change in time. However a more serious obstacle to the creation of a specifically female heroic ideal may be the absence of a usable prototype. The only Western equivalent to the Japanese *miko* is the witch, who is not only associated with evil, but also with New Age practices. Witches and even goddess-based female heroes are starting to emerge in underground comics and graphic novels like Neil Gaiman's *Sandman* series, but it will be a long time before more mainstream publications and the television networks risk alienating their audiences (or their audiences' parents) with such controversial material.

How deeply *manga* and *anime* affect America depends, of course, on how deeply they penetrate mainstream culture and for how long. At the moment, *anime* in particular is doing well in America. The recent release of *Ghost in the Shell*, a cyberpunk fantasy featuring a female hero, drew record audiences at art theaters. Even more recently, Disney Studios contracted to distribute Hayao Miyazaki's animated children's films, all of which feature strong female leads, most of them linked to *miko* traditions in some way. *Manga* are making their way more slowly onto store racks, but they are finding readers. Considering how short a time they have been around, the impact of *anime* and *manga* on the American comic book and cartoon industry has been profound. How much further it will go, however, is still in doubt.

BIBLIOGRAPHY

AAUW Educational Foundation Research. *Shortchanging Girls, Shortchanging America*. Washington DC: AAUW, 1991.
Battle Angel. Kishiro, Yukito. Houston, Texas: A.D. Vision, 1993.
Blacker, Carmen. *The Catalpa Bow: A Study of Shamanistic Practices in Japan*. London and Boston: Unwin Hyman, 1975.
Captain Harlock. Matsumoto, Leiji. Westlake Village, California: Malibu Comics Entertainment, 1992.
Devil Hunter Yohko. Aoki, Tetsuro. Houston: A.D. Vision, 1990.
Doomed Megalopolis. Taro, Rin. Santa Monica: Streamline Pictures, 1992.
GoShogun: The Time Étranger. Yuyama, Kunihiko. New York: Central Park Media, 1995.

---

[5] The same is not true in Japan, where almost half the top *manga* and *anime* artists are female, although men still dominate in production and distribution.

Kudo, Kazuya and Roichi Ikegami. *Mai the Psychic Girl*, trans. James D. Hudnall. San Francisco: Viz Communications, 1995.

Ledoux, Trish and Doug Ranney. *The Complete Anime Guide: Japanese Animation Video Directory and Resource Guide*. Issaquah, Washington: Tiger Mountain Press, 1995.

Levi, Antonia. *Samurai From Outer Space: Understanding Japanese Animation*. Chicago and La Salle: Open Court, 1996.

Morris, Ivan. *The Nobility of Failure: Tragic Heroes in the History of Japan*. New York: New American Library, 1975.

Mulhern, Chieko. *Heroic With Grace: Legendary Women of Japan*. Armonk and London: M.E. Sharpe, 1991.

My Youth in Arcadia. Matsumoto, Leiji. Hicksville, New York: Best Film and Video, 1993.

Reader, Ian. *Religion in Contemporary Japan*. Honolulu: University of Hawaii Press, 1991.

Sailor Moon. Takeuchi, Naoko. Burbank: Buena Vista Home Video, 1995.

Schodt, Frederik L. *Dreamland Japan: Writings on Modern Manga*. Berkeley: Stone Bridge Press, 1996.

———. *Inside the Robot Kingdom: Japan, Mechatronics and the Coming Robotopia*. Tokyo and New York: Kodansha International, 1988.

———. *Manga! Manga!: The World of Japanese Comics*. Tokyo and New York: Kodansha International, 1983.

Star Blazers, Episodes 1–39. Nishizaki, Yoshinobu. Englewood Cliffs: Voyager Entertainment, 1980. [The original *Yamato* series is also available through Voyager Entertainment, Inc.]

Tezuka, Osamu. *Adolf*. Trans. Yuji Oniki. San Francisco: Cadence Books, 1996.

The Venus Wars. Yoshikazu, Yasuhiko. New York: Central Park Media, 1992.

Wings of Honneamise. Yamaga, Hiroyuki. Chicago: Manga Entertainment Video, 1995.

4

The Hercules Complex: The O.J. Simpson Story

MARITA DIGNEY

> It is a fact that cannot be denied: the wickedness of others becomes our own wickedness because it kindles something evil in our own hearts . . . . Has it never occurred to anybody, for instance, that the vogue for the thriller has a rather questionable side?
>
> —C.G. Jung, *Civilization in Transition*

If it is possible for an entire culture to experience a common neurotic symptom, then surely a shared obsession was revealed in the American psyche in our response to the murders of Nicole Brown Simpson and Ronald Goldman and the ensuing criminal and civil trials of Orenthal Simpson. The tremendous psychic energy expended by the press to slake the insatiable thirst of the American public for details of this crime and the lives of those involved approached the amount of coverage given to major world events such as wars and famines. On many days network news coverage of the trial surpassed that given to international and political events. Both television and radio talk shows hummed with the voices of ordinary citizens debating fine legal points regarding esoteric scientific findings and the admission of evidence. This hysterical response, at times, rivaled the level of passion of the crime itself.

This shared madness revealed far more about us as Americans than about the people and events related to the trial. The whole phenomenon took on the unreality of a dream-like state in which the protagonists of the ever-unfolding drama reflected parts of the psyche of the viewers. These very current events told an old, familiarly haunting tale. Indeed, it is a tale which we already knew, about a pattern of masculine violence rooted in the distorted family system prevalent in our culture and clearly revealed in the lives of O.J. and Nicole Simpson.

This pattern, which I call "the Hercules Complex," is as contemporary as the "Trial of the Century" and as ancient as the heroic, mythological figure of Hercules. It refers to the relationship of love and violence. A human struggle as intense as this evokes the deepest levels of the human personality, Carl Jung's "collective unconscious," where myth, symbol, and dream reside. We all partake unconsciously in these patterns of shared fears and unrealized hopes. Someone like Mr. Simpson is not different from us on the whole, he is just more visible.

Difficult as it is to see, the shadow of our own violence was mirrored back to us in the figure of Orenthal James Simpson. What we saw in that mirror was the great American dream, a poor boy who became a rich man. Simultaneously his life revealed the great American nightmare; all the popularity and money in the world could not buy happiness. Sitting in those courtrooms, while the details of his uncontrollable rage and physical violence toward his wife were documented, he became the portrait of the man who had, it seems, gained the whole world only to lose his own soul.

As the cameras focused on his physical presence, what we actually saw was our own most sinister thoughts and hidden feelings. Some saw a man who was guilty of murder. Some saw a man who was a victim of the system. For all of our intensity, the vision of O.J. Simpson as a brutal wife-beater and perpetrator of a murderous crime of passion or as an innocent, wrongly accused, arthritic sports figure remains largely in the eye of the beholder. The present analysis of our response to this crime and trial will not directly address Mr. Simpson's guilt or innocence nor the myriad questions raised by the issue of race. The Hercules Complex refers to a level of the psyche which is shared. Our response to these events, though often split along racial lines, was beyond race. We may have reacted differently according to several cultural variables, but on the whole, it was as a culture that we reacted.

The drama of what has come to be known as "The Simpson Case" provided a plethora of archetypal symbols, stirring our imagination and emotions. The powerful presence of television cameras in the courtroom cannot be overestimated. It allowed the images of husband, wife, father, mother, child, and most of all, the archetypes of victim and vindicator to haunt all who watched. The physical beauty of those involved provided images more suggestive of gods and goddesses than mere mortals. As if they were Olympians, eternal questions regarding what it means to be human were part of what kept us mesmerized by this amazing sequence of events.

Problems of the human condition as fresh as domestic violence, and as old as whether a husband possesses his wife like chattel, confronted us. The struggle within each of us between violence and peace, love and hate, madness and sanity was waged afresh each day before our eyes.

As we gathered nightly around that new campfire, television, and watched the events of the day in court, we heard echoes of ancient tales and mythological motifs. We just could not move away. The emotions evoked were primal and familiar. Another way of saying this is that they were archetypal. Consciously or unconsciously, we were resonating with questions which have plagued humankind since the beginning.

The drama of brute strength wrestling with the values of civilized constraint harkens back in the human imagination to the mythological hero, Hercules. Hercules, son of the god Zeus and the mortal woman Alcmene, was the greatest and strongest of the Greek heroes, granted the gift of "Herculean" strength by the gods, but also tested and tortured in the same measure. Throughout his mortal life Hercules was seized by passionate, at times murderous, rages. In one of these rages he murdered his children and, in some accounts, murdered his wife. Hercules is eventually driven to suicide by unbearable wounds caused by the blood of an enemy, a Centaur, whom he killed for making advances to Deianeira, Hercules's wife.

Like all who have had their aggression provoked by a hostile environment, Hercules struggled with controlling his violence all of his life. For Hercules, who had to overcome poisonous vipers sent to slay him in his infant's crib, to Mr. Simpson, who fought malnutrition and then the hostile streets of the ghetto, where he was ridiculed because of the size of his head, the psychological truth that violence begets violence applies. What is true for these two figures, is true for each of us. The myth of Hercules was born out of the imagination and experience of the gifted human beings who created it. Just as the ancient Greeks created the Hercules myth, we twentieth-century Americans have created the "O.J. myth." As you will see, there are amazing similarities in these stories, which indicate we are still struggling with the same psychological material.

As the offspring of Zeus and one of his many mortal partners, Alcmene, Hercules was persecuted all the days of his life by Hera, the jealous wife of Zeus. Because of this troublesome parentage, Hercules's mortal mother abandoned him to the elements to die, an unusual fate for a healthy baby boy. Hera was tricked into suckling this abandoned male child. His paradoxical name means, "Glory of Hera." Hercules was conceived by the father god who very much wanted a remarkable son. To accomplish this, Zeus seduced a mortal woman. Abandoned, Hercules was raised and educated by men. It is odd to have his identity attributed to the immortal Hera who was betrayed by his very conception. Hercules, then, is the son of a woman who is not identified as mother but rather as consort of the father. This fact is the determinant of his fate. It gives him his name, creates his identity: son of the betrayed and therefore hostile mother. The mythmakers are telling us something essential here: the slighted child of a betrayed mother grapples with violence and aggression all of his or her life.

Hercules emerges as a man with a impaired relationship to the mother. He is a living symbol of the inevitable suffering in a culture where mothering is compromised. He is missing the primal bonding to a stable, care-giving other, male or female, who is dedicated to him and enabled by the culture to meet his essential needs. In this sense he carries the wound of the privileged son of the patriarchy, where women are dominated by men. In this system women are limited in the ability to mother freely in their own right because they are firstly identified as consort, and as they must remain consort in order to survive economically, the mother-child bond suffers. Then children experience what might be called a "hollow mother": the need for mothering exists, but the mother or mothers who are present in their lives are compromised in ways which prevent them from offering the nourishment and love necessary for the healthy and autonomous development of the child. As every mother who has ever birthed a child knows, good mothering and child care do not pay the rent: factors outside of the mother-child bond are necessary for this to occur.

The Simpson story mirrors this conflict—of woman as consort of the father versus woman free to mother—in the reports of Simpson rejecting Nicole when she was pregnant with their second child. Her diaries indicate that he called her a "fat pig," asked her to have an abortion, and was violent to her during her pregnancy (Butterfield 35). This is an example of the woman-as-consort/woman-as-mother tension which exists in all male-dominated relationships between parents. Here we see the Hercules Complex as an inter-generational phenomenon. The unmothered man, in a culture of male privilege, demands to be the sole focus of his wife's attention. This sets up a competition with his own child for the precious but limited resource of what is really, at its basic level, mother love. The National Clearinghouse on Domestic Violence statistics indicate that approximately three million women are battered each year. Statistics from more than one source indicate that 20–30% of battered women are pregnant (New Jersey Coalition 6). Lest we focus too closely on the Simpson case and miss the real point, keep in mind that there are millions of Nicoles battered each year.

Though Mr. Simpson appears to have a remarkable, loving mother, he experienced the hollow mother in the context of the wider culture. In childhood, Mr. Simpson had rickets, a disease related to malnutrition (Gibbs 29). Like Hercules, he was in a sense abandoned by his care-giving environment. Though clearly cherished by his personal mother, his broader care-giving community failed him. Indeed, it fails all children in such circumstances, by not providing the essentials which are necessary for healthy physical and emotional development. The individual person who would mother may be stressed, preoccupied with the father, abandoned by the father, ill, busy providing a living, or psychologically unmothered herself. For one reason or another, including poverty, the wider culture is not supporting her with the resources to mother well enough. That in a rich and abundant nation like the United States, poverty exists for a shockingly large percentage of children is an indication that the culture is manifesting a hollow mother to a significant number of its members. The results of this will, from an archetypal perspective, yield equally shocking future violence. This is also an indication that the Hercules Complex is a widespread malaise which unconsciously influences public policy and decisions about allocation of resources. We did not respond to the Simpson case by accident or solely out of our desire for melodrama; we responded because we know this story, in some personal variation, by heart.

In fortunate families mothers are not compromised. Moreover, what the mother provides can often be supplemented by people or institutions in the child's environment. From the perspective of the needs of the child, it actually matters little who carries healthy mothering to the child as long as someone does. It is clear that the Hercules Complex is not the fate of all in our culture. Some loving, egalitarian enclaves of sanity have, through the ages, resisted the prevailing ethos. Some women are valued in their fullness including as consort and mother. Some women are free to choose neither of those identities and live full lives. Some children are sufficiently protected and abundantly mothered by their personal mothers, fathers, extended families, neighbors, churches, synagogues, and schools.

For the truly unmothered, there exists a deficit which is never filled. For such a person the attachments to mother and subsequently to the unrealizable necessity of the constantly available woman are very strong because the need for mother has never been satisfied. It is said that Hercules once cavorted with and impregnated fifty women in one night. In the hyperbole of myth the point is made, that the appetite for sexual conquest, like the need for mother, can be insatiable. Often such individuals develop a sentimental overvaluing of the mother, even deification of her. This creates a psychological reality, or as the Greeks would say, fate, which colors the experience of a lifetime. But most importantly for our discussion here, the unmothered child, male or female, is aware of this betrayal and grows up an angry, hostile, and violence-prone individual. This child has been meanly cheated out of its birthright to thrive and knows this at some level of awareness.

Like Hercules, Mr. Simpson distinguished himself by his physical prowess. Before the trial, Mr. Simpson was considered a sports hero of considerable fame, a remarkably likeable and popular figure. From a mythological perspective such a designation is a loose application of the meaning of the word "hero." Both Hercules and Mr. Simpson were held in fond esteem by the wider culture. Hercules, however, is an example of the archetypal hero in that his accomplishments of danger and cunning often benefitted entire communities in substantial ways.

What is often ignored in the popular images of both Hercules and sports figures today is that the physical aggression necessary for their prodigious athletic feats spills over as violence into their personal lives ("Athletes" VIII, 1:2). Such men become over-identified with the unrelated aggressivity of the masculine side of their nature. It is said that Hercules claimed never to have picked a quarrel but always to have given the aggressors the same treatment as they intended for him (Graves 148). Mr. Simpson is quoted as saying, "I only beat up dudes who deserved it . . . usually once a week" (Gibbs 32). Both statements are examples of the mind-set by the which the violent ascribe their own motives to others and then blame the victim.

After murdering a teacher, Hercules was sent to the country where in time he became famous as a warrior. He was never defeated in battle. In a madness sent, it is said, by Hera, Hercules murdered his own children. As in all living myths, there are at least two ways of telling this part of the Hercules story. What is true for both Mr. Simpson and the mythological Hercules is that in some renditions, he is named as the murderer of his wife. In other accounts he is not found guilty of this crime.

Though a murderer many times over, the Hercules of the Greek myth is no unrepentant psychopath. Repeatedly throughout his life Hercules seeks guidance, performs service, and once is sold into the service of Queen Omphale, where he is required to do women's work and serve as if he were her handmaiden. These activities both punish Hercules and assist him to integrate his aggression with his desire to relate and be loved.

At one time, seeking the help of the Oracle at Delphi as spoken by the Sibyl, Hercules is instructed to go into the service of a lesser man for twelve years. In this ancient expression of community service, Hercules served Eurysthesus and performed what have become known as the "Twelve Labors of Hercules." This part of the myth represents the development of conscience, struggling as Hercules did with both his aggression and his desire to relate in a constructive way. At a later time he underwent the initiation of the Eleusinian Mysteries, another rite of intense ritual purification and hope of spiritual transformation. Hercules is paradoxically a vile murderer, a liberator, and a man with the courage to relate and develop beyond his aggression.

For all his repentance, Hercules lived to murder again. Eventually his infidelity in marriage led to his painful, self-inflicted death. In a prophecy, Zeus said, "No man may ever kill Hercules: A dead enemy shall be his downfall" (Graves 189). These fateful events came to pass. Deianeira, the wife of Hercules, tiring of his love for Iole and his extramarital exploits, decided to use trickery to put an end to his unfaithfulness.

While crossing a flood-swollen river, Hercules entrusted the care of Deianeira to Nessus, a Centaur. When Nessus attempted to violate Deianeira, Hercules killed him. Before he died from this wound, Nessus told Deianeira: "If you mix the seed which I have spilt on the ground with blood from my wound, add olive oil, and secretly anoint Hercules' cloak with the mixture, you will never again have cause to complain of his unfaithfulness" (Graves 186).

In time this is exactly what Deianeira did. We learn in the myth that Hercules, in the midst of a sacrifice to his father Zeus, put on the cloak soaked with the blood of his victim, thus releasing the poison which

coursed all over his limbs, corroding his flesh. As the pain was beyond
endurance, he tried to rip off the garment, but it clung to him so fast that
his flesh came away with it, laying bare the bones. "His blood hissed and
bubbled like spring water when red-hot metal is being tempered" (Graves
188). With the blood of his victim burning his skin, Hercules sought the
fire of death to extinguish the fire of guilt. He mounted a pyre and gave
orders for its kindling.

Being the natural son of Zeus as well as the suckling of Hera, Hercules
was welcomed, after death, to Olympus and the realm of the immortals.
Though he died, in some sense unredeemed, he worthily and fully bore
his fate. Hercules's heaviest labor was to integrate his enormous masculine
strength with his legitimate need to love and be loved. Clearly we are still
integrating the message of the life of Hercules. We seem to have missed
the point, and have passed through the ages the worst of the patriarchal
values, and must, in each generation, essentially fight once again the old
fight. Seen in this light, Hercules represents an energy of human potential
which can be used positively or negatively but which cannot be ignored.

In the development of consciousness, as the story of humanity continued to unfold, the unfinished task of Hercules was taken up again and
approached differently. Another hero, in another struggle of mythic proportions, faced the conflict of these two great forces in the human personality, power and love. In the New Testament account of the temptations
in the desert, Jesus of Nazareth wrestled with the issues presented to him
by Satan. He was tempted to use his considerable personal power to create food, earthly kingdoms, and security (Matthew 4:1–11, Luke 4:13). He
chose instead to honor the call of his divine father to proclaim the realm
of God and proceeded to use his power in the service of healing and
teaching. His kind of love, described by the Greek word *agape*, a spiritual
love, included women as well as men, the ill as well as the healthy, and
the outcasts as well as the socially acceptable. The unorthodox response
of this Galilean sage to use power in the service of *agape* demonstrated a
life lived free of the Hercules Complex. He was crucified for his efforts, but
he modeled a refreshing possibility available to the human psyche. For us,
the struggle continues as does the choice.

The fact that the well-loved Hercules, who never came to terms with
his violence, was deified in the Greek imagination, suggests a shadow side
to the patriarchal Olympus. We could say as well that the "myth" of O. J.
Simpson reveals the shadow side of the American sports world and its
wider cultural milieu. Likewise, family systems based on male privilege
institutionalize a violence which is passed like a curse through the generations. As long as a society creates a large percentage of hollow mothers,
the Hercules Complex will continue to be a dominant force.

As we enter another millennium, it is alarming to reflect that many people, if they know the history of the last thousand years, know best the history of wars and warfare. The sentimental historians' notion of the

progressive development of civilization away from violence and toward increased human rights died in the gas chambers of the Third Reich, as did many idealized religious notions. The power of the well written constitution which defends individual liberty ends wherever might makes right.

Today violence in both war and peace become ever more bizarre. Genocide, ethnic cleansing, terrorist attacks on the innocent, and rape as an instrument of war are frighteningly present in the news each day. In the midst of this violence, the family is ever more stressed. More and more women consider the world as we know it an unsafe place to raise children and hence by the millions they choose not to bear children. Abortion has become for some a form of birth control. Clearly, these are difficult times in which to mother well.

Violence pervades American culture. Sports contests, once a form of ritualized, controlled combat, increasingly cross the line into actual violence. Even as ritualized combat, participants are maimed and bodies broken as a matter of course. Recitation of the "Disabled List" becomes routine sports news. Talk shows incite participants to a screaming frenzy, occasionally, a fatal frenzy. Children watch uncounted hours of television in relaxed states and as their brains slip into receptive alpha waves, they are saturated with images of violence. Weapons go to school. Whole segments of the American populace, often deprived inner city residents, implode upon each other in drug wars and gang violence. Increasingly murder-suicide replaces a happy old age as the culmination of life.

Homes are revealed as battlefields of another kind. The civil trial of Mr. Simpson brought to the attention of the general public the detailed story of violence in the seemingly paradisiacal world of privilege. The phrase "domestic violence" labels a phenomenon as old as our civilization itself. Although academic and political battles of words over statistics rage, the FBI's Uniform Crime Reporting system states that men most often kill men, strangers, and those known to them in about equal numbers. Nine out of ten women who are murdered are killed by men—usually (78% of the time) a man known to them. Fully a third of women murdered are victims of husbands or boyfriends. And an estimated three to four million American women are battered each year by their husbands or partners. The Bureau of Justice statistics indicate that overwhelmingly (95%), victims of all kinds of domestic violence are women (NJ Coalition 2). In 1994, over three million cases of child abuse and neglect were reported in the United States (U.S. Bureau of the Census 1996). Hercules bore his fate valiantly and dwells in Olympus, but brutal rage still plagues the human psyche. We, like Hercules, remain unredeemed.

The lives revealed in the trial of Mr. Simpson, the diaries of Mrs. Simpson, the interviews of Mr. Simpson, and the substantial literature being produced about these lives and the trial itself are strong evidence for the fact that violence and lust dominate human life as much today as in the time of Hercules. These sources merely provide us with a dramatic

microcosm of the macrocosm of violence which surrounds and threatens
to engulf us. That is what was so compelling about this trial and the thousand spin-off stories it generated. We were hearing once again what we
already knew to be true, when inequality in personal relationships prevails,
the whole family and the culture are imbued with violence. We heard this
story and at some level, whether we stayed tuned or tuned out, knew this
to be our own.

Can we stretch our imaginations to grasp the possibility that it is not
only the real Nicole whom we mourn? Can we see her fate as the fate of
our own life-giving feminine soul? Can we imagine her as an aspect of ourselves which we often batter and abuse? Can we see the blood-drained
body of one woman as representing the millions of other victims of violent crime and through this, begin to comprehend the enormous hostility
toward the feminine within the Hercules mentality? Can we, in an imaginal way, sense the diminishment of the figure of the accused and know
him to represent our own unrelated, blindly brutal masculine urge for
power? And those beautiful, motherless children, can we look into their
faces and see our own? For it is in such imaginings we will find the core
of our shared obsession with this crime.

BIBLIOGRAPHY

"Athletes More Likely to Assault and Rape." *New York Times,* (3 June 1990),
    VIII, 1:2.
Bugliosi, Vincent. *Outrage.* New York: Norton, 1996.
Butterfield, Alan. "Nicole's Diary." *National Enquirer* 70 (24 October 1995),
    35–39.
Cavendish, Richard, ed. *Mythology: An Illustrated Encyclopedia.* London:
    Orbis, 1980.
Darden, Christopher, and Jess Walter. *In Contempt.* New York: Harper
    Collins, 1996.
Dershowitz, Alan. *Reasonable Doubt.* New York: Simon and Schuster, 1996.
Funk, Robert W. *Honest to Jesus.* San Francisco: Harper, 1996.
Gibbs, Nancy. "End of The Run." *Time* 143 (27 June 1994), 29–35.
Gleick, Elizabeth. "O.J. Feels The Heat." *Time* 148 (2 December 1996),
    60–67.
Graves, Robert. *Greek Myths.* London: Penguin Books, 1955.
Guirand, Felix, ed. *New Larousse Encyclopedia of Mythology.* London:
    Hamlyn, 1959.
Herman, Judith. Lewis. *Trauma and Recovery.* New York: Basic Books, 1992.
Jung, Carl. *The Archetypes and the Collective Unconscious.* Trans. R.F.C.
    Hull. London: Routledge, 1959.
———. *Civilization In Transition.* Trans. R.F.C. Hull. London: Routledge,
    1964.

Maples, William. *Dead Men Do Tell Tales.* New York: Doubleday, 1994.

Neumann, Erich. *The Great Mother.* Princeton: Princeton University Press, 1955.

NJ Coalition for Battered Women. *Fact Sheet on Domestic Violence.* Trenton: New Jersey Coalition for Battered Women, 1995.

Parry, Danaan. *Warriors of the Heart.* Cooperstown, New York: Sunstone Publications, 1989.

Resnick, Faye and Mike Walker. *Nicole Brown Simpson: The Private Diary of a Life Interrupted.* Beverly Hills: Dove Books, 1994.

Schindehette, Susan, et al. "Shadow of Suspicion." *People* 41 (27 June 1994), 94–102.

Shapiro, Robert. *The Search For Justice.* New York: Warner, 1996.

Simpson, Orenthal. *I Want To Tell You.* Boston: Little Brown, 1995.

Thurer, Shari. *The Myths of Motherhood.* New York: Houghton Mifflin, 1994.

Toobin, Jeffrey. *The Run of His Life: The People v. O.J. Simpson.* New York: Random House, 1996.

U.S. Bureau of the Census. *Statistical Abstract of the United States, 1996: 116 Edition.* Washington, D.C.: U.S. Bureau of the Census, 1996.

5
Coming Home: Hyper-Images of the Hero and Child in America

MARY LYNN KITTELSON

Culture shock is like being in a nightmare. Suddenly, your world has become perturbing, disturbing, even frightening. Things around you, the actions, rules, and even the language, have become outlandish. Your own expectations jump out from the shadows, startling you into odd awarenesses. At first, culture shock can overwhelm you with more than you wanted to know. But as the waves of strangeness recede, its afterwaves become interesting, even provocative. Just like a nightmare, which can help you understand yourself better, culture shock becomes a psychological opportunity to understand both yourself and the culture.

What I discovered during the process of re-entering the American culture was that these shocked reactions were bringing home deeper realizations about the culture, both on its surface and subterranean levels. Paying attention to the images of America, to these expressions of the cultural psyche which so vividly surrounded me, seemed necessary. They were, after all, affecting me in a particularly fresh and intense way in those first few weeks, as I encountered them in people's stories and verbal expressions, bestsellers, TV soaps, the evening news, graffiti, song lyrics, ads, and movies. So I began to gather the images of my culture shock experience and work with them in a Jungian analytic style, as if they were my cultural nightmare. And the two main figures I met with on this cultural scene were the active, strong *hero*, and the dependent, imaginative *child*.

But before proceeding, a word on the place I was coming *from*, in my case, Zurich, Switzerland. During the 1980s, I lived there for eight years, teaching English as a foreign language while completing training as a Jungian analyst. In Zurich, I was at the source, where Jungian psychology came into being, living in an atmosphere of careful observance of dream-life, shadow, and the unconscious, steeped in a deep sense of culture and history. In many ways, I left "the American way" quite thoroughly. My American-bought clothes, cosmetics, and household effects disappeared, piece by piece, and in a quiet, ghostlike way, Swiss-bought things replaced them. Even American money got funny. Dollar bills began to look strange, all green, all the same size, oddly dull next to colorful, many-sized Swiss franc bills. During visits to America, I now translated dollar prices into Swiss francs, to see if items were a good value. I became thoroughly unused to America.

In attending to the American images that I met upon returning, I invite you to approach them in an imaginative style, as I did, noticing the images carefully, and allowing them to live on together in an associative way during further observations and private musings. Images naturally tend to group together, formed by affinities and opposites which are deeply-rooted in the human psyche. Sometimes they shift to different layers of meaning, and sometimes, vision shifts to the archetypal patterns which loom in the background of these images.

Upon my return, things looked big and wide. American buildings, even familiar ones in my hometown, seemed oddly spread out. Streets and yards seemed wider, and in downtown areas especially, things felt oddly expansive or far apart. Sometimes things seemed less cared for, even ramshackle, as if everything were expendable. Americans in the stores and streets looked foreign, "heroic-sized"—both large and tall, and many were overweight. Personal space was also different, wider, more expansive, since people stood a bit farther apart while talking to each other. Over all, it seemed that buildings and people alike were "making themselves wide" (*sich breit machen*), a sense of taking up a bit too much space, as the · German expression goes.

Like a culture that does not know when to stop, stores, lights, machines, sound systems all seemed to be *open* or *on*, all of the time. Words like "more" and "super" held sway, in imperative tones, as if heroes—or children—were in charge. Getting food no longer meant going to the neighborhood greengrocer, but dealing with food factories and warehouse food stores. Within a few days of moving back, with empty cupboards, I went shopping at the monster grocery store. Overwhelmed, I had to hurry out, barely escaping its giant maw with my sanity, such as it was.

Sounds were also big, unstoppable, demanding. In stores and on the streets, things sounded loud and often raucous: the noise of radios, videos, TV, their endless chatter and announcements, and even louder commercials. To my perception, a strong sense of neediness and appetite was playing loud and hard, though no one, it seemed, was really listening. Talk shows cranked up every kind of issue and emotion, for cheap thrills. The theme of abuse was raging. "What an abuse of listening," I thought. "What an abuse of emotion!" Useless, manipulative, hyperbolic information abounded. Super sale, super power, super cool! As impressive as the assertion of power was the assertion of appetite and need.

So this was what finally coming "home" was like. I still felt like a stranger in a strange land, in a place where things felt oversized, overactive, loud, and unhappily grasping. Safe in the refuge of my own home, I found myself becoming a Trekkie, regularly watching *Star Trek: The Next Generation*, which is all about communicating with alien life forms. My country had become an alien space, and I wondered if I would ever feel this America was mine to live in again.

In moving to some sense of interpretation of my "nightmare" experience of the culture, the psychic "figure" or energy which "looms" most clearly in this scene, the most clearly dominant energy in the complex world I was observing, was *the hero*. We know this figure to be active, outgoing, single-minded, and impatient, with fervent belief in rationality and science, eager to conquer, control things, and win. These heroic attitudes, assumptions, and demands were loud and compelling, and also little challenged, in the culture. But pulling insistently on the hero's shirt-tail, strongly influential in "the cultural scene," was the opposite energy of *the child*—dependent, insistently hungry, needy, and personalistic, but full of imagination and creative potential.

These cultural images of the hero and child were not new to the culture, I realized, but their impact—their looming, overdrawn quality—were born of the hyper-reality of culture shock. These figures appeared to me in their nightmare aspect. The hero and child, as psychic figures in the soul of the culture, are all around and within us, shaping our attitudes and goals as Americans. And by the way, these two figures at the center of the culture are *not* wearing happy faces; they are in fact engaged in a monstrous split, one that strikes deep at the heart of our imaginative lives.

The Superhero

One dominant image that has formed America since its settlement by Europeans is that of the hero. Heroic images appear at every turn, not only in the stories and tales in the culture, but in the media and on the political scene. Our interest in maintaining our image as "guardian of the world," or "savior," is palpable in such projects as the Marshall Plan, Operation Desert Storm, and Operation Rescue to save Somalia, which captured and held the attention of the nation. Heroic types of the strongest magnitude claim the foreground in movies and on TV, in ads and in children's—and adult's—games and play, from the highly popular soldier and cowboy movies, to John Wayne and the Marlboro Man. These heroes are strong, active, and embody both right and might. It is as if things cannot be big enough.

America is a heroically proportioned country, with a hero's good luck—an abundance of land and natural resources. As we were taught from school and from immigrants' tales, settling America, coming across the ocean and setting up life in the New World, was a heroic act, full of great dangers—and rewards. This "hero" energy lived in both its constructive and destructive forms in frontiers-people and settlers, who upon arriving in the "New World," marched west, subduing—transforming—the land. Coming in droves, they conquered Native Americans and appropriated the land; they imported African slaves to do back-breaking labor. And along the way, they decimated whole species of animals, cutting down forests, ploughing and mining the earth, transforming the country into burgeoning cities and amber waves of grain. As these "new" Americans moved west in a giant swath, they ripped up the roots of trees, prairie grasses, and peoples alike. These are monumentally large, dramatic, and often brutal actions. And in the classical sense, "heroic" actions are all of those things.[1]

"The American way" has had a powerful impact globally too, through music and films, fashions, and a wide variety of goods and services. Pico Iyer in his travel reportage book, *Video Night in Kathmandu*, describes heroic-sized 5-foot cut-outs of Rambo, looming in ten Bangkok theaters. Rambo, he said, had shattered box-office records everywhere from Beirut to San Salvador (3–4). As a dominant force in industry, science, technology, and politics, America is now called "*the* super-power." Whether you call it foreign aid or power-mongering, imperialism, investing in developing countries, CIA meddling or rescue missions, this giant America is both admired and reviled in the world. The idea has thrived, both globally and internally, that America's horizons are limitless, that anything is possible. This is the heroic mode.

On the positive side, the hero is decisive, strong, and good in a fight. In accomplishing the impossible, he often saves the underdog, or the whole kingdom; he "does the right thing." We find all of these values prevalent in the rhetoric of politics, in fiction and nonfiction, in movies and in the media—in all of the plotlines of the culture. Nowadays, however, this hero is by no means unscathed. We face a backlash of superhero, a challenge to him as national icon, as our heroic "rightness" comes into question; and sometimes our "might" as well. It is, for example, a hot topic of debate not only about whether we wish to, but whether we *can* provide assistance to foreigners—or even help our own economically disadvantaged. While the definition of America as superpower remains firmly established, since the 1960s, and increasingly in the 1990s, the role of America as guardian of the world is lessening.

There may be some balance coming into play, some underlying sanity in these challenges. The assumption of an all-American, good-hearted altruism and generosity is much reduced, as we hear continual accusations

---

[1] I refer here to the archetypal image of the hero (as active, strong, controlling, warriorlike, on the winning side, in the right). Several of these essays in this collection discuss other definitions of hero, some emerging in the culture and some "imported: from different cultures. See especially Levi and Stewart. For resources which discuss the hero as archetype and image, see Campbell, Jung (*Symbols*), and Neumann.

and admissions of selfishness and greed, on both domestic and international levels. Personally and politically, cynicism is widespread, a get-what-you-can hardening, a drive to make a profit, a huge profit, grab power, any way you can. Whether on TV or in movies or in neighborhoods or gangs, those who take our hero roles have often turned destructive, criminal or violent, have become anti-heroes, their powers turned randomly violent or terrorist.

In point of fact, while our ideas are based on heroic assumptions and ideals, experientially we find ourselves having to face our limitations everywhere we turn: in questioning our role in international politics, in domestic policy decisions, and for many, the economic scene with its widespread down-sizing of companies; we have to fight to deal with entitlements and decrease the national debt, all much in the news. Welcome to the real America, the poor and minorities shout! Our ultimate limits confront us too in such issues as health care, in both the right to die and right to life issues. This giant country of right and might is taking on more darkness, trying to come down to size.

Fairy or folktales teach us that heroes must learn to honor the rejected, the animal, the vulnerable, or they will fail in their goal. They must perceive and honor the wider—and deeper—picture.[2] Indeed, without this larger base, without going beyond this clear focus or goal and listening for the unexpected, they will miss the mark, and their hard-won goals will turn out to be short-term, over-muscled monstrosities. America has the problems of someone "caught in the hero archetype," that is, too exclusively possessed by heroic attitudes.

Our Heroic Goals

The goals of this hero are straightforward. Clearly, America in general champions the outer and material world. With most of its considerable energy, intelligence, and resources going toward material progress, it is no wonder that American successes are so clearly recognizable. Truth be told, Material Gain is the true American dream. Without thinking, we equate money and material goods with freedom, happiness, recognition, and even personal value. Shopping in the malls and on TV seems to be the new center of American entertainment and culture.

We trust in facts and data; we feel it necessary to be practical, to get down to business. We are only comfortable with the "real," the "concrete"—having literally covered over much of our world with concrete! We want to be *proactive*, *grasp* life, make it *work* for us, *get rich*. If things are not marketable, profitable in some "material" way, they do not seem worth

---

[2] The classic kind of tale that makes this point is the "Dummling" fairytale, where the third and least favored "stupid" young man, the one who listens to animals and to strange advice, saves the kingdom. See Grimm, for example, "The Cunning Little Tailor" (N. 114) or "The Poor Miller's Boy and the Cat" (N. 106).

the effort. For even in matters of education and of the spirit, cost-effectiveness is often used as the first and most persuasive argument.

Symbolically, the material world belongs to the mother archetype (*Mater*, in Latin; matter, Mother Earth). In our culture, all this heroic energy functions like the powerful warrior-son who has, so he thinks, overcome the earth and matter. All that energy from the mother archetype then has no choice except to reassert its power indirectly, destructively, and we get "possessed" by materialism. This negatively obsessive power is a diseased kind of "worship" that shows us that "Mater" is not in her rightful place. In the hero myth, we could say that the American hero energy has remained astride Mother Earth, wielding sword and bulldozer blade, instead of getting on with the bigger story, which would have our hero coming into relationship with feminine energies, finding an equal feminine partner, rounding out his life. Instead, our American "can-do" heroic attitude is easily ensnared in a rigid, overly simplistic, and finally empty role of warrior, where the compulsive hero keeps fighting to acquire more, more, more, and win, win, win!

We live so inside our *obsession* with materialism in Western culture, that we can no longer see its grip. It really is more the case that material things possess us than that we possess them. Richard Heinberg calls our love of money "a particularly virulent form of cultural trance" (1). At some point, we must ask ourselves what sort of "gain" this is, when we are getting fatter, more angry, and more confused. How indeed does matter matter, if we lose our sense of worth and meaning?

In general, our approach is extraverted, outward; the inner world appears as suspect and too full of self-absorption. Popularly, American psychologies prefer cognitive and behavioral approaches, with rationally appropriate behaviors and thoughts. We trust in what is outwardly demonstrable, measurable, repeatable. You can hear the hero's strong and insistent tones in our demands for empowerment, proactivity, and immediate results. Any championing of passivity or irrationality makes most Americans suspicious. Mentally, Americans prefer the linear, the long, straight roads across the prairies of the mind. We want to discover causes, and thus control situations, objects, behavior—our lives.

Heroic attitudes make issues sweepingly simple. A "heroic" commitment means having no doubts. No wonder we suffer from black-and-white thinking! In her discussion of how we talk as a culture, with its predominance of masculine mode in many arenas, Deborah Tannen makes the point that ours is a culture of critique, where oppositionalism more than cooperation reigns (Tannen, *passim*). There has been much criticism of media coverage, which typically seems based not on what is important, or on processes of discussion, but on opposition and debate, an aggressive going-after the other guy. This is our familiar cops-and-robbers, black-and-white mode. Being "aggressive" in business, and now even in health care, is desirable; "compromise" in many quarters seems to have become a negative word. This issue lives in the ongoing debate around President Clinton, who is known for bringing sides together, compromising, finding the center. On the negative side, he is often criticized for "waffling," being slippery, and betraying promises. In dealing with this President, we are challenged to reassess this oppositional mode, to ask what might be possible in a new synthesis, or in some middle ground between opposing forces.

Rationality and will-power are two of the great traits of Western heroes, as many people have pointed out. But must these traits dominate to such a *heroic* extent? Depth psychology portrays the human psyche, in its individual and cultural aspects, as a multileveled structure with its own core, operating in a field of affinities and oppositions, structured and influenced by personal and collective forces and by archetypal resonances. In an arena like this, a "hero" needs breadth, balance, flexibility, a sense of participation and interdependence. Instead of the classical heroic goal of *perfection*, of climbing ever farther and higher in one direction, depth psychology suggests that wholeness is generally the wiser goal.

Without some place for this kind of recognition—the nonheroic kind —of the associative nature of the imaginative psyche, its deeper resonances of meaning, its shifting matrices of interdependence, these great ancient paths to meaning and wisdom will remain hidden in the unconscious. And according to the rules of psychic functioning, that means that we will continue not only to devalue these qualities, but even attack them when they "threaten" us, in others and even in our own selves. We need to hold both sides of an issue in our cultural consciousness. Splitting off one side leads to a Gulf War. And in our national psyche, nowhere is there a wider or more dangerous gap than between our heroism and our own childlike qualities.

The Shadow Child

Child energies are "shadow" to hero energies, that is, they carry the side of things that is opposite to the hero, and thus devalued. In its qualities of being small and dependent, in its playful, uncontrolled, and fantasy-filled ways, the child carries the dark or rejected side of the hero. For all of its survival skills, the vulnerable child, at the far end of the spectrum from the hero, grows only slowly into adulthood, into heroic energy, where psychologically, a person can stand alone, make decisions, claim a place in the world. Neglect and mistreatment characterize the way that people act toward their shadows, toward rejected qualities that they themselves possess too, but only see in others. It is a frightening fact in America, but until recently, our steadiest attention to children in the public forum has been on the topic of child abuse.

Our real children, with real live bodies and souls, are not only our future, but a wellspring of energy and authenticity in our present lives. It is an agonizing misplacement of values to hurt or neglect children, materially, mentally, or spiritually. Depth psychology adds another level to our concern for our outer cultural situation, a question which concerns our inner life too; it asks: "What does it mean about us that this level of abuse is possible?" Or we could phrase it more hopefully: "What is it in us that is finally waking up to the abuse of children?" Then, this burning issue has to do with our abused child energies, both within our own selves, as well as among ourselves, in families and society. Outer child abuse is happening; but child abuse is happening on the inside too. Both are real, inside and outside, and they are related.

There is an impressive nationwide celebration of independence, that quality around which our national holiday revolves, every July 4th. This is no empty ritual, since the cultural ideals of being strong, proactive, and courageous are all non- or anti-dependent. Yet it is its opposite, *dependence*, which is a basic trait of children: a developmental stage as well as a humanly necessary state. It is interesting to note that the major psychological movement or industry which crested before child abuse was chemical abuse or "chemical *dependency*." Indeed, our list of addictions/ dependencies gets longer and longer: alcohol, cocaine, heroin, amphetamines, caffeine, nicotine, food, video games, shopping, gambling, sex, and so on. This growing list suggests a deep hunger inside, an empty, starved need for interaction, for stimulation or comfort, for feeling filled up inside, but through substances and set activities. It is a tortured picture of dependency.

It is harrowing to contrast this cultural attitude of anti-dependency with the way that real children confront us with their dependence. Their undeniable needs require great amounts of familial and societal support, for many years. It takes a village to raise a child, as we hear from all corners. And as the popularity of James Hillman's book on the Acorn Theory suggests,[3] there is a truth we can all recognize in the idea that children have a way of having to be their real selves. Children also show us irrepressible imagination and intense emotionality. They are wonderfully, irrepressibly in contact with their inner realities and images, through fantasy and play. Using a depth perspective, we would do well to ask if, in our state of heroic overkill, these might be the qualities we are abusing, inside ourselves as well as in our children. If we as a nation meet our children with scant resources, with disrespect, neglect, and violence, are we not also reflecting what is also in our own souls?

For example, workaholism is "psychic neglect" at the very least; and many Americans basically never stop working. It is "psychic abuse" never to have time to attend to emotional and reflective life and dreams. It is

---

[3] Hillman's main thesis is that each soul has within it a core of what it must become, and this essence must express itself, even when it might come of in strange, uncomfortable, or furtive ways. Thus environment has a more limited influence than we had thought. See Hillman.

neglectful and torturous never to day-dream, or muse, or wander freely along a mental path. Now, in response to all of our workshops and technologies for fulfillment, we have "busy-holics," those who, week after week, use their "free time" for "growth" or professional workshops, or learning how to "relate." With no free time, inner life becomes bruised, starved. Imagination dare not reveal itself, be naturally interactive and reactive—playful—and especially not in relationship to other humans. Much of Americans' leisure time is regimented, set up by someone else, like TV or video games or theme parks. Then people do not actively discover what is inside of themselves; they neglect an individual sense of their inner lives. This lifestyle has become "The Chronic American Way."

The Monstrous Pair

The images of the child and hero may seem to be as far apart as they can get. Indeed, we have been viewing them as deeply split. Jungian theory has it that in the process of becoming more fully yourself, opposites are attracted or pulled toward each other by virtue of their being so opposite, with the hidden (unconscious) agenda of learning about "the other side." Many romantic couples look like this, but this process may occur between any two figures who need to come to terms with each other. If the two sides are relatively unformed, with little real exchange or respect between them, then instead of having a fruitful play of difference, they form an "unholy union," that is, a premature joining (Jung, *Practice* 202–323). They are not really developed enough in themselves to form a "holy" or "whole-making" union. On the cultural level, these figures of hero and child, whose ubiquitous energies are so split in society, form a monstrous pair, an unhealthy merging, in the "victim mania" in America. The role of victim unites a vulnerable person in a childlike position with the powerful, heroic cry of "Injustice!" Charles Sykes in his book, *A Nation of Victims*, chronicles the lengths Americans go to "get in on" being victims. He states that 374% of the population is now included as disadvantaged, counting all categories (12–13).

From a victim's perspective, all suffering is wrong, and potentially subject to legal action. Even though we litigate at the drop of a hat, still, no one seems to end up responsible. In our culture, not suffering seems to have become a right. If you stop to ponder, how "realistic" is this? The idea that suffering might be necessary, meaningful, or a valuable part of the human condition has become quaint or perverted in most quarters. In thinking thus, we have childishly—or is it heroically?—turned our backs on much of human experience, as recorded in history, literature, and religion.

Are we entitled not to suffer? Not to die? Is everyone? Always? With this mix-up regarding what we are entitled to, it is no coincidence that entitlement expenditure is the unaddressable issue in the national budget. Our judgment seems poor in assessing when suffering might be necessary;

thus, we cannot see where the real victims are, and whom we should champion. As the child is shadow to the hero, so too is the hero shadow to the child. Heroic energy tries to make things right and just, but when it looks too childish, too self-centered and naive to tolerate suffering and frustration, it reveals its possession by its vulnerable and personalistic shadow, the child.

Finding the "Real" American Dream

The assumption that only the outer world, only "objective" facts, and material things are important, is the core of the American heroic, black-or-white, materialistic illusion. Most adults in our culture would claim to know, clearly, the difference between what is real and unreal, and many would formulate that as the difference between what is outside and inside. However, as a psychologist and analyst, I work all day with how people deal with the outside world as *based upon their inner realities*. We interpret the world based on the necessities of our inner life, as well as outer: this is, plain and simple, how the psyche functions. Both the inside and outside worlds are "real," and they are interrelated.

The power, the "reality" of inner life, and the essential part it plays in our lives, goes largely unrecognized in America. There is little interest, for example, in this fundamental piece of data: People need to dream. If deprived of dreamtime during sleep, we get confused, irritable, and suffer memory loss. Eventually, we begin to hallucinate: that is to say that our minds force us into fantasy. Dreaming is an activity the psyche requires to function properly. Likewise, and like dreaming, imagination is an undeniable psychic necessity. Our imaginative lives, just like real children, need patience, gentleness, time, respect—and in our culture, they need somebody to stick up for them.

A majority of Americans try to meet their imaginative needs by engrossing themselves in television. They sit, mesmerized by the screen, restlessly switching channels. Video images are fast-moving and often extreme, with little chance to process things. In this highly active, even violent, style of imagination, in which we are so passive, where is the chance for active imagination and for reflection? How can imagination "open out"? No wonder then, with no real time for processing things or real relationship, that people have short attention spans and lack frustration tolerance. For a desperate enough person, it seems the next small step to random violence, to reckless, flashing acts, where it really does not matter at all where things come down.

The hero side, with its warrior energy, is prone to wield the light of consciousness as much like a weapon as a tool. Light which is too strong, too heroic, accounts for some of our most frightening images, involving catastrophic ruin: an annihilating flash of nuclear blast, or a hole in the ozone layer which is blinding, burning the Earth and her inhabitants. Such images are searing, terrifying, as outer possibilities as well as in our inner dreams and images.

What amount of health care could make things right? In attending to the needs of our soul, in honoring the inner world, there is a process, a journey of patience, trust, of natural interplay, which associativeness teaches. Through imagination, through the ideas and feelings and images that come, ongoing ways are found to have a meaningful world inside, one that can also bring meaning and healing to the world outside.

Could it be, in our Deconstructionist era, that in this Internet of possibilities, a new matrix of meaning is forming? Will we learn to balance technology and data as forces in our lives? It seems to me that in some way, we are going to have to reclaim a world that believes in mystery, that allows and even welcomes the fact that unconscious energies have a power and a purpose. New paradigms, new networks on the outside interrelate with new paradigms and networks on the inside. We need to get to know ourselves inside: to recognize, respect, work, and play with what is inside of our heads and hearts. In contemporary culture, in these times of increased transition and danger around the third millenium A.D., we need both the hero and the child, and all of the other "figures" as well, those whose energies form our lives, in the outer world and inside.

Some works of science fiction imagine our lives forward into successfully dealing with our world. Usually it is just in time. However, other works, and a preponderance of global history, tell a grimmer story. Like most species, we may well go down, big brains, opposable thumbs and all.

In America, our resources, our energy remain great. We are good in a crisis. No country knows better on some ground level that individuals make a difference. And our difficult struggles with freedom, with openness and diversity deserve more respect, and often more patience, than they get, considering the profundity. For now, it is true that nightmares loom, and frustration reigns. But the psyche, in both a personal and collective sense, is enormously creative and resilient. If we can wake up to its imaginative challenges, responding with heart and mind—and soul—it may be possible that some core, some essence of what we call "the great American dream" is not over yet!

BIBLIOGRAPHY

Campbell, Joseph. *The Hero with a Thousand Faces*. Bollingen Series XVII. Princeton: Princeton University Press, 1949.
The Complete Grimm's Fairy Tales. Intro. Padraic Colum. Comm. J. Campbell. New York: Pantheon Books, 1944 and 1972.
Heinberg, Richard. *Museletter,* January 1994 (N. 25).

Hillman, James. *The Soul's Code: In Search of Character and Calling.* New York: Random House, 1996.

Iyer, Pico. *Video Night in Kathmandu: And Other Reports from the Not-So-Far East.* New York: Knopf, 1988.

Jung, C. G. *The Collected Works of C.G. Jung.* Eds. H. Read, M. Fordham, G. Adler, W. McGuire. Trans. R. F. C. Hull. 2nd ed. Bollingen Series XX.

———. *Symbols of Transformation.* Vol. 5. Princeton: Princeton University Press, 1956.

———. *The Practice of Psychotherapy.* Vol. 16. Princeton: Princeton University Press, 1954 and 1966.

Neumann, Erich. *The Origins and History of Consciousness.* Foreword C.G. Jung. Trans. R. F. C.

Sykes, Charles. *A Nation of Victims: The Decay of America.* New York: St. Martin's Press, 1992.

Tannen, Deborah. *Talking from 9 to 5.* New York: Morrow, 1994.

6
Cinemyths: Contemporary Films as Gender Myth

TED E. TOLLEFSON

Film as Dream and Myth

Joseph Campbell was fond of saying that the recurring theme of mythology is that there is an "invisible world" which supports, sustains and shapes the "visible world" around us.[1] When a mythological system is in good form, we can visit that invisible world and return safely. There are agreed upon points of passage, tour guides, signs and symbols; there are some aspects of the journey which are necessarily solitary, but there is always the implication of community. There are trustworthy models for each stage of life and each gender.

By mid-twentieth century in many parts of the industrialized world, many of the traditional mythological systems began to break down. Large portions of the human community entered a "Wasteland," a place where the gods were silent or dead and traditional symbols had lost their meaning. The "invisible worlds" evoked by inherited mythology receded from view or were replaced by political counterfeits (Facism, Communism, Capitalism) and mass-market substitutes (Mickey Mouse, Coca Cola, L.L. Bean).

Despite these changes, or perhaps because of them, there have remained two rich zones for myth-making: dreams and film. It was C.G. Jung and his followers who pioneered techniques for disclosing the mythological significance of dreams. One breakthrough was to focus not just on an individual dream but a dream series where patterns can be detected and their evolution traced. A second innovation was what Jung

An earlier version of this essay appeared in Mythos Journal *No. 3, "The Mythology of Gender."* © *1994 Ted E. Tollefson.*

[1] For an overview of Campbell's understanding of the function of myth, see chapters 1–11 of Campbell and Moyers.

called "archetypal amplification," which sought the meaning of a dream image by placing it in the larger context of mythological symbols. Thus, for example, Jung's dream of the death of "Siegfried" is related to a certain heroic tendency in the German soul and thereby to the universal myth of the Hero. When these two methods are combined, they provide insight into larger trends in the dreamer's inner life and give a feeling of participation in patterns that are common to all human beings, that is, the archetypes.[2]

Despite Jung's innovations, dreams have often proved to be an insufficient basis for generating myths to organize community life. The private and often idiosyncratic content of dreams make them a problematic source for shared meanings. Jungian analysis may "bottle up" dreamwork in the private meetings of analyst and client. This may be productive for therapist and client, but the larger community is deprived of the healing wisdom of dreams. The limits of dreams to take on the traditional functions of myth also reflect the biases of Jungian theory, which may overlook the domain of culture in its head-long rush towards universal archetypes.

Film, a medium unique to the twentieth century, replicates many of the features of dreaming.[3] Film-goers enter a darkening space, leaving behind the familiar aspects of the waking world. In the darkness they partake of a world of flickering images ("movies") which create the illusion of a world somewhat larger than life. As has been often noted, the "stars" of film play a role similar to tribal gods and goddesses, eliciting fascination and adoration, establishing ideals of beauty, strength, or consumption, filling the tabloids with lurid half-true tales of their exploits. What film adds to dreaming is a public dimension: the theater is a place of *shared* dreaming. The responses of the audience become part of the spectacle. Thus film can take on both psychological and social functions once fulfilled by mythology. Some films have the power to create their own ritual process, such as the public enactments which accompanied showings of the *Rocky Horror Picture Show* in many American cities in the 1980s.

The rub with film-as-myth is that relatively few films exercise a lasting influence on their culture. *Snow White* or *Star Wars* may have imprinted a whole generation, but most traditional myths exercise their power over hundreds if not thousands of years. Films by their very nature ("movies," "flicks") reflect a world of impermanence, flickering images, adorned by rising and falling stars. Films may be an ideal medium for generating myths that map the rapidly shifting landscape of the late twentieth century.

In order to reveal the mythological dimensions of contemporary film, two shifts in perspective are called for. First, borrowing a page from Jung's

---

[2] For these and other dreams of Jung's, see Jung, *Memories, Dreams, Reflections* and *Dreams,* and also Hall.

[3] For more on the similarity of dreams and films, see Hobson and Hill.

dreambook, we must look not at the individual film but the *film series*. When we shift our attention in this way, more durable patterns begin to emerge. We see not just individual stars but constellations of meaning. Second, we need to recognize an intermediary layer between the traditional Jungian dyad of the personal unconscious and the collective unconscious. Between the personal unconscious, which changes repeatedly in one life-time, and the collective unconscious, which changes rarely if at all, there is the *cultural unconscious* which changes by the decade or the generation. If the collective unconscious is like constellations of stars, with relatively stable patterns of meaning, the cultural unconscious is like the intervening layers of earth's atmosphere, which both sustain life and obscure perception. We may be able to step outside cultural biases to see more clearly, but like the Hubble Telescope, only at great cost and with the help of corrective lenses.

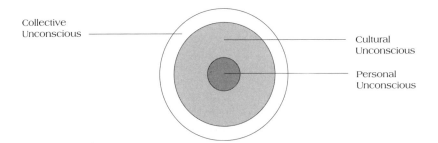

Putting these two elements together, we can say that the *mythological dimension of film is revealed by the film series*. Through a film series the cultural unconscious tries to find ways out of conflicts and contradictions which arise in a given time and place. These "cinemyths" may be related to archetypal patterns (the hero, masculine and feminine, shadow and evil) or the complexes of their creators, but they always bear the stamp of a particular time, place, and culture. It is in the cultural unconscious where the universal patterns of myth and the particularities of human life are joined to create images and stories which speak to our time. Without acknowledging this intermediary zone of culture, it is difficult to explain how archetypal patterns are acquired or how they might change. Our particular concern will be how relations between the genders are envisioned in American films of the 1980s and 1990s.

Gender War: Demonizing the "Other Woman"

Many cinemyths have arisen at the wounded boundaries between women and men, between pre- and post-feminist models of masculinity and femininity. It should not be surprising that some cinemyths struggle to preserve established models of gender while others attempt to break new ground. The most brutally conservative cinemyths are the "snuff films" and their slightly sanitized cousins which depict the murder, mutilation and rape of "uppity" women. Understood literally, these films may legitimize violence against nontraditional women or at least desensitize their viewers to such violence. Approached metaphorically, these films express the need of a reactionary sector of the cultural unconscious to "kill off" images of powerful women.

A more subtle form of conservative cinemyth seeks to demonstrate that "uppity women" (read: economically independent and sexually pro-active) are dangerous and must be tamed or destroyed. An especially vulnerable target is the "Other Woman," who lures men away from their wives or steady girlfriends into an intoxicating vortex of sex, secrecy, and violence. Indeed, one of the most popular American cinemyths is the demonization of the Other Woman. This is not a new story, for its roots go back to Biblical mythology and the legend of Lilith, first wife of Adam. Lilith was Adam's equal and therefore refused to lie down below him to make love. For her rebellion, she was banished from the Garden and replaced with Eve, a more compliant wife made from Adam's rib. As the legend of Lilith was elaborated in the rabbinic tradition, Lillith was turned from an uppity woman into a demon with the talons of a bird of prey. She was blamed for death in child-birth, she was the stealer of children by disease, and at night she stole semen from men by seducing them in their dreams.[4]

One incarnation of Lilith was in *Fatal Attraction*, starring Michael Douglas as a hapless Adam and Glenn Close as his demon lover. The opening and closing scenes of this film telegraph the values to be defended. In the opening scene, Dan Gallagher is shown at home with his son and dog sitting cozily on the couch watching TV, while mom sorts laundry in the bathroom (she's sexy but domestic). As the film unwinds, it becomes clear that Dad is a bumbler: he stubs his toe answering the phone, he can't open his umbrella in the rain. Like Adam, he is riddled with uncertainty. This makes him an easy target for a sexy Other Woman, fiercely played by Glenn Close. Few details are spared in emphasizing the Otherness of the demon lover: she's blond (Dan's wife is brunette); she smokes (Dan's wife does not); she's a working woman (an editor with the power to cut off men's words) while Dan's wife is a housewife. She has a man's name (Alex) while the wife is the ever feminine "Beth" (meaning "house" in Hebrew). What makes Alex a threat is her taking "masculine" privileges into the sexual sphere. Alex easily seduces Dan and can't get enough of him ("I feel you . . . I taste you . . . I think you" she moans on a tape).

When Dan tries to distance himself from Alex, she goes crazy. She slashes her wrists, then smears his face with blood (he binds her wounds). She claims that she's pregnant with their child (he believes her). When Dan

---

[4] For more about Lilith, see Ruether and Stone.

continues to withdraw, Alex is transformed from a sexually aggressive woman to a predator of Lilith-like proportions. She kills the family rabbit and leaves it boiling on their stove. She stalks her man. She attacks his car. She kidnaps his child for a joy-ride on a roller coaster. Alex is given some plausible lines ("I want you to acknowledge your responsibility to me."), but these pale in comparison with her demonic behavior.

The final confrontation between the faithful wife and Other Woman comes in a steamy bathroom. Beth is home from the hospital recovering from a car accident provoked by Alex's abduction of her child. She runs a hot tub while her husband tries to boil water for tea in the kitchen. When Beth wipes away the steam from the mirror, she sees behind her the ghostly reflection of Alex, dressed in white, carrying a very large phallic knife. Alex attempts some "girl talk" with Beth, while mutilating her own right thigh with the knife. Beth bides her time, then decks Alex with a stiff right hook. They fight, scream, and Dan comes to the rescue just as Alex is about to carve up Beth. Dan strangles Alex and then drowns her—as if he is trying to push the image of the Other Woman back into the unconscious. He succeeds and we see Alex's peaceful face beneath the water. But as Dan turns way, Alex rears up with super-human strength, knife in hand, ready to finish off Dan. He is rescued by Beth, who calmly shoots Alex through the heart. Thus, this cinemyth suggests, domestic tranquility is restored when the Good Wife murders the Other Woman. Just in case we've missed the point, as the closing credits roll, the camera dwells lovingly on a photo of the Happy Family framed by key rings as if to say: *the key to happiness is family unity.*

With minor variations, this cinemyth is amplified by several contemporary films including *Presumed Innocent*, *Dick Tracy*, and countless TV movies. The Other Woman is blond and almost always a working woman who is usurping pro-active social and sexual roles usually reserved for men. Often the Other Woman dresses like a man, has a man's name, or in the case of Madonna in *Dick Tracy*, masquerades as a male gangster. The male hero is usually a bumbling servant of the Law (a detective, cop or lawyer). Like Adam, he is passive, reactive and easily led astray. And almost always, the Other Woman dies to pave the way for a happy ending. Like the snuff films from which this genre is derived, the message of the cinemyth is clear: *uppity "masculine" Other Women must die for the sake of Family Values.*

Sooner or later, every myth spawns a counter-myth: so *Fatal Attraction* leads inevitably to *Basic Instinct*. Michael Douglas once again plays the male hero, a cop not a lawyer this time and a little smarter besides. He's not married, but his "steady girlfriend" is a co-worker who also acts as his shrink and defender. (He used to be married, but she killed herself when she found out he was unfaithful). The Other Woman is played to the hilt by Sharon Stone. She is a blond, sexually active, professional woman (a writer, not just an editor—even closer to the creative power of the Masculine Logos). In almost every way, the predatory qualities of this Other Woman are maximized: she not only screws men, but she ties them up and kills them with a phallic ice pick; she is not just sexually active, but shamelessly bisexual; she's not just a professional, but filthy rich; not just intelligent, but dangerously brilliant. Once again lust unites the hero and the Vamp, for a series of remarkable sexual romps (especially in the uncut version). And with each encounter, the question deepens: which basic instinct will be played out here—sex or violence? In short, we are set up to expect the predictable ending where the Vamp is terminated by the Good Girlfriend, who then marries the Guy so they live happily ever after.

The first crack appears in the myth when "Shooter" discovers that his girlfriend dyed her hair blond (a dangerous color!) during college when she had a crush on the Vamp. As the plot thickens, we learn that his girl-friend may have murdered her former husband and a cop who uncovered her secret life. Shooter confronts both women, but who can he trust? In a chilling climax, the cop shoots his girlfiend and discovers hidden in the stairwell the SFPD raincoat, blond wig, and ice pick she may have used to kill his partner. The closing scene only serves to deepen mystery. Shooter is in bed with the Vamp, who ties him up and seems about ready to repli-cate the killing scene with which the movie began. Instead, she embraces him. But wait, as the closing credits roll by, she reaches down below the bed and fondles an ice-pick. Has true love triumphed to tame the Vamp? Or is this just a temporary truce?

When these two tales of gender war are joined, an interesting and com-plex cinemyth begins to emerge. The men who embody the Law of Patriarchy (cops, lawyers, detectives) range from inept (Dan Gallagher) to dangerously semi-competent (Shooter) to cartoon caricatures of phallic male prowess (Dick Tracy and his spurting Tommy Gun). The dominant myth divides women neatly into two camps: faithful, domestic house-wives (brunettes or red-heads) and sexually and professionally pro-active vamps (always blonds) who usurp privileges and powers traditionally reserved for men. In the dominant myth, domestic tranquility is restored when the Good Woman kills the Vamp. In the subversive version, what draws men and women together is the ambivalent twin "basic instincts" of love and death (Freud's *eros* and *thanatos*). In this perplexing battleground, it is unclear whether any women can be trusted because they have claimed the power of the "killer phallos" (the knife, the ice pick, the handgun). In this unsentimental counter-myth, perhaps the best that can be hoped for is, in the words of Shooter: "to screw like minks and make the rug rats." When the blonde vamp says "forget the rug rats," the compliant Shooter agrees. The choice may come down to this: *preserving an outdated vision of domes-tic tranquility by killing off Vamps or to make one's bed on the battlefield.*

Pygmalion: Why Can't a Woman be More Like a Man?

A second genre of cinemyths takes up a theme inherited from the Greeks where male mentors are the creators of "good women." In the Greek myth, the sculptor Pygmalion fell in love with one of his statues. In her generosity, Aphrodite endowed the statue with life. In its modern versions, the male creator is more likely to be a professor or business man than an artist. The woman is not lifeless, but uneducated, poor, or from a lower class. The power of men, says this cinemyth, is to remake women in their own image and thereby enoble them. Professor Henry Higgins teaches Eliza to speak like an Englishman (*My Fair Lady*); an alcoholic professor played by Michael Caine teaches his student Rita to think for herself and write (*Educating Rita*); James played by William Hurt tries to teach his deaf student-lover to speak (*Children of a Lesser God*); Edward, a millionaire played by Richard Gere, raises the self-worth of his hapless hooker (*Pretty Woman*). In most cases the boon bestowed by male mentors upon their female creations is *Logos:* the power of upper class speech and rational discourse.

Circling the edges of these stories are hints that the education/initiation process is not entirely a one-way street. In each case, the woman teaches her mentor something about the transforming powers of erotic (though not necessarily sexual) love. Eliza weans Higgins from his bachelorhood; Rita weans James from his bottle; James gets a dancing lesson and gains respect for the deaf; Edward becomes a little more playful.

There is another possible version of this myth: the process of initiation is fully reversed and *the woman "makes" the man*. This is hinted at in three films. In *Risky Business* a young hooker teaches a suburban kid something about the arts of love and of business. In the process she frees him from the pristine orbit of his mother (her "glass egg"). In *The Graduate* the initiator is Mrs. Robinson, who easily seduces her daughter's fiancé and reduces him to pathetic whimpering. This initiation is regressive. In the closing scenes the young man, played by Dustin Hoffman, escapes the clutching thighs of Mrs. Robinson and approaches the altar with his young bride. In *Weird Science*, two teenage boys grow up with the help of a beautiful woman whom they conjure via their computer. The ancient story of women educating and initiating men in the arts of love and beauty (the realm of the goddess Aphrodite) remains a possibility still too risky to fully imagine.

Lilith Returns: New Places in the Heart

There is a recently rediscovered tradition of speculation which suggests that Lilith's abiding passion was for Eve, not Adam. The two of them met frequently at the Tree in the Garden, and sometimes Lilith appeared in the form of the phallic serpent. In the end, this legend says, Lilith and Eve went off together, leaving Adam to converse with his true lover: Yhwh (Reuther 607). A recent series of films has emerged which traces the amorous relations of Lilith and Eve, the wild woman and the domesticated woman. Many of these films are set in the steamy backwater country of the rural South which has also midwived Jazz, Blues, Cajun cooking, rock 'n' roll and much that is "soulful" in American life.

Each film begins with an attempted departure from the Old Order. In *The Color Purple* Celie flees her childhood home where she has been raped and beaten by her father. *Places in the Heart* begins with the death of a macho sheriff which creates a crisis-opportunity for his widow. *Thelma and Louise* begins when two women leave behind two insipid jobs and one insipid marriage. *Fried Green Tomatoes* begins with two interlocking stories. Evelyn Couch, who is trapped in an unhappy marriage, meets an elderly storyteller in a nursing home who regales her with stories of Idgie and a long-lost childhood. In each case, the threshold of adventure is crossed by leaving behind some of the strictures of patriarchy: an incestuous father, a husband/sheriff; a degrading job and marriage; a beloved sibling.

As each film unfolds, the wounds between women and men deepen. Celie marries a charmer called "Mista," who quickly turns her into a servant while he chases other women. The sheriff's widow, played by Sally Fields, is befriended by a treacherous banker, but eventually she is helped by a black hobo and a blind white man. Thelma falls for two cowboys: one who tries to rape her, the other who robs her. Louise shoots and kills the cowboy rapist. Idgie in *Fried Green Tomatoes* is helped and protected by two men she knew as a child: a black man and the town sheriff. What all of these films suggest is that romantic love between men and women reinforces old destructive patterns; the love which transforms begins with friendly love, rooted in the healing experiences of childhood.

The emotional center of three of the films is the love between women. Celie is first befriended and then seduced by her husband's live-in lover "Shug." Idgie bonds with her brother's fiancée by rescuing her from an abusive marriage and founding the "Whistle Stop Cafe." Evelyn is transformed and empowered by listening to stories of Idgie. Thelma and Louise transform each other from sleepy suburban waitresses into two savvy outlaws. In all cases, the relationship between the women combines friendship, passion, and compassion in a way that is liberating and transforming. Sadly all these films lack the courage to deal openly with sexual love between women. Their sexual love is tolerable only to the extent that it is kept undercover. Lilith is still banished to the margins.

Once women have been transformed by their love for each other, what relationship remains possible between women and men? *The Color Purple* offers the most pessimistic response. All the men in this film are brutal, inept, and unfaithful. In *Thelma and Louise* a certain rapport develops between the outlaw women and one of the policeman pursuing them. When Thelma and Louise are finally surrounded by an army of gun-wielding policemen, all the "good cop" can do is chase after Thelma and Louise, who join hands before plunging into Grand Canyon. *Fried Green Tomatoes* offers the most optimistic vision. In the stories of Idgie, Idgie develops a deepening friendship with the local sheriff, a friend from childhood. Perhaps most hopeful of all, Evelyn's husband is at least partially transformed. He stops drinking beer and watching television long enough to bring his wife flowers. He learns to make room for a wife who is at least his equal.

At the margins of each of these films, there is an unfinished meditation upon the Law of Patriarchy and its role in the new era. In each film a male character who embodies the Law stands at the crossroads of change. The sheriff must die before his wife's transformation can begin. The sheriff in *Thelma and Louise* can establish rapport with the outlaws, but is not able to mediate between them and his gun-wielding comrades. The sheriffs in *Fried Green Tomatoes* embody two stark possibilities. The local sheriff earns his place as a friend by bending the law on Idgie's behalf. The hard-nosed neighboring sheriff is tricked into eating Ruth's deceased husband, who is disguised as pork ribs ("The secret's in the sauce," the black cook tells him with a smile). The father, husband, and sheriff who embody the Law in *The Color Purple* are so brutal that they can neither understand nor share in the transformation of Celie.

Each of these remarkable films muses on the role of traditional religion in the emerging myths. *Places in the Heart* ends with a dreamlike communion scene in which all the film characters, black and white, male and female, living and dead are joined in a communion feast. It is as if the transformation of gender roles could release the power of love to gather up all our wounded parts into a larger pattern. *The Color Purple* culminates in a rousing gospel sing in which Shug (the wild woman, the Magdalene) is reunited with her father, the preacher. Both these films hold out the hope that the erotically charged ethos of Southern Christianity can be stretched to include women who are empowered and changed by the love of women. The love which saves unites passionate and self-sacrificing love (*eros* and *agape*).

Fried Green Tomatoes offers a more ambiguous vision. Idgie is finally persuaded to visit the local church by the parson who stretches the truth by testifying on her behalf. But the core of her tender power lies somewhere else. She is the "Bee Charmer," the wild woman who gathers honey from woods in unconscious service to Diana or Aphrodite: ancient Bee-Goddess and protector of wild women. Her friendship with her lost brother "Buddy" recalls Diana's love for her brother and companion Apollo.

Thelma and Louise presents the most provocative musing on the role of inherited myths in the new era. There is no place in this film for Biblical religion, its texts, sacraments, or representatives. But the central transformation of the film is cloaked in the language of Eastern religions. As the day dawns and Thelma and Louise speed towards their fate, they each experience an "awakening." They say they have never felt more awake or more alive; they have sensed under the desert sky a kinship with the stars that makes their final plunge over the cliff a journey of homecoming. This "awakening" to the unity of mind and nature lies at the heart of many Eastern and Primordial religions; "the Buddha" means "the awakened One." Awakening, writes Judith Christ, is a key moment in a woman's spiritual journey: "For women, awakening is not so much a giving up as a gaining of power. Women often describe their awakening as a coming to self, rather than a giving up of self, as a grounding of selfhood in the powers of being" (19). After such an awakening, there is no going back. Thelma and Louise choose to ride their Thunderbird into the Grand Canyon rather than submit to the Old Law and its gun-toting enforcers.

Cinemyths: New Horizons

Beneath the flickering surface of discrete films, a larger body of cinemyths is taking shape. So far, three mythological systems have been detected, all of them old stories in new garb. One emergent myth returns to the Garden of Eden. In the dominant version (*Fatal Attraction, Presumed Innocent, Dick Tracy*) Eve the good wife kills Lilith the wild woman and is reunited with her wandering husband, Adam. In the subversive version (*Basic Instinct*) Adam prefers Lilith, the wild woman and the seemingly helpful girlfriend reveals her own demonic side.

The second emergent myth is Greek rather than Biblical in origins. It represents the age-old fantasy that women can be retooled to a higher, male standard. As Henry Higgins laments, "Why can't a woman be more like a man?" In the dominant version reflected in films like *Educating Rita, My Fair Lady,* and *Children of a Lesser God*, woman are 'improved' by men who school them in the powers of rational, upper-class speech (Logos). In the subversive version of this myth (*The Graduate, Risky Business, Weird Science*) lurks a possibility too terrifying to contemplate: that *women may be the mentors of men, especially in matters of the heart*. It was after all the Goddess of Love, not Pygmalion the male sculptor, who endowed the statue with life. So far this erotic initiation is permitted only to teenagers (*Risky Business* and *Weird Science*) or other neophyte males (*The Graduate*). The mentoring power of women is limited by depicting them as aging *femme fatales* (*Mrs. Robinson*), youthful happy hookers (*Risky Business*), or computer-generated offspring of teenage lust (*Weird Science*).

The third myth returns to the Garden of Eden with a new twist. In films like *The Color Purple, Fried Green Tomatoes,* and *Thelma and Louise*, the focus of healing and transformation is the love and friendship between women. In mythological terms, Adam (the husband, sheriff, lawyer, or father) is left to wander alone, while Eve and Lilith, the Good Wife and Wild Woman, travel together. Those who take this path will be perceived as "out-laws," for they do stand outside the established construction of gender. But that is where change often begins—not within the strictures of the Old Law, but with the liberating power of Love.

These emergent cinematic myths offer no easy answers about the future of gender relationships. There will be many men and women who perish along the way. For those who have awakened there may be no way back to the Law of Patriarchy. Some like Thelma and Louise will choose to die free rather than live in prison. Others like Shooter and the Vamp will make their bed over the warring instincts of love and wrath, *eros* and *thanatos*. The Laws of Patriarchy must be bent, if not broken. Friendship between women and men and passionate love between women are gateways through which a new gender mythology is being born.

BIBLIOGRAPHY

Campbell, Joseph and Bill Moyers. *The Power of Myth*. New York: Doubleday, 1988.

Christ, Carol. *Diving Deep and Surfacing*. Boston: Beacon Press, 1980.

Hall, Stanley. *Jungian Dream Interpretation: A Handbook of Theory and Practice*. Toronto: Inner City Books, 1983.

Hill, Geoffrey. *Illuminating Shadows: The Mythic Power of Films*. Boston: Shambhala, 1992.

Hobson, J.A. "Film and the Physiology of Dreaming Sleep: The Brain as Camera-Projector," *Dreamworks* I (1980), 9–25.

Jung, C.G. *Dreams*. Princeton: Princeton University Press, 1974.

———. *Memories, Dreams, Reflections*. New York: Vintage, 1965.

Ruether, Rosemary. *Womanguides: Readings Towards a Feminist Theology*. Boston: Beacon Press, 1985.

7

By Jove! There's More to British Comedies Than Meets the Eye

ELIZABETH MASIÉE

I loved the series *Butterflies* from the moment the heroine announced she couldn't cook. Viewers watch again and again, making this one of the longest-running comedies on PBS; it's a classic. It should be, it's based on classical mythology and strikes an ancient chord. Mythology is timeless. We think of it as fiction but it's full of truth. Like Shakespeare, who also employed it, the stories fit in any age. It bridges not just time but it spans oceans, and its archetypical symbols reach each one of us. The underpinning of myth makes for strong drama and if a story catches us, we just might look for myth that's woven through it to which we respond.

In *Butterflies*, the star is a lovely mother of grown sons. Her family constellation includes her husband, Ben, an unsmiling oral surgeon, and her two lusty sons who lounge about, chase girls, and lament the fact that they cannot find jobs. Also in the star's sphere is Leonard, a dark-haired admirer who tirelessly pursues her. He watches the paths she takes and tries to intersect her trajectory so he can accompany her. She is definitely drawn to him, though each time she sees him, she finally, somewhat reluctantly, breaks away from his attraction, saying she must feed her family lunch.

Others who orbit about her are her sighing, tired cleaning lady, Ruby, a "jewel" of a domestic, and her admirer's chauffeur, Thomas, who doubts everything. Thomas is his employer's only conscience and though he is the chauffeur, he also serves as a "vehicle" so we can hear what his employer, Leonard, thinks.

The names of these two employees, Ruby and Thomas, echo the names of the servants in the Masterpiece Theatre series, *Upstairs Downstairs*, and remind us of socio-economic positions: who is up and who is down. The downstairs help in the earlier series never rose to the heights of the privileged heroes and heroines for whom they worked. In *Butterflies* the

characters at first seem merely mortal, destined to remain confined to earth
while the main characters are on the heights—the Greek gods—on Mount
Olympus. The characters are also like an eighteenth century comedy; the
servants are the opposite of their masters.

This wry and sometimes searing playfulness on how scruffy we can be
makes us laugh at our condition, or at least scoff at that of others, but it
also causes us to reflect and ponder. It is both funny and wise, like most
parents, and the focus on the mother and on women everywhere is one
intriguing theme.

The series has played almost continuously in the United States since
the late 1970s. There is no mystery why the series has a cult following; it's
based on mystery cults, the Eleusynian mysteries which revered Demeter,
or Mother Earth, and her daughter Persephone, and counted on these
female figures to provide abundant crops and keep us warm and happy
and well-fed.

The Mother goddess goes by many names in different cultures and in
different times. Ria, the television heroine, is named for the ancient mother
goddess, Rhea, who reigned before Demeter. The goddess Rhea may have
altered her spelling and shortened her name by one letter during these
thousands of years, but she has much in common with her ancient self.
On television she sighs, "I feel I've been a mother for thousands of years."
She has. She is Mother Nature, replacing Gaia, her own mother, Mother
Earth. Both ancient Rhea, whose followers regularly gave her a holocaust
of pigs, and modern-day Ria, whose oven billows smoke and disgorges
disastrous meals, are known for their burnt offerings. They have many
more similarities, as we shall see.

In myth, Rhea's consort was Cronus, the god of Time. On television,
Ria's husband is aptly named Ben, for what British symbol of Time comes
to mind more quickly than Big Ben? We often forget about Father Time,
that hooded figure, until New Year's when we see depictions of him carrying his hour glass and scythe. Ben listens to Gregorian chants, perhaps
to allude to a monk's robe, which suggests the long, hooded robe worn
by Time. Ben's other pastime is collecting butterflies, the title creature of
the series. In Greek the word for butterfly is *psyche*, and in Greek, *psyche*
has another meaning, soul; so Ben, like the father Time he is, collects not
merely butterflies, but Souls.

Ria, flitting about the house in her pastels, seems a bit like a butterfly
and also like a character from *The Bell Jar*, yearning for more freedom and
more meaning in her life. She performs her duties around the house, but
like the (Mother) Nature she is, she too abhors a vacuum. Usually it is her
cleaning lady who hauls the Hoover around and turns it on when Ben is
speaking. Ria has the machine with her only once and then, she barely
uses it; she's interrupted when she finds some drugs behind her couch
cushions.

What have these heroes come to in the present day? Rhea and Cronus were Titans, larger than life, giants in fact, the children of Heaven and Earth. Cronus was king of the Titans and Rhea was queen; their children were well-known gods such as Zeus, and wavy-haired Poseidon, or Neptune.

There are broad hints of who they are in the series, such as when curly-haired Russell has a child. The baby's mother, who bore the baby out of wedlock, asks him what name he would choose for their son. Instantly he answers, "Triton." "Triton?" she asks him with surprise. "Sure," he answers with a knowing smirk, "son of Neptune." Unless we look for them, these clues pass by us, forgotten with the next lines we hear, perhaps because the situations are not new.

The baby's mother, Jeannie, or possibly Genie, has much in common with Amphitrite, the wife of Neptune or Poseidon in the myth. Both the young women, one from television and one from mythology, were loved by a curly-haired god, both had a son by him named Triton, both were reluctant to marry the father and refused him for a long time, and like Jeannie, Amphitrite also had a mother named Doris. More than coincidence, one suspects.

But who is Adam, the scrawny son, the first born? Adam, of course, is the first man, and Zeus was the first manlike god. Before him, Titans and monsters "peopled" the world. Zeus was manlike in many ways: for one, he was well known for seduction. Zeus even changed his form to insinuate himself into his target's affection, transforming himself into a swan, a bull, even a shower of gold from the sky. Once he was attracted to a young man, Ganymede, cupbearer of the gods. Zeus changed himself into an eagle to carry off the boy. Could his disguises relate to Adam's T-shirts which state, "I am a sex object," "I am a UFO," and "I am a trans-vestite"? And Adam, like the over-sexed Zeus, certainly chases girls. But close-ups of the cars that Adam drives, the roaring engines and the faulty mufflers spewing smoke, indicate what little is now left of the god of thun-der, smoke, and lightning. What have these gods come to in the present day? They bumble about, skinny, horny, and incompetent. On television today they're merely comic figures, though manlike gods were far from perfect.

Butterflies seems sometimes to be asking, "How low can we go?" The Soul has become only a frilly, fluttering insect, a mere bug, rather than a winged immortal, raising humankind to greater heights, and if the gods themselves have metamorphosed into such small, insignificant creatures, no wonder the comedy is bizarre.

Butterflies is not the only British comedy based on mythic themes. In *Fawlty Towers*, behind the innkeeper, Mr. Fawlty, lurks old Procrustus, the ancient host who made everyone fit his measure. If guests were too short, he stretched them to fit his bed. If they were too tall, he chopped off parts until his guests fit perfectly.

Mr. Fawlty, the contemporary innkeeper in the television series, insists that everyone measure up to his odd standards. If guests come up short, he scorns them for not being big enough to suit his measure; he lifts his cringing waiter by the lapels until he is at Fawlty's level. But if guests are above him, Fawlty frantically tries to cut them down to size.

He is so judgmental that in each episode he either tries to measure up himself, or else he is not on the level and he hides the truth, tripping himself up in lies. This turns him into a buffoon and much of the comedy comes from his desperately trying to save face. In myth, once Procrustus's tricks were discovered, his punishment fit his crimes and his own head was lopped off. This fits too, for on television Basil Fawlty loses his head often, ranting, raving, and getting more frantic in each scene. Actually, there was a real Basil Fawlty, an innkeeper in England. As John Cleese mentioned in an interview on *Parkey at Christmas*, Monty Python's actors stayed in his small hotel and found him so unique Cleese named this series for him.[1]

In *Fawlty Towers*, the protagonist's name, Basil, means "King." His inn is his castle, although it is his wife Sybil who rules. His jester is of course his cringing bellboy and waiter, Manuel, who, like a court jester, speaks the truth. But in Manuel's case, instead of coating truth in humor to make it palatable, Manuel is frank and therefore not believed and usually punished.

Sybil, Fawlty's wife, is graced by one of the other names by which the Phrygian and Roman mother goddess (Cybele) was called, as well as for the Sybils, women who spoke the oracles at Delphi in Greece. As the ancient goddess was all-knowing, so Sybil Fawlty tells us that she, too, knows much. Her voice is amusingly smug and nasal, and as she speaks into the telephone, she says, repeatedly, "I know, I know, I know . . . I *know*."

And Polly, the pretty maid in the hotel speaks not only clear, fine English, but French and Spanish, and she writes poetry and draws portraits whenever she has time. She is a Muse, and like the Muses, whose mother's name means "memory," she frequently reminds Basil Fawlty of what he has forgotten, which happens often; his memory is as faulty as his name.

Muses, of which there were nine, expressed joy in dance, poetry, abundance, good cheer, comedy, fine arts, music, literature, and mime. Frequently Polly mimes behind someone's back to try to save Mr. Fawlty from making yet another mistake. She excels at language, and certainly

---

[1] John Cleese recounted how Eric Idle, well-known for "Say no more" and "Wink wink, nudge nudge" left his suitcases at the inn while he went away for a few days. On his return, the real Basil Fawlty told him he had moved the suitcases outside, to a safer place, behind a wall behind a shed. Why had he moved the cases, what was he afraid of, Idle asked him. "Bombs," said the real Fawlty. "Whose bombs?" asked Idle. Fawlty explained, "I've been having a bit of trouble with the staff."

The interview was vividly recalled by Laura Palmer of BBC World Wide America.

has good cheer. Because she incorporates the qualities of all nine Muses, her name is Polly, or *poly*, for these many qualities blended into her one character.

The Muses offered inspiration and attended celebrations such as weddings. Frequently, when someone boasted, the Muses punished him with blindness or the loss of memory. Mr. Fawlty is definitely blind to reality. Perhaps because of his arrogance, he suffers the ultimate loss of memory, amnesia. In one episode he is hit on the head, loses what little sense he has, and shockingly insults everyone who isn't British.

The Muses also turned arrogant people into birds, and if that didn't help they plucked the feathers out. Polly is definitely plucky. Her frilly apron is sometimes a pinafore and stands in for the muses' wings.

Many of our favorite series are threaded on the strands of well-known tales. Though British comedies use myth more frequently to propel and strengthen and inspire the drama, our own country also uses myth, of course. Here, one example is the character of Lilith in *Cheers*.

Lilith was the first woman, the first Eve, and the first woman patron of the bar in *Cheers*. On television Lilith usually keeps herself in check and seems as uptight as her hair, which is pulled back so severely it must hurt. But when she loosens it and lets it down, she gets wild and uncontrollable. She, like the ancient Lilith, the first Eve, is sexually passionate, a wild woman, and she frightens men. Wild hair equates with Medusa, that snake-haired Gorgon who turned men to stone. Wild women do that. Because the first Lilith was so strong, wild, and untamed, she was expelled from Eden; today, Thelma and Louise reveal their strength and power but, surrounded by men determined to subdue and control them, in order to retain their power they must soar off the rim of the Grand Canyon.

Butterflies is in good company, and certainly not the only series permeated with myth, for we all recognize archetypal patterns at a deep level. Some of our pleasure in drama is based on recognition, even if it is subliminal. But it is even more intriguing when we discover this and see it consciously.

In *Butterflies* the mythic parallels catch at us and we see more. The unsmiling father, Ben, has an apt job, extracting teeth, reminding us of what we leave when we have left this life. He says he feels as though he has washed up on the beach in some strange land. Indeed, he *is* all washed up; Ben does not change, but is as locked into his era as an insect in a piece of amber. Unhappy in today's world, and perhaps always rather glum, he constantly chews out his sons and finds everything they say or do as hard to swallow as his wife's cooking. To him, their every act is quite distasteful.

This fits the myth, for Cronus, also known as Saturn, devoured his own children. He was told that one of his offspring would overthrow him and to save himself, as each child was born, he swallowed it whole. Rhea was understandably tired of his kind of parenting and when Zeus was born she hid him, and handed Cronus a stone wrapped in blankets instead. Cronus swallowed it, blankets and all, although he did mention that the child seemed lifeless. Her ruse worked, however, and it worked so well that when Neptune was born she did the same thing, though this time she wrapped up a foal instead. It thrashed and kicked, Cronus swallowed it, and Neptune has been shown with horses ever since; he owed his life to one.

Cronus was king of all, gods and Titans, and perhaps today he does still rule, for who among us does not worship Time? Some people are enslaved by the ritual of their Franklin Planner or their electronic date book, we all have time strapped to our wrists and sometimes it beeps at us and moves us on from what we currently enjoy, the "faces" of clocks stare at us and "tell" us time in almost every room. Nowhere more than in our calendars do gods who we think ancient, reign today. We consult calendars with months named for Janus; Mars; Aprille (Venus); Maia the goddess of plant growth; and Juno, advocate of marriage for the month still so popular for weddings. Our days are named for Roman, German, and Old English gods. We easily speak of Tiw's day, Woden's day, Thor's day, Freia's day, Saturn's day, and then one each for the sun and moon. Of course the echoes of ancient gods remain strong; we hear them every day.

And dreaded Cronus trudges along, relentless, carrying his hour glass and bloody sickle. By the way, his manlike children, in their ten-year rebellion against Cronus and the other Titans, were helped by the Queen of the Amazons, usually called Antiope. She may also be referred to in the television series as the one girl Adam really cares about. Both young women "have to leave," both "have troubles" and both cope with extremely difficult situations. Antiope may be Adam's one true love, whom he and Ria refer to as "Annie."

The closing of the Golden Age which ended with Cronus's reign is hinted at in several scenes. No longer were good things abundant, no more was it eternal spring. Although the series was produced for four years, everything we see takes place in spring or summer. Yet, at the close of the series, in the last two episodes, the landscape surrounding Ria is suddenly autumnal, the end of growth. The season seems a closure and indicates the Twilight of the Gods, like the sun finally setting on the British Empire. The cyclical aspect of nature is also indicated though, for in the last scene, as Ria watches Leonard's plane leave England, another man tries to enter her life, and she does not discourage him completely.

There are other hints of the idyllic age gone by. The family name, Parkinson, may be a twist on son-in-park or children-in-Paradise. In one brief scene a poster on Adam's door states, "Another lousy day in Paradise." These "Olympians" are sick of Paradise and need more in their lives.

The serpent who tempted Eve is seen in this series as Leonard, the dark man who tempts Ria. He is the only character with a *leitmotiv,* for when he thinks of Ria or when they meet, we hear Albinoni's "Adagio." His name, Leonard, may be derived from the lion who accompanied the Mother Goddess, for she was shown with either lions or those helpful serpents who caught the mice and saved the grain. Egypt did not loan out precious cats for years, so elsewhere it was snakes, those symbols of renewal and of healing, that were worshipped. Leonard, the snake, lures Ria from her duties, although she always faithfully returns to feed her family, the family of mankind.

Leonard may play the role of Hades or Pluto, god of the underworld, who fell in love with young Persephone. He lured her from her playmates to a lovely flower, then surged forth from the earth in his chariot drawn by black horses, scooped her up in his arms and carried her back to the underworld. She was furious. She wouldn't eat. Finally, as you recall, her disconsolate mother, who refused to grow the crops until her daughter was returned, convinced the gods to make Pluto release her. But just before Persephone left the underworld, she was tricked and ate a few pomegranate seeds, learning too late that the snack doomed her to return to the underworld for a few months each year, as many months as seeds she'd eaten. And that explained why we have winter every year.

Mythic thinking is by its nature associative, one story or god merging into another. The ancient cultures saw Persephone and her mother Demeter or Ceres as one woman, who personified the seed which rested in the earth for months, then emerged in the spring. Later cultures divided the two into mother and daughter and sometimes added the third phase of a woman's life with Hecate, with her connections to the moon and underworld. On television Hecate is probably represented by Ruby, the tired cleaning lady who, like Hecate, has a dog and who, like Ria, is tempted by an admirer. So Persephone, Demeter, and Hecate, the three aspects of woman, all appear in the series and Ria plays two of them. Persephone too is connected with the moon, and like a lunatic, she flirts with the dark devil.

The television Ria has no trouble playing the roles of both Demeter and Persephone. At home, where she forces herself to feed everyone, her setting is ideal for Mother Nature: sky blue shades over flourishing plants on her windowsills. While she is with Leonard though, she is like someone else and as if possessed, she does not do her job of causing things to grow. Instead, she shreds the flowers of each centerpiece, spills or pours her meals all over Leonard, and even squashes her groceries in a trash can. Instead of nourishing the plants and wild creatures, instead of her crusade to save the fox from hounds, or her liberating a butterfly captured by her husband and imprisoned in a jar, with Leonard she not only lets things slide but throws her food away. Yet she refuses to eat with him, until, perhaps in the penultimate episode, she may, reluctantly, share some eggs with him, just like Persephone with Pluto.

Indeed, the television Ria is uneasy. Neither on earth nor in the heavens, it seems, is this feminine energy in its proper place. Her restlessness in the series may come from several sources. She yearns for a real job. Her feelings of uselessness may stem from the fact that we ignore her or misuse her and forget her, or even poison her, though once she received reverence from agrarian societies. Now, she has only occasional guest appearances on commercials, where with a flourish she raises her arms to cause lightning to flash as she declares, "That's not butter! You can't fool Mother Nature!"

But Mother Nature has her own shadow side, a side seen only in pale form in Ria. Mother Nature, like Kali, does more than nourish. She sends us hurricanes, droughts, floods, pestilence, and famine. She too, like Cronus, must sometimes destroy what she creates. The sculptor Charles Biederman has watched her for ninety years and says that she has changed. She will not stand for our abuse now. Fortunately, we are changing too.

It is true, and perhaps not surprising, that our focus on forgotten Mother Nature and our need to help her has coincided with another movement, the woman's movement.

Rachel Carson published her book, *Silent Spring* in 1962. It was ridiculed at first, as were Adelle Davis's books on nutrition, in the 40s, 50s and 60s. The first to quote these women's observations were labeled cranks, crackpots, and on the fringe. But in 1963 the *Feminine Mystique* became widely read. Women began to realize they had power, often latent, but it was there. By 1968 Simone de Beauvoir's *Second Sex* appeared here in translation. Soon Carson and Davis were taken very seriously by the public. News woke us, news that what we ate helped or hindered health, and what we put on fruits and vegetables had an impact on birds, on plants, and on our health too.

Perhaps our interest in the series resonates to this increased attention to Mother Nature. We define myth as false, as fiction, yet myth is where the truths reside. Myth strengthens drama, and it strengthens us. And the gods do have a sense of humor. It is no accident that these truths come to us in comedy and in comics; like court jesters the truth is sweetened by laughter of recognition, of others' silliness, and sometimes even of our own.

BIBLIOGRAPHY

Bell, Robert E. *Women of Classical Mythology*. ABC-CLIO, 1991.
Bettelheim, Bruno. *The Uses of Enchantment: The Meaning and Importance of Fairy Tales*. New York: Vintage Books, 1975.
Bolen, Jean Shinoda. *Goddesses in Every Woman: A New Psychology of Women*. San Francisco: Harper and Row, 1984.
Bonnefoy, Yves. *Mythologies*. Chicago: University of Chicago Press, 1991.

Burrows, David J., Frederick R. Lapides, John T. Shawcross, eds. *Myths and Motifs in Literature*. New York: The Free Press, 1973.

Campbell, Joseph. *The Masks of God: Occidental Mythology*. New York: Viking Press, 1964.

Campbell, Joseph. (1986). *The Inner Reaches of Outer Space: Metaphor as Myth and as Religion*. New York: Harper and Row.

Cleese, John, interview by Michael Parkinson, first aired 20 December 1996. BBC's *Parky at Christmas*.

Frazer, Sir James George. *New Golden Bough*. New York: Criterion, 1959.

Grant, Michael. *Gods and Mortals in Classical Mythology*. Great Britain: Michael Grant Publications Ltd. and John Hazel. New York: Dorset, 1973.

Graves, Robert. *The White Goddess*. New York: Farrar, Straus, and Giroux, 1948.

Johnson, Buffie. *Lady of the Beasts: The Goddess and her Sacred Animals*. Rochester, Vermont: Inner Traditions International, 1994.

Leeming, David, and Jake Page. *Myths of the Female Divine Goddess*. Oxford: Oxford University Press, 1994.

Nicholson, Shirley, Com. *The Goddess Re-Awakening: The Feminine Principle Today*. Wheaton, Illinois/Madras, India/London, England: Theosophical Publishing House, 1989.

Palmer, Laura. Telephone interview, BBC World Wide America, 12 and 19 April 1997.

Sjoo, Monica, and Barbara Mor. *The Great Cosmic Mother: Rediscovering the Religion of the Earth*. Harper and Row, 1987. (*The Ancient Religion of the Great Cosmic Mother of All*. Trondheim, Norway: Rainbow Press, 1981.)

Woodman, Marion, and Elinor Dickson. *Dancing in the Flames: The Dark Goddess in the Transformation of Consciousness*. Boston: Shambhala, 1994.

Part II

Shadows and Shades: Dealing with the Dark

8

The Mists of Lake Wobegon: The Archetypal Function of an American Storyteller

MARY ANN MILLER

> Every morning brings us the news of the globe, and yet we are poor in note-worthy stories.
>
> —Walter Benjamin, "The Storyteller"

An intriguing phenomenon has been afoot in the United States for over the last two decades: a storyteller named Garrison Keillor has been coming on the radio every Saturday night to give the news about a tiny, some say imaginary, Midwestern farm village called Lake Wobegon, Minnesota, "the little town that time forgot and the decades cannot improve." This "news" consists of the endless imaginings that draw on the small everyday details that make up life in a rural farm town. And we, an audience of millions, have been held as spellbound as Scheherazade's Arabian King, for even longer than one-thousand-and-one nights by now.

The remarkable fact is that Keillor employs the ancient storyteller's art, embedded in ritual and restricted to listening (he repeatedly rejects offers to go on television). The fact, too, that the tales seem so simple yet leave listeners with the palpable feeling that his tale-telling has fallen like rain on the parched ears of a story-starved people suggests that these stories have an archetypal function. Like fairy tales and myths, they are symbolic stories, our Grimms and our Greeks. This storyteller and his story cycle may have emerged because we have been ready for him. These "new" stories, it appears, are also the "old" stories we have missed, and craved, for a long time.

What follows will be an exploration of these ideas, using for illumination the oral storytelling tradition, the study of fairy tales, and analytical psychology.

Our Need for Stories

Joseph Addison wrote in the late seventeenth century: "But now the mystic tale/that pleased of yore/can charm an understanding age/no more." The scholar Henry Wiggins in the twentieth century says that for three centuries, since the beginning of the rise of the novel, we have been attempting to persuade ourselves that we could live without stories. This hasn't worked, and suddenly there has occurred a sudden and quite dramatic widening of interest (4). Depth psychology is one of the movements which has helped bring stories back, for it is by discovering and telling her story and the realization that it is an old story, that a patient is healed. We also have narrative theology, narrative psychology, oral history, and story telling revivals sprung up here and there.

For many of us, though, the stories which used to be culturally and spiritually sustaining are inaccessible now, at least as it appears. Keillor's art is not to simply reiterate the old stories, but to clothe them in the subjects that arise from the life of a community we all recognize. "If I am to discover the holy, it must be in my biography and not in the history of Israel," says Wiggins (17). This is Keillor's starting place; he has turned the ancient storyteller's art to the telling of "new" stories set closer to our time and place that are paradoxically the "old" permanent stories we have been hungering for for a long time. He is a great artist who can capture in his own stories the folk tale power of ages past.

One Saturday night, the News from Lake Wobegon is about a father, Kenny, staying at home with his five kids while his wife is out at choir practice. After a prolonged bout of happy rough-and-tumble play, which leaves the house in a shambles, the father lies on the living room floor, his kids on top of him, and tells them the story of Hansel and Gretel in the dark forest, from the Grimm Brothers' fairy tales we know so well. He tells them how their mother has gotten so sick and died, and their father, after great sadness, has brought home a new mother. But for Kenny, says Keillor, it is not easy to tell about a dad who lets his wife persuade him into leaving his dear children in the dark woods, to be eaten by animals. However, the story goes along fine and the kids are thoroughly engrossed. In fact, Kenny might sometimes forget a detail, but the kids remember every one, and correct him where needed.

> . . . if the bread crumbs on the path sparkle like diamonds in the moonlight in one version of the story, then the next time you can't say they glisten like pearls, you've got to tell it the same way. You can't disappoint them, but you've also got to surprise them, so each time he'll toss in something new and crazy— maybe the gingerbread house will have a garage this time, made of pepperoni pizzas, and the wicked witch will sit drinking coffee and watching T.V.—but Kenny has to be careful: next time he can't say the pizzas were sausage and onion. Stories are permanent. (Keillor, *Leaving* 221).

This story elucidation of our subject corresponds exactly to the rule for a storyteller's initiation among the Cree Indians: The initiate must tell a story, but if he tells it exactly as it is, he fails. If he changes it, he also fails. A story is a paradox; it is old and new.

We also need stories because they testify to the peril in which every generation stands, and Keillor does not shirk this task. It is hard for Kenny to tell the cruel parts to his children, but somehow he knows they need them. He knows that "shadow," as Jungians would call it—his own hateful feelings—are important, and must be acknowledged. It is a redemption story and he knows that, too.

Nevertheless, we love the fairy story not first for its wisdom. We love it for the manner in which it is told, just like Kenny's kids. Its external appearance, which varies from people to people, from narrator to narrator, delights us (Lüthi 26). We love to compare the Algonquin Cinderella with the Chinese Cinderella and the Grimms' Cinderella. But for a story to touch us, it is important that the surroundings be familiar. The archetypal yearning for story has not disappeared, as has been made clear by the response to Keillor's Saturday evening story. The symbols still come floating up, but the world around the symbols is different. In one of his stories Keillor tells us that Marlys and Harold . . . "grew up on Taft Street a block from the ballfield" (*Leaving* 50). The picture of a street a block from the ballfield conjures up in every American the once-upon-a-time of his or her mythical past, and carries an emotion that a poor cottage near a dark forest or a palace on the hill can no longer do. Keillor is doing what storytellers have always done: set his story in the landscape his audience knows. The Grimm brothers evoke the hayfield, the humble hut, the dark forest. In the Grimm brothers the castle is always on the hill, remote from the day-to-day lives of simple people. Their tellings reflect an era of romanticism and at the same time the loss of idealism and acceptance of reality following the Napoleonic wars, when there was little wealth. The ballfield is quintessentially small-town American, and this single image lets us walk right into the landscape of the story. No more description is necessary, for our memories and imaginations provide all the rest.

The ballfield places us on one of the last streets of town, where it is especially quiet, and you can see the sky, unobstructed by houses or hills, reach all the way down to the horizon. A small-town ballfield is an open patch of green, where the grass is worn away in the shape of a big diamond. Sliders-into-third have worn the ground around third base into a long deep oval pocket. The sandy patch in the middle is the pitcher's "mound." To the left of the diamond is a stand of wooden bleachers. Some big lights on tall poles light the scene for night games, and turn the dewy grass a deep emerald green. On a fine summer night the whole town might stroll over to see what is going on. It is a place especially suited for ritual meetings of young people whose "sap is rising." Most of the time, though, the ballfield is empty and then it looks vast or small, depending on your age and where you have been in the meantime. The sight of it makes you happy or sad depending on the fluctuations your heart performed on those rare summer evenings. For some then it is a lonely part of town, the empty ball park a constant reminder of faded romance or fleeting victory. To live near the ballfield would be like living near the heart chakra of a small town.

Though a storyteller must be spare with details, the name of the street, Taft Street, is a deft touch. "Taft" conjures up a quiet time in American history under a president of unspectacular achievements. It is a wry way of placing us more securely in the midst of quiet, conservative small-town Americana, in "the town that time forgot."

The Voice of Soul

The storyteller's voice is his instrument, singing out the musicality in a story. The Celtic and Homeric bards were renowned for their sonorous voices. One critic has said of Keillor, "above all else, he has got a perfect storytelling voice, lazy but powerful, deep and wide, full of natural drama (*Dictionary*, "Keillor").

Keillor himself describes his voice as "flat and slow. . . and there are long pauses, and sentences that trail off into the raspberry bushes." He relates that when he first entered the radio world in 1963 as the "friendly announcer of *Highlights in Homemaking*," he badly wanted to sound like Orson Welles, "as rich and smooth as my mother's gravy on Sunday pot roast." But he succeeded only so far as to sound "at least brown and thick and lumpy." But, he says, the pretense was hard to keep up, so by the time "Prairie Home" rolled along, his voice had drifted back towards center and sounded more like his dad's (*Leaving* xvi).

In simply describing his voice, Keillor is compelled to tell a story which contains the distinguishing feature of most of his stories, the motif of redemption. We see how he holds the tension between his unshakable tendency to automatic self-effacement, learned in his childhood, and his ambition. In the process, the father who had likely sown the seeds of his son's self-doubt, has been redeemed. The pious repressive father can now be loved for the gifts he has given his son.

Keillor reports having been hurt by his harsh puritanical upbringing. "Something happened to me when I was six or seven years old. . . . I have dim memories of it. I became fearful, always looking around, always checking, always alert. You never overcome it. You go on from there." (*Dictionary*, "Keillor"). Keillor's "going on from there" is his quest to heal his psychic wounding, and it takes the form of telling stories about himself and the world of his childhood. Said Keillor to an interviewer: "I think it takes an act of redemption to jump back into the old life, and I look for that redemption. I don't want to just tell funny stories about paradise (*Dictionary*, "Keillor")."

A comparison with Sinclair Lewis, who also described midwestern small-town culture in his scathing novel *Main Street*, can further illuminate how this redemption motif permeates the Wobegon stories. Whereas Lewis calls his small town a "town of a few thousand in a region of wheat and corn" (6), Keillor says his town "contains the *homes* of some 900 *souls,* most of them small white frame houses [italics mine]" (*Lake* 4). His aim is nothing less than soul-making, the work of storytellers through the ages. His town is a *temenos*—a container, or "holy space." It is full, not famously empty like Lewis's town.

The placement of the prepositional phrase in this loving summary also teases us a little and keeps us on our toes. We cannot be sure, at first, whether he means to say that the *souls* are small white houses or the *homes* are small white houses. But these are symbolic stories and the small white frame houses do signify souls—souls that are as neat and plain and serious and vulnerable as little frame houses on the prairie. They are the souls of god-fearing Protestant Fundamentalists who "believed there was a verse in the Bible, they couldn't find it, but it was there, maybe in 'Leviticus' somewhere, that forbade air-conditioning" (Skow 68).

Though it is clear Keillor values much of his heritage, "soul" carries a heavy burden of guilt and anger too, which are not to be swept under the rug. Sometimes he doesn't spare the town at all. One evening the "News from Lake Wobegon" was about an angry son who has returned to town intent upon nailing a list of his "popular grievances" against his repressive parents and neighbors to the door of the Lutheran church, like Martin Luther nailed his "95 Theses" against Rome to the door of the Wittenberg Castle Church in 1517. The disgruntled son calls his document the "95 Thesis 95," and the fourth thesis states:

You have taught me to worship a god who is like you, who shares your thinking exactly, who is going to slap me one if I don't straighten out fast. I am very uneasy every Sunday, which is cloudy and deathly still and filled with silent accusing whispers. (1985, 315)

The ninth thesis addresses "Minnesota nice":

You taught me to be nice, so that now I am so full of niceness, I have no sense of right and wrong, no outrage, no passion. "If you can't say something nice, don't say anything at all," you said, so I am very quiet, which most people think is politeness. I call it repression. (316)

In the words of his character, Keillor is no less cutting than Sinclair Lewis; but then as he goes on with the story, he gives the angry son second thoughts, so he does not carry out his plan exactly. Instead of nailing his "theses" to the church door, he slips them under the door of the one-man newspaper office, and they get lost in the clutter of the editor's desk, and never get published (313). In this story we can almost feel the bitterness and rage of a suffering man-child being transmuted into gentle laughter and forgiveness. The terrible emotions are redeemed, though not repressed. For they are still there on the editor's desk, in the clutter of the psyche, so to speak, but they aren't so soul-destroying now. "Neither ghosts nor demons shall have any power, whenever and wherever these tales are told," says story scholar Heinrich Zimmer (215).

Crossing Over

Storytelling gains special numinosity when ritualized; in ages past storytelling was not a separate event; it was always part of the entertainment at a festival, or surrounded by the bustle of the marketplace, or accompanied by the routine of household or field work. Likewise Keillor's radio story each week is embedded in a ritual two hours of folk music, jokes, skits, mock commercials, and all kinds of other light-hearted (and repetitive) shenanigans. Every Saturday at six or so we listen before we go out for the evening.

And finally the moment we have been waiting for comes: "It's been a quiet week in Lake Wobegon," intones the storyteller, without fail or variation. These words, an initial incantation akin to Homeric, Celtic, and folktale practices, usher us into the story zone. It is a real but invisible place. Keillor comments in the course of his stories that the county surveyors of Mist County, because it was so cold and the snow so deep, carried out their duties while sitting next to the cozy potbellied stove; in consequence the town and its little lake never made it onto any map (10). This "Mist County" then, puns on the mists of mythical places, concealed by fogs from the daily world. It is a place which is gradually disappearing, a kind of Avalon of middle America, which today only the storyteller can visit. Keillor is just like Merlin, bard and magician of Celtic lore, who could freely move between Avalon and King Arthur's Court because he still believed in the Druids and the Little People.

Mist County also touches on the *missed-out* character of these people and their place, their passed-over status as shy folk forgotten by the world and abandoned to their drab little backwater, and perhaps even plays on on "misty-eyed" nostalgia.

Etymology was of great significance for Jung, because it revealed for him something of the unconscious layers of the word. This seems also to be true for Keillor. Wobegon's English etymology points to sad-sackness—Middle English *wo begon,* beset with woe or "burdened with sorrows"—and to the folk tale motif of the village of fools. Keillor gives his own playful etymology of the town's name in a footnote. The name, he wrote, was given "as an attempt to be accurate while still putting the best face on things. To scholars of the Ojibway tongue, "Wobegon" or "Wa-be-gan-tan-han" means "the place where we waited all day in the rain. . ." (Keillor, *Lake* 48).

Listen how Wobegon vibrates with the sound of Native American names like Michigan, Waupeton, Sisseton. The Indian background is picked up by the psychic ear; it is shadow material for most Americans, offstage, even repressed, and instinctually other. It is part of what the "inner" ear picks up as it "crosses over" and engages with the shy folk who inhabit the heartland.

It is with great skill that the storyteller helps us cross over into shadow-land, where he goes regularly in order to bring back the "news." He offers precise directions, because even for him, it is not so easy to get there any more. "The turnoff is just before a sharp bend in the highway," he confides,

> and when you break for the turn, you think of the speeding truck that might leap from the bend and roll you flat as a pancake. This turn might be your last. You break and at the last moment you hit the gas and swerve left, as if cross-ing a hidden border. Where the county road leaves the highway, there is a dip in the road and a bump that lets you know you're back in the land of where you came from. You hit the bump and see George Washington's face on the schoolroom wall and hear the Nicene Creed, "I believe in God the Father Almighty, maker of heaven and earth, and of all things visible and invisible," and you smell tuna fish casserole. (unpublished radio broadcast)

The dip in the road and the bump demarcate the story space. It is Alice's rabbit hole or the wardrobe in C.S. Lewis's *Tales of Narnia*. This bump—a typical poltergeist phenomenon—lets us know that we are shift-ing psychic levels and, in Jungian terms, have "activated" the unconscious. And so, thence to the litany which ends Keillor's entry passage— Washington's face on the schoolroom wall, the awe-inspiring phrases of the Creed, *and* the smell of tuna fish casserole.

Keillor has called his performances "seances." This litany of things he sees as he "crosses over" outwardly signifies a sampling of the "news" that he brings back, but it also represents something inner and invisible. It anticipates humorous ordinary *ordeals*, and brings us closer to the truth about the difficulty of the teller's transition backward into shadow—a nec-essary journey if there is to be redemption.

One of the crossover details inspires a story about a small initiation ordeal. George Washington is looking down from his portrait with a severe and somewhat pained expression upon a shy schoolboy whose turn it is next to stand before the class and face death: make an impromptu speech about himself. But then he notices that Abe Lincoln, looking down from *his* portrait, seems kinder and gives some comfort, if not courage. What has been activated is typical of initiation sequences in any number of tribal cul-tures: the images of ancestors and the gods pass before the eyes of the ini-tiates who are about to undergo their ordeals.

There are also many stories inspired by the Nicene Creed, for example, the ones about the agonies of a young boy stuck with a family who are devout members of a fundamentalist Protestant sect, the Sanctified Brethren. They eschew anything so worldly as music, church buildings, or even clergy. They worship for hours every Sunday, sitting silently on hard kitchen chairs in Aunt Flo's living room until someone is moved by the Lord to speak, which is not very often. The boy can hear the organ and the singing from the nearby Roman Catholic Church, Our Lady of Perpetual Responsibility, and he yearns to be a Catholic. It would be so glamorous, especially on the day they bless the animals on the church steps, "right out there in the open" (Keillor 127).

But at the end of the long, plain service, the Sanctified Brethren will all sit down to Aunt Flo's pot roast and rhubarb pie. It will all end with the feast of reintegration into the community and a meal of celebration.

Storytelling, Archetypes, and Active Imagination

When we get to analyzing stories like this, it *seems* the storyteller has these things in mind. But in fact, the underlying structures in "true" stories, that is, the symbolic stories we crave, are archetypal, and are not simply "made up" by the conscious mind.

As many people know, Jung advocated a technique he called "active imagination," as a way of releasing psychic energy or "exposing unconscious contents." He described it as "dreaming with open eyes." Jung uses an example from his boyhood, when he would pay a call on an aunt in her old-fashioned house, where there was an impressive picture of his maternal grandfather in full regalia. "He was a sort of bishop," Jung says, ". . . and every Sunday morning I knelt on a chair and looked at that picture until grandfather came down the steps." His aunt would challenge this fantasy of her nephew's, but Jung knew he had seen grandfather walking down.

So, Jung says, "in the same way, when you concentrate on a mental picture, it begins to stir, the image becomes enriched by details, it moves and develops. Each time naturally you mistrust it and have the idea that you just made it up. . . But you have to overcome that doubt because it is not true" (*Symbolic*, par. 398).

Keillor's storytelling technique is like Jung's active imagination, and he describes it his own way: "Out of curiosity you follow where the unexpected turns take you," he says. "You get tired of being afraid of embarrassing yourself, and so rather than drawing back and going in a direction you are sure of, I think as a person gets older, you get reckless. I think you are supposed to get reckless" (Skow 72).

We might say that it is Keillor's inner Wise Old Man, counterpart to Jung's Child, who allows his "overcoming conscious doubt." Through the ages storytelling has been the office of the elder members of the community, those in the second half of life beyond the age where ego concerns dominate, but where he or she is able to recklessly follow the lead of the Self,[1] if you will. Young and ego-bound, we are cautious. Old and wise, we can trust the process and take risks; we can let in the unexpected and crazy.

Keillor also admits that part of his craft involves learning to talk

---

[1] "The Self" is the guiding center within the totality of the psyche.

until he thinks of something to say, that he and others in the ministerial profession sometimes do this. In this gentle poke at homily-delivering clergy he again reveals his sense of lineage with the ancient Celtic story-tellers who also held a spiritual office in their societies.

One story which illustrates active imagination in Keillor's storytelling is "The Ten Dollar Bill," which is also on the theme of suffering, shadow, and redemption.

In the story, an adolescent son, Jim, has just asked his father for ten dollars. Over his father's chair is an old family picture, which Keillor describes in startling detail, telling about the mundane family history, while at the same time slyly evoking archetypal undertones. It is a photograph of a prairie family in a dirt yard in front of a sod house, the narrator tells us. The husband and wife are on white kitchen chairs, and there are eight little kids, five barefoot, a tall boy with shoes, and twins, a boy and a girl, on the mother's lap. The father is holding a portrait of a girl who died a year before of influenza. Keillor manages to touch on the comic, surreal, tragic, and archetypal in his closing lines:

> Next to the tall boy is his dog, who jerked his head as the lens opened, and so in the picture he has two heads, and there is a cow grazing on the roof. It was the summer of 1876. In August the twins perished of diphtheria. To look at the parents, you might guess their ages as late fifties, but Karl is twenty-eight and Sophie is two years younger. . . . So you can see from the picture where people got their philosophy that life is hard. (*Leaving* 13)

The story returns to the present, and Jim asks his father, who is eating a bowl of ice cream, for some money. When the father protests that he has already given him money, Jim lies, saying he spent it on pizza and a movie. But the truth is that he has gone to the ballet in Minneapolis, and spent not only that money, but the entire one hundred dollars his uncle had given him for his birthday. At that point, Jim goes into a private reverie, reliving a special moment in one dance where a dancer danced all by himself, and "how he took three steps and a tremendous leap and hung in the air and you saw his face so clear, illuminated by grief, and then he vanished" (14).

But again, the present interrupts this exquisite memory, this time harshly, as the father, Byron, begins to rant, demanding to know why his son can't look at him when he talks, recounting how he sure never expected a handout when he was a kid because he knew what responsibility was, and accusing Jim of not knowing this.

Jim replies that he does know about responsibility, which sets off a full-blown lecture. Byron has however, peeled off a ten-dollar bill, and as he talks, he is gesturing broadly, bill in hand. Suddenly the unexpected enters: a young cat. He has been sitting next to the father, and now he becomes fascinated by the ten-dollar bill swooping overhead. The cat sees "a green bird" diving and fluttering, and he crouches. The father talks on, waving the bill in the air.

> "There was discipline then, I'll tell you, and a willingness to sacrifice, to wait for what you wanted, not to have everything handed to you right away on a silver plate." The bird dove and fluttered and the cat—waiting for what he wanted, not expecting it to come on a silver plate—tensed for the leap, winding his mainspring, as the bird flung itself through the air. 'I don't know how many times I have to say this before you finally get it through your head—" Byron shrieked. (15)

The little cat, in a move both magical and synchronistic, has made a tremendous leap, hung in mid-air, just like the dancer, and latched onto the father's hand. From there he is catapulted halfway across the room and lands neatly on his feet, running away into the dark (15).

Here is a picture of Keillor's ability to follow "out of curiosity" where the unexpected turns in his stories take him. Conscious doubt is overcome and allowance is made for whatever falls into consciousness—the cat. So he lets his attention go to the cat; he watches it. It has a life of its own. It behaves according to its cat nature—watches, waits, tenses, and leaps— and suddenly a new situation is created where unconscious contents come into dramatic awareness. Jung sees this as the collaboration of conscious and unconscious factors to produce a symbol.

Our symbol could be analyzed into next week for what it has exposed about the population of the storyteller's psyche. One figure we might readily discern is a father both wounded and wounding, whose psychic pain is expressed by the cat's attack on his withholding hand. The cat is known for its sensuous nature, and is commonly associated with desire, liberty, and chthonic or underworld powers. So we might see the cat as the father's own repressed libido. This little animal is also associated with the moon and hence with the less conscious and feminine. Byron's repressed feminine impulses of generosity and nurturing have turned negative. This is borne out by a third mythological characteristic of the cat: its association with powers of evil and witchcraft. We can gather from this amplification the ability of the imagination, drawing on the unconscious, to produce the appropriate symbol.

There is also an angry, rebellious boy inside the narrator, who feels helpless before the powers of his father—the father who "is helpless in the powers of time" (Heydt 138), as the picture on the wall so vividly testifies. The ten-dollar bill in the father's hand, with which he is so reluctant to part and which he fears his son will misuse, symbolizes the negative, overconservative father who inhibits the life of his son by resisting his desire. His power over his son is so great that it is impossible for Jim to say that he has gone to see a ballet. In Greek myth the image of this father is Chronos, who devoured his children because he did not want them to be in time and space. In Lake Wobegon, Chronos is the father whose philosophy and ideas are based on the collective attitude of past generations of fathers, represented by the picture on the wall over Byron's chair.

In the photograph is an animal image parallel to the cat: the two-headed dog. This is the mythical dog Cerberus (who can have from two to fifty-five heads), whose job it is to prevent return from Hades, the underworld, back to the world, where salvation and atonement are still possible. Though Jim's father lives in a new generation where you can eat ice cream and things are not so hard, the two-headed Cerberus, symbol of the older harsh collective attitude, has prevented his escape.

On both planes of time, in the past (photograph) and present (story), there is animal-in-movement through which life protests, and Keillor's active imagination captures that protest. The two-headed dog also magnifies the significance of the *leaping* cat and Jim's indelible memory of the leaping dancer. Jung says every symbol has within itself a contradiction, and the story's sad photograph is also alive with instinctual motion in the *moving* dog.

The Story World

Max Lüthi, the great Swiss folklorist, whose approach to the study of fairy tales has some of the magic of the tales themselves, says that the fairy tale is a world in miniature, in which are present the basic motifs of existence (73). Within "The Ten Dollar Bill" we can find all of the motifs Luthi finds in a fairy tale (73): life and death (the dead children); good and evil (Byron's sermon, the symbol of the cat); temptation and intrigue (the trip to Minneapolis); weakness and innocence (the son faced with the father); despair, guidance, and assistance (the Uncle's birthday present).

Moreover, in a fairy tale these motifs are accompanied by the range of human feelings (25). In our story privation, longing, grief, joy, horror, hope, bitterness, irritability, pain, and compassion are all expressed.

How is all of this embodied in such a short tale? Through its artistry and style, says Lüthi. Keillor's tales have a folklore power because he is a consummate artist working in the style of fairy tales. The structural element of repetition, for instance, is organic to the folk tale, and in our tale, the suspended animation of the dancer's tremendous leap and hanging in midair recurs again in the cat's tremendous leap. Fairy tale structures like this satisfy what Lüthi would call "our allegiances to the subliminal depth" of the psyche. They subtly deepen *from underneath* the satisfactions derived from our closer-to-conscious sympathy with the son, his feelings, and desire for freedom.

This structure also assists the fairy tale's artistic ability to sustain or vary a theme. Our story is based on the theme of suffering. Once stated, it is varied and intensified—the pioneer family, the dancer's grief, the father's clawed hand.

"The fairy tale loves action, clarity, precision and compactness," says Lüthi. The appearance of the characters is not described in detail, if at all. Nor are their inner feelings (51). Keillor says his tales are "starved for detail, in literary terms. You cannot supply that on the radio. The listener supplies it (*Dictionary,* "Keillor")." This is fairy tale style. "The tendency is for feelings and relationships to congeal into objects and thus become outwardly visible," says Lüthi (51). Notice what the father's eating a bowl of ice cream suggests to you. See how the relationship of the father and son is concretized in the ten dollar bill, how the dancer represents the boy's feelings, how animals can be seen as forces in the soul, as we've already noted with the dog and cat.

Moreover, even as the world in its essential elements is present in a fairy tale, "the supernatural world is clearly visible, [too]" (Lüthi 25). In "The Ten Dollar Bill" the figures of the dancer, the cat, the two-headed dog, and the cow (symbol of the great mother and moon goddesses) join the supernatural world to the world of humans, as the seven dwarfs do, or the thirteen fairies, or the golden goose. So we can see how Keillor's stories get their power.

Ritual Departure

Finally there is the *rite du depart*: "That's the news from Lake Wobegon, where all the men are good-looking, all the women are strong, and all the children are above average." At the end of each telling the storyteller recites these words. We have been participating in a ritual, and these ritual words reintegrate us into the outer world. We know the words by heart and know they signal the story's end. We regret that we must leave Lake Wobegon so soon, but we also feel, because the words are always the same, something of the permanence, even of the eternal about what has happened there.

A deeper look tells us more. First there is its ironic twist, which is like the traditional storyteller's little rhyme at the end of his tale, which seems to deny the seriousness of her or his business. Our storyteller reverses the traditional fairy tale scheme (as well as modern expectations) of beautiful women and strong men. He also understates the perfection of typical fairy tale offspring, who are so perfect, that "even the sun gazes upon them with astonishment," and so on. In the Midwest, "above average" is hyperbolic enough to describe perfection.

These closing phrases allude to legendary and mythical times when the land flourished because of the marriage of a good king and queen. Or to go back even further, "all the women are strong and all the men good-looking" reaches into the far past of goddess rule and to the old myths like those of indigenous peoples of the Americas. They tell of strong, willful women—women who chose to live separately from the men, whom they relegated to an island, or in some stories, to the sky, out of the way, yet available for pleasure and love-making when the serious work was done.

These beautiful men and powerful women are the distant cousins of the king and queen, whose exemplary qualities guaranteed the flourishing of the people, whose future lay in offspring who are wondrous, even golden, or translated into Minnesotan: "above average." With Garrison Keillor we have in our midst a storyteller who understands what soul-making is, who wants us to look at his people, and at the population of our own psyche, in new ways, so that they and we may be redeemed and our land may flourish once again.

BIBLIOGRAPHY

Benjamin, Walter. "The Storyteller: Reflections on the Works of Nikolai Leskov," in his *Illuminations*, ed. Hannah Arendt, trans. Harry Zohn. New York: Harcourt Brace, 1968.

Dictionary of Literary Biography 1987 Yearbook. Detroit: Gale, n.d.

Heydt, Vera von der. "On the Father in Psychotherapy," in *Fathers and Mothers: Five Papers on the Archetypal Background of Archetypal Psychology*. Zurich: Spring, 1973, 128–42.

Jung. "The Tavistock Lectures" in *The Collected Works of C.G. Jung*, Vol. XVIII. Eds. H. Read, M. Fordham, G. Adler, W. McGuire. Trans. R.F.C. Hull. 2nd ed. Bollingen Series XX. Princeton: Princeton University Press, 1950.

Keillor, Garrison. *Lake Wobegon Days*. New York: Penguin, 1985.

———. *Leaving Home. A Collection of Lake Wobegon Stories*. London: Faber and Faber, 1988.

Lewis Sinclair. *Main Street*. New York: Harcourt Brace, 1920.

Lüthi, Max. *Once Upon a Time: On the Nature of Fairy Tales*. Trans. Lee Chadeayne and Paul Gottwald. Bloomington: Indiana University Press, 1970.

Skow, John. "Lonesome Whistle Blowing." *Time* (4 November 1985), 68–73.

Zimmer, Heinrich. *The King and the Corpse: Tales of the Soul's Conquest of Evil*. Bollingen Series XI. Princeton: Princeton University Press, 1957.

Wiggins, James B., ed. "Within and Without Stories," in *Religion as Story*, New York: Harper and Row, 1975.

9
Taking the Dark with Open Eyes: Hidden Dimensions of a Psychology of Abortion

LYN COWAN

> If I can take the dark with open eyes
> And call it seasonal, not harsh or strange . . .
> And, treelike, stand unmoved before the change,
> Lose what I lose to keep what I can keep,
> The strong root still alive under the snow,
> Love will endure—if I can let you go.
>
> —May Sarton, "Taking the Dark With Open Eyes," from *Autumn Sonnets**

Say the word "abortion" in America and you light a fuse that detonates a violent debate—emotionally, and sometimes physically. It evokes a sweeping range of emotion: to some it is a blasphemy, to others a symbol of the most fundamental right to govern matters of a person's most intimate life. The way we Americans respond to abortion—the word, the concept, the fact—trumpets the existence of a fierce collective psychological complex. A complex of this depth and magnitude is a more-than-the-sum total of all our individual thoughts and feelings about abortion.

The *word* is loaded. The *idea* of abortion is deeply meshed with our ideas about power, control, and being "civilized." And though the capacity to regulate the timing and number of offspring is not unique to humans, when a female of our species willfully and consciously terminates a pregnancy, it is impossible for us to regard it as nothing more than a

---

* *Used by permission.*

biological response to environmental conditions. Such a termination always involves an intricate set of emotions, both on the part of the pregnant woman and of the culture in which she lives.

Most psychological and counseling professionals have been occupied with the ego-level decision-making process of a woman considering abortion, and with the aftermath of such a decision. The inevitability of serious depression as a consequence of aborting a pregnancy is generally assumed—a prejudice held over from the last century when it was irrefutable dogma that a woman can only be fulfilled and happy when she has children, and must become depressed and miserable if she does not. In 1888, the great Austrian psychiatrist Richard von Krafft-Ebing wrote, no doubt with an assured and benign smile, that a woman will not suffer with dread the coming of menopause and the end of her productive life if "her sexual career has been successful, and loving children gladden the maternal heart" (Krafft-Ebing 8). Even today we do not hear much about those women who consider abortion but decide, or are required, to carry to term *and then become depressed.*

The legal choice used to be: get pregnant and have children, or, get pregnant and have children. This "choice" was also a social requirement for women. In the public mind there was no *moral* choice, since no one, or no one who mattered, considered that the bearing of a child might in some circumstances be immoral. For married women, an abortion could never be a moral choice, for it contradicted the very purpose of marriage, and deprived her husband of *his* offspring. Even for unmarried women, the crushing shame attached to an out-of-wedlock birth was light compared to the moral horror of a woman terminating the tiny life in her own body.

In the public ravings about abortion, the deeper psychological point of view has been conspicuously absent. Psyche's perspective, which has to do with possible *meanings* of a woman's termination of pregnancy, is the hidden dimension of the complex that has been obscured by politics, religion, sociology, medicine, and the advertising industry. By positioning abortion in the religious sphere of morality or the political realm of social policy, everyone has a position on the matter. But psyche is not a position; it is that image-making faculty in us through which we perceive and understand our reality. To "understand" abortion, then, is to stand under it and try to see what fundamental psychological image, or idea, or necessity, is expressing itself in the social arenas of debate.

The psychological place to begin talking about abortion is in the psyche's own language, the language of image. Experience is differentiated through language, and each arena of debate about abortion has its own vocabulary. *Politics* uses the language of rights: who has the right to make decisions about other people's rights. *Law* talks about abortion in terms such as jurisdiction, criminality, liability, constitutional rights to privacy. *Religion* uses the language of morality: wrong or right, bad or good, sinful or acceptable in the sight of God. *Medicine* uses the language of biology:

fetal viability, genetic dispositions, congenital defects, risk to the mother's physical health. And so on.

The human psyche has its own language, which is less verbal than imagistic; it does not speak in concepts and categories, but in *images* that personify ideas and that animate us with their inherent emotional qualities. The *psychological* question of abortion is, "What images arise in the psyche of a woman who voluntarily aborts a pregnancy?" One way to find these images is to ask metaphorically, "Who does a woman who aborts a pregnancy look like?"

Recognizing Artemis

A woman who aborts a fetus looks like a woman able to live in the realm of the goddess known to the ancient Greeks as Artemis, to the Romans as Diana, to Candomble believers in Brazil as Oxum, and in other cultures by other names. The pattern of consciousness or attitude personified by this goddess is the backdrop against which a particular understanding of pregnancy, childbirth, and abortion is formed. In an individual woman (whose psychological disposition inclines her to that way of understanding), "Artemis" functions as that deep, remote pattern of energy, that particular perspective on the world that evaluates experience in terms of female intactness and bodily integrity. In the Artemisian world, anyone who threatens a woman's sense of completeness, psychological and physical, is deemed inimical to her life and honor. The consciousness personified by Artemis[1] is connected with virginity in the psychological, not sexual, sense; that is, a woman who is complete unto herself. But, strikingly, this Artemisian perspective is also concerned with wild, pristine nature and care of the young and most vulnerable creatures.

I suggest that the problem our culture has with Artemis is the problem we have with abortion. By looking into the nature of this divinity, we find a way to look differently at the experience of abortion, a perspective from the mythic depth of the soul, or psyche.

Our world is sophisticated, domesticated, and largely urban, and Artemis is not welcome here. She is not interested in intimacy and interpersonal relationships, nor in community. She does not know the meaning of "co-dependent" and has no "issues" to "work on." She would not be caught within fifty miles of any kind of support group. She reveals herself in those with a certain kind of wild and independent spirit. Queen Elizabeth I once said, "I will have but one mistress in this house and no master," and thus gave voice to living Artemis.

Artemis is known as the strange, distant one, the remote one, unapproachable, the one who comes from far away. When she does manifest

---

[1] For a psychology of Artemis and her style of consciousness, the following works are suggested: Hall, Downing, Bolen, and Paris. Some sources for ancient stories about Artemis are: Tripp, Kerenyi, and Michael Grant and John Hazel.

in our lives, there is often an ominous sense of mystery because she is so foreign to our "civilized" ways of being. She who loves the freedom of solitude and wilderness would go mad in a world like ours, full of arbitrary moral prohibitions and scientific manipulations that seek to override the *natural* course of life and death. In her realm, death and life are merely two aspects of the same thing—the cycle of nature. Christine Downing says, "Artemis is *herself* the wilderness, the wild and untamed, and not simply its mistress" (165).

Downing writes of Artemis as the one who is fearlessly self-sufficient, and when she manifests in a woman's consciousness, that woman is serious, committed, utterly uncompromising. Artemis brings to consciousness the necessity of choosing *oneself,* a choice that confronts every adolescent entering adulthood. But it is a choice especially difficult for girls, who are still taught from birth to choose someone else—a husband, for example. Artemis is the personification of a woman's essential, core integrity of which she becomes conscious by choosing herself. And though our culture professes to value these qualities of self-sufficiency, integrity, and incorruptibility, they are often still judged as liabilities in women: the Artemisian woman is thought to be aloof and cold, hard and ruthless. Our culture fears and discredits Artemis when she makes her epiphany in a woman. And if you doubt this, you haven't read a newspaper or watched television lately.

Artemis unites seemingly incompatible values. She personifies that awful and awesome solitude where a woman is utterly alone and inaccessible, yet she attracts to herself companions who are like her. As hunter, her kills are quick and clean, because while death is natural, the unnecessary suffering of wounds caused by the hunter is not. And though her arrows never miss their aim when they pierce our consciousness with the demand for adult independence, she herself becomes the hunted one who flees the voyeuristic encroachment of those who seek to possess or destroy her. As constrained nature, she will strike ruthlessly and suddenly against any who violate her. But she is also the great maternal protector of all young, wild, and vulnerable creatures: animals and children.

I suspect that abortion was a more straightforward thing in the old times now gone from living memory, that time when women honored Artemis by living congruently with their instincts—including self-preservation. That time may have no documented history, but lives in us through mythic tradition, just as Artemis the Goddess is not a historical figure but a mythic, psychic pattern of behavior. In those mythic times women kept their own counsel, their own wisdom, about matters that did not pertain to men, such as moon and blood cycles, birthing, and the particularly female kind of sexual pleasure that men could not imagine.

Women had abortions in those times for most of the same reasons women have them now, because they could not or would not ensure the child what it needed for viability: they could not get enough food for one, or for one more; they were sick; if they got sick they could not work; they were poor; they were too young, or too old; they were afraid the child would be born deformed or under a curse, that it would not live long or well; the father was unknown, or unwilling, or untrustworthy, or too poor, or dead; they were afraid of not knowing what to do; and they were afraid of dying.

In those ancient times, law and religious sanctions and economics and the male need for proprietorship were no less forceful than they are now; in some external ways they were even more so. But women had not yet completely absorbed those man-made laws and theologies and medical dictums; they had not yet so totally *intro*jected, or accepted within themselves, the values of the male world that they were cut off from the original source of their own female physical wisdom, as many women are today. They had not yet lost contact with the deepest female knowings of when it is time for life, and when it is time for death.

All female animals know this. In nature, the reproductive cycle of most female animals changes when food supplies become scarce or environmental conditions become too harsh to support young life. Female birds and mammals do not ovulate then, in effect preventing untimely reproduction in spite of the males' blind urge to mate. Once, human females could do this too, by ingesting certain herbs and roots to induce miscarriage. They acted from the same natural instinct, that instinctive response that serves Artemis and is preserved by her.

Artemis was also known as the midwife, invoked in ancient times by women in labor because her own mother Leto bore her with no pain. As soon as Artemis entered the world, the Fates appointed her to midwife the birth of her twin brother Apollo. And so she is the goddess who is present at every birth and every death, midwifing the transitions, the death of the old and the birth of the new. In particular, she presides over the passage of young girls into womanhood—which is both a birth and a death—because she embodies and personifies the most elemental natural rhythms and transitions of the life cycle. Indeed, she is present whenever a woman of any age prepares to undergo yet another step in maturation. And in the way of the virgin, Artemis remains unmerged with and separate from those young girls and women who are her chosen companions; her sexuality is for pleasure and is in the service of neither reproduction nor relationship.

The Bible says that to everything there is a season: a time to be born, and a time to die. But the times of being born and dying are, for us humans, times of profound mystery. Abortion is a death that a woman experiences in her own living body, usually by her own will; often it happens privately, almost invisibly. The Latin root of the word "abortion" means, literally, "to disappear." In our culture the public debate and rhetoric and positions are open and loud and everywhere visible in our national life, but the *experience* of the woman who aborts her pregnancy too often disappears. Not only her pregnancy is aborted, but her experience of its termination is aborted and disappears as well. We have to keep in mind that the Latin root of the word "experience" means "to lead out of peril." Here again Artemis is to be invoked, for as with all other birthings, she presides over perilous transitions in a woman's life as she midwifes meaning in the psyche.

A few years ago, at a large public debate at Columbia University, Illinois Congressman Henry Hyde—a well-built, white-haired, white-skinned, well-groomed sixty-something gentleman—declared that he opposed *all* abortion except to save the mother's life. When asked why he would not make an exception even for a conception resulting from rape or incest, he replied that there should not be a secondary victim of the crime; the unborn child's "claim [to life] is equal [to the mother's]—a life for a life." I think it is precisely this inability—or refusal—to differentiate between mature life and nascent life, between conscious, responsible, independent life and unconscious, reflexive, dependent life, that constellates Artemis and draws her to the scene. It is Artemis in me who wants to ask Henry Hyde if he considers his life equal to that of a ten-week-old fetus.

Artemis and Men

One of the reasons Artemis is feared in our sex-obsessed culture is because it is forbidden to men to look upon the beautiful Artemis naked, to try to penetrate her mystery, to trespass in her private, interior realms. Artemis does not suffer voyeurs. When he trespasses into questions that belong in the domain of Artemis, the civilized Congressman Henry Hyde, for example, is potentially a modern Actaeon, the legendary hunter who gazed upon Artemis bathing nude. The goddess punished him for this trespass by turning him into a stag so that his own dogs tore him to pieces. She who midwifes life and also brings death will have her revenge if her domain is violated by intruders. She is as capable of killing in vengeance as she is of killing in mercy, and the arrows of Artemis, whose name means "She Who Slays," always find their mark.

There is a profound mystery in abortion, a mystery of female power, which is still something of a contradiction in terms. It is a mystery of death, which we fear and deny; a mystery of life, which does not yield its secret meanings easily; and a mystery of sacrifice, which we have so much trouble understanding because it has to do with love, about which we know so little.

That a woman may bring her re-creation of her own flesh and blood to death before its birth is, in the deepest sense, a sacrifice. It is one of the great mysteries. Perhaps the reason we become so inflamed about abortion in our time is not because it is so controversial, not because it is so political, and not because it is inherently moral or immoral. We become inflamed because it is a mystery that we do not understand, do not want to face. We are terrified. It is a mystery like Artemis, protector of the young and yet, "She Who Slays."

At the heart of this mystery is the power of women over life and death. Men may have a harder and more fearful time with this mystery because the primal power of life belongs to woman, and most certainly then she wields the power of death. That primal power of life is a biological impossibility for a man. He can never be a true matrix of that mystery. It is possible that at least part of what fuels patriarchy—the rule of the fathers—is a belligerent, resentful, compensatory response to the fathers' fearful and precarious position.

In a culture which has no significant female deity and is ruled by a male god, this life-and-death power has been appropriated to *him*. The giving of life through women still retains a sense of *mystery, but the taking of life by women* is a *sacrilege*. When this power is exercised in abortion, legally or not, it contradicts our most cherished and exalted image of the male-defined meaning of "mother."

Artemis and Mother

If we expect "Mother" to be the source of abundant nourishment, the model of infinite sacrifice for the child's well-being, and the fount of limitless love and devotion—all of which we *do* expect—then the mother who voluntarily aborts her child utterly destroys those expectations, destroys paradise. She is a monster, an abomination, an unnatural woman. This is simply not how we expect women to behave. However, our expectations of men betray an appalling double standard and hidden contempt: though we feel shock and grief and rage when *they* act like monsters, we secretly expect a dark side and are not really surprised when it appears.

A woman who aborts presents us with an image of the mother who has the godlike power to destroy each of us, who ejects us coldly from the womb as from the safe, life-giving haven we think nature intended it to be. Such a godlike woman becomes a person of ultimate consequence. It is a profoundly tragic irony that a woman's sacrifice of her fetus is counted of far greater import in our country than the fact that this same woman is likely to be raped, beaten, or murdered in less time than it takes for me to write this sentence. And *her* death will have little more than statistical significance in the national collective mind. It is equally chilling to consider how many are raped, beaten, and murdered *because* they have this fearsome godlike power.

For centuries, the rhetoric of abortion, and particularly religious rhetoric, has condemned women who abort for selfishness, unnatural selfishness, and sinful selfishness, making it clear that the real crime a woman commits is not the termination of her pregnancy, but the prerogative of valuing her own life, her own viability, over another's. Again, this flies in the face of everything we expect a mother to be.

We can see just how deep this cultural expectation is by the prevalence, for example, of Jewish mother jokes: the stereotypical Jewish mother is completely antithetical to Artemisian consciousness. When she prepares the family meal, the "Jewish mother" is expected to eat only a few ounces so that there will be more wonderful food for her children—and still she will worry that they will starve. This is the immeasurable devotion of her self-sacrifice. Jewish mother jokes are funny because they express as exaggerated truism how devoted mothers are to children. But the humor also provides insulation from the deeper and secret sense of fear that at any moment, that same mother may turn on her children and eat them instead.

The depth of our expectation of the mother as supremely self-sacrificing is embodied in the image of the Virgin Mary, a central image of "femininity" in our culture. In her, virginity is exalted because it makes *divine* motherhood possible: in her, motherhood is the essence of femaleness that makes biology into destiny. Every woman who aborts a pregnancy appears as a polar opposite of the Virgin in the collective view: she is not all-embracing life-giving mother; she is selfish, very selfish, totally selfish. She does not acquiesce, and this is the second worst crime women can commit. The *first* worst crime is to imagine that she actually, not rhetorically, has power over her body—that she has the power and *authority* to decide whether to bear or not to bear a child conceived in her womb—even a divine one.

Artemis and the American Child

And here is another compelling reason why abortion has become a painful collective complex for us. We have such trouble with Artemisian consciousness, and women who at times act from that consciousness, because our culture is held in thrall by the archetypal image of the Child. As long as the image of "child" is made the supreme value of one's inner life, there is little hope of resolving the abortion complex. For if the child is the primary divine figure, then to kill it is not only infanticide, but *deicide*; and if it demands so much narcissistic attention as one's *central* inner figure, then to abort it is to commit a kind of suicide.

On a less profound level, cultures of longer histories than ours accuse Americans of youth-worship and of indulging in the longest collective adolescence on the planet. While we elevate the child's longings for comfort, safety, and feeling good as our highest values, the rest of the world regards us as irresponsible, undisciplined, and self-absorbed. It is no accident that the so-called "abortion pill," RU486, was developed outside the United States.

Consider the astounding proliferation of "help books" on the theme of "the inner child" or "the child within." One such advertisement in a psychology catalog assures us that by reading this book, we will learn that if you feel anxious, depressed, or angry "*without reason*," then you have probably "identified with a childhood experience." (As if there were no reason to feel this way as an adult in the present world!) Further, the author will teach you to find your inner child, whereupon you will "learn to love, nurture and respect this little person."

But Artemisian consciousness resists this infantilizing of the adult psyche. *My* child has not read Shakespeare, has not been entranced by Michelangelo's sculpture, been moved by the language of Toni Morrison, or been delighted by a Mozart opera. My inner child remains a child, uneducated and illiterate, and while my attitude toward it is important, it is not the *only* imaginal figure that is important, and not the *most* important most of the time. And much of the time it is not very interesting, either.

Sacrifice

It is true that in the world of Artemis, that world of wild nature, there is no place where death may not enter. There is no law that says it is illegal, immoral, unnecessary, or unjust that young things die: that fawns may not freeze in the cold or that rabbits may not be eaten by wolves, or that lionesses may not kill some of their young if food is insufficient. This "natural law" is much older than man's theistic inventions and "civilized" constructs, and this is probably why Artemisian consciousness appears to us as cold, cruel, and psychopathic. Such deaths, we think, are avoidable, or with modern technology, at least postponable. But a woman who is moved by Artemis to abort her pregnancy presents us with a different understanding of death: death as sacrifice, death of a living part of oneself as a sacrificial offering.

Since we moderns have lost nearly all contact with Artemis, with that way of understanding life and death and the inviolability of women's bodies, we view abortion as an avoidable, unnatural, wasteful death rather than a sacrificial death in which there is meaning. Our culture says the woman who chooses to abort becomes like Artemis, remote, cruel, heartless, a woman far away from conventional morality and social norms. Or else she is young and immature, sexually wild, promiscuous, and irresponsible—by either of which we mean a woman who contradicts all the cultural expectations of what a "mother" should be.

Because this condemnatory collective judgment is very old, and reinforced through daily repetition in our newspapers and courts and clinics and churches, the woman who terminates her pregnancy may have a very rough time returning to the integrity of her interior self and appreciating *herself* as sacrifice to Artemis. A woman who has had an abortion by choice has made a sacrifice; she has also become a sacrifice. For a woman is not separate from her pregnancy, any more than Artemis is separate from her virginity. A pregnant woman is not merely a carrier, a walking womb, any more than a man is merely a life support system for a penis. When a woman aborts, something of her life, her living body, has been killed. She also has had to offer up on the altar of Artemis something of her old way of being, in whatever way that mattered: she has passed through sorrow and loss; she has given up one of her futures. No longer is she innocent, naive, all-nurturing. No matter what her age, she is no longer truly young and inexperienced; she may even sacrifice love and respect in a relationship or marriage. Sometimes she may sacrifice her own deep desire to bear the child because her mate is unable or unwilling to help provide the love and sustenance that is a child's birthright.[2]

Whatever it means to her, having an abortion changes a woman. In the best of circumstances she discovers her capacity to sacrifice, and sacrifice is one way we measure the capacity to love. Perhaps it is the consciousness of abortion as a meaningful sacrifice that takes it out of the realm of personal selfishness and puts it into the context of some deeper necessity, some deeper purpose she must serve. For where there is meaning, there is a divine presence.

There are a thousand reasons why women decide to abort a pregnancy; but in every instance, a sacrifice is being made, consciously or unconsciously. And it is only the individual woman who can say, if she knows, what that sacrifice is and what it means to her to offer it. Accusations of murder, selfishness, promiscuity, and irresponsibility are all ways of *avoiding* the meaning of the woman's experience, ways of refusing to regard her decision to abort as something more than self-indulgence, something less than criminal, something other than bad judgment. Such accusations are, at bottom, judgments that her sacrifice is unworthy and so is she; and I for one cannot understand how a woman can be condemned for *her* sacrifice, while we hold as a spiritual ideal of obedience the old patriarch Abraham with a knife to his thirteen-year-old son's throat.

When Artemis comes to a pregnant woman, she comes either as midwife or as "She Who Slays," she who requires sacrifice for the sake of the mother's integrity, physical well-being, or for the sake of any young for whom there may be fates worse than death. The concern of Artemis as midwife is not based on a morality requiring that life be preserved in all circumstances at all cost; it is not a morality that glorifies Life with a capital 'L', transcendent abstraction without regard to the quality of individual life. And it is not a morality that conceptually extracts individual life from the collective context and environment that must support it.

Artemisian morality knows, as every mother knows, that nothing is more cruel than the suffering of children. For a woman to bear a child she does not want is a violence perpetrated upon the child. The bond of love and desire which should provide the psychological environment in which the child may thrive is broken or contaminated even before birth, because the mother is not right with herself and cannot willingly provide psychological nourishment to the child. The child comes into the world already wounded. A woman who overrides her maternal instinct not to bear a child damages the child as much as she damages herself.

---

[2] For a full and rich discussion of Artemis, with particular attention to childbirth and abortion, see Paris, "Artemis," chapter 8.

The conscious decision of a woman to abort a pregnancy involves, to some degree, recognition of a collective good. And in this, too, Artemis is present in the woman's concern to protect and spare the young and vulnerable from unnecessary suffering. From the perspective of Artemis, it is a violation of nature, an affront to the goddess whose special province is the care of small and helpless creatures, to bring children into a family or community or country or world in which they will not be given all those things that make for true viability. In this sense, viability is a psychological concern, not a medical definition. From the Artemisian perspective, the debate is not about when the embryo becomes a fetus becomes a baby becomes viable, but rather the circumstances under which it is good for the child to be midwifed from the womb to the world.

Viability, until quite recently, meant something much larger than whether a fertilized egg with no developed neurological system was "viable," or whether a six-month-old fetus was physically viable outside the womb. Viability means, literally, the ability to live, and "life" is always something more for human beings than mere existence, more than the lung capacity to inhale and exhale, more than the brain's ability to produce a blip on a monitoring screen. A viable child is one who is welcomed into a larger body than its mother's, who comes well into a community able and willing to receive it and sustain it for years. In the absence of provision for the child's food, housing, medicine, future education, the promise of meaningful work, and/or the absence of love, desire, and responsible maturity in the procreators for their child, the maternal concern for the well-being of the child may consider abortion the best course. In such an instance it is, again, usually Artemis, the unseen, ancient, intact wisdom of nature, that moves a woman to act on behalf of her child by aborting it. She makes the decision in maternal consideration of the child's viability— the same consideration that moves Artemis to kill a wounded fawn rather than force it to live crippled and defenseless.

As with any deep, painful complex in an individual psyche, there is little likelihood that our national abortion complex will be thoroughly untangled, let alone finally resolved. As long as women get pregnant, some pregnancies will be aborted—by accident, by coercion, or by choice. Neither legislation, nor religion, nor politics, nor social disapprobation will prevent women from seeking abortion: none of these have ever done so historically, do not now, and will not in the future. Rather than look for solutions to the so-called *problem* of abortion, we might productively look for meanings in the experience of abortion. We become trespassers in the domain of the great goddess Artemis and her mysteries of primal life and death when *our* laws are forcibly imposed on her. Like Acteon the hunter, if we try arrogantly to penetrate her mystery, we risk having our collective national body torn to pieces. And indeed, the tearing is well under way.

So long as human beings attach meaning and dignity to individual life, there will be sacrifices made to preserve meaning and dignity. Our first responsibility is not to condemn, outlaw, and bemoan abortion, but to ensure that such sacrifices are not made in vain.

The story I close with here was given to me by Clarissa Pinkola Estés. It is a very old story that comes from the psyche's mythic ground, and therefore is a true, but not literal, story. The people of Mexico know of the goddess named Tsati, who always appears carrying a great bowl. Her bowl is both breast and grave: when turned one way, the bowl is a great breast pouring out life-sustaining milk; when turned another way, the bowl is a coffin. The goddess Tsati comes when you are dying; gently she sets you in her great bowl and begins to swirl you around. And as she swirls around and around, you become smaller and smaller, and younger and younger, and then she pours you from her bowl into a woman's womb so that you may again come forth into life.

BIBLIOGRAPHY

Bolen, Jean Shinoda. *Goddesses in Everywoman*. New York: Harper Collins, 1985.

Downing, Christine. *Goddess*. New York: Crossroad Publishing, 1984.

Grant, Michael, and John Hazel, *Who's Who in Classical Mythology*. London: Weidenfeld and Nicolson, 1973.

Hall, Nor. *The Moon and the Virgin*. New York: Harper and Row, 1980.

Kerenyi, Karl. *The Gods of the Greeks*. London: Thames and Hudson, 1951.

Krafft-Ebing, Richard von. *Psychopathia Sexualis*. Trans. Franklin S. Klaff. New York: Stein and Day, 1965.

Paris, Ginette. *Pagan Meditations*. Dallas: Spring, 1986.

Tripp, Edward. *The Meridian Handbook of Classical Mythology*. New York: Penguin Books, 1970.

10
Deconstructing the American Shadow: A Review of *Pulp Fiction*

JOHN BEEBE

Bullet holes appear in the wall behind Vincent and Jules, hit men who have come to discipline a flat full of collegiate drug dealers for holding back a stash that they owe to the drug lord Marsellus Wallace. For the viewer of *Pulp Fiction*, the pattern punched out by the bullets—five-fold and symmetrical in the longest-held image—is like Quentin Tarantino's signature, a promise that an intuitive, visionary energy will drive this aggressive movie to a spirit-affirming finale.

Discovering that they have survived an unexpected counterattack from a hidden cohort of the frightened students, the two hit men react quite differently. For the coolly slack Vincent (John Travolta), just back from hiding out in Europe, the close call is another occasion to express his dismay at the way things go in our unmannerly American society. The viewer is so inclined to agree with him that it comes as a shock later in the film to see his viewpoint utterly undercut.

The more reflective Jules, played by the eloquent African-American actor Samuel L. Jackson, takes the sparing of his life as a religious sign, a sort of writing on the wall that God wants to keep him alive so that he can bring life, and not death, to others. His is a totally original character for American movies. Usually, in our films, the character in touch with a private religious symbolism is suspect, at best a proto-fascist and more often some kind of serial killer, like Robert De Niro's Travis Bickle in *Taxi Driver,* or a cynical sadist, like John Lithgow's Liberty Bell Murderer in Brian De Palma's despairing *Blow Out.* But Jules takes his serendipitous glimpse of

This is an expanded and revised version of a review that first appeared in Volume 13, No. 3, 1994 of The San Francisco Jung Institute Library Journal, *which has kindly granted permission for it to be printed here.*

a transcending pattern as an opportunity for a reappraisal of his own relation to the culture of violence. That he is initially a mocking trickster who
cites Ezekiel, the prophet of divinely sanctioned vengeance, to justify his
own reprisals for hire but ends by seeking to shape himself into a New
Testament shepherd suggests an unsuspected possibility in the American
shadow. Beside Jules's moral energy, Vincent's fashionable cynicism
begins to seem lazy as the movie progresses.

This is the film for anyone to see who wants to understand better what
our violent, fear-ridden society may unconsciously be aiming at beyond its
own self-destruction, but, like the two hit men, viewers are often split on
how they experience the film. From one side of the ambivalent feeling it
sets off, *Pulp Fiction* is a sharply funny satire of the violence of our culture, offering itself, with its vulgar language and tense set-pieces, as a
supreme occasion for indulging our regret at the deterioration of the culture's values. From the other side, *Pulp Fiction* feels like a weirdly hopeful, even religious, film, an angel carrying the message that our collective
weariness with violence marks a shift in the narrative structures of
American power, the sign of a transformation in this country's historical
valorizing of heroic vengeance.

The most straightforwardly vengeful character is Bruce Willis's
Coolidge, a reasonably competent boxer approaching the end of his
career. He has accepted a bribe from Marsellus to throw a particular fight.
Instead, he knocks his opponent out dead. Tucked into the movie's parade
of quirky, intrusive humiliations to the body, this boxing fatality, the most
clean-cut of the physical violations on which the messy action of *Pulp
Fiction* turns, creates a melancholy pause. This interval of reality allows the
viewer to reflect on the way this movie, in which numerous men and
women suffer corporeal battery, suggests wholesale injury to the American
body politic. The man Coolidge kills is never clearly seen, but his name is
given as Wilson, and Marsellus's grieving for him is a rare, somber moment
in the flight of movie ideas. On the arena marquee, the announcement, as
the main event, of "Coolidge vs. Wilson" had seemed no more than the
director's playfulness in pointing to the political shift that occurred after
World War I, when Reagan's favorite president, Coolidge, came in. But the
lethal kayo of Wilson brings unexpected force to the notion that liberal idealism has been knocked out as a governing value on the American scene.

Pulp Fiction's vision is rooted in the post-traumatic wake of American
idealism scuttled to make a sweeter deal. The way director Tarantino
underlines this event in the political psyche, which is to circle the victori-
ous Coolidge with a full 360-degree turn of the camera, makes clear how
important it is to him that we take a good look at the quasi-conservative
attitude which congratulates itself for having overpowered our former sen-
timent of liberalism. As played by the can-do Willis, Coolidge is the pragmatic present-day American egoism; he has the mean, crafty look of a
sharp-eyed senator who, despite the snakiness of his integrity, can still

summon up an angry nostalgia for the conservative past. By enfolding this
hero's story into the circular structure of the film so that events that actually precede it chronologically are allowed both to follow and come before
it in the telling, Tarantino undercuts the heroic narrative and moves us into
a post-heroic perspective. From that perspective, the black Marsellus
(played with austere understatement by Ving Rhames) is strangely
respectable; like Brando's Vito Corleone, he still evokes loyalty to the nos-
talgic ideal of the good father. His stern godfatherliness, like his deep ora-
torical voice, is Roman, and his contracts, like Roman law, are reasoned
and clear: it is his clients' own fault if by violating them they occasion his
reprimand. His name recalls the Marcellus who opposed the imperial ambitions of Julius Caesar, dooming the Roman republic and thus the Western
tradition of representative government for a millennium and a half. It is not
surprising that almost everybody in the film, including Coolidge, eventually wants to honor Marsellus: saving his honor means rescuing what's left
of the patriarchal order from the queerer sorts of self-designated vigilantes
who would use American freedom abusively.

Marsellus's wife Mia is another story. A hard-pouting high-tech doll
with a lacquered pageboy hairdo like the one Miranda Richardson wore in
The Crying Game, her feeling is impossible to find, and she seems to be
all seduction and trouble. She has a way of coming on to Marsellus's men,
but for one of them to respond even minimally is to risk his life.

On Marsellus's orders, it's Vincent's turn to take Mia out for a good
time. He shows up stoned on heroin while she is revving up with cocaine.
Uma Thurman's Mia has a suspicious nose, and through her long date with
Travolta (an excursion into an absurd "period" club where doomed fifties
gender prototypes like Elvis and Marilyn are blithely passed off as fun and
sexy) she is frustrated by Vincent's laid-back, self-protective manner. They
dance—a wonderful chance for Travolta to pay homage to his own mythic
movements in *Saturday Night Fever* and *Grease* and in so deconstructing
his own image to convey the reinvention of self that from Poe to Monroe
has been America's spookiest talent—but they do not meet emotionally.
Finally, Mia gets Vincent to achieve a heart connection with her by sniff-
ing into his special stash. Terrified as she overdoses that she is dying and
that he will end up a "grease spot" when Marsellus finds out, Vincent
plunges a long needle filled with adrenaline through her sternum: like the
bride of Frankenstein she starts up and reveals the vulnerable feminine
creature that had been hiding behind the mask.

The characters in Quentin Tarantino's *Pulp Fiction* are cynics, but command (at least among an American audience) a rapt, entertained attention,
because we can see our present anxieties so baldly mirrored in them. That
so many of them are in dysfunctional, narcissistic couples suggests the frustration of our attempts to find anyone else who can truly see us. There is
a scene in which Vincent plots his strategy for ending the date with Mia
without going to bed with her. Reasoning with himself in front of a mirror,

he exactly echoes the private thoughts of most of us in an erotic situation we don't want to be compromised by—which is most erotic situations nowadays.

More upsetting, these characters' complicity in conspiracies of violence hooks deep into our tendency to insist on patriarchal values such as obedience, rhetoric, and property rights at the cost of terrible violations of others. Tarantino confronts us with very exact personifications of the attitudes that fuel the assaults that are launched in the name of loyalty to patriarchal forms, but he is also fair to the hunger within those attitudes for a safer, if not more ideal, expression of the father principle.

The first spoken words of the film are "It's too risky," and this seems to be a leitmotif of the entire movie. The final section, whose middle class surrealism is worthy of Buñuel, involves the mess made in a car by an accidental killing. The car winds up in the garage of one of Jules's friends, played by Tarantino himself as the middle class homeowner who at one point quietly wags his finger at the two hit men dripping with blood and bone, bits of brain stuck to their hair. One of Marcellus's experts, Winston Wolf (wonderfully played by Harvey Keitel), is summoned to clean up the mess so that the friend's wife won't find out what has gone down.

The cover-up, like most American cover-ups, works, but the message is clear: the fallout that accompanies a violent intervention, whether individual or national, is just too messy. As part of the clean-up operation, Jules and Vincent are hosed down and dressed down too. In shorts and short-sleeved shirts they suddenly look like chastened high school students, more immature, and absurd, than the college boys they terrified when the film was young, and echoing all the other pairs of characters in the film who are reduced to human size after an initial strutting inflation of their cool. This scene prepares us for the stunning finale, in which the narrative circle returns us to the frame—to the Genesis story of the film itself—and Jules gets his moment to play Angel of the Lord opposite the first of the film's posturing pairs. Pointing his gun like a flaming sword to usher Pumpkin and Honey Bunny out of the Eden of mayhem they promised to open up for us at the beginning of the film, Jules transcends black-exploitation shadow figure and enters the role of dark Cherub. A mercurial messenger who epitomizes *Pulp Fiction* itself, his mission is finally clear: it is to deny legitimacy to the Bonnie and Clyde pattern that Honey Bunny and Pumpkin are trying to perpetuate. As this archetype surrenders to Preacher Jules's insistent shaming of it, we can feel that, with all due respect to the likable Vincent, gratuitous violence will never be quite so cool again.

11

Pulp Fiction: From Shadowland to Heartland

LYDIA S. LENNIHAN

> . . . I saw some shit this mornin' made me think twice. . . . Now I'm thinkin',
> it could mean you're the evil man. And I'm the righteous man. And Mr. .45
> here, he's the shepherd protecting my righteous ass in the valley of darkness.
> Or it could be you're the righteous man and I'm the shepherd and it's the
> world that's evil and selfish. I'd like that. But that shit ain't the truth. The
> truth is you're the weak. And I'm the tyranny of evil men. But I'm tryin'. I'm
> tryin' real hard to be a shepherd.

—Jules, in Tarantino's *Pulp Fiction*

P*ulp Fiction*, a *film noir* written and directed by Quentin Tarantino, has
captured and held the imagination of the American culture. Known for its
extreme violence, *Pulp Fiction* offers a reference point in our journey to
know and deal with ourselves as Americans. This film illustrates through
its imagery and characters that our healing lies deep within the very wound
which sears us.

The film centers around the lives of several small-time criminals living
in the contemporary underworld of Los Angeles. Time is mythical and circular rather than linear as we return to the beginning of the tale at the end
of the film. The film is divided into three stories, each one a vignette with
its own beginning, middle, and end, yet they are all connected and interdependent. Several Jungian principles are suggested throughout the film.
The tales themselves are about each character's call to self-investigation,
usually brought on by an out-of-the-ordinary experience which results in
the integration of portions of the character's shadow or dark side. In addition, there is an alchemical motif woven throughout, in which gold plays
an important role both visually and symbolically, and redemption is found
in the separation and later rejoining of opposites.

The marginal and intriguing figures in *Pulp Fiction* represent what has been rejected by the consensus reality of American culture; they symbolize our collective shadow. We tend to look away, and certainly would not pay the price of admission to view acts of violence such as mob discipline, heroin overdoses, and heads being blown off. Yet these same figures populate our dreams and nightmares at times; the life-urge that drives us also powers the fictional characters of our cultural imagination. Images are the natural language of the psyche; whether created in our dreams or in films, they compel us to follow. In our times, film as image defines and creates our mythology. Whether expressed orally, in books, or in technicolor, stories present us with our greatest moments as a species as well as our darkest impulses.

The film opens with a casual conversation between Jules and his friend Vincent, who are partners working for a crime boss, Marsellus Wallace. They have been sent to retrieve a briefcase of money which has been stolen in a drug deal. There is little feeling in either one of the men as they nonchalantly murder almost everyone in the room, dispensing mob justice to naive college students who have dared to cheat them. A man who has been hiding in the bathroom of the apartment bursts out unexpectedly and unloads his gun directly at Vincent and Jules. Not one bullet finds its mark, and they survive this outrageous reprisal. Jules believes this to be an act of God, but Vincent is cynical and denies that anything besides a freak accident has occurred. By the end of the film, Jules has had a spiritual awakening, and decides to quit his life of crime and to wander the earth "like Cain in *Kung Fu*," waiting to see where God sends him (Tarantino 147). Vincent, on the other hand, doubts both divine intervention and Jules's sanity, and sees no need to scrutinize his life; he continues to work for Marsellus.

The ramifications of this tale as a myth for contemporary American society are fascinating, especially since we seem to be collectively obsessed with preventing criminals like Jules and Vincent from meting out mob justice, fixing fights, selling and using drugs, and breaking the law. But we also love antiheroes like the Godfather and Marsellus Wallace, characters who hold our nation's projections and shadow; we are drawn to them and compelled by their world. Something about them repulses yet seduces us as they draw us closer, down and out, into a world of smoke and mystery we know nothing about. As a society and a nation we need to address our shadow, portions of which these characters represent. What is it about the personalities in *Pulp Fiction* that attract and repel us so strongly? What can they tell us about our culture, the times we live in, and our own shadow?

The vignettes which make up the film revolve around the absorbing character of Marsellus Wallace. The mysteriously glowing golden case is being retrieved for him, and like the fisher king of the Grail legend, he is also wounded in the groin when he is sodomized by extremely evil men, darker even than himself. Like the Grail king, Marsellus represents a region of our collective mind, a shadowland where portions of the psyche of our culture have been rejected and marginalized, waiting for consciousness to address them and bring them to light. A modern-day King Arthur, Marsellus cannot completely hold onto his beautiful wife Mia, and unwisely has his lieutenants attending to her while he is out of town. His fate is to be rescued from his attackers by Butch, the prize fighter "palooka" who has betrayed him and stolen money from him. As Marsellus's savior, Butch is linked with him in terms of gold and money imagery, which symbolically brings the two together in the story. This theme of the union of opposites is at play throughout the film, particularly in the redemption of good through evil, which relates directly to the idea of our cultural shadow and our attraction to the intrigue of the cinematic underworld.

Jung's concept of individuation involves the relationship between the ego (the conscious part of the personality) and the Self (the core but also the circumference or totality of the psyche), between consciousness and the unconscious. Jung believed that for the whole self to develop, the ego had to attempt to integrate, as much as possible, aspects of the unconscious, both personal and collective, so that they become related parts of the personality. The ego assimilates the unconscious contents, and the more numerous these contents are, the closer the ego is able to move toward the Self (Jung, *Aion,* pars. 43–44). As a result, individuals can more authentically express themselves and broaden their experience of the outer world and the inner psyche, thus enriching life immeasurably. One of the most important methods of this integration includes assimilation of what Jung called the shadow, which represents parts of our psyches which have been split off because they are unacceptable and too painful to us. The attraction to the shadow will always exist because it is so enriching to our lives, when it is integrated, that is, when it can be used in adapted and constructive ways. Perhaps this is why these characters appeal to us so strongly; they symbolically represent instincts which we find unacceptable in ourselves.

This theme of expansion is hinted at in the structure of the film, which is made up of three stories. Edinger discusses the significance of the number three in *Ego and Archetype* as being a symbol for creativity, growth, and the stages of development in the individuation process (182). This process at times requires alienation and inflation, which are needed for the development of the individual (7). Alienation makes us realize that we are separate from our family and society, which is essential if we are to discover our own meaning and journey in life. Inflation and its partner, deflation, help us to explore and discover what our real powers and limitations are, within our self and in the world. Without hubris, many of the heroes of mythology, such as Odysseus, or Adam and Eve, would not have embarked on their journeys. In *Pulp Fiction,* Jules is alienated from the rest of society as an underworld criminal, and is inflated in the sense that he feels completely justified in taking people's lives as an act of retaliation for perceived wrongs. He behaves as if he were God in this regard, although he is just following orders from Marsellus. In terms of individuation then, he is ripe for expansion.

The character of Jules is being called to develop beyond the boundaries of his ego, to deepen and incorporate aspects of his shadow. When he is not hit by any of the bullets of his assailant, he experiences what he refers to as a miracle. He has encountered what he believes is God, the holy or the divine. This is what Jung defines as "numinous." While he is acting out his shadow by unconsciously and nonchalantly murdering people, he experiences something out of his normal realm of perception. When Vincent questions if this was truly a miracle, he replies, "It's not about *what* . . . . You don't judge shit like this based on merit. . . . What is significant is I felt God's touch. God got involved." And this perceived contact changes him profoundly (Tarantino 146).

Witnessing the numinous acts as a catalyst for confrontation between the ego and the shadow, we see that Jules's "self, in its efforts at self-realization, reaches out beyond the ego-personality on all sides" (Jung *Mysterium*, par. 778), confronting him with a man whose murderous instincts are equal to his own. This event begins the integration of portions of Jules's shadow, bringing them into the light where he can more consciously deal with them. Jung observes that even with a small amount of understanding, an experience of wholeness can be achieved (par. 777). This nascent experience for Jules is the beginning of a spiritual awakening, which he describes to Vincent when he says: "I had what alcoholics refer to as a 'moment of clarity'" (Tarantino 148). Emma Jung writes in *The Grail Legend* that the experience of the numinous is "usually accompanied by a profound emotion which the ego senses as an epiphany of the divine. For this reason it is practically impossible to differentiate between an experience of God and an experience of the Self" (99). Jules illustrates this when he tells Vincent that he felt God's touch.

When Jules is being robbed in the restaurant at the end of the film, his behavior shows that he is a changed man. Normally, he would think nothing of killing someone who was attempting to rob him. He was in fact doing just that when he witnessed the miracle earlier that day. This time he changes his behavior. A piece of Jules's psyche which murdered without remorse has been made conscious, and he can no longer kill without repercussions; he cannot, as he tells Vincent, "go back to sleep" (Tarantino 146). He now realizes that what the world is asking of him has profoundly changed; it now challenges him to try "real hard to be a shepherd" and his brother's keeper; to be a guide through the valley of darkness (157–58). Jules with his new awareness confronts and consciously synthesizes that part of him which is "the tyranny of evil men" (158). Instead of killing the thief, he gives him the contents of his wallet and lets him go, but without the briefcase, which still needs to be given to

Marsellus. Jules says he feels that he has bought this man's life. But Jules's process has only begun.

We can apply the metaphor of alchemy to Jules's psychic expansion. Jung discovered that alchemy was a valuable tool for describing the process of individuation. It gave him images with which he could symbolize the work of human development. Jung tells us that the rich symbolic content of alchemy is comparable to one's life's work (*Mysterium*, pars. 790, 792). This task starts with the raw material of the imperfect individual, and then through several processes, becomes the "Philosopher's Stone" or gold, that which is of highest value in ourselves. It becomes the incorruptible substance which symbolizes the Self (par. 356). What is essential in understanding Jules's experience alchemically is that the starting place of the work is dark and murky like the shadow, that portion of ourselves that is cast out as despicable (Edinger, *Anatomy* 12).

The characters in *Pulp Fiction* portray the shadow-criminal world of our culture; they symbolize our most murderous and violent urges which repulse us emotionally. The alchemical transformation of growth and development requires that we begin with raw material, in this case our cultural shadow. Yet there is also a morality and sense of justice in this marginalized part of society. For complicated and sometimes opposing reasons, we find ourselves drawn to some of the characters and their world. We are looking at Jules specifically because he has an experience of redemption, but there are many shadows populating his world, from the absolutely evil men who rape Marsellus to the quirky and appealing Vincent. We are reminded by Tarantino's film that not all things in the work of development get integrated successfully and safely, and that evil exists which cannot be integrated at all, such as the men in the pawn shop.

There are three stages in the alchemical work. The first of these is the *mortificatio* or *nigredo* stage, also known as the *massa confusa*, which enmeshes the soul and the body before separation between the two can take place (Jung, *Mysterium* par. 696). The work of development begins in this dark and confused state. The *mortificatio* period is associated with the color black, death, putrefaction, defeat, and disintegration (Edinger, *Anatomy* 148). In terms of Jules's individuation, it is important to know that unlike the other alchemical stages with their chemical processes, *mortificatio* literally means death and killing (147). Jules not only kills people who cross him or his boss, he is also surrounded by death, and by the imagery of the *nigredo* phase of individuation. At one point, Vincent accidentally shoots the head off one of the college students in the back seat of the car he and Jules are travelling in, literally decapitating him. This image is an important detail in light of what Edinger points out, that "the skull . . . is an emblem for the operation of mortificatio" (168). Jung also discusses the idea of the skull in relation to alchemical processes. In alchemy, the raven's head represents the darkness of the human soul, but it also represents the beginning of the work of individuation, and the dark incubation period that is required for the process (*Mysterium*, pars. 727, 729). The Osiris-king is associated with the raven's head, and it is the severed head of the king that is boiled and turns to gold in Rosencreutz's *Chymical Wedding*. The beheading is symbolic for the necessary separation of logos from eros, of mind from heart, thinking from feeling, which is essential before the different sides of the personality can be brought into play, and the raw material can be transformed into gold or wholeness (pars. 727–30).

It is important to remember that the process of development, especially when dealing with the shadow, can be treacherous. Not everyone, even those who are trying hard, will succeed traversing the blind sides and doubts along the way. The character of Vincent illustrates this clearly, as his heroin addiction and inattention get him into serious trouble. As Jules responds to the confrontation by his shadow, Vincent is oblivious, recurrently going into various bathrooms throughout the film. But when he could perhaps have had some brief encounter with his own dark side, he blithely emerges, pulp fiction paperback in hand, only to find chaos breaking out all around him, and finally his own death confronting him.

Vincent's character does not respond to the call to broaden and deepen himself and his role in the world as Jules's does. He and Jules argue about what they have both witnessed and survived. Jules has had a powerful experience and he knows it. Vincent is dubious. The viewer is being offered two possible outcomes of this encounter. One is the "miracle," which can shake up the conscious attitudes of the ego and let in the dark and as a result, more wholeness. There is always the potential for great beauty or huge disaster when our sense of who we are is questioned or disturbed. Vincent's visits to the bathroom evoke the symbolism of the unconscious plumbing into the depths of the psyche, and always precede disaster. The first time he descends, he comes out and Marsellus's wife, who is his charge for the evening, has overdosed on heroin and is dying. Another time he ventures to the restroom, and when he returns, Jules is in the midst of being robbed. The man who surprises Jules and Vincent in the apartment and nearly kills them both is hiding in the bathroom. Vincent is finally undone, though, when he emerges from the bathroom obliviously one last time, and Butch kills him.

Although there is something about him that we really like, Vincent is spiritually bereft and cynical. He continues on his way, fumbling through his life, unaware of any changes he may need to make, and like Parsifal in the legend of the Grail, he forgets to ask himself "the vital question" because he is not aware of his own participation in the action (Jung, *Mysterium*, par. 753). Jules tells Vincent in their debate about their experience, "If you find my answers frightening, Vincent, you should cease askin' scary questions" (Tarantino 148). Vincent's fear is about his own life and the unknown. He does not like Jules sitting quietly and reflecting; it disturbs him. He advises Jules, "Lighten up a little. You been sittin' there all quiet" (145). Jung observed that the individual must recognize his or her own involvement in the process, or the potential for change remains in the imagination; the psyche stays the same (*Mysterium*, par. 753). When one consciously realizes one's involvement, as Jules does, the unconscious elements such as the shadow can be integrated and assimilated. The ego is expanded and deepened, and the individual can then make choices which have meaning for that person's life. Jung called this integration *unio mentalis*, or insight. He believed this insight was the beginning of individuation, which is accompanied by symbols of totality and the Self (par. 753).

Pulp Fiction can be seen on one level as being simply a film about good and evil. It is also about the redemption of good out of evil, about transformation, about the individual being called to action and being held accountable for becoming conscious of participating in life and its outcomes. The film acknowledges that there is a dynamic cycle of opposites at work in the world, and that nothing can exist without its shadow. Campbell observes that the "legends of the redeemer describe the period of desolation as caused by a moral fault on the part of man . . ." (352). Perhaps this moral fault is that, like Vincent, we are unable to confront our shadow, which has created such cultural desolation. The contemporary setting of the film illustrates very well the "wasteland" we live in today. Campbell makes a crucial point about the dark times we are experiencing, in terms of humankind's history and mythology. He sees that "the golden age, the reign of the world emperor, alternates, in the pulse of every moment of life, with the waste land, the reign of the tyrant. The god who is creator becomes the destroyer in the end" (352).

We see this same cycle occurring in the individual. Jung realized that for evolution to occur, there must be tension to induce movement, and that the shadow provided this energy. He observed that the contrast between opposites was essential for psychic energy to become available to the individual (*Mysterium*, par. 707). Jung knew that the ego had to come to terms with its shadow. As a culture, we need to do the same.

Tarantino illustrates this concept in the interplay of opposites throughout the film. The characters of Butch and Marsellus and their relationship is a good example of the tension, separation, and subsequent redemption of opposites. Butch has been paid a large sum of money by Marsellus to take a dive in a fight. Butch ends up killing his opponent with a fatal punch and wins the fight. He plans to run off with Marsellus's pay-off and the money he has won in many lucrative bets from the fixed fight. But Butch discovers that his great-grandfather's gold watch has been inadvertently left in his apartment. He decides to risk his life returning to retrieve the magical gold watch. Of course, Vincent and Marsellus are waiting for him to return, so that they can kill Butch for double-crossing them. When Butch and Marsellus have their run-in, they end up trapped together in a very dark situation where Marsellus gets raped. Butch frees himself, and there is a pivotal moment where he almost leaves the raging, wounded, and helpless king-pin to his fate, but returns with a Samurai sword to kill the attackers, thus saving Marsellus.

This cycle of one side and then the other being on top is what the conjunction of opposites is about. First the separation has to occur of upper- and underworld, consciousness and the unconscious, thinking and feeling. Only after this separation has happened can development take place. Jules, for example, has to see his own tyranny before he can behave differently. Butch and Marsellus have to be dragged into the underworld and violated in order for their relation to be anything other than simplistic and oppositional. Then a dignity occurs for both the characters; it is a dignity, says Jung, "which makes it morally possible for a man to stand by his soul, and be convinced that it is worth his while to persevere with it. Only then will he realize that the conflict is in him, that the discord and tribulation are his riches, which should not be squandered by attacking others" (par. 511).

These two who are sworn enemies have now gone through a profound experience together. Once Marsellus was the king and held the power, but in the end Butch holds his life in the balance in the underworld. Butch does not have to save Marsellus; in fact, it is against his nature. Like Jules, he does the opposite of what he would normally do. He had been trying desperately to kill Marsellus before Marsellus killed him, right before they got kidnapped. Yet we see that this is what the conjunction of opposites produces; "if a union is to take place between opposites like spirit and matter, conscious and unconscious . . . it will happen in a third thing, which represents not a compromise but something new" (par. 765). Now their roles are reversed; Butch and Marsellus are shadow and light, two aspects of the one, shifting roles and changing. A third thing is now produced; a kind of intimacy arises out of the behavior that has been up to this point alien. Through Butch's rescue of Marsellus, a different relationship is created between them. It is neither sworn enemy nor friend, but something else which their intimate union has produced. The situation then is no longer black and white, but many shades of gray, with peculiar nuances which demand our attention and response, not blind reactions from thoughtless habit and one-sidedness. Butch then takes leave of Marsellus and rides off on his attacker's motorcycle named "Grace" to Knoxville, Tennessee, where our nation's gold is stored under the earth.

What is happening to Jules and Butch is also happening to us as we view the film. Slowly the simplistic, primitive, and one-sided contents of their normal way of thinking differentiate as they become complex creatures, both good and evil, darkness and golden, a union of sublime complexities which we all relate to on a deep level. We can feel for Butch and Jules. Perhaps, like Jules, we are all "tryin' real hard to be a shepherd"; perhaps we too are on our way to recognizing the "tyranny of evil men" in ourselves (Tarantino 157–58). After all, maybe we can be redeemed as well. The characters in this film tell us, as Jung has, that this redemption cannot be achieved without acknowledging our collective and individual shadow.

Pulp Fiction serves as a reminder of where we are as a society. We have collectively come to a place of extreme separation between forces of hatred and forces of humaneness. Productivity wars against creativity. In our politics and in media reportage, the tension between the two opposite poles of a question becomes mired in rigid, simplistic, black-and-white thinking, so that creativity fails us, both as a nation and individually. We become convinced that our beliefs, and only our beliefs are right, even though they are questionable. A counterbalancing usually occurs, one which is done against our will and our conscious values, until balance is restored, and we can hold opposite views simultaneously. The more rigid one mind-set gets, the more loudly, and sometimes violently, will the opposite opinion be expressed. Jung reminds us, "Wisdom never forgets that all things have two sides, and it would also know how to avoid such calamities if ever it had any power. But power is never found in the seat of wisdom; it is always the focus of mass interests and is therefore inevitably associated with the illimitable folly of the mass man" (*Mysterium*, par. 470).

As Romanyshyn observes, "film portrays the mythology of an age. It is a shared myth, a cultural daydream" (19). *Pulp Fiction* serves as a mythical reminder to us of what our potential is, both positively and catastrophically, both individually and as a culture. To avoid Vincent's fate, we need to participate in our own process and awakening.The underworld characters which haunt our dreams and populate the pulp fictions of the world need to be seen; we need to know what they have come to tell us about ourselves. Without their essential darkness, we will become lost in the one-sidedness of the daylight world. Without consciousness, without knowledge of our own participation, both on the micro and macro levels, we will be deluged by our shadow and the unconscious. Without awareness of the whole cycle, we see only one part, and thus never attain our full potential as human beings and as a culture.

BIBLIOGRAPHY

Campbell, Joseph. *The Hero with a Thousand Faces*. Bollingen Series XVII. Princeton: Princeton University Press, 1972.

Edinger, Edward F. *Anatomy of the Psyche: Alchemical Symbolism in Psychotherapy*. La Salle: Open Court, 1985.

———. *Ego and Archetype: Individuation and the Religious Function of the Psyche*. Boston: Shambhala, 1992.

Jung, C.G. *The Collected Works of C.G. Jung*. Eds. H. Read, M. Fordham, G. Adler, W. McGuire. Trans. R.F.C. Hull. 2nd ed. Bollingen Series XX.

———. *Two Essays on Analytical Psychology*. Vol. 7. Princeton: Princeton University Press, 1966.

————. *Aion: Researches into the Phenomenology of the Self.* Vol. II. Princeton: Princeton University Press, 1969.

————. *Mysterium Coniunctionis: An Inquiry into the Separation and Synthesis of Psychic Opposites in Alchemy.* Vol. 14. Princeton: Princeton University Press, 1970.

Jung, Emma and Marie-Louise von Franz. *The Grail Legend.* Trans. Andrea Dykes. Boston: Sigo Press, 1970.

Romanyshyn, Robert. *Technology as Symptom and Dream.* New York: Routledge, 1989.

Tarantino, Quentin. *Pulp Fiction: A Quentin Tarantino Screenplay.* New York: Hyperion, 1994.

12

Vampires, Eroticism, and the Lure of the Unconscious

NANCY DOUGHERTY

> Mystery and manifestations
> arise from the same source.
> This source is called darkness.
> Darkness within darkness.
> The gateway to all understanding.
>
> —The Tao Te Ching (Lao-Tse 1)

As the twentieth century comes to a close and as a new millennium begins, we are witnessing a reappearance of the popularity of the vampire. His immortal undead presence is again evident in pop literature, prime-time television, and movies. His shadowy presence is also evident in our children's interest in the undead motif. Vampiric motifs appear in the music, comics, and the clothing preferences of our contemporary "children of the night" (consider the popularity of the gothic look). Even closer to the bone and embodied in their flesh is the resurgence in popularity of tattooing, piercing, and branding.

A parallel development in consciousness, evident even in the daily rounds of talk shows, is a heightened awareness of how we act out the victim and perpetrator roles in interpersonal relationships. Exploring how we victimize others, and how we participate in our own victimization, requires looking into the darkness. The psyche of the culture, like the psyche of the individual, needs to do its collective shadow work, that is, to face and to some degree integrate its dark side, in order to grow.

While many contemporary works of fiction expand on the legendry of vampires, the vampire is an ancient archetypal theme. The trail of the cursed undead goes beyond Transylvania back to ancient Egypt. In literature and film, this restless, subterranean theme shows us how it lives in the psyche by taking surprising sensual and violent turns. What is the meaning of these dark powers that arise from the unconscious? These are forces that are capable of seducing us into desiring death over life, war over peace, addiction over creativity, and in a completely concretized kind of valuing, consumerism over spirituality. Our deadening exploitive materialism has the power to trick us into seeing everyone and everything "other" as a concrete object to be manipulated. Vampire motifs challenge us to come to terms with these energies.

In art as well as in the psyche, the potential for renewal becomes possible when we turn within, with an inquisitive and respectful attitude, to meet the shadowy figures who reside there. Even in the bloody realms of imagery in the horror genre, the light in the darkness can unfold into the mysteries of healing and transformation. In considering the image of the vampire, I invite us to consider the powerful shadow side of our heroic national ideal. While the vampire casts no shadow, every hero casts one directly. Every nation does also. Culturally, the vampire's presence may be beckoning our society to kill off the adolescent conception of ourselves as innocent heroes and heroines who desire only the best for the world. The image of the vampire embodies potential life energy pressing for the destruction of outworn stages of development and adaptation (Estés 231).

Symbolically, we can imagine vampires as unconscious energy that sucks us dry of the will essential to desire life. Vampires portray predation; they are images of dark and needy beings, preying on the weak. Predatory energy depicted in these symbols expresses archetypal themes. At the same time, predatory impulses are an integral part of our human biological heritage. All humans are biologically "hard-wired" for instinctual responses that correspond to the behavior of predators or prey. These biological drives arise from the brainstem, also called "the reptilian brain." It is from this structure in the human brain that impulses for "fight or flight" arise. Early experiences and predispositions lead us to preferring one option over the other. However, we all have the biological resources either to fight or flee (Meloy 66).

The image of the vampire and its victim as it appears in the psyche of American culture leads us to flesh and blood considerations. The psyche and body are of one piece, and while symbolic vampire motifs arise from the psyche, the human conundrum of sex and violence arises from the body and the somatic unconscious.

Before we descend too deeply into this material, let's acknowledge that there is a desire in existence itself to bring about wholeness, balance, and growth. Jung refers to this whole-making urge in the cosmos as the "Self," and describes it as the central ordering principle in the psyche. This idea appears in all of the world's religious traditions, is evidenced in the harmony and balance of the cycles of nature, and most recently appears as well, in contemporary conceptualizations of systems and chaos theory. In vampire motifs the portrayal of redemption leads us to consider the mysterious and paradoxical nature of the cosmos's movement towards wholeness and balance.

Imagine for a moment the vampire representing the unconscious consequences of our "over-heroic" uses of power as a nation. The unconscious use of predatory power exacts a high price. When power is used in an unrelated or intrusive manner, it either plunders what is weak in the environment, or if it is projected onto the world, it is attributed to those "dangerous and violent others." Acting out against those "others" is then rationalized.

The raw powers of the instincts clamor for integration. When one is unconscious about human predatory instincts, it is not possible to have a moderating, conscious influence on them. In his *Vision Seminars*, Jung advises that if instinct goes unheeded, it grows in the dark (423). This unconscious predatory energy can fuel territorial furor, driving the horrors that individual and global conflict entail in our time.

The problem is not with instinct itself, but rather with the lack of a conscious attitude towards predatory instinct. When basically predatory feelings and thoughts, driven by the urge to power, are left in the unconscious they gravitate towards negative and unadapted uses, overwhelming our conscious lives. Unconscious of this powerful drive, we set ourselves up to be overrun by it. On the other hand, predatory aggression can be consciously mediated and directed towards constructive goals. Creativity, assertiveness, as well as the power to assert a rightful sense of territoriality are all examples of conscious use of power. Unconscious predatory energy exists as raw power in the collective, as well as in the individual psyche. Until power is integrated, and put to conscious use, it will be fueled by motives that we do not recognize and have no control over. And when we are in a state of unconsciousness, we will not know this, but only feel ourselves in the grip of something strong and unfathomable.

Feelings of fear and the experience of horror are appropriate companions when considering the management and use of both personal and global powers. Human use of power split off from the experience of fear easily becomes sadistic. Similarly feelings of fear split off from a sense of empowerment can become masochistic. Using power in an integrated and related way is a delicate and important human task for an individual, as well as a formidable challenge for our country at this time in the world. In order to create balance, what has been relegated to darkness needs to be reflected upon, and reconsidered. While telling a story about predator and prey, vampire tales unearth the "return of the repressed" that allows us to peer into the mystery of growth and participate in universal cycles of regeneration.

There are many contemporary examples of the vampire as a symbol of predatory instincts. It is of note that there is the frequent thematic connection of eroticism and violence in vampire stories. In the 1979 film version of *Nosferatu*, starring Klaus Kinski, the Count heatedly speaks to the young English lawyer Harkner about going hunting together in the woods.

Dracula says, "Do you enjoy the chase, Harkner? It's the greatest living sport! Ah, to have the power of life and death over a living being!"

Horror movies about vampires offer us the opportunity to feel a dark release and to experience a sense of mastery over primitive fears. It is always a relief to laugh over something that is truly horrible. However, in our inner lives and in the world, the dark energy of the vampire is no laughing matter. Unless we are numbed or misled, its power to suck the life's blood from what is good and true really should strike a chord of horror.

Vampire motifs often illustrate an abuse of power: the strong over the weak, the jaded over the innocent, the adult over the child. Because of the United States' wealth and dominance in global politics, the possibility of the abuse of power is an issue of which we as a nation must constantly be aware. The cowardly abuse of power is accurately represented in the 1922 classic vampire silent film called, *Nosferatu*. Most frequently vampires are associated with wolves or bats, yet in the movie *Nosferatu*, Dracula's appearance is announced by hyenas. The hyena is a flesh-eater whose bristly mane gives it a hog-like appearance. It is considered cowardly because it only feeds off carrion, dead meat. With a real shudder, the image of the hyena brings to my mind my enjoyment of my moderately priced new Nikes. Shortly thereafter, I noticed in the newspaper photographs of children in sweat shops in Thailand who manufactured them.

Vampire lore can be camp and ridiculous as well. I have watched lots of bad, but funny, vampire movies researching this theme. There are highly amusing moments in these films. For example, in a 1972 black exploitation film called *Blacula*, our hero at the disco says, "Make mine a bloody Mary!" In a broad sense, the vampire symbolizes the heavy, seductive lure of the unconscious itself, that force which works to keep consciousness captive in unconsciousness. We might call it the slow, sensual suck of inertia that lures us into living an unconscious life because it requires less effort and risk. In our American arrogance, too easily and passively identified with being the hero, "the good guy," we create a vacuum that quickly fills with our own dark motivations.

My interest in vampires deepened while reading Anne Rice's novel *The Witching Hour*. In that novel, the tale is told that since the sixteenth century, generations of women in the wealthy Mayfair family are possessed by an inner vampiric spirit named Lasher. In Jungian thought, the dark energies of the psyche can have a purpose, an awakening effect. This dark possession could symbolize a challenge from the unconscious to establish a solid, mature identity out of a drowsy, unexamined existence. Imagine Lasher as a dark, powerful force that needs to be confronted along the path of development. Especially troubling to many readers are the erotic notes in the text. How and why is submission to this dark figure so often experienced as erotic? How do these women become prey to unconscious forces? And, most importantly, can this cycle be transformed? And if so, what might the transformation of the predator/prey opposition look like?

In the novel *The Witching Hour*, generations of first-born daughters in the Mayfair family are seduced, then possessed by Lasher. Over centuries, living vicariously through these host carriers, the entity Lasher is strengthened, becoming more powerful, knowledgeable, and sinister. His power collects over time, and grows in the dark. In return, he rewards the large extended Mayfair family with fabulous monetary gain. He lures their first-born daughters into consenting to a withdrawal from participation in life, into passivity, into reverie, and finally into insanity. The loss of consciousness is the price these women pay for the masturbatory eroticism offered to them by this demon lover. His dark incarnation recurs over generations, enabled by his victims' passive submission. In many folkloric traditions, a vampire cannot enter a place unless he has been invited. Possession cannot occur without consent of a victim, even if the consent is given in the form of passive submission. Lasher feeds off his victims' vitality. This demonic possession extends into the current generation of Mayfairs. However, some of the current generation of female relatives have the courage and cunning to forgo his gifts and challenge his sensual allure.

The battle between the dark regressive forces of the unconscious and the courage and cunning needed for development occurs in each of us as individuals, as well as in our culture. Allowing predatory instincts to remain unexamined in the unconscious, impulses that have been frustrated and ill-educated, is like leaving a psychopath free to roam in your neighborhood.

Unconscious addictions vampirize an individual as well as the collective soul. Addictions dull our perceptions, and always serve to keep feelings and thoughts unconscious. Addictions sedate our senses and our psyches out of healthy instinctual responses (Leonard 77). Self-destructive behaviors drain instinctual vitality as directly as if they were sucking our blood. We anesthetize ourselves to pain with addictions. This fleeting anesthesia enables us to remain passive and compliant in situations that require ethical mobilization. As individuals and in families, we have an ever-longer list of addictions, and dealing with them has become a major societal focus. On the level of the culture, rampant addictions include our materialism and consumerism, our ignorance and arrogance about cultures less industrialized than ours, and our one-sided appetite for science.

But how and why is self-destructiveness erotic? In contemporary American culture, witness the heroin addict's notorious love affair with the needle, the battered partner's desperate and erotic need for the abusive spouse, the bulimic's excited preoccupation with the need to binge and purge, the self-mutilator's tragic need to pierce flesh to find some relief from inner demons. All of these addictions partake of the same undifferentiated mixture of eroticism and violence; they emerge from the same primitive layer of the psyche. The long-term result of addictions is an anesthetized consciousness, concretely grasping its fix. All the while it is separated from the living wellsprings of the deepest layers of the psyche, separated from authentic creativity, spontaneity, and instinctual sexuality.

Cultural gender role stereotypes can be seen in operation by noting that the most prevalent combination is of a male vampire with a female victim. In our culture, it is more common for the male to be identified with the aggressor and for the female to behave more passively. The hierarchy of power abuse can also be noticed by the fact that male vampires most often feed off females; however, in a new twist, in the 1992 Francis Ford Coppola movie, *Bram Stoker's Dracula*, the female vampires feed off children. And while the original Count Dracula was a male, there also exists a female folk heroine from Transylvania, recently fictionalized in a novel by Andrei Codrescu entitled *The Blood Countess*. In a particularly feminine abuse of power, Lady Elizabeth Bathory, another historic as well as literary figure, is said to have killed 650 virginal girls in her time in order to bathe in their blood to preserve her fading youth and beauty.

When the dark energy that works against life has the upper hand, the energies that can generate constructive creativity and ethical action are enmeshed in the culture's unconscious. A major weapon of the dark force is the erotic release that it provides to many at the moment of surrender. The dark force seduces us into trading life for death, trading our feelings of desire for the supposed bliss of unconsciousness. Individually and culturally, we trade our life's blood for the fleeting moment of peace as we turn our collective heads in arrogance at what we perceive as "other."

Although werewolves and vampires are present in ancient and classical literature, the specific character of Dracula was inspired by a real person, the mad and sadistic sixteenth century Transylvanian count, named Vlad the Impaler. Vlad was a feudal baron who was famous for his custom of punishing local debtors and enemies by impaling them on stakes and leaving their corpses exhibited to serve as a lesson to local peasants (Mascetti 121). He is said to have cut, roasted, and eaten pieces of flesh from their still living bodies.

Vlad engendered such irrational unconscious fear in his serfs that, long after his death, they believed that he would return from his grave to plague and torment them. Their terror was so great that even Vlad's death brought them no sense of release from his tyrannical control. This folkloric story introduces several motifs that recur in the vampire motif: dismemberment, the consuming of flesh, the return from the grave, and the mechanisms of fear and of trance as means of control.

Vampiric "penetration" is oral and most accurately reflects an infantile stage of development and relationship to conflict. In the most primitive unconscious, the opposites are experienced as intermingled. Love and hate, pleasure and pain are still energetically enmeshed. What is desired is merger, fusion, not union. What is desired is incorporation, not insemination. What is desired by vampires is suck, not sex. Sucking up directly the vitality of the other through ingesting their blood is oral erotic satisfaction, not genital sexuality. Since blood is already in usable form for the body, vampiric parasitic leeching even bypasses the digestive system: what occurs is direct transfusion. This is truly a dark symbiosis. This dark enactment is concretely enacted in the film version of *Dracula*, starring Frank Langella. In this movie, the vampire pierces his own breast to feed the newly vampirized Nina with his own blood.

These gory and compelling motifs arise from an ancient layer of the psyche. Developmentally, an infant's individual consciousness and identity exist only as a delicate flickering candlelight, while the unconscious looms in all its primitive intensity. Depth psychologist Erich Neumann designates the imagery of the vampire to "a pre-egoic state where chimerical beasts and fantastic creatures lurk in a more infantile state" (12). In the first few years of a child's life, pre-egoic consciousness, that is, the state of mind before consciousness is differentiated from unconsciousness, has yet to fully separate inside and outside, its own self from people or objects outside of it

Cultural shadow energy can be hard to perceive, especially when we are engaged projecting it onto others. We humans frequently define the unconscious fusion of sex and violence as other, "not-I", and then treat it with loathing, disgust, fear, or contempt and yet fascination when we meet it in the world. For a fragmentary or weak consciousness, the fear of being engulfed and overwhelmed by the "other" is experienced as a constant danger. The fear of fusion is a fear of annihilation (Carroll 43). The dark side of this early oral layer of consciousness can be juicily illustrated with several literary examples. The drowsy and vulnerable state of emerging individual consciousness, as well as the fantastic and erotic threat of being overwhelmed and engulfed by the other, is caught in the following vignette by Bram Stoker, author of the original 1897 novel, *Dracula*. In an earlier story entitled, "The Guest," the first-person narrator tells us how he was awakened by a werewolf:

> This period of semi-lethargy seemed to remain a long time, and as it faded away I must have slept or swooned. Then came a sort of loathing, like the first stage of sea-sickness and a wild desire to be free of something. I know not what. A vast stillness enveloped me, as though the world were asleep or dead—only broken now by the low panting as of some animal close to me. I felt a warm rasping at my throat, then came a consciousness of the awful truth. Some great animal was lying on me and was now licking my throat. (19)

Perceived with a psychological eye, we could view this scene as a call to consciousness, to awaken to the instinctual psyche, to the animal consciousness within us all. In the following passage from an H. G. Wells story, "Sea Raiders," we can see the dynamic interplay between self and other, sex and violence, aggressive attack and eroticized passive submitting to the aggressor. Listen to the narrator's shocked response at the discovery of some unsavory, glistening, tentacled creature eating his human companions. He says, "I was horrified, of course, but also intensely excited and indignant at such a revolting creature preying upon human flesh" (116).

Another example of the fusion of opposites in primitive consciousness surfaces in Jack Finney's novel *Invasion of the Body Snatchers*. The following is dialogue uttered by the narrator, Miles, when he first encounters the alien pods. "At the feel of them on my skin, I lost my mind completely, and then was trampling them, smashing and crushing them under my plunging feet and legs, not even knowing that I was uttering a sort of hoarse meaningless cry—Uhhh! Uhhh! Uhhh!—of fright and animal disgust and passion" (136). As we can tell from these passages, descent into this dark place in the psyche generates lived experiences of pleasure, humor, passion, and relief as well.

Whether conscious or unconscious, humans feel an instinctual impulse to annihilate whatever threatens. Among nations, we have seen that our adolescent cultural identity gives rise to preoccupation with defense, demonizing of other cultures, paranoia regarding internal and external enemies, as well as phases of highly militaristic, intrusive, and oppressive concern about controlling citizens through the mechanisms of fear. The excessive brutality of authority figures generates the psychological phenomenon of trance induction. The ability to induce a hypnotic trance in a victim is a frequent weapon of the vampire, as it is with any predator. The vampire's power to paralyze its victim with a glance is congruent in the animal world with the predator's ability to immobilize its prey with a stare. As a deer caught in a car's headlights, a chicken hypnotized to hold still for its own execution, or lambs that proceed silently into slaughter, humans become seduced into the loss of consciousness and entranced into willing self-sacrifice.

The predator's power to paralyze prey is the same power used by sociopathic leaders to suspend the will of his or her flock, and induce the devotees to sacrifice themselves for the leader's personal vision. In the not-too-recent past, the Branch Davidians encountered David Koresh's apocalypse. But we have seen a long list of others: Jim Jones, Charles Manson, and to serious but not yet fatal proportions in Montana, Elizabeth Clare Prophet. Most recently in the Heaven's Gate Cult, suicidal devotees of Do and Ti terminated their lives, hoping to be beamed up on the tail of the Hale Bopp comet.

Splitting, along with a fierce competition that seeks to destroy, occurs between genders, between generations, as well as between countries. Fear and loathing of difference is generated by an unstable consciousness, one that has to hold on tight to its own "good" side, and attack the other side. Constant one-upmanship and competition are signposts of an immature sense of personal and cultural identity. Cultural shadow energy can be hard to perceive, especially when we are engaged in projecting it onto others.

With conscious effort, it is possible to become aware of that which we perceive as "other," merely as "different." In this way, for example, people of other races or ethnicities can be appreciated for the differences that enrich our world, rather than as threats to our existence. However, when identity is unstable, fear and hatred of whatever is considered "other" is easily evoked. Weak consciousness carries with it the moment-to-moment fear of being overwhelmed and annihilated. In this weakened state, humans quickly and unconsciously resort to dominating or submissive behaviors. The possibility of equality and mutuality require further development.

Another way to conceptualize vampiric imagery and its presence on the American pop culture scene is through the lens of fusion. In our media-charged familiarity with psychotic abuse scenarios, primitive, intrapsychic conflict is acted out in the interpersonal realm. The abuser acts out his or her inner drama on the victim. Thus what is inside is experienced outside. In horror movies and murder mysteries, we explore these dark and violent parts of our psyches a few steps removed from the action. At its darkest, undifferentiated sexualized violence that is acted out on another is the stuff of psychotic homicide. Bereft of the experience of human relatedness, and filled with the scary dark contamination of sexualized violence, serial killers enact what is perhaps the most tortured layer of the human psyche. These are cases of severely arrested development, where a child's developing consciousness was overwhelmed by chaos and neglect. For these people, the capacity for human attachment was never developed, and the dark archetypal inner world was the child's closest companion. Unmediated by human relatedness, primitive archetypal material erupts into life. In the concretized moment of violence, the difference between self and other is obliterated in a fleeting experience of contact, mastery, and release.

Whenever it seems we have finally seen the worst acting out of the perpetrator/victim dynamic, we are greeted with another one that is worse. Perhaps taking the phenomena of enmeshed relationships, domestic violence, and potential homicide to the limit is the true story of serial killer, Dennis Nilsson. His story is published in a book entitled *Killing for Company: The Story of a Man Addicted to Murder* by Brian Masters. In a case very similar to that of Jeffrey Dahmer, Nilsson was a loner who rented two rooms in a rooming house. Like Dahmer, Nilsson kept his victims' body parts in his apartment "for company." He would dress and bathe them and act out his internal fantasy life with these dismembered parts. As in any violent assault or homicidal enactment, the abuser "proves" that he is no longer a terrified, abandoned, victimized child, but rather a powerful and energized predator, preying on those who appear weaker.

According to the most severe critics of our culture, our motivations and actions in relation to the nonindustrialized world is characterized by these dynamics. Just as if we were locked in the mesmerizing embrace of the demon lover, Americans can remain unconscious of our position of privilege in the world, while our shadow may cast the pall of poverty, discrimination, and violence. Economically, we see this parallel in the global hierarchy, as we benefit from the cheap labor of second-, third- and fourth-world nations. Thus economically, we become vampires.

Another way to conceptualize vampiric imagery and its presence on the American pop culture scene is through the lens of incest, of staying fused. In Anne Rice's *The Witching Hour*, the inheritance of the vampiric spirit Lasher is accomplished through physical, incestual liaisons. The novel tells of numerous incestual couplings—father/daughter, mother/son, between twins, between siblings, between uncle and niece. Symbolically, our struggles with incest and the vampire can refer to hungry, young, fused energy in the psyche. This dark force of unconscious inertia works to keep us sleepwalking through life, unaware of our own individual identity, unaware of our collective responsibilities. Comparable to unconscious shadow contents that clamor for attention, vampire energy is Nosferatu, or undead.

To review the qualities peculiar to the vampire, this predator represents psychic energy that exists outside consciousness, parasitically sustained by the vitality of its host. The vampire cannot be seen in mirrors, since it has no body in this world. Thus the vampire, like the internal bad object, is incapable of the self-reflection that humans take for granted. Without a body, the vampire casts no shadow. Yet paradoxically, it is an image of the archetypal shadow. The vampire exists in the land of shades and whispers, unable to tolerate sunlight or the light of consciousness. Dracula and vampires frequently live near or in insane asylums. The line between loss of consciousness and insanity is very narrow. Vampires are accompanied by plague and contamination fears. Psychologically, contamination fears are akin to fear of fusion, fear of being engulfed by what we experience as "other."

Challenging vampiric seduction requires specific skills. Vampires can be kept at bay by the use of garlic, wild rose, and rowan, as well as a crucifix, bells, and sunlight. Vampires are vanquished by the specific and intentional use of power against the forces of dark: a stake through its heart, a silver bullet, destruction by fire. The use of silver, fire, and a sword-like stake refers symbolically to kinds of light, penetration, and consciousness. This is true in vampire stories, as well as in our cultural psyche. Making conscious all of our uses of power and aggression would represent a cultural coming of age.

Most recently, a vampire tale has shape-shifted from film to prime time television, in a series that conveys the transformative and potentially moral and empowering energy that can be found within the vampire motif. In the 1997 prime time comedy/drama, *Buffy the Vampire Slayer*, a delightful play on cultural gender roles has the main character as a beautiful blond cheerleader who is the latest incarnation in a long line of vampire-slaying heroines.

In the beginning of the tale, Buffy is a pretty but empty-headed Valley girl who is consumed with consumerism, personal issues, and is casually cruel to those in her high school who are not in the "in" crowd. Over time, however, she has been transformed by witnessing the random violence of vampires, and moved by their unfair abuse of otherworldly power. So she

has begun a disciplined study of the ancient tradition of vampire van-
quishers. As she learns to take her feelings and her studies of power seriously, she herself develops into a more complete person. She blossoms
into a sensitive young woman who can handle herself in the dark, and still
get to the prom with her favorite guy. Sometimes she even lets her guy
help fight evil.

In the world of fiction, and wildly popular fiction, I might add, let's
return to the current generation of Mayfair witches in *The Witching Hour*.
This is the first generation with the intention to forgo possession, and
change the family history in a powerful way. How does this generation go
about consciously using power?

In 1990 the vampire spirit possesses Deirdre, before her Antha, but
before Antha, he wanted Carlotta. Carlotta was the first to fight back and
refuse Lasher, the first to use her own will against the force of the vampiric
will. Carlotta refuses both the incestual advances of her charming Uncle
Courtland and the erotic otherworldly temptations offered to her by Lasher.
Carlotta is strong, smart, willful, and religious, albeit rigidly so. She is dis-
gusted by generations of decadence, wealth, weakness, and insanity.
Rebuffed by Carlotta, Lasher seduces her weaker sister Antha instead.

As an adult, Carlotta manages the vast Mayfair legacy and New Orleans
household. Her possessed sister Antha commits suicide when Lasher
directs her to do so. Lasher intends to possess Antha's daughter Deirdre
next. Carlotta has other ideas. She continues to refuse to be tempted by
Lasher's favors and gifts. She warns her niece Deirdre of Lasher's seductions. However, Deirdre, like her mother before her, is too weak to resist.
At a very young age, Deirdre becomes pregnant, seduced and raped by her
Uncle Courtland, while outside Carlotta's vigilant protection.

The now pregnant Deirdre becomes more feeble and withdrawn. When
she gives birth, Carlotta names the baby girl Rowan and sends her off to
be raised in California, with the stipulation that the child be told that she
is an orphan. (Rowan, by the way, is the formal name for the Mountain
Ash tree; its berries are traditionally used as both a vampire and witch
repellent.)

Since Rowan's birth, Carlotta keeps Deirdre heavily sedated and at
home. Many ghostly sightings of "The Man" are seen in the household
around the possessed and sedated Deirdre. Carlotta observes Deirdre in
her drugged delirium and possession, moaning in indecent ecstasy while
being aroused by her demon lover. Meanwhile in California, Rowan is now
thirty and has become a very successful surgeon and healer. Through her
persistent use of a private investigator, synchronistically Rowan finds out
about her family roots in New Orleans and her mother Deirdre's death.
Rowan shows up for the funeral.

The spirit Lasher, no longer able to live in and off her mother Deirdre,
begins to tempt and seduce Rowan. Rowan is more than adequately
warned about Lasher and the Mayfair family legacy from both Carlotta and

an ancient secret order of "watchers" called the Talamasca. This secret order has recorded and kept the entire history of the Mayfair witches since the sixteenth century. The "watchers" represent the incremental presence and power of observing consciousness.

Now the real power of evil begins to show itself to Rowan as Lasher begins to tempt her directly. Rowan is erotically tempted by delicate and warm touches in the darkness as she sleeps, by a demon lover who will not show himself. Made vulnerable by her feelings of estrangement and her orphan status, she is tempted by Lasher's real connections and knowledge about all of her family ancestors. She is tempted financially by her family's vast financial holdings. He tempts her intellectually with articulate promises of supernatural knowledge about medicine, health, and genetics. Finally, and most tempting of all, Rowan is drawn to Lasher's desperate need for her. He pleads with her that in order for him to survive, she must allow him to possess her.

And to what end? Well, I won't tell you the end of this story, but I will tell you that the choice is entirely in Rowan's hand. How we as individuals and as a nation, relate—or refuse to relate—to our own primitive, dark energies is a choice that is in each of our hands. Unconscious predatory energy can be used constructively or destructively. To choose not to claim this instinctual power is to lose control of it. An unconscious national power drive bears no goodwill towards "us" or "them." Conscious passivity about power feeds the evil of shadow. And who amongst us wants to end up as vampire fodder? At the root of the psyche's most primitive energies lies a source of potential consciousness, strength, and creativity. But we cannot know this source until we have traveled deeply into its darkness.

BIBLIOGRAPHY

Badham, John, director. *Dracula*, with Frank Langella. Universal Pictures, 1979.
Buffy the Vampire Slayer. Fox-TV, Burbank. 1997.
Carroll, Noel. *The Philosophy of Horror or Paradoxes of the Heart*. New York: Routledge, 1990.
Codrescu, Andrei. *The Blood Countess*. New York: Simon, 1995.
Coppola, Francis Ford, director. *Bram Stoker's Dracula*. Col/American Zoetrope/Osiris Films, 1992.
Crain, William, director. *Blackula*. American International, 1972. Transcribed by the author.
Estés, Clarissa Pinkola. *Women Who Run with the Wolves: Myths and Stories of the Wild Woman Archetype*. New York: Ballantine, 1992.
Finney, Jack. *Invasion of the Body Snatchers*. New York: Simon, 1989.
Herzog, Werner, director. *Nosferatu*, with Klaus Kinski. Filmproduktion, 1971. Transcribed by the author.

Jung, C.G. *The Vision Seminars*. Book Two. Zurich: Spring, 1976.

Lao Tse. *The Tao Te Ching: A New English Version with Foreword and Notes by Stephen Mitchell*. New York: Harper, 1988.

Leonard, Linda Schierse. *On the Way to the Wedding*. Boston: Shambhala, 1986.

Mascetti, Manuela Dunn. *Vampire: The Complete Guide to the World of the Undead*. New York: Viking, 1992.

Masters, Brian. *Killing for Company: The Story of a Man Addicted to Murder*. New York: Random House, 1993.

Meloy, J. Reid. *The Psychopathic Mind: Origins, Dynamics, and Treatment*. Northvale, New Jersey: Aronson, 1992.

Neumann, Erich. *The Origins and History of Consciousness*. Trans. R.F.C. Hull. Princeton: Princeton University Press, 1973.

Murau, F.W., dir. *Nosferatu*. Prana Films, 1922.

Rice, Anne. *The Witching Hour*. New York: Knopf, 1990.

Stoker, Bram. *Dracula*. New York: Bantam, 1981.

Stoker, Bram. *Dracula's Guest: Nine Stories of Horror and Suspense*. New York: Irish, 1990.

Wells, H.G. "The Sea Raiders." *Great Tales of Terror and the Supernatural*. New York: Random House, 1944, 116–37.

13

The Dragon and the Man-Machine: Reflecting on *Jurassic Park* and *Frankenstein*

JAMES W. MAERTENS

The Dragon Emerges

Michael Crichton's novel *Jurassic Park* and its subsequent film adaptation seized the imagination of a nation grown just a little weary of Barney. *Tyrannosaurus rex* strode across movie screens as the terrifying shadow of that lovable, purple, singing dinosaur with the flawless white smile. Dinosaurs have been a fascination for generations of young boys and girls, but in our time, the juxtaposition of Barney and *T. rex* illustrates the profoundly ambivalent nature of our experience with this mythic figure.

Crichton's Professor Alan Grant speculated in the novel that children liked dinosaurs "because these giant creatures personified the uncontrollable force of looming authority. They were symbolic parents. Fascinating and frightening, like parents . . . " (115). Parents have the power of life and death over their children, so they seem godlike, at least to the child's unconscious imagination. The murderous father, the devouring mother: these are the dark fantasies of infantile fear that persist in one's adult life as unconscious phantasms.

The monstrous parent evokes an even more primordial fear: the fear of Nature itself—larger than the self, a living reality that is built upon eating and dying: one life consuming another. Like fairy tale giants, dinosaurs represent the dark side of human eating; they are predators large enough to eat us at one gulp. To push the symbol further, the huge maw of the

---

An earlier version of this essay appeared in Mythos Journal *No. 6 (Summer 1996).* © *1996 James W. Maertens.*

dinosaur is the shadow of the human desire to consume: food, energy, property—*consumerism*. It is ironic that John Hammond and his genetic engineers call their artificial offspring "consumer biologicals" to be sold as entertainment and accompanied by all the spin-off tee shirts, toys, and goodies that feed the modern economy of children's amusements. The dinosaurs turn out to be much better at consuming human beings than being consumed. Behind these Titans is the dreamworld of the infant's desire to ingest its environment and even devour its mother. In this dream, one becomes powerful by eating the world.

Ubiquitous in myths and folklore, dragons may be good or evil, sources of superhuman benefit or superhuman dread. They may be, like the Dragon of St. George or Beowulf, a force of destruction that threatens the fragile order of human culture huddled in its circle around the village fire. They may also be, like the Chinese Dragon, the spirits of the mountains and the flow of water in mist and rain—a symbol of good fortune and power. The undulating form of the dragon resembles rippling water, bringing life and fecundity and rebirth to the land. Depicted in the midst of terrifying thunderstorms, the dragons of *Jurassic Park* are more obviously like the Western tradition's "fire-drake," a personification of lightning and fire in its destructive aspect.

The dragon is a variant of the serpent motif, often used in myth to symbolize primordial wholeness, an enveloping, self-feeding power like the worm uroboros.[1] In this guise, the dragon is the source of the material world. It unifies the opposites—or more precisely, it signifies a union of light and dark, fearfulness and nurturance that precedes the cognitive division of the universe into the categories of "good" and "evil." The Jungian psychologist Edward Edinger discusses the dragon-serpent as a symbol of the sacred marriage itself, the union of spirit and body, soul and sexual pleasure, light and dark. These dichotomies exist in united form in the primordial energy of the universe. In the Eastern tradition, this primordial, underlying, and unifying energy is *chi*, often called the vital energy. It is the union of yin and yang, the balance of dark and light. In such a mythology, the dragon is a good thing, emblematic of the bounty of limitless potential, the source of being, the Tao itself in its flow. In the West, where philosophy has tended to polarize life into contraries, the dragon ends up being slain as an enemy of goodness. The Light wants to slay not only the Darkness, but also anyone who would dare suggest that the two are really one.

Splitting the Cosmic Egg

Dinosaurs emerged from the obscurity of prehistory in the late nineteenth century. There was a sharp shift in collective self-image during that period. On one side of the historical shift was a culture with no knowledge of the

---

[1] "Uroboros," a mythological motif of a serpent coiled into a circle, biting its own tail.

millions of years and thousands of species that had populated the earth prior to the existence of humans. The Biblical account of Genesis was taken as the whole of existence. After the shift in consciousness one finds a culture that sees itself as one small phase of an unimaginably long evolutionary process. The rigorous classification of life forms by modern biologists led to the imaginal extinction of the old mythical beasts: the giants, chimeras, lamias, and dragons of old. Yet, the same science uncovered even stranger creatures inhabiting a new expanse of time too vast to be grasped by anything but a mythic imagination. In this way dinosaurs have taken the place of the mythical beasts in the mythos of the scientific worldview.[2]

Modern Western minds have woven an imaginative space, a "mythic field," from scientific factuality and reason. This field of imagination goes beyond mere facts to fulfill the deep desires of human imagining. Popular fiction now occupies the zone of myth, expressing all our hopes and fears. Genres such as science fiction, fantasy, detective fiction, and techno-thrillers are our modern myths. As scientists have replaced priests as authorities given the ultimate power to name and explain how the world works, they have assumed the mythic roles of savior, wise man, and miracle worker. They have also, however, inherited the more uncomfortable archetypal roles of mad ruler (the technocrat) and bungling demiurge— that creator-god (or angel/demon) who, in the Gnostic tradition especially, was blamed for fouling up the perfect universe.

Faust is probably the earliest form of the destructive scientist motif which flowered with Goethe and then takes on an even more secular form with Mary Shelley's *Frankenstein*. Today the novels of Crichton operate as part of a pervasive and vast mythic field that includes animated action-adventure heroes for children, comic books, the whole genre of science fiction stories, novels, and films. It also extends into the realm of cultural criticism, from academics to popular critics, whose voices expose an insidious corporate society that uses scientific language to rationalize the most horrible crimes against individual humans and against Nature herself.

Without advocating any part of this mythic field as "objective" truth, the student of myth and soul realizes that such myths are charged with psychological truths, with largely unconscious assumptions we rely on to make judgments. Three-year-olds believe that Power Rangers are superhuman saviors; middle-aged executives and politicians believe just as strongly that thermonuclear fission can save the world economy. Modern chemical elements such as uranium, titanium, and neon have as much mythic power invested in them as did the gold, lead, and sulfur of the medieval alchemists in their time.

---

[2] One of my favorite recent manifestations of the mythic status of dinosaurs is James Gurney's illustrated fantasy *Dinotopia*, which describes an island where humans and highly intelligent dinosaurs live in harmony.

She's a Man-Eater

Crichton's Alan Grant is based on the real-life paleontologist Robert Bakker, whose scholarly studies were popularized in his book *Dinosaur Heresies*. Bakker and his colleagues turned the interpretation of dinosaurs on its head. In the debate surrounding Bakker's work, one can see that scientific discourses, for all their intention to stick to "reality," often end up serving the needs of their cultures for cosmological stories. The old view of dinosaurs was that they were slow, stupid, isolated creatures all of whom became extinct after "ruling the earth" for millions of years. The moral lesson implicit in this tale of fallen giants was not deliberately concocted by the scientists telling the story. They were just interpreting data, putting together skeletons. But they were also re-writing the cosmology of Western culture. They were creating a new mythic age populated with monsters. The hero of the old story of dinosaurs was not St. George but Natural Selection, and the extinction of these supposedly cold-blooded giants stood as a monument to the superiority of warm-blooded mammals—especially humans.

Evicted from Eden by nineteenth-century Biblical scholars, human beings were made by paleontologists into the rulers of an even more wonderful prehistoric Garden—a Jurassic Park, as it were—from which they did not fall, but rose up and conquered the world with big brains and technology. This myth took the place of the Genesis myth's insistence on human supremacy, as well as neatly explaining why technologically advanced Europeans had a natural right and duty to rule over, raise up, or make extinct all the "less evolved" brethren populating most of the rest of the globe. They were "primitive," still living in a prehistoric past and enslaved to incorrect stories—myths.

On one level, *Jurassic Park* shows us a fictional version of one of the scientists who stood up to scholarly orthodoxy. Bakker's arguments have changed our view of dinosaurs. Now they are not only warm-blooded, but smart, capable of complex social organization, and eminently successful. After all, however extinct they are now, dinosaurs dominated the natural world for millions of years, while mammals have dominated for only a fraction of that time, and humans, only a comparative blink of the eye. The lesson of this morality play has been reversed. In the old myth of the dinosaur, they were ponderous creatures whose defeat meant the triumph of brains over brawn, the new over the obsolete.

In the new myth developed by Bakker and his colleagues, the dinosaurs are a grand and glorious race of creatures who successfully adapted themselves to the ecosystem around them. The new lesson seems to be that the dinosaurs were smarter than we who are poisoning our habitat and threatening the whole world with nuclear winter. So, in *Jurassic Park* the monsters are really the heroes. By the end of the book, one can't help admiring the velociraptors with their intricate society and communication, their desire to escape their prison. Theirs is an elegantly adapted and far-seeing intelligence. Hammond and his scientists, by contrast, have only what Ian Malcolm (Crichton's eccentric chaos theorist) calls "thintelligence."

> They see the immediate situation. They think narrowly and call it "being focused." They don't see the surround. They don't see the consequences. . . . [Y]ou cannot make an animal and not expect it to act alive. To be unpredictable. To escape. But they don't see that. (284)

Womb Envy

This motif of the monster stitched together from dead matter (DNA fragments in this case) hearkens back to one of the seminal tales in the scientific mythology: Mary Shelley's *Frankenstein*. Victor Frankenstein and his monster have become universals of Western popular culture. Is there anyone who cannot instantly picture Boris Karloff's interpretation of the monster, even if they've never seen the film? Yet, the genre of the monster movie drains Frankenstein's creature of most of its blood. In the original by Shelley, the creature is drawn with compassion, so that his murders are almost excusable. The reader is meant to sympathize with the monster, even as chills run down her spine. A similar feeling emerges in *Jurassic Park*. There is something in the technique used by Crichton's genetic engineers that suggests an illicit *resurrection* and consequently evokes the uncanny for us. The prehistoric monsters that ruled the earth are brought back from the grave of extinction by extracting traces of their blood from mosquitoes preserved in amber. They emerge as test-tube babies from a dinosaur factory-laboratory, just as parentless and bewildered by the world as Frankenstein's artificial man.

Jurassic Park thus, on one hand, taps into the archetypal stories of creation, and, on the other hand, into a tradition of human inventions that become disasters.[3] To recreate the Jurassic Age is an archetypal usurpation of godlike power—that is, the creation of a primordial world. Scientists, like the Greek titan Prometheus, steal the fire of life and generation from the divine and turn it to their own uses. Of course, when scientists make this Promethean move, Zeus has long ago vanished in a puff of logic, and so they escape divine vengeance. Or do they? We see that hubris, that foolish overreaching, still leads to destruction.

---

[3] One of the earliest artifices gone bad was Pandora, the artificial woman created by Hephaestus for Prometheus and Epimetheus. The theme of Pandora's Box lies behind *Jurassic Park* and its association of the opened box of troubles with the monstrous Feminine. Another famous classical story of invention gone bad is the story of Daedalus and Icarus.

John Hammond's "consumer biologicals" come from the ultimate fantasy of masculine creativity—male parthenogenesis.[4] The Greek gods also suffered from such womb-envy. Take Zeus swallowing Metis to claim sole parenthood for Athena, born subsequently from his head. Or his other trick of snatching Dionysus from the ashes of poor Semele and sewing the godling into his thigh to gestate. Indeed one of the perennial themes of patriarchal traditions is the usurpation by men of female reproductive power.[5] In the Western tradition the act of usurpation usually results in the death of the mother. The (devalued) female is sacrificed in order to permit a claim of male supremacy.

This myth of male supremacy, or even monopoly, in matters of creativity persisted well into the nineteenth century as a serious "scientific" argument. The logic goes like this: Creativity is active; masculinity is active; therefore men are inherently more creative. The best women can hope for is to be immortalized in song or visual arts as the inspiration of men's creativity.[6]

Percy Shelley (with inspiration from Milton and Aeschylus) took up the character of Prometheus and made him a symbol of rebellious mankind, struggling in the face of tyranny. In *Prometheus Unbound*, the Titan is a suffering genius fettered and persecuted by the narrow-minded despotism of the Establishment. But it was Shelley's wife Mary who turned that modern Prometheus into a more complex and ironic tragic hero. For it was Mary Shelley's *Frankenstein* which first suggested that the modern Man of Science was the creator of his own shadow: his creation was itself doomed to be monstrous because of his short-sighted megalomania.

Like John Hammond in *Jurassic Park*, Victor Frankenstein believes he is artificially procreating, making something marvelous, the wonder of his age that will leave all other men breathless with admiration. For young Victor, his artificial man is his Adam, his hope for a whole race of androids (as we should call them now) who will worship him as a father and a god.

---

[4] "Parthenogenesis" from the Greek *parthenos*, meaning "virgin." Reproduction from gametes but without fertilization. The omission of one of the parents, usually the father, but in this usage, the mother, which is replaced often by a machine or artificial womb.

[5] On one level female reproductive power is itself a symbol of women's *social* power generally, and the usurpation of parturition through scientific theories is a way to subvert women's social value.

[6] "Original Genius" as the Romantic tradition celebrates, is distinctly male. In her book *Gender and Genius*, Battersby explains that, although artistic genius is often given stereotypically "feminine" traits, it is nevertheless reserved for men.

> The genius's instinct, emotion, sensibility, intuition, imagination—even his madness—were different from those of ordinary mortals. The psychology of woman was used as a foil to genius: to show what merely apes genius. Biological femaleness mimics the psychological femininity of the true genius. Romanticism . . . developed a phraseology of cultural apartheid... with women amongst the categories counted as not-fully-human. The genius was a male—full of 'virile' energy—who *transcended* his biology. (Battersby 3)

Frankenstein usurps God's place as creator, as Mary Shelley indicates through her many allusions to Milton's *Paradise Lost*. This act of over-reaching is not the admirable rebellion against tyrants espoused by Percy Shelley. Rather, it is a dangerous hubris Mary Shelley sensed in the scientific ambitions of Romantics such as her husband.

In the Frankenstein story, a creature is produced who is superior to his creator: bigger, stronger, faster, and even more sensitive than his supposed master. Contrary to later film portrayals, Frankenstein's monster is highly intelligent and articulate, arguing eloquently that he deserves to be treated humanely, to be loved and respected. Although Crichton's velociraptors and tyrannosaurs do not speak to us in the poetic voice of a wounded child raised on *Paradise Lost*, the character of Frankenstein's monster is nonetheless present in their alien intelligence. They are not commodities, but living children of their human creators. The dinosaurs are more cunning, faster, and stronger than their human creators. They are also repulsive, terrifying, and at the same time, sublime.

Fathering and Control

The missing emotional bond between father and son is not so overt in *Jurassic Park* as in *Frankenstein*. At first, the dinosaurs are icons of the alien, utterly nonhuman, and so the lack of emotional relationship between creator and creature is no surprise. However, as the story unfolds, the dinosaurs (particularly the predatory raptors) seem more and more "human" because of their intelligent behavior. They are distinctly *not* abandoned *sons* seeking to murder their fathers.[7] The dinosaurs are explicitly *female*, engineered in an attempt to control their breeding. Science naively reproduces the culture's patriarchal assumption that females are more passive, easier for men to control. Jurassic Park becomes a kind of bestial harem with electric fences to keep its female charges inside and continually available for the pleasure of their masters. The (potentially) male embryos are neutered, made into eunuchs, as it were, to preserve the genetic engineers' monopoly on reproduction. But, as with so many harems, some of the eunuchs turn out to be all too fertile. Moreover, as the story teaches, when it comes to velociraptors and tyrannosaurs, the females are at least as dangerous as the males. They refuse to let their reproductive power be usurped.

Like Frankenstein's creature, Hammond's dinosaurs symbolize the tensions inherent within modern masculinity. The monsters possess unexpected patricidal desires, desires partly spawned by the cruel imprisonment they undergo. But they are also desires which resonate as a

---

[7] Note the Oedipal pattern. Oedipus is deliberately deformed by his father, lamed and left to die on a mountainside. The power of this ancient myth is apparent in the textual unconscious of *Frankenstein*.

shadow-side of the scientists themselves. Like Frankenstein's monster, the dinosaurs outwit their creators.

Both stories depict an egotistical technocrat who rushes headlong into the application of a new discovery on the grandest scale he can conceive. Hammond is like Frankenstein in his naive inability to conceive his creations as *subjects*, as living beings, rather than as *objects*, mere machines, or worshipful playthings. Both men assume the place of god, not just in the act of "playing god" but in the way they view their control and expect passive obedience from their creatures—as if they possessed God's omnipotence. But they not only lack omnipotence and omniscience, they lack God's love. Neither Frankenstein nor Hammond proves capable of loving and respecting his "offspring." This is emphasized in Hammond's case, in the novel, because Crichton makes him almost entirely unsympathetic.[8] He is a scheming impresario who uses other people's money to hire scientists and technicians to carry out his dream of stealing the fire of life.

The Factory Eden

Hammond creates a modern version of Eden, the enclosed garden. This garden possesses all the primordial mystique which the Jurassic era conjures in twentieth-century minds. It is a world without humans, which, if it can be controlled and commanded, places its master squarely on God's throne.

Isla Nublar is a world of all females controlled by a brotherhood of elite men. It is an island of purified Nature, entirely removed from (but imprisoned within) civilization. It embodies the mysterious potency of the archetypal Feminine, which is both Woman and Nature, while at the same time attempting to omit Motherhood entirely. The power to reproduce, to create life in Nature is lodged with the man behind the curtain and his machines. In this respect, Jurassic Park symbolizes the ultimate fantasy of technological civilization, a totally *controlled* Nature.

One of the theories of Alan Grant is that modern birds descended from the dinosaurs. Birds symbolize freedom, soaring, and flying; they are the image of happiness in their spontaneous songs. One of the most sublime scenes in the film version of *Jurassic Park* is when, waking up in the tree where they have sought refuge, Grant and the two children hear the brachiosaurs calling to each other in titanic voices that echo through the misty jungle. Calling back to them, Grant makes the dinosaurs in the herd raise their thirty-foot necks above the treetops to turn and look. This act of communication signifies a connection, a relationship of one speaking subject to another.

---

[8] In the film, Hammond is revised into a lovable, if naive, grandfather, who seems to admit his mistakes in the end. In one scene, in the dinosaur hatchery, he says that he insists on being present at the birth of the dinosaurs so they will bond with him. In the novel, the dinosaurs view Hammond as potential prey just as much as every other human they encounter.

For Grant and Sattler, and the children, these creatures are not mere machines to be controlled and disposed of by computers and corporations. They are living beings with powerful instincts, intelligence, and life. In the novel, the most powerful scene comes just before Isla Nublar is destroyed by aerial bombardment. Grant has insisted that they find the cave where the velociraptors are breeding so that they can count the hatched eggs and have some idea how many animals have escaped the island. As the humans enter into the subterranean nest of the raptors, the scene turns sublime. For under the earth the velociraptors have recreated their own social forms, complex and deeply mysterious, apparently including migration patterns and nurturing of their young among their strong instincts.

In the novel Hammond is not rescued (as he is in the film) but falls down a hill in a moment of panic and is bitten by the cute little compysaurs, who inject him with their anesthetic venom. Hammond, the great master capitalist who would have conquered the world and made billions off his Titanic zoo, becomes himself the object of consumption for the compysaurs. The dragons prevail.

In *Jurassic Park* dinosaurs represent a Nature that human society has worked hard to destroy over the last hundred years: the Nature that eats humans. *Tyrannosaurus rex* epitomizes this rampant predation, so large that even human machines are hard-put to fight back. But *T. rex* also symbolizes primal rage[9] and destructive aggression—that is, Nature fighting back against the selfish and "thintelligent" control of corporate technocracy.

The technicians of Jurassic Park (not surprisingly, all men who seem to have no families) have reduced themselves to a confident rationality which believes it can predict all outcomes, evade all consequences that are contrary to its will. Theirs is a fat and arrogant masculinity that is represented by Nedry, the greasy and unscrupulous computer security specialist.[10] The counter-maleness that emerges spontaneously among the dinosaurs, despite the bio-engineers' high-tech castration, is Nature itself in all its chaotic sublimity. The nonrational is a positive, creative force larger than human will. Nedry, Wu, and the other technicians have not just lost the Feminine and its ability to be in relation to others; they have lost Nature and the understanding that they are part of it. Removed from the natural world into their air-conditioned control room (control womb?), the technicians play out a game of absolute mastery: they know it all and so are slightly bored with even their own creations. They are just doing their jobs, just trying to make a buck.

---

[9] There is a popular video game called "Primal Rage" which includes among its battling characters a tyrannosaurus.

[10] "Nedry" is, of course, an anagram for "nerdy."

The Abandoned Child and the Masculine Sublime

When one reads Shelley's *Frankenstein*, similarly, one sees a man who has so devoted himself to rationality and the lust for control over Nature that he has lost touch with domestic life and friendship. One feels that Victor has lost part of himself, indeed that the monster is his better half—strong, courageous, loving, sensitive, and conscious of his need to be connected responsibly to a family. Victor has lost a sense of wholeness and his response is to try to restore it by recreating that giant man inside himself, his shadow, his lost embodiment in Nature. When he confronts his double, he is horrified and flees its "ugliness," just as the modern mentality flees the natural world because it contains ugly, messy, powerful things.

Frankenstein and the scientists of *Jurassic Park* attempt to be perfect reasoners, perfectly conscious, wholly *subjects* manipulating others who are wholly *objects*. They hope to do this through a pure mastery of Logos—logic, words, signs—but to their dismay, such action only leads to chaos and fragmentation. In psychological terms, these men are investing all their energy in their egos, or indeed even more shallowly, in their personæ, the masks they wear. As Technicians, Lawyers, PR Men, Men of Reason, Men of Business, they are shrunken fragments of a whole soul.

Yet, Ian Malcolm, the chaos theorist in *Jurassic Park*, represents another view, a science that has cast off its hubris and sees wholeness in Nature with all her chaotic unpredictability. Like a Taoist or Hindu, Malcolm sees Nature as inherently uncontrollable because it is inherently unpredictable and infinite. The universe is the manifestation of the vast unmanifest; its soul is pure potentiality and so anything might happen. No longer is the universe a finite machine that works on clockwork principles, ultimately predictable and controllable, no matter how complex. Science's obsession with "laws" of nature and Western culture's blind faith in "law and order" are revealed as intimately related in *Jurassic Park*.

Jurassic Park epitomizes Foucault's image of the "panopticon" described in *Discipline and Punish*—the island park is a prison in which the inmates are all constantly watched by their captors who are themselves positioned at the center of the prison. Ironically, the guards are the most deeply imprisoned of all, in the concentric circles of their surveillance and control. Anthony Easthope uses a similar circular fortress as a model of the modern masculine ego. Ego constructed as complete control over external forces is entrapped in its own defenses, unable to escape the barriers it has raised against a universe that can only be conceived as an enemy.

The abandonment of offspring is as strong a theme of *Jurassic Park* as it is in *Frankenstein*. It is a spiritual abandonment that lies hidden within Hammond's grandiose belief that the vast theme park is really for children. The infatuation of the technicians with their own mechanical prowess begets the abandonment of family. Indeed any genuine relatedness to others is replaced by the artificial and strictly hierarchical relationships of the corporate org chart. These men take refuge in what I will call the Masculine Sublime. Its inflated egoism stands in stark contrast to the Natural Sublime, which is that encounter with the vastness of the universe that leaves the ego feeling small and insignificant.

Frankenstein is a timorous and nervous young man, introverted and ill-adjusted to the world of male competition. Is it any wonder that he reacts to his own insecurities with overreaching ego-inflation? The monster he encounters is the shadow of this inflated ego. To identify with the universe, to say "I am the universe" or "I am the center of the universe" is paradoxically to become utterly disconnected from the material world. This form of irrationality grounded in rationalism is Hammond's fatal disease. Alan Grant is symbolically redeemed from this technician mentality by his being forced to protect Lex and Timmy as they make their Dantesque journey through the park. He becomes the symbolic Good Father—the Protective Father—in atonement for all the bad fathering of his fellow scientists.

Crichton displays the evils of the Masculine Sublime that underlie the desire to unlock the "secrets" of the genome. In modern industrial culture, the myth of masculine independence as a *worker* separates men (and to some degree women) from the domestic sphere, from tender emotional expression, and from a nurturing focus on relatedness to others (rather than competition with them). These are the gendered characteristics out of which the myths of science are molded—myths of masculine power, control, rationality, objectivity. The relationship between *control* and *fear* is made clear in *Jurassic Park*'s repetition of the word "control" as a chapter heading, when the action shifts to the innermost interior of the panopticon. Seeking the immortality of fame, the technician-heroes die, one by one, prey to their own alienation from Nature and the rage implicit in their own lack of relatedness. Denying connectedness to their offspring, they refuse to believe in their own vulnerability. To be in relation to others—to care for others, or to be cared for—is seen as vulnerability and vulnerability is the ultimate enemy of control and mastery.

One should not think that *Jurassic Park*, any more than *Frankenstein*, is only a critique of scientific institutions or their attendant ideology of control. Both stories go beyond this to recognize that these mentalities pervade modern political culture. The panoptic mechanisms of control that Hammond's men construct could just as well be turned on human societies. The dream of controlling Nature has led to the dream of controlling criminals, the underclass, foreigners, children, and women. Ultimately it is rooted in a desire for absolute *self*-control, the ability to recreate oneself into a predictable machine, one which, if it does break down, can be fixed. *Will power* triumphs over the dragon—the body and the unconscious. Encased in the heroic armor of high-tech security systems, the will power of these men eliminates human vulnerability—to disease, to error, to pain, to defeat, even to death.

That is, until the dragon emerges again.

BIBLIOGRAPHY

Bakker, Robert. *The Dinosaur Heresies*. New York: Morrow, 1986.

Battersby, Christine. *Gender and Genius: Towards a Feminist Aesthetics*. Bloomington: Indiana University Press, 1989.

Crichton, Michael. *Jurassic Park*. New York: Ballantine, 1990.

Easthope, Anthony. *What a Man's Gotta Do: The Masculine Myth in Popular Culture*. Boston: Unwin Hyman, 1990.

Edinger, Edward F. *The Mysterium Lectures: A Journey through C.G. Jung's "Mysterium Coniunctionis."* Ed. Joan Dexter Blackmer. Toronto: Inner City Books, 1995.

Foucault, Michel. *Discipline and Punish*. Trans. Alan Sheridan. New York: Vintage, 1979.

Gurney, James. *Dinotopia*. Atlanta: Turner, 1992.

Jung, C.G. *Mysterium Coniunctionis: An Inquiry into the Separation and Synthesis of Psychic Opposites in Alchemy*. Trans. R.F.C. Hull. 2nd ed. Vol. 14. Bollingen Series XX. Princeton: Princeton University Press, 1970.

Shelley, Mary. *Frankenstein, Or the Modern Prometheus*. 1818. Ed. M.K. Joseph. World's Classics. Oxford: Oxford University Press 1980.

Spielberg, Stephen, director, *Jurassic Park*. Universal Pictures, 1992.

14
Ain't No Angel: AIDS and the Abandoned Soul

JUDITH SAVAGE

Since the shocking arrival in 1980 of what has been called our first post-modern plague, one of our greatest struggles has been with the prevention and cure of AIDS. It has challenged us individually and in our collective humanity. Although recent medical advances have led to some hope for a cure, AIDS continues to defy optimism, not only because it kills, but because it confronts us at our core: at the heart, in love, in sexuality, in relationship. However, there is a worm in the rose of our compassion. AIDS is more than just a disease. Like a social terrorist operating in a climate of fear and distrust, it malignantly separates humankind into opposing camps of "us" and "them." With some of our most vociferous preachers clamoring for the condemnation of AIDS victims, even religion cannot provide clear and compassionate answers.

Many writers before me have struggled with the problem of sustaining love and compassion in the face of hate and fear. In the second century, Apuleius tackled the topic in his *Metamorphoses*, in which the tale of "Eros and Psyche" is found. Frequently a subject for artistic interpretation, the myth has also been examined for its psychological meaning. Jungians such as Neumann, von Franz, and Hillman have interpreted the characters of Psyche and Eros as personifying *daimones,* angel-like intermediaries between the human and divine realms.

In the myth Eros, the Greek god of love and son of Aphrodite, was sent to punish the mortal maiden Psyche because her beauty had incited Aphrodite's jealous wrath. As if pierced by one of his own arrows, Eros became so captivated by Psyche, he rescued her from the very punishment he had concocted for her. After he snatched her from a suicidal leap, he took the maiden to his Olympian home where he became her invisible lover. Once there, she was warned not to look at him but eventually she succumbed to the insinuations of her envious sisters who accused Eros of being a monster, not a God. Disobedient, she spied upon him and accidentally wounded him with the wax spilled from her candle. Enraged, Eros abandoned her. Forsaken and bereft, the young and mortal Psyche was deserted by the god of love. Before being reunited with him she had to complete many difficult tasks to prove her worthiness. When we look upon the face of AIDS today, we are faced with a dilemma similar to Psyche's. We can see either a divine daimon or an evil monster. Are AIDS victims being punished for betraying the will of God, as some have suggested, or doesn't such a belief only reveal hubris, an arrogant assertion that we can know the intentions of God?

The Story of A Soul/A Spirit on Earth

In human history, it is not unusual to invoke the Muses or to call upon the spirits of lost loved ones as angels whose power can enhance the creative process. The muse of my thoughts on the subject of AIDS is my dear friend, Peter Kunz, who died of AIDS in 1989. He was a talented artist with an indomitable spirit, a genuine personality easily at home in the company of the artistic Muses.

In February 1980, my husband and I hosted his farewell party. Peter was off to New York City to earn his way in the "real" art world. Some years earlier he had left his Swiss birthplace, the Kunz family farm known as *Opfersei*, and traveled to America. I have always imagined Peter like an earth sprite, born from the snowy loins of the Alpine mountains that surrounded the verdant farm. Passed down through many generations, the acreage inevitably became one with the family.

We visited Opfersei in winters while its snowy pastures were dotted by tawny milk cows, their foggy breath transforming them into ghostly images of ancient bovine beasts. Inside, gathered with the family in the kitchen, we were warmed by the radiating heat of a huge tile oven. At night we slept in freezing bedrooms beneath billowing down quilts. Peter's brother, Urs, ran the town's only *Gasthaus* where old men smoked crooked cigars and played endless rounds of cards under his kindly proprietorship. The family cemetery, where Peter is now buried alongside his parents, is just steps away from Urs's inn.

I have wondered since his death, if Peter had never left the safety of Opfersei, would he still have contracted AIDS? Could the insulating snows and sheltering family have protected him from the AIDS virus? I look back upon Peter's departure to New York City with helpless regret. Had his fate already been tragically foreshadowed in the namesake of his birthplace? In German *Opfer* means "offering" or "victim" and *Opfersei* thus has to do with being sacrificed.

Peter left his tranquil family farm in the 1970s, as a young man seeking the promise of his generation. It was, after all, the Age of Aquarius. A generation was singing its hope for harmony and understanding, for the promise of peace and sexual freedom in a new dawn. Two decades later the song has changed from the hopeful refrain of a liberated generation to one better sung in the prayerful lyrics of Bruce Springsteen's anthem for the nineties, the *Streets of Philadelphia*. Its highly popular lyrics have brought home the tragic reality of AIDS sufferers who "have walked a thousand miles just to slip this skin." At the end of their anguished journeys, these are abandoned souls. No angel is there to greet them.

Like a prayer from the pop charts, Springsteen's song laments our broken dreams. The dreamed-for, sexually liberated community has disappeared beneath the fear of disease, contamination, death. Sex is no longer free. Homosexuals are no longer just gay. Now they are members of a risk group fearing their possible designation as P.W.A.'s, the dreaded acronym for people with AIDS

Forsaken Soul: Becoming One with AIDS

In Springsteen's haunting lyrics, the AIDS victim laments that no angels are there to greet him as he leaves this world. The missing angel is Eros, the Greek god of love. Like Psyche, we have viewed AIDS victims under an alienating and doubting light and mistaken them for monsters. The harsh glare of moral judgment renders homosexual love and attachment perverse. AIDS becomes a gay plague. Tolerance and understanding are sacrificed to fear and blame. The victims of the disease become the disease . . . they *are* AIDS. Like the disease they have been forced to become, they too are banished.

This merger between a disease and its victim has happened before, but the victims of other epidemics have not always been vilified. Since polio struck mostly children, they were not blamed for their illness (Sontag 144). Because the victims of tuberculosis were often gifted and talented people, it eventually was regarded as a disease of genius.

Like syphilis, AIDS is regarded as a disease contracted through contact with "dangerous others," members of marginalized social groups: Haitians, prisoners, homosexual men, IV drug users (Sontag 114). Associating illness with the divine will of God is one of humankind's oldest ideas and is the basis of our experience of sickness as an infliction or a punishment. When disease occurs in large-scale proportions, it is more easily attributed to the wrath of God. According to Sontag, "The fact that AIDS is predominantly a heterosexually transmitted illness in countries where it first emerged in epidemic form does not prevent [it] from being depicted as a visitation especially aimed at Western homosexuals." As Jerry Falwell claims, "AIDS is God's judgment on a society that does not live by his rules" (149).

Once a contagion is associated with dangerous "others," contracted from the enemy, the immigrant, or Third World refugee, a foundation for prejudice is laid. According to Sontag, in the fifteenth century, the English called smallpox "the French pox," while the Parisians named it "*morbus Germanicus*" and the Florentine called it "the Naples sickness." Sontag makes the point that projection and blaming go beyond mere chauvinism; they are the result of this "crucial association between imagining disease and imagining foreignness" (136).

If a virus cannot be medically contained, it is society's vain hope that an immunity could at least be socially constructed. When forbidden sex and drugs are associated with a contagious disease, a society feels more free to blame and reject the miscreants. A social death created through prejudice and isolation may then precede the patient's physical dying by many years (Sontag 122).

Plagues have always been associated with moral judgments and, like unenlightened citizens of the Middle Ages, we too are lost in demonology. We see Satan in this disease. AIDS patients are perceived as dark demons, likened to Succubi and Incubi, Medieval devils who sought sexual intercourse with men and women while they slept. With the historical shift from paganism to Christianity, as sex was excluded from the nature of God, all manner of perversions was attributed to these night stalkers. Now, the AIDS epidemic makes it clear to us that a desexualized God cannot help us understand our sexuality. Russell Lockhart wrote while discussing cancer in an era before AIDS: "If the Gods wound, and if Gods become diseases, as Jung used to say, then it is necessary to understand sickness as a wounding and to go in search of the God at work in it" (14). He too evokes the Eros and Psyche myth, pointing out that it is "the mortal Psyche who must bring the God into view. For this she is afflicted, tortured, and put through impossible tasks" (15). If we imagine AIDS as only a demonic God, we cannot envision it as a *daimon* or guiding spirit personifying our forsaken human sexuality. As a daimon, an image of our banished sexuality is revealed and we can see how human sexuality is suffering in its alienation from God.

Trauma and Splitting in the Body Politic

In psychoanalytic literature, splitting is described as an infantile defense. Its objective is to rid oneself of undesirable impulses and fears by putting them into another. Once the undesirable trait is deposited into the other, its recipient is then hated as something bad. Splitting mechanisms operate in the community psyche as they do in the individual. However, within the collective, splitting transforms individual prejudice into custom. Prejudice enters the public realm.

As with all disastrous events that strain our comprehension, death in epidemic proportions is a profound trauma to society. Given the magnitude of the AIDS epidemic, the desire to associate this disease with the omnipotent will of God is understandable. But this standpoint requires the splitting of good from evil. It is this splitting then that allows the fundamentalist minister and the homophobe to make their cruel claim that AIDS is a punishment for a sexual sin. These insinuations can work in the collective as Psyche's sisters did in the evolution of Apuleius's tale. Through the lens of their misunderstanding and envy, love is turned into hate.

It is a profound shift to imagine AIDS and by association, the repudiated AIDS victims, as bringing before our eyes a rejected *daimon* personifying a misunderstood God. Because of the difficulty of this imaginal leap, it is easy to understand how we might mistake this divine messenger, the AIDS victim, for a monster.

C.G. Jung conceived of a psychological way of being where duality, splitting, and infantile defenses against annihilation fears were resolved. Through the study of alchemical and shamanistic practices, he discovered a psychological attitude able to break down the boundaries between matter and psyche. This is the imaginal dimension of the shaman, who allowed himself to be infected, to take on a sickness, to facilitate a cure. The Psyche of Apuleius's myth was also a shaman. Her initiatory trials, her descent into the Underworld, and her eventual reunion with the divine Eros, replicated the spiritual descent and ascension of a shaman along the *axis mundi* the imaginal axis that connects the divine and mortal worlds. Psyche was the human counterpart in this mythic tale. It was her task to restore the lost relationship with the divine Eros and, like her, we too must bring the God hidden in this disease back into view.

Taking the Cure

As a dreaded disease whose very nature reveals that we have no real immunity, AIDS threatens to become a social trauma too large for our comprehension. Given the magnitude of the problem, it is natural to seek a defense against its overwhelming power. We cannot fully live, however, as a culture or as individuals, if we are defensively split. Something important belonging to ourselves becomes lost to us when it is projected onto another.

By blaming the AIDS victim, we have created what James Hillman describes as a *sickness daimon,* "a being that carries the evil so that others may remain pure" (151). It bears mentioning that righteous moral superiority cannot provide us immunity from other diseases threatening us such as an Ebola virus, which does not need sexual contact to infect, or "flesh eating" bacteria that can enter even the smallest of wounds. The cure is not in constructing a delusion of immunity through social rejection or by creating scapegoats. Like the shaman, the cure resides in our willingness to become psychologically infected by our own mortality.

In antiquity, Eros was imagined as a hermaphrodite, a beautiful adolescent boy with a rose and a lyre. In our times, this is a "gay" image and if we reject it, fear it as a monster, he will turn the same face to us. Then he will abandon us as he abandoned Psyche. The wax from our judging candle can burn the god and make him flee. Yet, abandonment should not be the end of the story. Mythic currents run deep here, and they suggest that we must take up Psyche's tasks, follow her trials and drink of our own mortality. As Nietzsche suggests, by affirming our own mortal subjugation to fate, we can become wise. When we assume Psyche's burden in order to be reunited with Eros, human love can be transformed into *agape,* a spiritual love that can only be gained through the grace of God.

I do not know the ultimate meaning of AIDS. We are still in the midst of the story's unfolding. Pandemics such as AIDS frighten us and cloud our vision. This article is also a confession, a regret born from my own failed eros that allowed me to know more of Peter's life than I did of his dying. While I had enjoyed his vigor, I feared his decline. Peter, like Psyche, was one of the initiated. While dying of AIDS he produced hundreds of drawings that went into his *Book of Transformation*. He painted the images of his own dying, transmuting AIDS into human suffering. Ultimately, his life was a work of soul. Much like the last great visitation of the Seraphic choir of angels who helped humanity through the power of their love, we are now visited by the souls of the thousands of AIDS victims who have suffered and died. They are angels too. Each of them has deepened humankind's search for meaning and wholeness.

B I B L I O G R A P H Y

Field, Nathan, "Projective Identification: Mechanism or Mystery?" *Journal of Analytical Psychology* 36:1 (1991), 93–100.
Franz, M. von. *A Psychological Interpretation of the Golden Ass of Apuleius*. Zurich: Spring, 1970.
Gmrek, Mirko D. *History of Aids: Emergence and Origin of a Modern Pandemic* Princeton: Princeton University Press, 1990.
Godwin, Malcolm. *Angels: An Endangered Species*. New York: Simon and Schuster, 1990
Gollnick, James. *Love and the Soul: Psychological Interpretations of the Eros and Psyche Myth*. Waterloo, Ontario: Wilfred Laurier University Press, 1992.
Hillman, James. *A Blue Fire: Selected Writings by James Hillman*, ed. T. Moore, New York: Harper and Row, 1989.
Lockhart, Russell, "Cancer in Myth and Dream: An Exploration into the Archetypal Relation Between Dreams and Disease." *Spring* (1977), 1–26.
Mogenson, Greg. *God Is a Trauma: Vicarious Religion and Soul Making*, Dallas: Spring, 1989.
Monick, Eugene. *Evil, Sexuality and Disease in Grunewald's Body of Christ*. Dallas: Spring,1993.
"Sex and Sexuality." *Encyclopaedia Britannica*, 1992.
Sontag, Susan. *Illness as Metaphor and Aids and Its Metaphors*. New York: Doubleday, 1989.

15
Looking Through the Keyhole: Recollecting and Reflecting America's Soul in *Paris, Texas*

GARY D. ASTRACHAN

> You know what side of the border you're on? You got a name boy?
>
> —The doctor to Travis in *Paris, Texas*

In this beautifully crafted 1984 film, *Paris, Texas*, the German director Wim Wenders gives us a richly evocative glimpse into our own personal and archetypal beginnings. Through both a variety of cinematic techniques and through the narrative content and imagery of the story, this filmic tale provides an entire myth of origins, in fact, several different kinds of creation myths for our times, revealing something about where we've come from and what we are as human beings and as Americans.

It is also a story about rage and hate, generational failures and despair, conflagration and destruction and passion, and perhaps finally, acceptance. We will "re-view" it together, especially though, as a film about memory and identity in America and how they are lost and found. *Paris, Texas* allows us to believe, however fleetingly, in the possibilities of relationship and redemption, even while wandering within the personal and cultural deserts of the soul. The film offers us the clue that to know about our past

---

A different version of this essay on Paris, Texas *for people especially interested in analytical psychology can be found in two parts in* Quadrant *XXVII:I, Winter, 1996–97, 22–33 and in the following 1997 summer issue under the title: "In the Eyes of the Beholder: Recollection and Reflection in Wim Wenders's Film* Paris, Texas.*"*

allows us to more fully claim and own our lives and surroundings in both the present and for the future. *Paris, Texas* tells the story of a man found wandering in the desert who reunites with his brother and young son and instigates deep encounters with his own inner demons and his former wife. The film indicates that this process of recollection allows him to possibly both recover his obliterated soul and begin healing his destructive marriage.

As reflected in the title, the film is a European and American collaboration. Sam Shepard completed the screenplay in 1982. The actors are predominantly American with several major exceptions, notably the two female leads, Nastassia Kinski, who plays the mother, Jane, and Aurore Clément, who plays the stepmother and sister-in-law, Anne. Since it is actually a German-French co-production, most of the film's technical crew is European. Despite, or maybe paradoxically, because of this strong European influence and viewpoint, particularly under the authority of the director Wenders and his photographer Robby Müller, *Paris, Texas* appears as one of the quintessentially American "road" movies of all time. The lonely romance, gritty glamour and popular iconography of that genre here act to carry and contain authentically harrowing and devastating themes. The story and the images weave in and out, both glorifying and idolizing desolated American pop icons, while at the same time critiquing them within a context of emptiness and alienation. All of these are essential parts of this peculiarly American hero (or, anti-hero) myth.

The *topos* of the film, that is, the psychological place where it occurs, its inner geographical space of enactment, is unmistakably, unremittingly, and frighteningly America, the United States. The visuals are clearly telling: the scenes shot in Texas and California and along the many roads in between, in Arizona and New Mexico; the freeways of Los Angeles and the traffic cloverleaves of Houston; airports, huge jets in the sky, and car-rental lots; all the familiar and strange stretches of plains, deserts, and hills of the Southwest; and of course, the so-recognizable diners, the neon-signed motels, laundromats, night clubs, and seedy bars. This is America at the end of the twentieth century. All those great open spaces and decaying urban areas virtually cry out "America," and then in sarcastic refrain, "land of the free and the home of the brave." And their back-up is the nasal twangs of the actors and the accompanying slide guitar on the sound track.

But all those literal scenes and settings only help us to arrive at the true *topos* of the film, the place "America" occupies in our souls, how it has become us and we inseparably it. And it is precisely the interactions of the characters within their typical American environments that convey a strong sense of place, a locale, a local color. We find here a real myth of place, one that both reveals and hides the truth, like any good symbol would, or like an oracle or a dream would, or a film, for that matter. *Paris, Texas* appears as a film before our very eyes. It captures this U.S. of A. in powerful and polyvalent ways we overlook only at our increasing peril.

Paris, Texas portrays a contemporary landscape that is dying from spiritual thirst, that is arid, parched, and meaningless, that is ravaged, barren, and ugly, nearly bereft of human warmth, emotional support, or soul values. And here, in this place, we are all dislocated, vaguely fearful, and ill at ease.

Shorn of much of the easy nihilism of other road movies, this film lays bare where we are most hurt: in our deeply wounded capacity for loving and in our brutal cynicism and hopelessness about creating either meaning or beauty in our lives. We see in this film an America that has seriously lost its way. Beyond and within the pop cultural images on the screen, we feel our own unsettling confusion and disorientation mirrored back to us. It is both poignantly sad and occasionally humorous at the same time; but it is a weirdly disenchanted humor, as it concerns the erosion and fragmentation of our memories and identities.

As the story begins, we see a man stumbling, dazed and desiccated, through a vacant, baking desert. We don't know who he is or where he is. We don't know where he is coming from. And we surely have no idea where in this awesomely empty plain he is going. We, like Travis, are lost in a wasteland. We, like Travis, live in a culture and in a time that has lost its memory.

The vast grandeur of the American Wild West, filmed in all those John Ford and Howard Hawks westerns with their limitless vistas of promise and hope, strength and courage, have become, in the short span of time since the 1950s, just empty, lonely spaces, littered with the hulks of rusting cars, plastic fuel containers and fast food wrappers blowing like so much tumbleweed along the highway.

In grappling cinematically with this nostalgically appealing and still obviously attractive American hero myth, Wenders draws upon what is perhaps, for better *and* worse, its single greatest product and most highly valued contribution to world culture: technology. The American mania for producing and consuming this technology, cut loose from the moorings of meaning, continues to fill the world with both pragmatic and ingenious emblems of ultra-contemporary American know-how, as well as with overwhelming amounts of toxic and highly destructive, death-dealing trash.

In *Paris, Texas*, Wenders redirects technology, however, to further and deepen the viewer's own experience of film as a medium for reflecting the multileveled nature of consciousness itself. He employs a wide variety of technical means to both symbolize and amplify the actual processes of seeing, hearing, reflecting, and especially, remembering. These images propel the film along towards its ultimate goals of recognition, recollection, and reunion.

They are in a way metacinematic techniques and images, in that they reflect upon the film even while it is going on, a style used by many directors and to great effect by Fellini and Bergman, for example. Here with Wenders, the techniques have a particularly postmodern, that is, vaguely paranoid and industrially edgy, resonance. The images act to interiorize and deepen psychological space both within the film and within the viewer by adding layers of reflective possibilities. Often it is done both literally and visually, as with mirrors and glass windows, or acoustically, with voice-overs from telephones, tape recorders, and microphones. These mechanical means present us with visual and auditory analogues to the actual processes of memory. They represent what the ancient Greeks meant by the word *techne*, the "imitation of nature." The Greeks regarded *techne* as the true province of art, and *techne* still *is* a work carried on by artists, alchemists, and analysts, just to name a few, the imitation of nature, whether inner or outer, in order to transform it. Serving this purpose, Wenders additionally uses as technical elements photographs, home movies within the film, radios, walkie-talkies, and in two climactic scenes, one-way windows and microphones.

Besides this set of symbols about the dissociated nature and disconnected working of our postmodern consciousness, which he re-uses for associating and connecting, another secondary set of signs populates the film as Wenders's own reflections on American culture. This group of images, which iconically set off many scenes, includes billboards, advertising sculptures and structures, road signs, maps, pop cultural artifacts galore, and of course, the ubiquitous Cyclopean shrine of the great American cult religion, the television screen.

There is, however, an intense ambivalence which belongs to all of these technological images. While offering possibilities for reflection and deepening, the means themselves, particularly television, video, and computer screens, also create distance and duplicity. Hermes, the Greek God of both communication and commerce, moves within these images and techniques,[1] and like him, they bear the capacity to deceive and trick the unwitting consumer. Wenders's repeated focus on these American implements deconstructs the actual culture while he reframes it within a provocative context of desolation and despair. He portrays the emptying out of the American soul as it gets sucked through the screen, devoured by the consuming gods of materialism masquerading as tawdry bread and circus for a depressed and powerless people. There is no nourishment for the soul in these sterile motel rooms, TV soap operas, sitcoms and talkshows, or plastic-laden truck stop diners. What then, we have to ask, is their continuing allure[2] (Kearney 322–32)?

Human communication via technology, Wenders shows us, becomes more rich and complex as it also becomes more fragmented, oblique, and

---

[1] On Hermes as patron god of communication, commerce, and connivery among many other attributes, see Brown, Kerenyi, Lopez-Pedraza, and Otto.

[2] Richard Kearney discusses the fundamental paradox of postmodern cinema, as exemplified in *Paris, Texas*, which attempts to deconstruct the cult of the media-fabricated image from within the cinematic image itself.

refracted. Hermes, the thief, connives against and steals from us even while providing the means for brilliant and instantaneous connection-making. He cons us while we marvel at his cleverness. Technology leads us astray when *techne* is divorced from *telos,* or "meaning," when the human mind transforms nature without its serving a truly human and meaningful purpose. In archetypal terms, this is when Hermes the thief becomes separated from his other roles as Hermes the servant, or the initiator of sacrifice, all of which are necessary if he is to guide our search for soul. America's unmediated passion and anti-Hermetic exploitations of human and natural resources through technology, however, contain the seeds for proliferating ecological catastrophe and cataclysm. Where once Americans were proud of their role as international leaders and its consequent political and economic imperialism and technological hegemony, it is now exceedingly difficult for us to accept responsibility for the cultural leveling and global ravaging we have created, as we abandon others to their Coca-Cola and Disney-colonialized fates.

Scenes From a Film

Turning now to the film, we begin our exploration of its artfulness with the image of the mirror, how we need mirrors to reflect ourselves, to tell the truth and to communicate. Art as image is itself one such mirror, and so the film *as film* is already a mirror for our reflections.

The first appearance of the mirror in this film accompanies, appropriately enough, a one-way dialogue between Walt, who has come all the way from Los Angeles to bring home this recently found brother, and Travis, the main character. Travis was discovered passed out in the middle of nowhere, in the Texas desert. Strangely reunited after five years, Walt is then quite understandably questioning Travis, who has been presumed dead. Travis, however, is mute. He is stonily silent and appears confused and severely withdrawn.

In one scene, as Walt talks to Travis, he hands him a small plastic bag filled with Travis's worldly possessions, retrieved from his pockets when he had passed out in the desert. In this beautifully filmed interchange, we see mainly the eyes of the men reflected back and forth in the rear view mirror.

There is possibly a reference in this scene to Jean Cocteau's film *Orphée* (1950), where Death and Orpheus are chauffeured in a limousine by a Charon-like driver. The mirror in *Orphée* is there the entrance to the underworld. Cocteau shows us that to look into a mirror is to see ourselves transformed, to see our own death. Travis, like Orpheus, has returned from the land of the dead[3] and he appears still to inhabit a nonhuman realm deep

---

[3] There are bountiful references in the film which support the hypothesis that Travis, like Orpheus, has journeyed to the realm of the dead and furthermore, has returned with secrets from the wellspring of archetypal/collective memory found there. The first scenes of the film

within himself. He looks shell-shocked, burnt out and hollow. As he watches and listens, it is the eyes and voice of his brother which slowly seem to kindle his soul back to life throughout the early part of the film. And it is done entirely with mirrors. He begins truly to see himself for the first time, literally, in the car mirrors and in his brother's eyes.

The next mirror scene occurs when the two brothers stop at a motel and Walt goes out to buy some clothes for Travis. Travis now sees himself in the bathroom mirror and has a shock of recognition and he immediately flees out of the motel, clutching his small plastic bag of possessions. Unable to relate to his own image, as if some part of himself has died, Travis is on a threshold and has not yet come back into life.

The bag contains the only clues to Travis' identity. Its contents allowed the doctor to locate Walt. One of the key images in the bag is a photomat strip taken of a more youthful and smiling Travis with a woman and a young boy, all crammed into a photo booth. They look playful and care-free. The other important image is a postcard-sized photograph of a vacant lot amidst scrubby desert wasteland with a FOR SALE sign on it.

In the first of the ensuing car rear-view mirror dialogues, Travis, sitting in the back seat, is looking at this frayed and tattered photograph along with two maps when he says his first word: "Paris" (Sievernich 20).[4] It sounds like someone learning to speak. In the next of these scenes, Travis, still in the back seat, again says "Paris" (25) and then hands the photograph of the empty desert lot to his consternated brother, who is driving. All of these scenes of driving, being driven and remembering are largely composed of shots of both Travis and Walt reflected in the rearview mirror. At first Travis, now talking, cannot recollect why he bought that forlorn lot of land. And then during yet another mirror shot, he remembers: that is where he was conceived, in Paris, Texas. He recalls their parents talking about where they met and when they first made love and then more poignantly, his father's standing joke that his wife is from Paris . . . (pause), Texas, followed by laughing a lot (31). "That is where I began," Travis says. "I started out there" (30).

So we return with Travis through these images and reflections to a

---

are actually shot in the Devil's Graveyard, Big Bend, Texas. The first shot is a bird's-eye view of the landscape and Travis stumbling through it; the second is a hawk landing on a boulder; and the third is Travis staring at the hawk. The hawk as a symbol of the soul and solar transfiguration points to the possibility that Travis has been initiated, transformed, and resurrected during his long wandering in the desert. His thirst echoes the "thirst of the deceased," a motif corresponding to all descents to the underworld from Plato through Dante to postmodern fiction. There the soul of the initiate is counseled to drink deeply the water of the spring of Mnemosyne, the great Goddess Memory in ancient Greece, in order to completely escape the wheel of reincarnation, or else like a Bodhisattva, return to this world to teach the mysteries of life and death. For other references to postmortal and underworld journeys, see Astrachan, Eliade, Harrison, and Vernant.

[4] All the direct quotes are taken from the handsomely illustrated screenplay in three languages, *Paris, Texas*, edited by Sievernich.

place of origins, to his place of beginnings, to his motherland. He has managed to keep a literal shredded picture of it with him among his scant belongings. His wanderings, his journey, has been guided by a compulsion to return to the place where he began, as if he could begin all over, perhaps do it differently this time. As a seed in his mother's belly, he now might be reborn out of the ashes of his own immolation on the altar of forgetting. In recalling the fantasy of his birth, Travis in this scene begins to retrieve and literally own his actual place of beginnings. He recreates the myth of his origins (Lopez-Pedraza 27–29).

In the film, remembering is associated thus far with mirrors and photographs, reflections and the inflections of human speech. Its opposite, forgetting, gets assimilated with Travis's emptiness, the desert and his initial lack of images and human language. Remembering and forgetting are constantly playing off against each other throughout the film, in dialogue as well as in the contrasts between interior and exterior scenes, the internal space of emotions and relationships, and the external world of desert, highway, skyscrapers, and urban sprawl. The film is able to contain and hold this strange juxtaposition which constitutes our lives, and show how it is forever oscillating between inner and outer, both the human and the nonhuman realms.

That we can create a *topos*, a world, so devoid of soul is one of the terrifying messages of this film. That we can create a world in which it is barely possible to recognize our humanness is the horror we face in looking at this American scene. The actual images of this landscape seem in a way to be designed to further forgetting and to abolish memory and recollection. For the most part what we see around us, especially in and around cities, are monumental advertisements created to sell products. Virtually the entire skyline of any major American city consists of corporate business buildings, like insurance companies, architectural idealizations dedicated to cupidity, avarice, and greed. The human background of cultural memory in America is being torn apart and buried by useless information, sensory bombardment, literal mistruths, and meaningless facts.

Travis's process of slowly recollecting the shattered fragments of his identity from the shards of the dispersed world's soul builds up to his return to Los Angeles with Walt. There Travis lives with Walt, his sister-in-law Ann, and his own son Hunter, who was left at Walt and Anne's house years before by his mother. So far unable to connect with his son, the justifiably wary Hunter, one evening at Walt's suggestion, Travis sits down with the family after dinner to watch home movies. Walt had filmed them five years before when they were all on vacation at the Texas coast. The film within the film is faded and grainy and shows them all, including Jane, Hunter's mother and Travis's wife, playing and enjoying themselves at a beach.

In this emotional scene of film-watching, Travis's eyes well with tears as he looks at this once sane and happy segment of his own past with his family unroll before him. It portrays an idyllic time and the viewer still does not know what has torn it all to shreds.

The home movie scene facilitates a rapprochement between Travis and his own dismembered identity. Watching Travis react, Hunter is drawn for the first time to acknowledge him as his father. Standing beside him after the movie, he says, "Goodnight, Dad" (44). The whole scene creates a continuity, a thread through time. Wenders here uses the film-within-the-film technique as a magical and healing umbilical cord bonding the participants with each other and with their own selves in time.

As the relationship is renewed between father and son, yet one more mirror scene intervenes to facilitate Travis's truly coming into his role as father. It is similar to the much earlier scene of Travis's first major transformation, in a motel room shaved and outfitted in new clothes, when he looked at his radically revised self in amazement. So too does this later scene use the mirror's reflecting image as a vehicle for changing deeper aspects of identity and the self. Here at this house in L.A., Travis tries on lots of different clothes in his effort to look like "the father," with the help of the Mexican cleaning woman and via the mirror. He literally dresses up in different father costumes in trying to adapt his deconstructed inner attitude to the mirror's reflected persona image of himself (Leonard 152).[5] In the following scene he and Hunter are looking at photos of the grandparents, further reconnecting the family links to their shared past.

The theme of the quest for origins and human beginnings is echoed on a grander level through the boy Hunter, who takes up the creation myth, this time putting it into a vast phylogenetic, astronomical, and even cosmic perspective. As Hunter is going to bed the night of the home movies, he casually observes to Anne that Travis, his father, still loves Jane. He comments that it is not Jane, however, that Travis was seeing on the screen. "That's only her in a movie, a long time ago, in a galaxy far, far away" (Sievernich 45). So the young boy's imagining of a time when he was together with both of his parents, and especially his mother, places it in an intergalactic space and in a distant mythological era. Hunter's musings on space and time stretch the dimensions of the film's narrative to archetypal proportions. His child's perspective locates the interpersonal drama of the family in the grand context of cosmic creation. Filmed against infinite horizons, mountains, and plains, all actually created during eons of geological time, personal and historical time gets repeatedly contrasted with archetypal and natural timelessness.

The road movie across America becomes an unfolding search for the mother, as well as a search for a vanishing mother nature, an external, ever-receding matrix of identity. Threatened by the huge spaces of this country, the American hero myth treats nature as something to be domi-

---

[5] Linda S. Leonard also discusses this cinematic quest for the father in her *On the Way to the Wedding*.

nated, controlled, and exploited, so as to avoid being engulfed by it. The misplaced focus in the American search for selfhood becomes outer-directed, material, horizontal, from sea to shining sea, manifest destiny, or, it gets projected into outer space, as in "star wars." Running from the terror of limitlessness, we seek boundarilessness and mistakenly call it freedom.

Later, in a very brief scene, Hunter and Travis are driving together towards a distant mountain range on their way back to Texas to find Jane, the mother. The young boy tells his father how the galaxy and the universe were created out of a tiny dot. In a few sentences he elaborates the big bang theory of creation, beginning with the explosion of matter out of a compressed spot, swirling gas, the sun heating the gas to form the hardened earth ball, the surface of the earth as watery oceans, sea animals, and then volcanic explosions and lava hitting the water to form rock and finally land.

After this amazing creation story, the scene which immediately follows shows Hunter and Travis strolling past a truck stop diner towards two large plastic dinosaurs that were put up as tourist attractions. With this shot, the dinosaurs quickly take up and continue the image of pre-history and the connectedness of all living things. At the same time, this scene literally and visually places Hunter and Travis against a backdrop of a fantasied geological past. The dinosaurs get juxtaposed with the truckstop and the present; cosmic eons of unimaginable length collide with the banality of the present and history. The relativity of time and space assumes immediate significance along with the creation of matter, energy, and life; we see that this journey backwards and forwards involves the necessity of pure creation, out of emptiness, out of nothing.

The creation theme becomes very specific as the journey towards the mother begins to focus. In a later scene, Hunter relates the following "fact" to Travis as they talk on walkie-talkies from the back to the cab of their moving pick-up truck. Hunter explains that if a guy traveling at the speed of light put a baby down for an hour and then came back, "in an hour, he would be an hour older, but the little baby would be an old man" (65). Again the relativity of our normal time-space reality here gets projected as the backdrop against which the pressingly human and emotional issues of birth, abandonment, time, and the life cycle get played out by both Hunter and Travis. We feel our vulnerability. Hunter was abandoned by both his father and his mother. His father has returned after five years and now together, in a totally changed relationship, they search for the mother who left both of them at different times in the past. Life for each of the characters in the film becomes a series of losses and reunions. The telescoping of time in the film works always in both directions, towards the past and from the past to the present. In *Paris, Texas*, time is portrayed like a ball of string which keeps getting unrolled and rolled as primary relationships get lost and found.

We arrive now with Hunter and Travis in their 1958 Ford Ranchero pick-up at the penultimate, climactic scene of the film. In these next three sequences we encounter one of the great depth probings in cinema of the possibility and limits of human relationship. True to the unfolding styles of recollection and reflection Wenders has been utilizing up to this point, capturing the deconstructed, angular American viewpoint through oblique, indirect, refracted communications, these three scenes build towards their tragic recognitions in gradual, back-and-forth, overlapping time sequences.

The actual images and techniques are once again mirrors and windows. In these three scenes, Wenders explores these images' fullest range of shading and nuance, which deepen and symbolize the intense conflict we all experience between the needs to connect to and distance ourselves from the "other."

These crucial scenes get played out in one of the true underworld locales of the American psyche. The image of the American unconscious is a seedy sex club in Texas where detached, impersonal, masturbatory sexuality takes its usual form of casually exploiting and degrading women. This autoerotic and schizoid atmosphere becomes at the same time, however, a meeting place of the utmost intimacy between the film's two main characters, Travis and Jane. Deep communication occurs at this mundane intersection of body and soul. Soul is forged in the underworldly depths of the erotic. Sexuality, banished to the shadow realm of our culture, then becomes the hidden place in ourselves where we must go to meet, relate to, and work with our own souls.

Hunter and Travis follow Jane from the bank where they have traced her to a dilapidated building. As she goes into the side entrance, we see painted on the huge wall a monumental Statue of Liberty portrayed against a background of blue-gray water and the New York City skyline. So even from the outside of this place of ultimate rendezvous, this place of meeting projections, we are welcomed by the American image of promise and hope, Liberty, opening her arms to the poor and suffering. What the image actually adorns, however, is a sleazy and pornographic fantasy world of derelict urban despair.

Leaving Hunter in the truck, Travis goes into the same side entrance door to the Keyhole Club that Jane has entered. From an infernally red and mirrored staircase, he emerges into a bar and club area where a band is rehearsing and people are standing around. One of them is Jane. He is confronted by the club manager and asked to leave. He goes downstairs as it seems to dawn slowly on him what is going on in this place.

Throughout the segment Travis hears over the loudspeaker system "Sergeant Jojo, booth 22," or, "Nurse Bibs, call for you, booth 19," or, "Mother Dana, booth 18, please" (73–75). Travis now finds himself in a long corridor lined on both sides by curtained booths.

The booths are peep shows with one-way mirrors, a microphone for the male customers to speak with the women, and a few rudimentary props associated with the room's fantasy name. Travis goes into "Poolside." Once in the dark booth, he sits down in front of a large mirror. There is a small clock on the wall and he picks up the telephone receiver in front of the mirror. After he describes Jane, a woman dressed like a nurse enters. It is not Jane. Out of breath from just coming from another booth, she playfully tries to engage Travis, who is still attempting to figure out how the mirror turns into a window. Travis, like Orpheus in Hades, the nocturnal realm of the shades, requests to see his beloved and can only view her through a glass darkly.

When Nurse Bibs comes in and turns the light on in her side of the room, Travis's mirror becomes a one-way window, so he can see her, but she cannot see him. The woman explains that to him since he sounds so puzzled. He gets up and leaves Nurse Bibs soundlessly talking. Her voice is cut off on the loudspeaker when he hangs up his receiver. He again walks out into the long, double-rowed corridor.

After a moment's hesitation, he takes a deep breath and walks into the booth marked "Hotel." He sits in the nearly identical booth for quite a while before a light goes on the other side and a voice comes over the loudspeaker. It is Jane's voice. After waiting so long for this encounter, the effect is quietly shattering.

Jane appears open, friendly, receptive, and engaging. Travis, however, seems to be smoldering, enraged at finding her in this place. He is quiet and non-responsive, so much so that Jane repeats that it is okay for him not to talk and that she is a good listener. Silence, or whatever he wants, she says, would be fine. Though she is light and genuinely accepting, Travis clearly cannot handle his emotions. When she offers to take off her short red dress, he gets furious. Now openly angry, accusing, and condemning, he starts quizzing her about the extent of her (implied sexual) activities with the customers.

His sudden eruption is frightening and she stammers responses. As he verbally presses further, his intensity makes her get up to leave, but then he anxiously apologizes and she stays. Looking put off and confused by this peculiar customer, she again sits down and becomes calming and understanding. It is too much for Travis though, and he leaves the booth while Jane is still talking to the mirror, as he left Nurse Bibs speaking to an empty mirror.

The scene is a relatively short one, but it ignites the pent-up expectations, energies, and tensions which have been building throughout the film. Something important has happened. Though it may not be visible or manifest in behavior, the remaining story line has crystallized itself in broad contours in Travis's mind: he knows roughly now what he must do. The search for his lost soul, the linchpin of his identity, has reached its goal and it is found, as usual, with the "other." He has come up against his limitations. As much as he has finally and agonizingly encountered his wife Jane, even more has he begun to come to terms with some of the split-off parts of his own self. What these fragments are only emerge in the next cluster of eight short scenes.

In the first of these brief, transitional scenes, Travis and Hunter are driving down the main street of a small town after the meeting with Jane. Later, Hunter and Travis are alone except for the bartender in a western saloon, and Travis is drinking hard. The picture of Travis's vacant lot in Paris, Texas, lies on the bar counter. Travis tells Hunter he thought they would live there together with his mom some day. Soon after, Hunter, in disgust with his father's drinking, walks out of the bar. The photograph of the empty lot in Paris, Texas, flutters to the floor. Travis orders another beer with a chaser.

The next scene, one shot, is at night and Hunter guides his completely drunk father down the deserted main street to a laundromat, the only illuminated building in town. Then, in the next scene, Travis is lying stretched out on a couch in the laundromat, telling Hunter about his own mother, Hunter's grandmother. She was, Travis says, a "plain woman," "plain and good," not at all "fancy." "But," he continues, "my daddy had this idea in his head that was kind of a sickness . . . he looked at her, but didn't see her. He saw this idea. And he told people she was from Paris. It was a big joke. But he started telling everybody all the time and, finally, it wasn't a joke anymore. He actually believed it. And, one day, he actually did believe it" (84–85). After this recollection, Travis falls asleep snoring to close out the scene.

The last three short scenes in this section are unified by a cassette tape recording. On the tape, Travis is telling Hunter he wants to bring him and his mother together, but he cannot be with them. What happened between him and Jane, though he can hardly remember it, cannot be healed. It has torn them apart, he says, and left them alone in a way he cannot get over. Travis finishes his message by expressing his love for Hunter.

We now know the outlines of the tragedy of their shared past—a passion which has turned to paranoia; a need for connection and confrontation which has turned into madness, jealousy, and delusion. And once again we are at the Keyhole Club and the culminating scene of the film. Travis is sitting in a peepshow booth. Jane comes in, flips the light on, and again the mirror becomes a window. Her booth is decorated like a typical American coffee shop. She seems happy and sits on a bar stool next to the counter. Travis, her anonymous customer, greets her and says he would like to tell her "a long story" (87). She does not seem to recognize his voice and says she has got plenty of time.

Now, finally, Travis slowly remembers. He starts to tell their story. He begins to recollect his and Jane's whole life together, their early happiness and youthful love and then his own increasing obsession with her, a possessiveness and jealousy so intense he stops working to be with her. He recalls his continued drinking and fits of rage and then Jane's pregnancy. He stops drinking and starts working again, but he is beset by the constant fear that she does not love him. He stops working and stays home because he cannot trust her enough to stay away from her.

When their child is born, Jane is more irritated and unhappy than ever. She feels imprisoned by him, now with a child in their trailer. She regularly dreams about running away. Becoming even more mad in his alcoholic fits of jealousy and anger, he ties a cow bell around her ankle so she cannot escape at night while he sleeps. She tries once to flee. He catches her, drags her back to the trailer and ties her to the stove with his belt. She is crying and their two-year-old child is screaming and he falls asleep.

When he wakes up, he is on fire. Their trailer is all on fire. He runs into the kitchen for the only people he loves and Jane and Hunter are gone. He runs outside and rolls on the wet ground, putting out the blue flames licking his arms. Then he runs into the darkness and keeps on until the sun comes up. He runs for five straight days, until there is no longer any sign of humankind.

Travis delivers this whole harrowing recollection monologue with his back turned to the window, so that neither of them can see the other. His is a disembodied voice coming over the loudspeaker, creating an agonizing clash between the deeply intimate and painful details of their life story and the unrelated and impersonal nature of their way of remembering together.

About midway through the recollection, Jane begins to suspect that it is Travis. As the events of their life together and their apocalyptic finale unravel, tears start to stream down her face.

Now at the end of Travis's narrative, she walks to the window, speaks his name, and he turns to face her. For one excruciating moment their faces are reflected in each other's on the screen. Together they make up one image of one person. There is one complete face in/on the window/mirror/screen. They talk. She turns off the light on her side so that she can see him. Travis turns his table lamp directly onto his face and the mirror reverses. Now Jane can see him, his ghostly, lit-up visage, and he can see only his own reflection. But he still cannot bring himself to look at her. Again, like Orpheus, he has recalled her from the dead and yet feels forbidden to look at her.

When Travis starts to leave, she pounds on the window with both fists and implores him to stay. He does. And now turning her back towards him, she has her turn to remember. Jane tells her much briefer, in a way, much sadder story: how she ran away with Hunter, gave him up because she could not take care of him, and came to work at the Keyhole Club. She recalls how she thought of Travis for long afterwards, how she would rehearse what she would say to him and what he would say back, and then how his image and his voice slowly disappeared, until there was nothing of him left. She ends her story by saying that now he has completely faded for her: "Everything stopped. You just disappeared. And now I'm working here. I hear your voice all the time. Every man has your voice" (95).

Travis tells Jane that he has brought Hunter with him and that he wants to see her. She is stunned at first, but quickly agrees to meet Hunter and take him with her if that is what Hunter wants. Travis tells her she will find him in room 1520 of the Meridian Hotel.

In the final scene of the movie, the coda, she goes to pick up Hunter. Travis watches the hotel from a nearby parking garage roof. Hunter and Jane embrace. Travis drives away. There is a red sunset. The film ends.

In Search of Soul

Turning now to a psychological discussion of the two great climactic scenes between Travis and Jane, we will see how the medium of *Paris, Texas* reveals the deeply patterned and poignant search for soul going on in America. We will focus on those aspects of their relationship which reveal how we project important parts of ourselves upon others and how we may need to recollect those parts for ourselves. As we watch Travis and Jane grope their way towards a kind of individuation in the entrails of the Keyhole Club, we become forcefully aware that the peepshow booth, despite its unlikely character, is *the* place of encounter, reunion, and separation. It reveals itself as a true source of soul-making, wrenching us from the daylight world down to our subterranean depths, to the labyrinthine coils of our own darkest passions. This most impersonal, detached, and unrelated of all places becomes, through their meetings, the locale of the most excruciating and painful mutual knowings and intimacies. In the realm of wounded sexuality where we all live, we too are lost souls, wandering in a hall of mirrors and forbidden doorways. There we too might hear the whispers of disembodied voices and see the powerful torments and bliss of our own imaginings. In the illusory world of the Keyhole Club, Travis and Jane meet behind windows which are also screens and shifting mirrors, ones which enable them to see their own reflections, as well as fleeting glimpses of the other. There, hiding behind microphones and muffling speakers, in that darkness of departed souls, they are able to speak the necessary words with each other. The paradoxical clash of opposites which *is* the sex club—distance and intimacy, impersonality and the most personal revelations, fears and wishes—becomes the focal point for recollection. This garish, illicit world is where remembering takes place.

Paris, Texas arrives at its denouement in a psychological hell,[6] in a world of ritualistic compulsions, debased fetishes, and voyeuristic fantasies. Among these many rooms for the thwarted and mirrored reflections of frustrated desire, Travis and Jane are finally able to re-member themselves.

---

[6] One of the last lines of Jean-Paul Sartre's play, *No Exit* (1944), is "L'enfer, c'est les Autres," "Hell is other people." Or the last scene in Luis Bunuel's film, *Simon of the Desert* (1965), after the devil has finally seduced Simon, the ascetic stylite, to leave his perch, they end up in a loud disco.

Remembering, as these scenes suggest, is done indirectly, with averted gaze, without direct looking. Recollecting is a ritual which is undertaken only obliquely, as one would make offerings to gods, or to the deceased. Remembering resists the direct, heroic approach. It does not yield to a John Wayne, Rambo, or Terminator. Descending to these depths, to the bowels of the club, one also risks dismemberment, madness, or death; and therefore, what is called for in the darkness of sexuality is reflection. One approaches the Medusa, the intolerable face we cannot bear to see within, armed like Perseus, with a sword *and* a mirror. The most horrible truths of our own past sometimes cannot be challenged face on—they may often demand careful and slow reflection.

The Keyhole Club of the unconscious, like the psychological consulting room, or Plato's cave, or the movie theatre itself, is a potential space for reflection and the recollection of projections in relationships, where seemingly outer things move to the inside of our lives. Each time we emerge from these depths blinking into the light of day, as we do each morning from our dreams, trying to adjust to the harsh glare of the upper world, we traverse a similar psychological ground. We all ascend to a grim day with the shreds and filmy tatters of dream images still clinging to our scattered limbs. As we stagger out of these most revealing of encounters, we are entangled in a binding web of projections, images, and shadowy reflections. The task remains the same: to sort through and separate out those valuable portions and pieces of our self, from the distorting projections woven out of the fear-based needs of our past.

What we gradually come to learn about Travis during the course of the film concerns his past. He has painstakingly replicated the disturbed bonds of his own original family in his relationship with Jane. His driving wish to regain his piece of paradise, that barren plot of land in Paris, Texas, where he was conceived, reflects his deep need to possess the loving mother he seemingly never had.

In marrying Jane, Travis's jealousy and possessive delusions come to the fore in his wish to have a completely exclusive, merged relationship. He unconsciously identifies with his father and his strange joke about Paris, city of eroticism and romance, and with the more serious, underlying need to turn the wife into the fantasized sexual partner she is not. He thus cannot let Jane out of his sight.

In buying a piece of land where he was conceived, Travis seems to want to crawl back into the womb of his mother, thereby recreating the paradisiacal state of union with her. This urge renders Jane totally passive, a fantasy object for his hypervigilant scrutiny. And so, also like his father, inexorably, he becomes mad, possessed, and ends by completely enslaving his wife, driving her to demoniacal acts.

Travis's delusional fantasies cross the invisible threshold from jealousy to paranoia as his childlike longings are challenged by Jane's increasingly desperate attempts to escape his suffocating clutches. The conflagration that follows appears inevitable. He must recollect his own soul, or become completely mad. Though he projects upon Jane the possibility of his redemption, his controlling persecution and torture of her arouses only hate and fear. She therefore, for her part, must flee his tyranny or die trying.

Years later in the peep show booth, when Travis is finally able to recall some of his projections upon Jane, he tells his story with his back to her, that is, by looking within and not at her at all. When at the end of his story, they do look at each other, we have that one amazing instant when their faces merge on the window/mirror/screen.[7] We see one Travis-Jane, male-female face. Their faces reflect each other's as their fates are intertwined. As their faces become one face, their stories become the same story. This kind of reunion at this depth, however, also makes possible a true separation; though agonizing, it is a more conscious sacrifice of their projections.

When Jane takes her turn to reclaim what shreds and fragments of her soul still adhere to Travis, she too turns her back to him, the better to recall her inner landscape. What is crucial now for both of them is to dissolve the enthralling mesh of projections they have upon each other; via the reflecting screen and mirror, they must get it right between them this time. They must try to fulfill their fates without the crippling distortions of each other they carry within.

In re-collecting themselves, their souls, in the presence of the other, speech, language, words, and hearing become paramount. It is as if articulating the words allows us to re-member our dismembered, dissociated bodies. We embody our projections and we need to remove them just as much from our own limbs and organs, gestures and postures, as we do from the significant others who carry them in our lives. These others, after all, live in our dreams, in the nonmaterial organ of our soul. Body and soul come together in remembering and we remember what we hear, voices, words, feeling tones, and sounds. Our entire collective and personal past lives in us in a vast sea of murmurings. It comes with the soft pounding of waves in our salt-tinged blood streams. The archetypal fabric of our souls is woven with words. Human speech and talking exists in order to tell our stories, where we have come from and where we are going. The voice, the tellings as the vehicles of the soul, must make our words bear the weight of our being.

---

[7] This scene rivals the literal and symbolic merging of identities and faces we find also in the much earlier film *Persona* (1966) by Ingmar Bergman. This merging and blending into one which precedes a separation and recollection of the projections, in films, takes place of necessity on a screen, in a mirror which can hold both identities as one and separate at the same time. The screen/mirror becomes the necessary medium for reflecting upon the soul, particularly for regaining the contrasexual portion of the personality which must become projected upon the other, be it parent, partner, or analyst. By recalling projections, one regains one's soul.

Our human way of relating and attempting to find meaning in our lives with others, in a community, within a culture, and in partnership, present us with both a mirror and a window to the soul. When two people meet with words in the depth dimension of the soul, mirror and window become indistinguishable. There we realize the inviolable truth: that we are each other. We as human beings are windows and mirrors for each other, that we might see, hear, and touch our own and each other's souls. The soul's deep, unceasing voices quietly and constantly urge us to be fully ourselves, to be and at the same time to know the deep ground of our being, our not-being, our sexuality, our darkness, our deaths, that we may truly fulfill our lives this time.

BIBLIOGRAPHY

Astrachan, Gary D. "Orpheus, the Lyre Player." *Harvest 38* (1992), 95–112
————. "Remembering, Holding, and the Soul." *Harvest 39* (1993), 60–70.
Brown, Norman O. *Hermes the Thief.* New York: Vintage, 1969.
Eliade, Mircea. *Myth and Reality.* New York: Harper and Row, 1963.
————. *A History of Religious Ideas*, Vol. II. Chicago: University of Chicago Press, 1982.
Harrison, Jane Ellen. *Prolegomena to the Study of Greek Religion.* London: Merlin Press, 1980.
Kearney, Richard. *The Wake of Imagination.* Minneapolis: University of Minnesota Press, 1988.
Kerenyi, Karl. *Hermes—Guide of Souls.* Zurich: Spring, 1976.
Leonard, Linda S. *On the Way to the Wedding.* Boston: Shambhala, 1987.
Lopez-Pedraza, Rafael. *Hermes and His Children.* Zurich: Spring, 1977.
Otto, Walter. *The Homeric Gods.* Great Britain: Thames and Hudson, 1979.
Sievernich, Chris, ed. *Paris, Texas.* Berlin: Road Movies and Noerdlingen: Greno Verlag, 1984.
Vernant, Jean-Pierre. *Myth and Thought among the Greeks.* London: Routledge, 1983.

Part III

The Mirror of Culture: Finding Ourselves Within

16

The Piano: From Constriction to Connection

DONALD WILLIAMS

Jane Campion says of *The Piano*, "I think that the romantic impulse is in all of us and that sometimes we live it for a short time, but it's not part of a sensible way of living. It's a heroic path and it generally ends dangerously." Certainly American culture shares this romantic impulse, and despite the Victorian setting of *The Piano*, we are no less isolated, constricted, even contorted, than the characters animating Jane Campion's film. We want to hear stories of passion but most of us learned to smooth over conflicts, to mute our excitement, and to express our sexual and loving selves guiltily or immaturely. Our values and impulses are as tangled as any Victorian tale. As a culture we value compassion and "good works" but we reward self-aggrandizing ambition. We value independence but reward the corporate deferential self. We champion individualism but submit to work in cubicles and go home to confining cells of credit card debt. We seek liberation from isolation and emptiness through the acquisition of money and consumer distractions, and when security and purchased pleasures fail to satisfy us, the fear of emptiness prompts a renewed, often more costly pursuit of happiness. As Americans we are much like Stewart in *The Piano* whose brush with passion leaves him saying, "I want myself back; the one I knew" (Campion 115). He wants the self who stoically tolerated isolation while steadily working to acquire more land. *The Piano* holds a mirror to our constricted lives while at the same time sparking a silent burning will to feel passionately alive and to love fully.

The Piano won the Cannes Palme d'Or Award and eight Academy Award nominations. Jane Campion received the Oscar for Best Original Screenplay, Holly Hunter the Oscar for Best Actress, and Anna Paquin the Oscar for Best Supporting Actress. The film provokes opposing reactions— a transcendent experience for some, a distressed or bored "didn't get it" experience for others. It is strangely difficult to say with conviction what this film is about. We remember its emotional tone and its images longer than its storyline. Images are the language of the psyche. We remember the image of an abandoned piano on an isolated beach, the surf sweeping around its legs, far from rescue, and the image haunts us. Or we see the piano plunging into the ocean, floating down in the water to a bed of perpetual silence.

The moving force of *The Piano* is Ada McGrath (Holly Hunter), a woman mute—no one knows why—since she was six years old. Ada leaves Victorian England for a marriage arranged by her father to join a husband-to-be in New Zealand. Traveling with Ada are her daughter, Flora (Anna Paquin), whose history remains a mystery to us, and her piano. Her husband, Stewart (Sam Neill), arrives a day late at the desolate beach where he arranged to meet Ada and Flora. When Stewart and his Maori helpers begin carrying her belongings up from the beach, Ada writes on the pad she carries around her neck, "THE PIANO," and Stewart, mistaking muteness for deafness, shouts back, "Too—heavy." There the piano will remain until Stewart leaves to survey his land and Ada, through force of will, prevails upon Baines (Harvey Keitel), the rough-looking Englishman turned half native, to take her back to the beach where she can play her piano. Ada's passion and will then proceed to endanger and transform everyone she touches.

Jane Campion said that she set out to explore the transforming power of eroticism and passion with three Victorian characters who had nothing—no words, stories, or codes of conduct—to prepare them for the power of sexuality. Yes, this sounds like the film I saw. The film, however, seems to be about many things, about the isolated, constricted self, about women in a patriarchal culture, about native culture and natural instincts under Western colonialism, about sexual and emotional repression, about loneliness and longing, about the relationship between passion and intimacy, about love and sacrifice, and about the failures of love.

The Victorian setting of the film places it close in time and theme to the sexual repression that generated Freudian theories of the unconscious and eventually psychoanalysis of all persuasions. The oppressive constraints on women, sexuality, and emotions forced life to assert itself in tortured symptoms. Remember that psychoanalysis began with an exceptionally intelligent and creative young woman who was confined as was customary to a "monotonous existence" in a puritanical family. She was left alone with no place to turn but to her "private theater," where she entertained and comforted herself with creative fantasies—not unlike Ada with her music. After tending her father, who was dying of tuberculosis, "Anna O." (Bertha Pappenheim) developed hysterical symptoms, and Dr. Josef Breuer (Freud's one-time mentor) was called in to treat her.

Breuer asked to be left alone with Bertha, then closed the wooden shutters, and pulled a chair close to Bertha's bed. He placed his long, sensitive fingers on her forehead, hypnotized her, and asked her to talk to him. He did not, however, instruct her to give up her symptoms, which

The Piano: From Constriction to Connection

was the usual treatment for hysteria at that time. Instead, Josef instructed her to talk to him in any of the languages she knew. And she began to talk.

With each succeeding visit, Bertha told her story, sometimes in German, sometimes in English. When she was angry and would not speak, Josef asked her to talk about her anger. When she would not eat, he fed her. His genuinely kind and gentle presence day after day soothed her. She looked forward to his visits, and she continued to talk. She introduced him to her "private theater." When Josef was present, the world was real, and she was alive and "in contact." Finally, she had found someone to follow her in a foreign language—hers—and to enter her world and match her intelligence and passion. Dr. Breuer, however, was frightened by the passion aroused in his patient and in him. When Bertha hysterically claimed to be pregnant with his child, Dr. Breuer fled her house and never treated hysterics again. But Freud was inspired by Breuer's experience and found there the seeds of psychoanalysis—repressed memories, talking, and listening. Psychoanalysis began at the turn of the century as sessions still begin today—with stories of constriction, isolation, and the emotions we defend ourselves against.

Jane Campion emphasized the power of sexuality—as Freud did—but I want to suggest another complementary interpretation of *The Piano*, one more compatible with Jung's broad insight that every individual, family, and culture casts a shadow, a cluster of emotions, ideas, and behaviors that are forbidden. The shadow is anything judged unacceptable or incompatible with our beliefs. As much as we have changed since the Victorian era, we still forbid certain feelings and ideas, and these forbidden "lives" will still seek some way, however contorted, to find air and light.

The Piano confronts us—passionately—with the harsh restraints that we face even in a "therapeutic" society. Every family, for instance, permits the expression of some emotions and some ideas while prohibiting the expression of other emotions and ideas. In one family it is acceptable, even necessary, to express aggressive criticism, competition, and ambition but forbidden by example and by fear to express tenderness or empathy. In another family, just the opposite is true. In a great many families sexual and angry feelings, thoughts, and impulses are unacceptable—they cannot be talked about. The restriction is often so complete that everyone acts as if such experiences did not even exist.

A great many people enter therapy saying, "I had a fairly happy childhood, a normal family," when in fact, to maintain their membership in the family, they had to believe that they were happy, normal children with normal parents. Perhaps they had to "shut down" in order to accept a father's beatings or a mother's emotionally vacant eyes. Perhaps they shut down any hint of intense emotion in order, at all costs, to protect and spare anxious parents. These are the familiar stories that therapists hear. No matter how rich our cultural soil may be, most of us are still surrounded by

entangled families at home, by workplaces where we must contort ourselves to survive, by impossible bureaucracies, unspoken rules, endless
telephone menus, and if we fall ill, the managed healthcare we pay for will
become as elusive as Kafka's castle. As Americans we like to see ourselves
as self-contained individuals (Cushman 2), but as Jung long ago diagnosed
us, we suffer from a loss of meaning, value, and soul. We can feel as easily trapped, empty, and bereft as do Ada, Stewart, Baines, and the others
who must struggle as they move through the unyielding tangle of vines,
tree trunks, and branches as they trek their way through the mud that
sucks up their steps, holds them back, and splatters their dark, binding,
Victorian clothes.

The Piano shows us abandoned, isolated, constricted characters who
suffer in silence but who will do almost anything to feel alive and to preserve that aliveness. Jane Campion's characters are as emotionally constricted as the crated piano on the isolated New Zealand beach, as isolated
as Ada who can play the piano but cannot or will not speak. The piano
can express the full range of human emotion—playful, sad, romantic, spiritual, passionate, lonely, violent, tender—but not when it remains boarded
up, not when it is bartered away for land. Words can express these emotions, too, but not if we do not know the words or cannot speak them—
and this is often our fate today, our cultural heritage. As Americans, we
grow up with forbidding restrictions—so forbidding often that we cannot
know that we are angry, or sexual, lonely, creative, or passionate. The constrictions work so well that we scarcely notice them.

Consider for a moment Flora's improvisation on her mother's muteness.
She tells the following story:

> "Mother used to sing songs in German and her voice would echo across the val-
> leys . . . That was before the accident . . . One day when my mother and father
> were singing together in the forest, a great storm blew up out of nowhere. But
> so passionate was their singing that they did not notice, nor did they stop as the
> rain began to fall, and when their voices rose for the final bars of the duet a great
> bolt of lightning came out of the sky and struck my father so that he lit up like
> a torch . . . And at the same moment my father was struck dead my mother was
> struck dumb! She—never—spoke—another—word." (Campion 31–32)

Flora's insight is penetrating. In this fantasy her father died and her
mother was struck dumb as punishment for their passion, for the joy of
their own voices. Many people and families do not tolerate passion well,
not in the Victorian era nor in America today. As much as we may long for
passionate experience, it is too frequently considered dark—shadowy—
and dangerous to our security. Passion, too, is easily confused with sex in
our culture, and we know that sex is dangerous.

The Piano is not restricted to its theme of sexual passion. Other emotions, thoughts, and actions are constricted, reined in: anger, fear, despair,

spontaneous play, joy, adult tenderness, empathy, compassion, gratitude, jealousy, ethical conflicts, and so on. The release of sexual passion in *The Piano* both incites and inspires other emotions, lifting the restrictions that have kept these emotions in check.

At the beginning of the film, we hear Ada's childlike voice, the voice in her head, saying, "I have not spoken since I was six years old. No one knows why, not even me. My father says it is a dark talent and the day I take it into my head to stop breathing will be my last. . . . The strange thing is I don't think myself silent, that is, because of my piano" (9). Her voice is cut off, her memory is repressed, and she presents us with a mystery that no one can fathom. Ada will do anything to have a voice—she stops at nothing to reach her piano. When pressed, she uses Flora for her voice, and when released by Baines, she uses her hands and her body to say what she must say. Most of us in Western culture, however, are more like Stewart than Ada or Baines: We prefer our stoicism and order to the dangers of excitement or love.

In the first onscreen image we see Ada in England, looking at the world through her splayed fingers, just as later she will see everything through boarded windows or through the tree trunks, vines, and branches of the New Zealand bush. In the background, we see a man trying to lead Ada's daughter, Flora, on a pony that stubbornly refuses to move. Later, Ada stands at a window in the moonlight and touches the curtain in an unconscious farewell.

Immediately the film cuts to an underwater view of the bottom of a long wooden boat cutting across the sea. Silence. Down under. Dreamtime. In another moment we see the "riotous"—passionate!—sea pounding an empty stretch of the New Zealand coastline. The beach is framed by steep cliffs and a dense forest. Seamen carry Ada McGrath in a large Victorian skirt on their shoulders through the rough surf to the beach. Others carry her ten-year-old daughter. Ada watches anxiously as the men struggle to carry her crated piano to shore. We see Ada sign to Flora and Flora speak to the seamen for her mother: These two feminine figures present a stubbornly united front, intending, if necessary, to stay where they are until they starve. Ada's husband is not there to meet them, and they do not know if he will ever arrive.

Later, with the boat now looking small in the distance, Flora becomes "aware of herself and distant, from both the boat and her mother" (16), and she runs frantically back up the beach to her mother. Cut to Flora sleeping in her mother's lap beside the piano while Ada's hand finds a way through a hole left by a broken board to reach a small stretch of piano keys. The camera shows us her hands close-up on the keys, hidden behind the boards. She begins the notes of the melody that will haunt the film. The comfort of the piano heightens their isolation. Suddenly, the rising tide sends a wave rushing under the crated piano—nothing is safe. This opening image captures the isolation that torments each character, and this isolation is the emotional core of the film. Great distances divide everyone. Later, sexuality breaks through all obstacles—Campion's theme—to transform people and open channels to every stifled impulse or feeling.

While pursuing the theme of isolation and constriction, I want to mention how and why screenwriters create clusters of emotional images and achieve psychological depth. Good writers do not weave images tightly because they learned to do this in English departments or film schools; they do it because this is how the psyche works. Good drama possesses a core conflict and an emotional tone that will inevitably influence a writer's choice of characters, actions, images, settings, and dialogue. As psychoanalysts affirm daily, images, words, and actions are not arbitrary; they carry unconscious but intelligent, meaningful responses to the world we experience. As Jungians assert, images are the natural language of the unconscious, of the unconstrained Self.

The multiple images of isolation and constriction in *The Piano* point to a central psychological complex. Carl Jung considered any unresolved conflict or ongoing psychological injury a "complex." A psychological complex (originating, say, with childhood neglect) can be triggered by any related experience (rejection or loss, for instance). When an experience approximates the original wound, the complex intrudes unexpectedly and can suddenly dominate our thoughts, feelings, and actions. The awakened complex carries an emotional tone or a familiar set of feelings. Psychological complexes commonly organize what we see, hear, remember, think, and feel. They attract specific feelings and repel others. When depressed, for example, we naturally notice experiences, ideas, and memories that confirm our depressed convictions, and we fail to notice anything too hopeful.

Within the first minutes of this consummately crafted film, we see images of the core complex that structures and colors everything that follows. The injury shared by each of the major characters—Ada, Flora, Stewart, and Baines—is emotional isolation. Along with this isolation comes the threat of loss, abandonment, loneliness, and failed connections with others. Ada and Flora are abandoned, left alone to wait at the edge of a wild sea for a stranger to arrive, God knows when. Their smallness and loneliness in this epic setting haunts us.

Other images of isolation, constriction, and failure to connect are just as movingly portrayed. These images seem fated and grow in power as they cluster and accumulate:

- Ada and Flora are isolated on a desolate beach waiting for someone they may not like and who may never come. Flora says, "I'm not going to call him Papa, I'm not going to call HIM anything. I'm not even going to look at him" (17).
- When Stewart does arrive with Baines and the Maori helpers, Ada does not respond to Stewart's questions, and he foolishly shouts, "Can—

you—hear—me?" Ada nods but is unresponsive. Stewart decides that they will carry everything with them except the piano.

- Ada shouts by writing in caps: "I NEED THE PIANO" but Stewart refuses (23). This is one more of many failures to connect, and a major one.

- When they have all climbed up the cliff from the beach, Ada looks down with anguish at the isolated beach and her piano as if she is leaving her soul in peril. This is a vision of loss that we all carry away from the film.

The next scenes show us people who are encumbered by the constrictions of culture, of unnatural Victorian clothing in a harsh natural environment. Ada struggles through mud and dense bush with petticoats, pantaloons, a hoop skirt, bodice, and delicate boots. Stewart's suit is splattered with mud but he wears his best clothes and a formal top hat nonetheless. This is a tortured wedding processional. After arriving at Stewart's home, it is time for the wedding pictures, and Ada, in a wedding dress, weaves her way over planks and logs while torrential rain pours across the mud and the dense bush outside Stewart's hut. She and her husband pose for their wedding photograph in the drenching rain. Clearly, nature is stronger than culture. Once inside, Ada pulls the dripping wet dress from her, ripping part of the gown in contempt.

Along with the constrictions of culture that separate people from themselves and from each other, there are the limits of language. Stewart cannot speak the Maori language and misunderstands their motives almost as often as he misunderstands Ada. Neither does he understand Baines, who identifies more closely with the Maori than with their small group of English companions. Baines, unlike Stewart, can speak the Maori language but he cannot read. Ada hears and understands everything that is said but she does not understand with the heart: painfully we watch her fail repeatedly to appreciate the separate needs and feelings of her daughter and of others. Ada treats Flora often as an extension of herself, often as her voice, as the one who speaks for her, and at other times she neglects her. The Maori are clearly puzzled by the English, but on the other hand, they may be the only people who know themselves: they are in their world, unashamed, freely curious, free to think their own thoughts.

Ada, more isolated in her own world than anyone, nonetheless experiences the most intense passion. Despite her silent will, she will do almost anything to express herself through the piano. Virtually autistic and separated from her piano, she carves piano keys onto the wooden table top in Stewart's kitchen and "plays" these piano keys she has etched. Flora sings, accompanying the silent piano. Ada hides the keys with the tablecloth when Stewart enters. Stewart reaches his hand under the tablecloth—as Ada reached through the crate to her piano—and his hand explores the keys. Along with him, as he discovers the intensity of her passion, we feel the emotional and erotic tension.

Despite the hold that the confined Ada has on our attention, Stewart and Baines in their own ways will also do almost anything to break their isolation, to feel alive and not alone. Stewart marries, sight unseen, a mute woman from England and dedicates himself passionately to the acquisition of land. Baines, on the other hand, seeks the society of the Maori, learns their language, forges genuine friendships, and marks his face as they do. Much like Ada, Stewart, and Baines, we contort and constrict ourselves, repress our vitality, and yet we still look for ways to feel alive as relentlessly as plants look for the light.

Everyone experiences some sense of being cut off from others, disconnected, but we see the greatest tension within Ada as she suffers the separation from her piano like a child separated from her mother. Finally, in an exercise of indomitable will, she prevails with Baines, and he takes Ada and Flora back to the beach while Stewart is away. When her fingers touch the keys and she begins to play, we see Ada smile for the first time, a warm, animated, and unexpected smile. And in the distance we see Flora dancing with grace and innocent joy as she waves seaweed from her outstretched hands, and the seaweed is caught up in the wind like beautiful ribbons. As Baines stands by and watches, he is drawn irresistibly to Ada. Upon their return, Baines trades Stewart land for the piano, and with the help of Maori friends he brings the piano to his hut. He barters with Ada and offers the piano back to her in exchange for "lessons." In his lessons he will study her, but never the piano.

If we follow the rest of the film, we experience one obstacle after another that interrupts self-expression, understanding, insight, and almost any clear human connection. And when Baines and Ada do finally learn to love each other, it sets off emotions that no one is prepared to manage.

The following is a list of moments—images—that continue to capture feelings of isolation, failed vision and empathy, frustrated desire and love, despair, rage, and loss.

- The piano is out of tune.
- The blind piano tuner feels for his glasses with an uncertain hand.
- The piano is a Broadbent, a fine piano and the only one on the islands—another hint of isolation. Now the piano is "tuned, but silent."
- When Ada plays the piano for Baines, Flora has to wait outside and endure her loneliness.
- While Ada plays the piano, Baines lies underneath the piano and watches Ada's stockinged calves as her feet work the pedals. One of the stockings has a small hole. Baines touches the white skin of her calf through the hole in her stocking. He reaches through to her skin the way she reached through the crate to find piano keys and music.

- Similarly, Flora looks through cracks and holes in Baines's hut. She sees the naked bodies of Baines and Ada but never fully.
- Stewart discovers his wife's affair, and he, too, succumbs to curiosity and watches them through a crack in the wood of Baines' hut. Wood planks separate him just as boards kept Ada's hands from the piano.
- Enraged by Ada's betrayal, Stewart barricades Ada inside the house and nails boards over the windows. Again she is cut off, isolated.
- The piano is returned to Ada at Stewart's hut but she will not play it.
- When Flora begins to play for Stewart and her mother, Ada walks away. She abandons them.

All of these images cluster around the core sense of isolation, silence, and loss. The characters are isolated by emotions and longings they cannot express, by physical obstacles, by misunderstandings, and by the constrictions of character that are as inevitable as fate. Ada maintains her isolation by willfully not learning to speak. She isolates herself with her piano and her daughter whom she uses as an intermediary between her and the world. Strangely, it is Ada, who is self-absorbed, ruthlessly willful, and more attached to her piano than to any living person who transforms everyone. Virtually autistic except at the piano and only erratically connected with her daughter, the most emotionally unattuned character forces each person out of their isolation. She awakens sexual passion in Baines, and without knowing it, inspires his love. He in turn teaches her to love and to experience feelings and thoughts that sometimes transcend the music she plays. Her passion and emerging ability to make contact with others besides Flora also forces her daughter to experience herself independently of her mother and to experience her own will, her own longings for a family.

Stewart barricades Ada in his hut and prevents her from seeing Baines. One night she walks into Stewart's bedroom with a candle (echoes of Eros and Psyche).[1] She pulls the sheets back while he sleeps, and tenderly strokes his neck, shoulders, and chest. Stewart's eyes well up with tears as he experiences her "like a nurse spreading ointment on a wound" (89). Stewart breaks their connection—the emotions are too overwhelming for him. He decides to trust Ada but it is short-lived, and the images of isolation, longing, and passion move toward their finish:

- Ada inscribes her love for Baines on the side of a piano key which she wraps up and gives to Flora to take to Baines.

---

[1] In this well-known myth about the soul's relationship with love, the lovely mortal Psyche is taken to the god Eros's castle to be his lover, but told she must never gaze on him. When she finally must look, in the night, she is amazed at the beauty of this great god of love. But she spills oil on him from her lamp, and he awakens and flees. She must undergo long and difficult trials to win him back.

- Ada's unrelenting passion for Baines forces Flora to choose between Stewart and Baines. Flora betrays her mother and gives her loyalty to Stewart and to her desperate hope for a family. She calls Stewart "Papa," and for the first time experiences herself independently of her mother. Flora gives the piano key to Stewart.
- Baines discovers the piano key being worn by one of the Maori as an earring—out of place, disconnected.
- Baines trades a gun, his glasses, and his belt for the piano key but then he cannot read the writing Ada has inscribed.
- Baines asks some young children to read the writing for him but it's difficult for them because this is "running writing," script. The girls repeat the words without understanding.
- Stewart, in a wild rage, drags Ada out of the house through rain and mud to the chopping block where with an axe he cuts off the index finger of her right hand.
- Stewart wraps up the finger and tells Flora to take it to Baines.

Stewart enters Ada's room, disconsolate, remorseful, still angry. He holds the lamp up to see Ada in bed, and he studies her face (another reference to Eros and Psyche). Ada hears nothing that Stewart says. When he straightens her gown, he touches her leg, keeps his hand there, and becomes unexpectedly aroused. He undoes his belt as he watches her, feverish and unconscious. When he begins to move on top of her, he is startled and ashamed when he sees her staring directly at him. He quietly withdraws but not before sensing that Ada is "speaking" to him.

In the scene where Stewart's sexuality suddenly asserts itself, he is shocked to "see" Ada for the first time. He leaves carrying a candle in a lantern and walks past the ghostly tree stumps to Baines's hut. Stewart has come face to face with a mystery beyond words. Ada has opened Stewart to his loneliness, to jealousy and rage, to sexuality, and finally to an uncanny compassion. He asks Baines, "Has Ada ever spoken to you?" Then we learn how she has spoken to Stewart. He explains, "I heard her voice. There was no sound, but I heard it here," as he presses his forehead with his open hand. He continues, "She said, 'I have to go, let me go, let Baines take me away, let him try and save me. I am frightened of my will, of what it might do, it is so strange and strong'" (115).

Stewart has experienced passion, despair, intimacy, and understanding beyond anything he ever imagined. But he wants himself back. He will rely on his goal to acquire land and prosper to contain the loneliness and the longing he cannot satisfy. He is unattuned to others but not insensitive. Stewart knows how terribly alone he is. Out of love for Ada and an awareness of his limits, he chooses solitude. He tells Baines to leave and to take Ada and Flora with him.

Only through their sacrifices do the characters resolve their internal conflicts and unexpectedly transcend their isolation. We again see a growing coherence to the images that cluster around the act of sacrifice. To appreciate the sacrificial theme we need to return to the theme of the symbolic association between the piano keys and Ada's fingers, to the piano keys that possess Ada's love and Ada's fingers that erotically touch the keys and later touch the naked bodies of Baines and Stewart. Baines is aroused watching Ada's fingers stroke the polished ivory. The piano keys are bartered and sacrificed, piece by piece, in the agreement between Ada and Baines: Baines agrees to return the piano in exchange for one visit for each black key. His generous sexuality, affection, and open curiosity first awaken Ada's sexuality, later her love.

Later, Ada betrays Stewart when she sends a piano key to Baines with the words engraved: "Dear George, You have my heart, Ada McGrath" (94). Flora betrays her mother's wish and gives the piano key to Stewart. In a rage Stewart chops off Ada's index finger with an axe. When he tells Flora to give the wrapped finger to Baines, it is with the warning that "if he ever tries to see her again I'll take off another and another and another!" (104). Stewart's violent threat is a hellish transformation of the bargain between Ada and Baines. With each variation in this cluster of sacrificial associations, we sink deeper into grief and despair.

When Baines, Ada, and Flora leave on a boat ferried by Baines's Maori friends, Baines insists on taking the piano despite Ada's protests that the piano is contaminated and the protests of his friends who believe the weight of the piano will tip over the boat. In the rough sea Ada signs to Flora: "She says, throw the piano overboard." "PUSH IT OVER," she mimes, and the oarsman echoes her, "Yeah . . . push the coffin in the water" (120). The Maori maneuver the piano into place and heave it overboard. As loose ropes once holding the piano "snake" past Ada, she curiously places her foot within the loop. The rope catches her up, pulls her over, and she hangs in the water as she sinks with the piano. Suddenly she begins to fight against the rope, she slips it off her foot along with her shoe, and she struggles to the surface. This is the final sacrifice. She sacrifices her willful isolation for an attachment to other people and to life.

Later, she will even learn to speak: "I teach piano now in Nelson. . . . I am learning to speak. My sound is still so bad I feel ashamed. I practise only when I am alone and it is dark" (122).

Sacrifice precedes the powerful resolution of the impossible conflicts in this film. Stewart sacrifices Ada to restore her and he regains himself. Flora finds her own voice when she risks the complete sacrifice of her mother's love. Baines sacrifices land, then the piano, then Ada, and after regaining her, finally sacrifices his old identity entirely for Ada and her love. On Ada's side, she sacrifices the piano for her love of Baines, for Flora, and for her own will to live. She unexpectedly finds the voice she silenced as a child and the love she perhaps never knew.

Affectionate hands and violent hands, erotic impulses and emotional longings, sexual fingers, piano keys, obstacles of every kind, and unexpected sacrifices are bound tightly together in this film of isolation and the transforming powers of sexuality and love. The film moves as relentlessly as the rough swells that pound the beach and wash up to and rush around the piano. In the final dream-like scene, we see the piano on the floor of the sea with Ada floating in surrender above it, and we hear her voice: "At night I think of my piano in its ocean grave, and sometimes of myself floating above it. Down there everything is so still and silent that it lulls me to sleep. It is a weird lullaby and so it is; it is mine" (122).

The universal acclaim for *The Piano*, its many awards, and the depth of reactions of those who liked the film touch a hopeful chord. The characters in this film speak powerfully to us with their actions, their hands, a piano, and few words. How different this is from our American never- ending and always-talked-about quest for relatedness and our determination to confront and resolve family "issues"! This film finds its depth with a small but universal story and with recurring, shifting images that accumulate emotional force. With these images *The Piano* takes us into the director's dream and a dream of Western culture. In the opening minutes of the film, when, from underwater, we see the hull of a long wooden boat move swiftly above us, we know that we have entered a dream wholly. We can hope that this film of isolated, disconnected selves who risk everything and transform will inspire emotional courage in us to touch others and risk being touched. This film may help us to respect our dreams and stories and to say about them, like Ada: Mine is a strange story and so it is; it is mine.

BIBLIOGRAPHY

Campion, Jane, director. *The Piano*. Videocassette. New Zealand: Miramax Films, 1993.

Campion, Jane, and Jan Campion. *The Piano*. New York: Miramax Books, 1993.

Cushman, Philip. *Constructing the Self, Constructing America*. Reading, Massachusetts: Addison-Wesley, 1995.

Freeman, Lucy. *The Story of Anna O.* New York: Paragon House, 1990.

Rosenbaum, Max, and Melvin Muroff, eds. *Anna O: Fourteen Contemporary Reinterpretations*. New York: The Free Press, 1984.

17
Another Look at Co-dependency

JOHN DESTEIAN

Over the last decade or so I have heard countless allusions to this behavior or that behavior being "co-dependent," from mental health professionals, newscasters, media-types, psychotherapy clients, and the average Joe and Jill on the street. As I have heard it discussed, more often than not the context is pejorative, co-dependency being an affliction from which we need to recover. Husbands have said to wives: "You're co-dependent," if she has shown interest in their children's school work. Wives have said to their husbands: "You're co-dependent," if he has wanted to take his elderly mother grocery shopping. I hear clients diagnose their desires as co-dependent and their solution is to say to themselves, "Knock it off!"

Co-dependency has become big business, with book sales shooting through the roof, and weekend workshops and psychotherapy groups springing up everywhere. But, co-dependency is not a new phenomenon. For decades it was called hostile dependency. I want to debunk the myth that co-dependency is a disease. Rather, when we strip away the masks we show the world, we see in ourselves the ebb and flow of hostility and dependency (co-dependency) which is at the heart of our human longing to be attached individuals.

Come Close—Stay Away

Hostile dependent relationships have been brought to life in popular works like the play *Who's Afraid of Virginia Woolf*, the radio series *The Bickersons*, and the film *The War of the Roses*. We don't have to be professionals to see the salvos of hostility lobbed back and forth, but if we look closely we see other dynamics, as well: intolerance, tyranny, blaming, rigidity, rejection, pleading, demands, threats, low self-esteem, narrow self-image, depression, anxiety, and sexual inhibition or low sexual drive. Strangely, if we see these people individually, without their partners, they often appear utterly different. Some may appear independent, capable,

231

warm, caring, and friendly; others may appear quiet, reserved, anxious, guilty, and insecure. Only some maintain their combative demeanor.

This description omits any mention of love. Where is the love? A couple came to me after forty years of marriage. They and their children, now mature adults, described year upon year of conflicts. Now he had cancer. During the course of the therapy, while they were saying good-bye to each other, as death approached, an outpouring of love and affection, tenderness and warmth flooded the family. The adult children were amazed. They had suggested divorce since they were youngsters, but now they saw a love that had never been apparent before.

A woman became severely depressed and suicidal when her former husband, from whom she'd been divorced for twenty years, died in an auto accident. They'd been divorced four times longer than the brief five years of their marriage. Their divorce had been bloody, and had carried over into post-divorce litigation that went on for years.

How are we to understand these stories? They seem to suggest that we love each other in the midst of our hatred, or vice versa, we hate each other in the midst of our love. What keeps these couples emotionally connected?

A woman in a couple's therapy session describes to me how she had cooked dinner the previous night, but her husband had shown up an hour late, without calling. The kids, screaming from hunger, were fed after half an hour, but she waited for her husband. "Why?" I asked. She said she waited because once before when he was late she had gone ahead and eaten and he had become furious. I turned to the husband and asked, "What about that?" "Yes, of course, that's true, and I would have been mad if she hadn't waited last night, too." The woman was hurt and angry that he didn't call. And he was angry that she was upset. This is a common and maddening stand-off.

Don't you have to wonder why couples like this stay together, or how they got together in the first place? If we listen to the co-dependency people and read their literature, we are told that upwards of 96% of the American population suffers from this disorder of co-dependency, and the underlying addictive disease process (Schaef 14). Ann Wilson Schaef says in her book, *Co-Dependence: Misunderstood—Mistreated*, that we mental health professionals who do not see the co-dependency problem as it is are blinded by our own disease (4, 7, 31).

It is clear that "co-dependency" problems exist in the intrapsychic, interpersonal, and spiritual realms. However, if so many people exhibit a particular set of attitudes and behaviors, can they be termed sick? How can something that happens to everyone be called sick? I hope to show that hostile dependency is typical expression of being human.

Going back to the couple I just mentioned: the woman can't stand her husband's anger and pouting for days. He won't talk to her; he won't look at her; he makes snide comments about her to the kids, to her face and behind her back. What is she so frightened of? If he were her seven-year-old son behaving this way, she might be angry, limiting, or even amused. What is stirring in her when her husband acts like a child who has not gotten his way? This is about her psychic structures.

From the other side, he'll be "damned" if he'll account to his wife for his time. What's so threatening about accounting for his time? Does he really want her not to care if and when he comes home? Of course not, otherwise he wouldn't be mad if she went ahead and ate without him. His dependency is expressed here by his anger when she acts independently. He refuses to be "hen-pecked." What stirs in him that to behave otherwise risks loss of his manhood? These conflicts have little to do with the partner, but rather with his psychic structure. However, they are only seen as they become visible in the relationship.

Not all marriages exhibit the gross symptoms of the frankly hostile dependent relationship. Take a type of modern marriage, for example, where the woman and man live in different cities, meeting only for weekends and vacations. They lead separate lives and come together only when it is convenient for both. They seem pleasant and chummy, have their own circles of friends, career interests, and activities, and respect one another's independence and integrity. They commingle nothing, except when they are having sex. These people may well be hostile dependent too. Only they compensate by creating a union that is no union. These marriages hit snags if either partner expresses an unexpected feeling or desire (a baby, time together, insecurity, jealousy, for example), and hostility is soon to follow. In such a case, whether it is couched as "feedback," or "constructive criticism," or analysis of the other partner's psychological condition, the partner's response is felt, and meant to be experienced, as hostile and disapproving.

Hostile dependency is a continuum, from the grossest example of overt hostility and dependency on one extreme, to the independent, uninvolved compensation on the other extreme. Hostile dependency underlies all relationships, just as Shaef says, not because it is the expression of an addictive process. It is because it is the expression of the two primary goals of individuation (i.e., coming to consciousness of oneself in the world). Those goals are *autonomy* and *attachment* (Desteian 55ff.).

It is here that the co-dependency "experts" fail us. The idea of autonomy as a return to health presupposes an original or earlier state of autonomy. When has a human being ever been born autonomous? And the idea of attachment as a return to health presupposes an original state of attachment. When has a human being ever been born attached? While we are all born predisposed to the possibility of autonomy and attachment, we were, in fact, born as hostile dependent babies. As infants we felt a wealth of undifferentiated needs (dependency), and had tools like screaming, crying (hostility), and smiling available to express them. We used some of those same tools to express our disappointment and anger if we didn't get our needs satisfied.

Bowlby has written extensively on child development, based on years of observation of infants and toddlers. Essentially, he says that we are born predisposed to form attachments when we encounter attachable behaviors in our caregivers. But these attachments may be strengthened, weakened, or even terminated, depending on the kinds of reactions we get from our caregivers. This predisposition, he says, expands after birth into the discriminating and sophisticated relational systems of later infancy, childhood, and adulthood, mediating attachments for the rest of our lives (210ff.).

Bowlby spurns a word like dependence because it is not only pejorative but inaccurate. "Attachment" provides a better description of the phenomena of early relationships, and is more likely to evoke our sympathetic responses. He says clinicians are apt to use dependency terminology to apply judgments to those who show "inappropriately" frequent and urgent attachment with little regard for the internal and environmental factors affecting the person at the time of observation (228ff.).

Equally likely to skew observations are the cultural and subcultural norms of the observer. If we believe independence is the ideal way to be, we will see dependency as abnormal, at best, or pathological, at worst. Bowlby contends that the observer's biases play an important role in categorizing individual behaviors (228ff.).

Of course, there are people who seem to be more likely to express urgent desires for attachment, and to feel crestfallen or even devastated when the attachment is broken when someone leaves, disappoints, or withdraws. These are the people we find in the most obvious of hostile dependent relationships, like the woman who didn't eat dinner until her husband came home. But Bowlby, here too, denies us the satisfaction of the dreaded label "dependent." He says these people are not truly dependent either; they suffer the effects of "anxious attachment" (230ff.).

There we have it! The dependent end of the hostile dependent relationship is, in fact, anxious attachment. Our whole attitude toward these behaviors changes if we see the fear and anxiety to maintain attachment which motivates them.

If we can recognize the purpose and sources of anxieties and fears, we can also understand the angry end of the hostile dependency continuum. Understanding the connection between anxiety and anger, however, doesn't necessarily make acceptable associated behaviors like battering or verbal cruelty. Indeed, we hear and read about too many instances of anger crossing over the line to assault and even murder. Fears are a natural part of human experience, beginning in infancy, and stay with us to one degree or another throughout our lives. Bowlby suggests that pathology exists where fears are absent or where fear is aroused with unusual readiness and intensity. Fears and certain behaviors associated with them are a natural expression of the survival instinct, he says, and anxiety serves the function of warning that danger is present, and that the individual must be on guard (119ff.).

Anger is an instinctive and predictable response to separation and the fear of separation. So, we could also say that we become aggressive in the service of attachment. Bowlby describes the process of moving from a state of affection to anxious attachment with resentment, as attachment needs are disappointed (245ff.). Marital therapists see this kind of resentful behavior with couples who, almost every night, come home from work and argue. Having been apart the whole day, their first encounters with one another will often degenerate into anger: who will cook, who is late, and so on. These couples' arguments stem from anxieties around attachment and separation. It is the particular realm of depth psychology to elucidate how conflicts like these live within a person, while at the same time they are expressed as behavior in relationships.

The Intrapsychic View: The Bloody Room

The fairy tale which epitomizes the internal tensions which are the source of anxious attachments is "Fitcher's Bird," a Grimm Brothers' tale (216ff.). It is about a wizard who took the form of a poor man and went begging from house to house, hoping to catch and kidnap pretty girls. One day the wizard, in poor man's disguise, appeared at the door of a man who had three pretty daughters. When the door opened, he begged for a little food, and when the eldest daughter came out to hand him some bread, he touched her and she was forced to jump into his basket. He carried her back to his house in the forest and provided her with whatever she desired, promising that she would be happy with him and that she would have everything that she could want. After a few days, he announced to her that he would have to leave for a brief while. He gave her the keys and told her she could go anywhere and look at anything in the house except for one room, which a little key opened. Into that room she dare not go on pain of death. He also gave her an egg and said, "Preserve the egg carefully for me and carry it continually about with you, for a great misfortune would arise in the loss of it" (Grimm 217).

She took the key and the egg, promising to obey him. She went through all the house and when she came to the forbidden room, her curiosity got the better of her. She took the key out, opened the door, and walked in. Horrified, she saw a bloody basin in the middle of the room, and in it lay human beings, dead and hewn to pieces. A gleaming ax lay atop the basin, blood dried to its sharp edge. She was so alarmed that she dropped the egg she carried with her, and it fell into the basin. Grabbing it out of the basin, she wiped at the blood, but it wouldn't come off. She washed and scrubbed it, but it would not come clean. When the man returned, he asked for the key and the egg; she gave them to him, but when he saw the red spots on the egg, he knew she had been in the bloody chamber. So he took her into the room and cut her up into little pieces. Her blood oozed on the ground, and the wicked wizard threw her dismembered body into the basin with those of his earlier victims.

Looking for another bride, the wizard returned to the same poor man's house and snatched his second daughter. The same course of events repeated itself. He left after a short while, and gave her the key and the egg, and the same warning. Upon discovering her disobedience he hacked her to pieces too and threw her into the basin. Now, he returned for the third daughter. When the time came for him to leave her in the castle alone, he handed her the key and the egg, and departed. However, the third daughter put the egg in a safe place, with great care, and only then did she examine the house. At last, she entered the forbidden room. She saw her dead sisters there, murdered, cut into pieces. She gathered their limbs together and put them in order: head, body, arms, and legs, and when she finished, the limbs began to move, and both maidens opened their eyes and were once more alive. On his arrival, the man again demanded the keys and the egg. Since he could see no trace of any blood on it, he said, "You have stood the test. You shall be my bride." He had no power over her now and from then on, was forced to do whatever she wanted. Needless to say, what she desired was his destruction, and the rest of the tale is taken up with the attainment of this goal.

What is this locked room, this bloody center around which the tale forms? It is an image of the place in our development that is so painful, so bloody, and so disturbing that we keep away from it at all costs. Whether we pathologize it by calling it co-dependency, or leave it as a fairy tale image, it is nevertheless the room where repressed parts of our personality lie, hacked to pieces, a place we dare not go, without the feeling that we may die.

How can we understand the construction and contents of this room? In childhood, interactions between our developing personalities and our environment produce collisions. The child's personality does not develop only from the outside in, but also from the inside out. We not only take on traits from what we see in the world, but qualities in the personality arise from inside us as well, from the unconscious. This is what Bowlby meant about our having a predisposition to attachment, and a set of behaviors organized to further attachment. The unconscious predisposition becomes conscious through collisions and encounters with the outer world. Encounters with people who satisfy the child's desires contribute to the development of the capacity for attachment. However, collisions with the environment may also be experienced as conflict, certainly where disapproval is present, even when there is no apparent conflict. We often experience our differences (traits, desires, attitudes, and so on) from others (parents, friends, teachers, and so on) as inferiority or inadequacy, and thus, as unacceptable. We feel shame or guilt and try to hide the difference in order to preserve the attachment we feel it threatens. We call this attempt to hide parts of ourselves *repression*.

The more the repression, the more we inhibit our personalities. It doesn't necessarily happen all at once. We may try to keep a trait/desire/attitude alive, but repeated experience may cause so much tension that we finally let go of it. Attachment to ourselves collides with attachment to another. With repression, anxiety and the trait/desire/attitude go into the locked room. It, then, contains the disjoined, split-off, repressed possibilities of personality which are hidden away from consciousness.

Who, then, is the Fitcher's bird? He is someone who takes people into intimate relationships, but cuts them to pieces when they enter his locked room. But he is also shame: that mean-spirited, magical guardian of our deepest secrets, longing at one moment, dismembering the next. Schaef and others, Gershom Kaufman among them, are quite right in seeing shame as the basis for co- or hostile dependency. Shame is the wizard, locking away unacceptable desires or traits, standing guard lest they escape.

Shame's psychological function is to preserve adaptation to our environment. Like anger, it is a survival instinct with the goal of preserving attachment: for the child, it is relative to their parents, friends, teachers, and the world at large; and for the adult, it is relative to their outer world, spouse, children, employer, and so forth. Shame serves an inner function as well: to preserve attachment to a tolerable image of ourselves. The locked room, its bloody contents and the Fitcher's bird, shame, are the inner dangers that we sense the presence of. We react with an instinctive survival response, either withdrawal (motivated by shame) or anger (motivated by defense). The sensed presence of the locked room is the source of our anxious attachment, not only to the spouse, but also to the self-image (the wizard's castle) we have constructed over the years expressly to protect us from knowing our whole selves, neediness and all.

When we fall in love we often, or perhaps always, take the beloved on a tour of our locked room, our most poignant and intimate places, as we express our disappointments and hurts about our families, teachers, and friends. But then, the room closes up and the stories fade in our memory as we try to get on with life together. Our partners don't forget. They often silently vow never to bring up these stories in a misguided attempt to make their spouses feel better, aware on some level of the shame wrought by memory of the locked room. But this vow also keeps them out of their own room. In effect, they say to each other: *I won't do to you what I don't want you to do to me.* An unspoken and unconscious compact results, with the purpose of keeping both partners out of their respective bloody rooms.

Taking the partner into the locked room is an act of attachment and staying away from that room requires detachment, distance. With distance comes loss, and with loss comes anger. It is not anger consciously experienced as the longing for attachment, but angry demands, for example, that the partner stay home more often. The loss of intimacy brought about by avoiding the locked room creates detached distance. Over time, unconscious despair of ever again feeling attached collides with the fear of the locked room. So fights about who takes out the garbage are the anger of despair, the expression of loss of hope for intimacy, interpersonally and also intra-psychically, with those parts of ourselves locked away in that bloody room.

The "Happy" Ending

"Fitcher's Bird" is not so much about a love gone wrong as an inevitable bloodbath. The equilibrium designed to preserve a safe attachment is bound to break down. If we can remember that both partners have this room, and each wants the other to stay out, we see that both are headed for a collision between their need for attachment and desire for autonomy. When he is hostile, her room is threatened, because in that room are all her experiences of abandonment and rejection of herself. He becomes the threatening, abandoning, and devouring mother or father. Her attachment is threatened and she behaves like a child with anxious attachment. She becomes "dependent." But when she becomes hostile, and if she cannot be bullied out of her anger, he becomes like a child, experiencing his own anxious attachment.

In a couple's session, a male client was confronted by his wife about his lack of responsiveness to her. Although ever-vigilant to care for their functional lives together, Bob could not respond at all to Hazel's emotional needs. She pressed him in that session, never letting up on her demand that he connect to her emotional life. He tried to squelch her by becoming angry, but this did not shut her down. He tried blaming her, but this didn't work either. She had placed her egg in a safe place before she pressed on into his room.

Finally, he began to cry and talk about his loneliness, which brought a flood of memories of fear, abandonment, and despair. Without knowing this fairy tale, he even talked about how he felt as if a room had opened up in him and he hated what he saw. They talked warmly; she comforted him and he became very responsive to her as well. However, by the next session, the door had closed. Neither Hazel nor Bob brought up what had happened. Then, and in later sessions, she could recall what had happened, but was not the least bit interested in going back there. He had amnesia; when graphically reminded, he had vague pictures, but no memory that had any feeling with it. This standstill went on for weeks.

A while later they came to a session wanting to talk about their children. The kids were beginning to exhibit the same frustration, impatience, and anger as the parents. That night, after our session, the man had the following dream. *He and his wife had left their four-year-old daughter alone in a house, in a room, and when he realized this he rushed to the house. The door opened and a mass of hundreds of children's bodies, dead and dismembered, dumped out of the door, and he knew his daughter's body was among them.* Not only was Bob disturbed by this dream, but so also was Hazel. The dream brought them both back to that place we had been to earlier. He was terrified by the dream, but also beset by feeling-filled memories he had repressed from that earlier session. She talked about her locked room also, where she found her own cut-up bodies. She remembered the loss of a brother in a fire as a child. The grief she and her parents had felt was overwhelming. She was only five at the time, with needs of her own, and her parents were not available to her because of their grief. She learned to get along by letting herself be forgotten, by fading into the woodwork. Hazel, herself, could only stand being in need so long before shame overwhelmed her, before she would close the room up again. The result was that she didn't press him either. She followed a pattern, her needs fading, becoming concerned only with day-to-day events.

When partners can reach a place of relative security, it is amazing to see how resourceful they can be in figuring out how to solve life's daily problems. However, when couples and individuals want to argue about what he said and what she said, or what he did and what she did, the dread of the locked room is apt to be looming in the background.

Anxious attachment seems to be an underlying psychological situation in relationships because a primary motivation for relationships arises from the shrieks and moans emanating from the locked room. That is, whatever affection we feel for someone at the outset of a relationship is far outweighed by the unconscious anxiety meant to be quieted by being in a secure-feeling relationship. A misguided notion, not only of the co-dependency movement, but also of our culture generally, is that we *ought* to be secure by the time we reach adulthood, and that we *ought* to know how to love in a mature, adult manner. But this supposition fails to consider the inevitability of the locked room, and the protective behaviors which surround and emanate from it.

The hostile-dependent condition is an attempt at self-healing, with the unconscious goal to transform the contents of the locked room, and contribute to the development of love as a primary factor in the relationship. The attempt at self-healing can be seen in the predictability of the "comings together" and the "comings apart." Marital therapists recognize this, and if you reflect on your own fights, you may also notice that when one of you says this, the other can be counted on to say that; and then you will say this and the other will say that; and so on. The progression has the character of an unconscious ritual. Like a ritual, hostile dependent behaviors have a predictable course and goal. Like a ritual, the goal of these behaviors is to make something known.

The unconscious ritual occurring in hostile dependent relationships seems to revolve around images of death and transformation. Since the locked room may be at the center of the ritual, it is understandable that death images might be an active ingredient. The motif of death and resurrection, as in the fairy tale, seems to speak to something that is very deep in the human psyche: the necessity for life to be torn apart in order for it to be reborn anew.

The hostile dependent dance around the locked room is an unconscious attempt to renew passion in our lives. In the early days of our love relationships, we feel a wellspring of passion. We are enamored of each other: we talk to each another, we attend to each another, we do things together we have never tried before. But inevitably, tension between passion and the anxieties of attachment results in the imposition of an equilibrium, which is, in fact, a repression of passion. The passion of relationship becomes unconscious, and stability, predictability, and apparent security replace it, based on rules like: I'll do this, and she'll do that. Following these rules results in "trust."

Trust which is based on these rules, however, may inhibit interaction between individuals. Often, trust is an unconscious foreshortening of the phrase, "I trust that you will follow the explicit and implicit rules of our relationship, so I can avoid suffering." It means, "I won't talk about your locked room if you won't talk about mine." It may also mean: "You'll call me when you're going to be late for dinner." It certainly means, in the vast majority of relationships, "You'll be true to me." Whatever the underlying agreements are, the longing to trust expresses the desire to become unconscious. It is the desire to let go of the anxiety which requires humans to be alert. If we trust, we needn't pay attention. If we trust, we can fall asleep. We needn't attend to the locked room.

Since humans are fallible, we are, by definition, untrustworthy. What happens, then, when trust is breached? Our man, from an earlier example, doesn't call at 5:30, knowing he will be late. When his wife says, "I trusted you to call," she is really saying, "I trusted you to call so I didn't have to work at finding *my* response to your not calling. I don't trust *myself* to know what to do in that situation." When we trust, we place our anxiety in the hands of another person. Then, if we can manage them, we don't have to deal with our anxieties.

The psychological (in contrast to the instinctual or economic) goal of relationship is gaining entry to that room, putting the bodies back together and breathing life into them. But it is also a life task. Co-dependency theory recognizes the locked room and sees the importance of entering it. Some may even correctly describe its contents: anxiety, envy, jealousy, competition, and other so-called petty feelings. But co-dependency theory is just as likely to add new bodies to the locked room as it is to breathe new life into the dismembered bodies still there.

As I mentioned at the outset of this essay, we are not born autonomous, but dependent. If anxious attachment is repressed in adulthood, more bodies are added to the room, recapitulating earlier developmental experiences. The ideals and goals espoused in co-dependency theory are essentially dominated by patriarchal images of separation and detachment. Attachment and involvement (read, traditional feminine/ maternal desires) are seen as neurotic. Like the JUST SAY NO slogan of the Reagan years, the co-dependency movement has come to expect suppression and repression of so-called dependency impulses. These mechanisms require the heroic attitude of Herakles,[1] when he dismembered the seven-headed Hydra, and we risk developing a compulsive independence.

From a depth perspective, co-dependency theory has an almost exclusive reliance on the personalistic, literal outer aspects of a person's life. That means that individuals fail to come alive to their inner world, their own relationship with the pain of being themselves. The practical importance of this failure lies in the fact that individuals are victims (or survivors) of their development, with no sense of secure attachment to themselves, let alone to another human being.

Finally, the most disturbing failure arises out of the fact that the so-called cure for common co-dependency is essentially anti-nature and anti-development. The real healing arises out of its own seeming impossibility. Clearly we find too little nutrition in detachment and independence to sustain ourselves. We need the nourishment of attachment and relationship. In the end it is the heat of the hostile-dependent condition, that is, the anger and the anxiety, which is attempting to feed (or heal) us, with the unconscious goal to transform the contents of the locked room, and to contribute to the development of love as a primary factor in the relationship.

BIBLIOGRAPHY

Bowlby, J. *Attachment and Loss.* 2 vols.
    Vol. I: *Attachment.* New York: Basic Books, 1982.
    Vol. II. *Separation.* New York: Basic Books, 1973.
The Complete Grimm's Fairy Tales. No. 46: "Fitcher's Bird." London: Routledge, 1978
Desteian, J. *Coming Together—Coming Apart: The Union of Opposites in Love Relationships.* Boston: Sigo Press, 1990.
Schaef, A. Wilson. *Co-Dependence Misunderstood—Mistreated.* San Francisco: Harper and Row, 1986.

---

[1] Also known as Hercules.

18
Dirty Politics, Clean Voters?

MARY ANN MATTOON

Since 1932, when American theologian Reinhold Niebuhr wrote *Moral Man and Immoral Society* and, in fact, as far back as classical Greece and Rome, there has been a debate about how much political involvement is necessary and good in the life of an individual. No matter what is good, political participation in our time seems to be in a serious downtrend.

"I've had it up to here with politics," we often hear. "Politicians! They don't say what they are going to do. And if they do say, they don't do it." People complain that politicians are out of touch with their constituents, that they do not address the real issues and—as the number of political scandals mounts—that corruption reigns. A remarkable proportion of the population stands apart from political processes and does not even vote, in many cases with the excuse that "all politics is dirty."

Yet politics is vital to the health of our society. Decisions important to everyone are made via political processes. The right to speak and vote in a political forum is the very stuff of democracy. We must all ask ourselves: Are my hands really clean if I refrain from participating in these decisions?

My answer is that I cannot refrain; I disagree with the "politics is dirty" view of many of my compatriots. In addition to family influences (my parents' preoccupation with community/political affairs), I grew up in an era when responding to political events was inescapable. The Great Depression and the Second World War affected everyone, directly or indirectly.

The news media of those times carried political images that are still in the collective memory. Before the television era, we saw—in newspaper photos, magazines such as *Life*, and movie newsreels—lines of Nazi soldiers goose-stepping, reflecting the war orientation of their government. On the radio we heard Adolf Hitler's lengthy, harsh, German-language speeches and Franklin Roosevelt's reassuring voice. Woman suffrage was a decade or two old in the United States, with its memories of the movement's hunger strikes and brutal force-feeding. In the 1960s the unconventional attire of the hippies accompanied protests against the Vietnam War. How can I not take a stand on issues like these when they affect my life so profoundly and I have the privilege of citizenship in a country as powerful as the United States?

Many other life experiences that are not encapsulated in images point to the need for concern with the political world. Many of us experienced the uncertainty of economic and perhaps physical survival during the Great Depression. Those of us who are middle-aged or older have felt the threat—on the battlefield or the home front—of the bloodbath of the Second World War, which was waged to settle political issues. The controversy still rages over the political decision of the United States to drop not one but two atomic bombs. Even more of us have lived through what are called now the Black (or Civil Rights) Revolution and the Women's (or Feminist) Revolution, and we have seen their impact on the lives of virtually all blacks and women—and on whites and males. We have experienced the disruption of our society over the political issue of the Vietnam War.

All these phenomena are political, or are treated politically. It is governments—political institutions—that decide to drop bombs, arrest protesters, send men and, increasingly, women—to war, close banks arbitrarily, administer relief funds, and legislate on civil rights. Given the amount of destructiveness and even evil in the world, there are times in an individual's life when nothing is more important than participation in the political process.

Nevertheless, the "politics is too dirty for nice people" school of thought seems to be saying that political activity is destructive to an ethical individual stance. In addition, people who are intensely involved with their own psychological processes often find it distracting to give attention to outer matters, including political ones.

The psychological concern is legitimate. Individual decisions often can be made according to fairly exacting standards, whereas political decisions must take into account a broad spectrum of values. But not to participate is to give support, by default, to whatever forces are stronger.

Psychologists' Attitudes toward Politics

Psychologists such as Lawrence Kohlberg and Carol Gilligan have pointed out that ethical/moral development, and its accompanying willingness to make decisions, is a crucial aspect of psychological maturity, the basis for mental health. As a friend of mine—a deeply inner, spiritual person—put it: "How can I individuate [become psychologically whole] when my neighbor is starving?"

Individual ethical standards call for concern for one's neighbor in a narrow sense: family, friends, people living nearby who are known to us. The Christian ethic (for example, in the story of the Good Samaritan), along with that of other religions, specifically expands that concern to strangers, even to adversaries. To see individual and ethical concerns as in opposition results, I believe, in a split within the psyche. Concern on an individual level for my neighbor's need can be expressed also via political decisions: economic policies (in response to unemployment), provision for public assistance, trade policies—and my stance toward war.

The necessary connection between inner and outer, individual and collective is found in our language. *Depression.* Do you think first of an emotional state or an economic condition? Whichever occurs to you first, the other may follow close behind. *Inflation.* Psychological, or economic? *Integration.* Psychological, or socio-political? Each term denotes a potential both for the individual psyche and for the body politic.

James Whitney, a Jungian analyst, pointed out that psychotherapy itself has parallels in political life. "Both [politics and psychotherapy are] concerned with bringing about change," he wrote. "Both combine pragmatism and idealism, accommodation and principle. . . . While the patient may be wrong in particulars there must be something essentially right . . . and worth preserving. I take the body politic to be a human organism, sick perhaps, wrong-headed, short-sighted and selfish, and yet in some intrinsic way worthwhile and deserving of life" (16).

Whitney's attitude is similar to that of many clinical and academic psychologists who are active in political causes and are likely to give their support to such organizations as Psychologists for Social Responsibility, through which members express and implement their political views.

However, some psychotherapists have reservations—for professional reasons—about political activity. Much of such activity becomes known in the community. Hence, clients may come to know or infer their therapists' political views. If that happens—especially if those views are not compatible with a client's own—the therapeutic "vessel" may be damaged; extraneous material has entered it.

Other therapists disagree with this reasoning or find the need for political participation more compelling. They may take the position that all reality—including the client's knowing some of the views of the therapist—contributes to the therapeutic process. Indeed, psychological maturity requires accepting the fact that the world is the way it is—even while attempting to change it.

Jung spoke out on the importance of political activity. He expressed two views that sometimes are seen as conflicting but can be seen as complementary. One is that power is an instinct—innate to our humanness. Consequently, politics, which embodies the use of power, is an inescapable part of life. Second, if an instinctual response is not "integrated"—made conscious and its expression channeled—it is almost certain to be repressed (pushed into the unconscious). Repressed contents, of course, do not disappear but tend to burst forth in destructive form. A repressed desire for power may express itself, for example, in a grab for control of a person or a group, solely for the satisfaction of having power.

(Students of Alfred Adler, along with some other psychologists, emphasize the power "drive" even more than do Jungians.)

The outer use of power, for Jung, must be confronted by an inner force. Indeed, in an oft-quoted statement during the early years of the Cold War, he held that the avoidance of a Third World War depends on how many individuals can bear within themselves the tension of opposites.

Some of the disagreement about the appropriateness of political activity arises out of a too-narrow view of what constitutes politics. Its most obvious manifestation is in organizations built around political causes, parties, and campaigns. Individuals' behavior in these organizations reveals openly their desire for power, and can be met on a conscious level. In contrast, a repressed power wish may be hidden when one is participating in an organization which has other primary aims than gaining power or control. Families, schools, religious institutions, businesses, professional societies, and voluntary groups often are afflicted with covert, unacknowledged power motives that prevent the open resolution of policy issues. Indeed, when I mentioned to a few colleagues and friends my interest in the relation of politics to Jungian psychology, each responded with, "Oh yes, I've been trying to understand what was going on in . . . [name of organization]." Each had been experiencing the power motives of a well-intentioned group. These organizations varied from small, local associations to national professional bodies.

Understanding Political Issues Psychologically

The events and forces that I have mentioned are contemporary expressions of the underlying archetypal reality of the relation between psyche and polis—the soul and the city—which were inseparable in the Greek and Roman worlds. The connection between God and Caesar, like all pairs of opposites, is a tension that must be maintained in order to make life a balanced whole.

How can we apply psychology to political structures, events, and forces? A major contribution is in the understanding of shadow projections: seeing one's own unacceptable qualities as outside oneself. According to Jungian theory and experience, projections are functions of the projec*tor* and, to a lesser degree, of the projec*tee*, and affect the psyches of both. These widespread types of projections can be institutionalized by means of political decisions—or their effects can be eased by the same route. A few decades ago, for example, school segregation became recognized officially as institutionalizing the projection of black inferiority, by providing black children with inferior education and by implying that they were not good enough to go to school with white children. Desegregation and other means of equalizing public education were political efforts at withdrawing that projection. (Current moves toward "community schools" address the unintended consequences of desegregation, while working to sustain equality of educational opportunity.)

Projecting the shadow onto "the other" is obvious in race relations, but such projection also takes place from almost any group onto another group that is considered different: respectable middle-class people onto political dissidents, religious sects, and those with a counterculture life style, and vice versa; heterosexuals onto homosexuals, and vice versa; men onto women, and vice versa, and so on. The commonly experienced psychological impetus for these projections seems to be the projector's uncertainty about self-worth.

Poverty is another condition of life in which politics reflects psychology. The projections on the economically disadvantaged make it difficult for them to find their way out of this condition. When they are told that they are inept and inferior, they carry a psychic burden along with their economic deprivations. Efforts can be made, via political decisions, to give them an opportunity to better their self-esteem in the process of bettering their economic situations.

A direct influence of governmental economic policies on psychological development is through the presence or absence of mental illness. Research (Brenner ix) indicates that instabilities in the national economy have been the single most important source of fluctuation in mental-hospital admission rates. It appears that, when people feel themselves to be in danger of poverty, they are more likely to become mentally ill.

The Need for Consciousness in Political Life

We are social animals. Psychologists have shown how profoundly people can be affected in attitudes and behavior by their social environment. In one experiment (Asch), for example, "normal" (that is, nonpsychotic) subjects were asked to judge the length of a line. After hearing the unanimous false judgment of others, over half the subjects changed their correct judgments to incorrect ones. Thus, they acted contrary to their perceptions.

In another experiment (Milgram), subjects administered to other persons what the subjects believed were painful electric shocks. They did so because they were told that participation in the experiment contributed to science.

In both experiments, subjects succumbed to social pressures. Such pressures act on us when we make political decisions. We are likely to succumb if we lack ego-strength—the psychological capacity to know our positions and act accordingly. Thus, individual psychology is reciprocally related to political participation.

Examples of major political structures that have been skillful in using social pressures to influence behavior are not hard to find. In Nazi Germany, Hitler aroused hysteria uncharacteristic of many of the individuals who succumbed to it. Then, through his Gestapo and other quasi-military organizations, he provoked fear which, in turn, precipitated behaviors that were against the ethics and religion of many of the participants. These behaviors included: (1) persecutions and mass-murder of Jews, other non-Aryans, gypsies, homosexuals, mental patients, and retarded people; (2) the conception of children without regard to family structures and relationships, and (3) the denial of responsibility for the policies and actions of government.

In 1935, Sinclair Lewis published *It Can't Happen Here*, a novel based on the insight that the citizens of Nazi Germany were not unique in their capacity to fool themselves when the political structures required inhumane behavior for physical or economic survival. To test Lewis's hypothesis, a high school teacher (Jones) designed a "learning experiment [that] ended . . . as a nightmare." In response to student skepticism that the citizens of Nazi Germany were people like themselves, Jones led the class, step by step, in one hour a day for only five days, from discipline, to unquestioning obedience, to betrayal of nonconformers, to mass responses to a fictional leader. Jones's observation was that the students "bargained their freedom for the comfort of discipline." Whatever their motives, the students, in a context of political manipulation, behaved exactly like the people they had been condemning. Thus, a quasi-political structure changed attitudes and behavior; that is, it changed the participants psychologically.

The same hypothesis—that "normal" people are capable of totalitarian behavior—is supported by a study conducted shortly after the end of World War II. Rorschach tests were administered to Nazi leaders awaiting trial; the results showed that they were not psychotic. Rather, they were psychologically normal people whose attitudes and behavior were distorted by political forces. Such studies speak loudly for the idea that, *when politics is dirty, citizens—voters and nonvoters alike—do not remain clean.*

There have been a few heroic individuals who were able to maintain their principles and perceptions in the face of Hitler's "big lie." It seems evident, however, that psychological development for most of us—at least in its early stages—is enhanced by, if not dependent on, adequate economic security and political freedom. Both of these conditions depend on political structures and events.

Coming to terms with the shadow, personal and collective, is an important part of psychological development. Collective manifestations of the shadow are evident in a now-classic book, *The Autobiography of Lincoln Steffens*. It skillfully delineates situations in which people, honest in their private dealings, were corrupted by political and economic structures. Steffens chided the reformers of the time (the early twentieth century) for asking repeatedly, "*Who* did it?" The correct question, as he saw it, was "*What* did it?" Political and economic structures formed environments in which evil deeds were done by whichever official or leader was in a position to do them. This is not to say that all politicians are alike; they vary widely in integrity, commitment, and wisdom. But as Steffens demonstrated, the shadow side cannot be destroyed. It can be hidden or even repressed, but it reappears eventually, with all its power.

Many of us seek to be conscious in all aspects of our lives, and we know that much of this consciousness is gained through relationships with other people: parents, children, spouses, co-workers, friends, adversaries. Unconsciousness of our will to power complicates these relationships. But the power shadow that inhabits the political arena is much larger, less personal and even more of an impediment to our societal and individual wholeness.

As individuals, we may not be interested in political power—at least in the sense of governmental or party office—but others *are* interested in such power. If we are not to be damaged by political power, we must bring some consciousness to its use. We have seen many political leaders forget their original constructive goals in favor of the lesser one of being re-elected. Some enjoy the "perks" of office so much that they take advantage of them and are challenged, eventually, by an ethics committee or by their constituents. Voters often lose sight of their own values and vote for a charismatic but unprincipled candidate. Reinhold Niebuhr, whom I mentioned earlier, wrote: "Man's capacity for justice makes democracy *possible*; but man's inclination to injustice makes democracy *necessary*" (p. xiii; italics mine). That is, the willingness of citizens to be concerned about each other and to cooperate with their chosen leaders makes democracy possible. But a democratic system is necessary so that no one group can consistently impose its will on the rest of the population.

Many people, including me, can become highly emotional over political opinions. As I mentioned, my family—especially my father—was deeply involved in political activity and was quite dogmatic in his particular point of view. A large part of my psychological liberation as a young adult, therefore, was to find my own political point of view and to stand for it. Most young adults have comparable experiences, often full of intense emotions, of needing to establish their identity by taking views— on a variety of topics—opposing those of their parents.

Even without such experiences, however, a powerful emotionality seems to be present in nearly everyone who has any interest in the world of politics. It may be that the Republican party reflects the "father archetype": maintenance of structure, order, absoluteness of the belief that spending must never exceed income. Conversely, the Democratic party may reflect the "mother archetype": nurturing, generosity, and caring for the weak and helpless. As with all archetypal phenomena, each has a negative side: justice without mercy, and nurturing to the point of prolonging dependence. It is conceivable that avoidance of participation in politics is motivated partly by fear of such powerful archetypes. Psychological development, however, requires dealing consciously with these deep archetypal forces.

Political activity can contribute to psychological development through the consciousness, expression, and integration of a basic human need. Jung called power an instinct. Other psychologists call it a need to participate in one's own destiny. This basic need must be taken into account in order for development to proceed. Except, perhaps, for the few persons who have a vocation to monastic solitude, wholeness includes the realization of one's relation to the power structures of the political world.

Indeed, wholeness includes recognition of the archetypal bases of all human relations. As Jung is famous for saying, "One cannot individuate on Mt. Everest." That is, the responsibility of human beings for each other's welfare is essential to the wholeness of each of us.

As in all factors in psychological development, the participation in the political world is not an "either-or" matter. I do not suggest that anyone ignore dreams in order to run for precinct chairperson or to become a member of the policy-making board of a professional organization. I do recommend a broad view of psychic reality that excludes neither the "outer" nor the "inner," the individual nor the group.

A woman's dream that I mentioned elsewhere (Mattoon) shows this inter-relation: *The Kennedys were having a sale to raise money for political campaigns. The congressman from the dreamer's district and his wife were there, buying some things. The dreamer was interested in the jewelry, but bought none, even though it was inexpensive.*

The valuables were going from the Kennedys (the family of President Kennedy), a power-oriented group, to the congressman, a compassionate person with little interest in power. Although some energy (money) went to the Kennedys, the valuables (worth more than the money paid for them) went to the congressman. At the time of the dream, the dreamer was a leader in an organization and had been concerned that, although she sought to give democratic leadership, she might be too dominant. The dream seemed to be confirmation of her conscious attitude: She was expending less energy on domination than on people-oriented, democratic leadership.

The use of power is potentially creative as well as potentially destructive. Political activity can correct the highly individualistic, inwardly oriented stance that ignores the power shadow and evades a valuable part of life. Indeed, the sense of connection with a larger world is both necessary and enriching. It can even be an exhilarating experience.

BIBLIOGRAPHY

Asch, Solomon E. *Social Psychology*. Englewood Cliffs: Prentice-Hall, 1952.

Brenner, M. Harvey. *Mental Illness and the Economy*. Cambridge: Harvard University Press, 1973.

Gilligan, Carol. *In a Different Voice: Psychological Theory and Women's Development*. Cambridge: Harvard University Press, 1982.

Jones, Ron. "The Third Wave: Nazism in a High School." *Psychology Today* (July 1976), 14–16.

Kohlberg, Lawrence. *The Philosophy of Moral Development*. San Francisco: Harper and Row, 1981.

Mattoon, Mary Ann. *Understanding Dreams*. Dallas: Spring, 1984.

Milgram, Stanley. "Some Conditions of Obedience and Disobedience to Authority," *Human Relations* 1 (1965), 57–76.

Niebuhr, Reinhold. *The Children of Light and the Children of Darkness*. New York: Charles Scribner's Sons, 1944.

Steffens, Lincoln. *The Autobiography of Lincoln Steffens*. New York: Harcourt, Brace, 1931.

Whitney, James. "Psychology of the Negro-White Revolution," *Inward Light* (Fall 1965), 15–34.

19

False Memories, True Memory, and Maybes

LYN COWAN

Once upon a time, a long time ago, far away, the great Goddess Mnemosyne, whose name means *memory* in our language, lived in the high mountains of Greece, and was greatly honored through her nine daughters, the Muses. Zeus was their father, he who discerns the truth in all matters, and so the Muses inherit from him their truthfulness, expressing it in many forms. For everyone knew that the most necessary "truth" of the human soul was found not in science laboratories and data banks, but in poetry and song, in fine art and drama, and chorales: all those modes that give voice to what humans remember and envision.

Mnemosyne keeps all remembrance, all history, alive within herself. Her beautiful daughters, the Muses, serve and honor her by rendering her substance, history, into art, so that what lives in memory is made into images that speak truthfully of the human condition. The Muses take individual memories, and the collective memories of a people, and turn them into the chorale of history, so that we know who we are and where we come from.

But the Goddess of all remembrance, Mnemosyne, is not simply a repository, a stone mausoleum for the storage of dead things. And the Muses are not mere attendants perpetually dusting off the coffins of forgotten events. Mnemosyne is more like a theater, upon whose stage the Muses perform what we recall of our lives. They take a person's or a people's history and shape it, reshape it, animate it, sculpt it, draw it out, set it to music, give it color, set it free through verse, release it into the air of spoken words so that it may fly ahead to become images of the future.

While Memory is the keeper of life through remembrance, the Muses are keepers of remembrances through art. We do not talk much in our time about Mnemosyne, Memory, as a mother, preserving and protecting images of our past; still less do we call upon the Muses to make the world beautiful and joyful. Ours is a culture where the arts are considered fun but not necessary, where creativity is equated with special effects, and where the true value of artful things is determined not by their lasting ability to delight us, but by how weird and salable they are. Years ago Jung observed sadly, "The Gods have become diseases" (par. 54). Much of what used to be recognized as the difficult gift of creative passion is now treated as curable pathology.

Mnemosyne too has become a disease: not a preserver of the memories that make our histories secure, but a disturber of our illusive peace. Now, she is thought to assault us intrusively, or elude us in a maddening way. How did once-divine Memory become a patient of modern American psychotherapy, abused, disturbed, needing to be recovered and released from repression? And how is it that Memory, mother of the arts, has become a defendant in American courtrooms, accused of being unreliable, distorted, manipulative, contrived, giving "false" information? When Memory is abused or mistreated—that is, taken literally, conceptualized as a filing cabinet, or computer bank for data, or as a merely mechanical function of the brain—then we *all* suffer, individually and collectively. We suffer from amnesia: loss of *memoria*, the capacity to make images and to see life imaginally. We suffer loss of soul.

In her book, *Pagan Grace*, Canadian scholar Ginette Paris says, "Mnemosyne is a voice, the voice of an oral culture. . . . It can come in the night as a dream, in a car as a project or longing, in bed with a lover as a sudden recollection" (121). Paris observes that memory does not just reproduce the past: it evokes a sense of meaning, it comes with poignancy, it constructs an image—which may or may not be literally true. But our culture is not an oral one anymore—talk shows and sound-bytes notwithstanding—and neither is it anymore a culture of the book, or written memory. We have become a culture of technological memory, a computer culture. Paris laments, "Memory more and more is restricted to accurate records and documented events, while each of us is left alone with private memories and the culture has no voice" (125).

Memory now comes to us not as the bringer of our past and compass to the future, but depersonified and mutilated into bytes that fit invisibly on floppy disks. Life is compacted to fit into ever smaller spaces, its bits and pieces assembled with blinding speed, a virtual reality to which we have but random access. Most of our programs are run on a hard drive, not on heart drive. Just as wisdom has been reduced to information, and thoughtful education has been reduced to learning skills, so has the goddess Mnemosyne, living memory, been reduced to a silicon chip.

In the eighteenth century, the great rabbi known as the Baal Shem Tov said, "In remembrance is the beginning of redemption." *Redemption* here comes not through sacrifice or self-denial, but through remembrance—through not letting experience be lost and forgotten. Redemption comes through being able to carry the past, however heavy the burden, because forgetting means to become uprooted, one-dimensional, flat, psychopathic.

The capacity to feel deeply is in part dependent on the ability to remember *images* of deeply felt experience. One of the great advantages of growing older is that one has more history, more memories, a wealth of images stored in that living psychic temple named Mnemosyne.

Given this ancient recognition of Memory as a divinity, as the matrix of art and history, and as the beginning of redemption, we can see how American psychology's debate about false memory syndrome has been poorly framed, to the disservice of both Mnemosyne and those wounded souls who must bear her difficult images for a lifetime. The question which has generated so much heat is whether memories of childhood abuses recalled years later in adulthood are accurate recollections of literal events, or whether they are distortions: vague, confused half-fantasies, or even downright false fabrications. But since all perception occurs by way of the psyche, *the psychological truth must lie in the psyche, that subjective, imaginal realm* where Mnemosyne and her daughters craft and fix their images of an individual's experience—that realm somewhere in the middle where even absolutes have blurred boundaries: the realm of "maybe," "if," and all their surrounding possibilities.

This is the realm in which psychotherapy should be done: not in a legal framework of truth or falsity. By supporting victims of childhood sexual abuse, psychotherapists of all persuasions have become involved in litigation and have often served an important function in bringing perpetrators to justice. But there has not been adequate differentiation made between the primary role of the therapist as one who attends to the soul and the very different role of one who advocates for a particular outcome in a judicial process.

There are two distinct sets of questions here, one for the courtroom and the concern for justice, and one for the consulting room and the care of the soul. They are certainly not mutually exclusive questions; but they are distinct, as "justice" and "meaning" are distinct. The requirement placed on memory in a court of law is vastly different than in a psychotherapeutic situation. Memory on the witness stand in a courtroom must be precise, linear, accurate, clear, absolutely truthful. But in the consulting room there is always a *psychological ambiguity* which preserves complexity and depth, where lived experience reveals the subtle work of the Muses in particular ways, and where such experience has multiple meanings.

The emotional heat generated by the debate tells us there is a powerful archetype, a deep, underlying pattern, driving it. The debate is conducted from literalized oppositional positions: we/they, us/them, abused children/abusive adults, believing therapists/skeptical theorists. The polarization of these positions is very possibly the result of the *archetype of the child* showing yet another aspect of itself in the American collective psyche.

Until the middle of this century, the child archetype dominated American consciousness through its vision of limitless progress, unshadowed idealism, endless growth. This was the pubescent youngster who never grows up and is thus eternal in its youthful vigor and hope—always heading toward frontiers, in earlier times toward the Wild West, now to the frontier of space: like Peter Pan, always taking the second star to the right and going straight on 'til morning. This was the child who is playful and inventive, at baseball or space stations, self-indulgent, optimistic, sometimes a bully to smaller nations, but basically a big hearty kid who unashamedly ate too fast and took up a lot of space. And at Christmas we still celebrate another, sweeter aspect of the archetype, the divinity of the asexual, pure, innocent Child.

In the last decades of this century, however, the aspect of the archetype we now see is the face of the child as victim: bruised and bloodied, frightened, rapidly losing hope in an adulthood worth living toward. The archetypal child of our time is neither the gentle divine redeemer in the stable manger nor the sly pickpocketing street urchins of a Dickens tale, but the child as victim, and also the horrific visage of the child as psychopathic criminal.

The archetypal child—which by definition never grows up but merely comes to inhabit an adult body—now manifests in a nation of victimized adult children. It is no wonder that our politics, psychological theories, and therapies are developmentally arrested at a child's level. It is no wonder that those approaches that please children—causal explanations, simple solutions, literal thinking, and singularity of viewpoint—gain quick currency in modern life. Children, having short histories, have short memories. But it is part of the dignity and vocation of adulthood to remember as many events and poignant experiences and disappointments and dreams and jokes and betrayals as one can. These make up the history of a life which is more than the sum of its parts.

The substance, or subtext, of the false memory debate concerns redemption. And what needs redemption in America, right now, is not only the child, the adult child, the family, but *Memory herself*—the faculty of imaginal memory, the capacity for holding many images of ourselves as individuals, as families, and as a people. Part of memory's redemptive value is its flexibility to remember this or that *way*—everything prefaced with a "maybe." The "maybe" helps protect us from literalizing ourselves into hard facts, keeping alive the sense of possibilities, which is perhaps the beginning of art, creativity, and imagination.

Most psychotherapists, of course, do not attempt to induce or insinuate false memories in their patients, and most patients who come to them are seeking relief from psychological pain. But to the extent that the false memory debate has fallen into the hands of literal-minded psychologists, the patient's need for psychological redemption has been turned into a demand for vindication, for confrontation and legal action. There are those few patients who come seeking not relief but revenge, through legal and social redress. They are in the wrong place. They have no questions, no maybes.

Persons who have been violated in any way need redemption, which comes through remembrance, in order to find meaning for themselves in senseless brutality. And they deserve justice, as any victim does. We have placed the burden of accomplishing both redemption and justice on memory. And by so doing, we have not respected the character of memory, which is as much a faculty of creative artfulness as it is a reliable record of events. Mnemosyne, keeper of images in the soul, is not concerned with literal truth or falsehood; still less so are her daughters, the Muses. Like the art they inspire, the Muses evoke truths of experience and wisdom, not necessarily a singular truth of fact and sworn testimony. For the Muses, as in art, truth is complex and ambiguous. And like art, what is true may also be deceptive, and what is false may nevertheless be experienced as real. True memories have many sides, multiple meanings, blurred boundaries with facts and events. They are like the scenarios on the holodeck of the starship *Enterprise*—virtual emotional reality, but not literal truth. The Muses tell the ancient Greek poet Hesiod, "We know enough to make up lies which are convincing, but we also have the skill, when we've a mind, to speak the truth" (ll. 27–29).

The reality of *psychic* life is that many contradictory things are true at once, and in different ways, more like in dreams than in data reports. In the imaginal realm, most things prove false at one time or another in different ways. There is always a maybe. Maybe it was this way and meant that; or maybe it was that way and meant this. Maybe it was, and maybe it wasn't—but what the soul wants to know is what it would mean either way. How would my life be different if I remembered or forgot? How would *I* be different if I remembered an event from my childhood in a particular way, attaching a particular meaning, than if I remembered the same event with a different meaning? How would I be different if I forgot a particular childhood event entirely?

These are questions for psychotherapy; they are therapeutic questions, because, like the Muses, they attend to the real need of the wounded soul, which seeks to provide redemption through the art of making remembered experience meaningful. Such questions are not legal ones, and so they shift the false memory debate from the courtroom to the consulting room. *More importantly, these kinds of questions shift the memories of a childhood to an arena where the child need no longer be crucified between opposite poles: not absolutes of victim/perpetrator, abused/abuser, child/adult, right/wrong, innocent/guilty, and on and on.*

Confronting one's abuser, family, spouse, may indeed lead to some sort of redemption. But in attending to the soul's deepest need, the essential question is not so much *what* I remember, but *how* I remember it.[1] How has such a memory image given form to my life? How has it helped form

---

[1] See Hillman and Ventura, pp. 22 ff., to undersand this idea more deeply.

my character? How have I been psychologically *de*formed by such a memory image? How has it encouraged, or ruined, my ability to trust, to think well of myself, to love? To redeem the memory image means to find meaning in it. This is what makes the future possible. I recall a Holocaust survivor, possibly Elie Wiesel, once saying: "Memory is the possibility of becoming more of a human being. Memory is a way of redeeming your past. Memory is for the sake, not of the dead, but of the future."

In the old days in Greece, the Muse named Clio was the matrix and crafter of history, which was imagined not as a chronological sequence of literal events, but as a great epic of human entanglements with Fate and divinities. The Muses create history by shaping and preserving images of what has happened, or more accurately, what has been *experienced*. Clio's task, with her musing sisters, is to craft or paint or narrate a pattern of a life where one can see the entanglements.

In a real sense, the purpose of deep soul work is to reveal the unfolding pattern of one's life as a series of divine interventions, or intrusions, from those archetypal powers that govern the soul. Each of us can remember moments when it felt as though some divinity, some unseen hand, moved to turn events a certain way—a letter sent too late, a wrong turn that led to a strange opportunity, a single intuitive decision that changed the course of our life, a sudden impulse that destroyed something of great value, an inheritance that came in the nick of time, a chance meeting that became a romance. The big and the small of one's life may be felt as equally fateful, all woven into the tapestry that gives each individual life its own unique design.

In the beginning, there were three goddesses, the Fates: one to spin the thread of life, one to measure it, one to cut it. Not only mortals, but even the gods were subject to the decrees of Fate. But the ancient Greeks had a saying that *the Muses—and only the Muses—can change the weave of Fate.* This is a remarkable psychological idea, and a redemptive one—for it suggests that one is never trapped by one's fate, never permanently imprisoned in the pain of one's childhood, never completely bound by the limitations of one's present circumstance.

But it is important to note that what brings redemption and freedom from the heavy hand of Fate is not the frenetic activity of data-gathering, and not a heroic egotistic attitude that tries to break down all barriers, all limitations, trampling over one's history in the determination to dictate all the terms of one's life. No: what brings real change, real redemption from entrapment in the deadening sense of fatalism that stops all creativity, are the Muses. These beautiful daughters of Mnemosyne are able to take the most horrific and anguished experiences of our lives and work their artistry upon them. The Muses enable us to make poetry from pain, lyric from loneliness, literature from personal tragedy. This is what releases us from the sense of meaninglessness that keeps us stuck in pain.

Please note: the Muses cannot undo the horror of brutal childhoods nor minimize the anguish of loss and grief; but they can change the pattern of how one perceives and responds to what Shakespeare called the "thousand natural shocks that flesh is heir to." In other words, the Muses spin the thread of which our lives are made; the threads of experience cannot be changed—but the Muses can change the way the design of the fabric is woven.

The Muses can change the psychological design of one's life because, if we allow them, they inspire us to work with the images that live in our memories; they inspire us—and sometimes *drive* us—to search for a sense of continuity and meaning in what has happened to us. Through our memory images, the Muses show us where we have been, help us reflect on where we are, and muse imaginatively on where we are going. As Mnemosyne is the keeper of the psychic archives that keep our history intact, so her offspring the Muses use the archives as the raw material from which to fashion images that return us to who we are and turn us toward what we might become.

Psychological history is different from literal history, in that it is a collection of images made from subjective experience and not exclusively from external events. It is the difference between an impressionist's painting and a journalist's photograph. Memory and imagination go together; the one is hardly possibly without the other. Mnemosyne is not much interested in mere record-keeping, faultless accounts—nor accountability. She is concerned with imaginal life, the life and preservation of images. Above all, she is devoted to remembering the gods, the powers, the ideas, or the archetypes that form the patterns of our lives.

Modern Americans, in particular, have a distinct dislike and distrust of history. And our conception of the human psyche is a reductive, materialistic one. So Jung's startling idea that "image is psyche" is practically incomprehensible to us (except to confirm our collective suspicion that Jung was something of a mystical eccentric and not to be taken seriously). Our sense of history is reduced to the recollection of literal facts. And this is where the false memory debate has led us astray, for the recollection of literal facts can never bring genuine healing to a wounded soul. The soul does not want mere recollection, literalism, or certainty; it wants living images full of emotion; it wants art that evokes these emotions; it wants history solidified as remembrance. And the soul wants redemption.

Our modern ability to remember has been so atrophied, our sense of history so foreshortened, that the idea of "ancient" now applies to anything that happened a few years ago. (Recently I heard a sportscaster on television refer to some record that was set "back in 1996"—which, relatively, would put *my* childhood somewhere back in the Middle Ages). It was *way* back in the mid-1980s (I think) that the so-called "false memory syndrome" debate began to gain currency in the national awareness of child abuse and the role of psychotherapists treating adults. From the beginning, the

debate focused almost entirely on the question of the correctness of recall
of incidents that might have happened in childhood.

The controversy over repressed memories turns not only on the accuracy of memory, but also expects that incidents of childhood abuse about
which one might have a true or false memory are of a sexual nature. This
fact alone should make us stop and wonder why we assume that *sexual*
experiences are so much more harmful to children than continual verbal
condemnations from parents, public racial slurs and humiliations from
schoolmates or teachers, or force-fed religious and ethnic bigotry from the
child's community. All of these childhood experiences constitute "child
abuse," and each of them is a violation, a violence perpetrated upon children that leaves scars for life. Some may be even deeper than those we
expect from sexual trauma.

*From the deep perspective of the psyche, the most pressing question in the
debate is not about the accuracy of memory but about the interpretation of
what has been experienced.* And in soul work what has been experienced
is a matter for interpretation, not verification. What does it matter that a
woman or a man in pain comes to therapy and remembers, thinks they
remember, isn't sure they remember, wants to or doesn't want to remember, that they were sexually approached, coached, touched, seduced,
molested, or raped twenty, thirty, forty years ago?

It matters greatly because they say it does. It matters because for human
beings the subjective reality of pain and emotion has primacy of value and
importance. It matters because their psychic experience is real, and true,
even though it may not be perfectly factual. It matters because their experience and their interpretation of it continues to affect the course of their
psychic, social, sexual, and physical lives.

The Muses, divine daughters of Memory, shape experience into images
and then, like true artists, preserve them in such a way that neither time
nor neglect will destroy their substance. The importance of the Muses in
human life is every bit as important as Mother Memory. For while it is
Memory that records, it is the Muses who give meaning to the record. This
is why we may have only a vague, fleeting memory of the literal circumstances of a long-past event, but the emotions attached to that wisp of
memory are still sharp, piercing, lodged permanently and precisely in the
imagination and in the body. And it is with these emotions that the Muses
must work to create new meaning, not only to relieve the pain, but to redi-
rect the psyche's creativity so that we may get on with life.

Those who have suffered a difficult or painful past (which includes
many of us) need to recall and make conscious the episodes and/or the
climate of that past. It is not necessarily useful just to recall and rehearse
the actual details, over and over again, year after year. The problem is how
to stop living *in* and *from* that wound and how to start living *with* it.
Redemption begins in remembrance, but its continuing effect depends on
the ability of the one who remembers to imagine forwardly, to re-call or

call again upon those possibilities for one's life that have not yet been considered or allowed into consciousness. No one is only one-dimensional; no one is only a victim.

A careful therapy of an adult who was wounded as a child requires not just regression to recall and relive the wound; it also requires progression through remembrance of what that child has, and might have otherwise, become. This is a remembrance not of all that was true or false, but of all the maybes, the thousand maybes and might-have-beens. As long as that early painful experience remains the central and defining experience of one's life, no real creativity is possible; life is lived in reruns—no new ideas, no new characters, no new plots, no new possibilities.

This is not blaming the victim. It is rather de-victimizing the person who has suffered painful blows in childhood; it is a refusal to tag the person with an eternal label of "victim," a label of choice by too many therapy clients. This label has been handed out by psychologists, journalists, and lawyers, who keep referring to such persons as victims—not as adults, not as individuals who have experienced anything else, not as persons, but as victims. The Muses assist us to *dis*identify with the victim archetype by calling us to reshape the context and import of those experiences of childhood which wounded us, so that we may honor the wound without having to suffer it daily, centrally, eternally.

You cannot look at Michelangelo's sculptures or read Maya Angelou's writings and *know* for certain whether they were abused as children. What matters is what they have made, the enduring images in stone and words they have given the world. Their works are full of suffering and power and so they speak to everyone, regardless of personal history or individual circumstance. But we know that Michelangelo suffered all his life from the mean-spirited and self-serving manipulation of his father, and we know that Maya Angelou had endured enough shattering pain by the time she was ten to fill a lifetime. But Maya Angelou is not a victim: she was our national Poet Laureate. And Michelangelo became immortal when he first struck chisel to stone.

They did not live *in* their wounds, nor *from* them, but *with* them, and from those tortured memories, gave us beauty. It is not necessary to remember accurately, or even literally; it is enough that one remembers imaginally, carries images embodying an experience of childhood pain. Most of us have little or no particular artistic inclination or talent—nor do we need it. The Muses are not elitist. They do not compare a person who sings off-key in the shower with one who performs with the Metropolitan Opera. They do not decide that one person's crude stick figure drawing is less worthy than a Rembrandt painting. What matters is that we *reflect on our experiences as if we had the eye of an artist*—that we wonder, muse, ponder the ways we could render and interpret our experiences. The Muses are not interested in legal or objective truth or scientific accuracy; they are interested in making life-sustaining images that express what has happened to us. These are the deepest images that give us voice.

Perhaps the greatest gift of the Muses is the restoration of language to those rendered mute and inarticulate by violence. Trauma makes one speechless; the full horror and violation of personhood that victims suffer cannot be expressed in words. To lose the ability to speak, to tell one's story, is to be condemned to hell, which is solitary confinement in silence. Elie Wiesel, Auschwitz survivor at fifteen, stayed silent, locked in his memory with unbearable images, for ten years after his rescue from the camp. Maya Angelou, raped at seven, became completely mute for years. A thirty-eight-year-old man I see now in analysis, accomplished, educated, successful, speaks for the first time in thirty years about humiliating sexual molestation in grade school. A woman I have worked with for nearly four years, a psychotherapist who was herself sexually violated twice as a young girl, began to write her dreams and there found a language to express her reality. For each of these people, and countless more, remembrance in the form of speech means the beginning of redemption.

Redemption, however, is not the same as justice. The false memory argument has confused the two, assuming that legal action accomplishes psychological redemption. Acting from this assumption, the first impulse is to *externalize* a person's past experience into an interpersonal confrontation with the perpetrator—before it is fully understood how the experience has been psychologically formative. And the second impulse is to *literalize* the memory of abuse and take the perpetrator to court.

There is no doubt that the need for justice in human affairs is as essential as the need for food; but the kind of justice a victim may expect from the legal system is not remotely adequate to bring about genuine healing or permanent change in the person who has been wronged. This kind of healing and change, since it is of a psychological nature, must happen in the psyche, in the interior. *One must come to terms with one's experience.* In this sense, justice is only a part of the therapeutic process, and possibly not the first part.

The child in the psyche wants a return to innocence, a return to a time before wounding. It does not want redemption, it wants injury undone, bad things and bad people banished. No amount of justice or confrontation with literal perpetrators, no apologies from the abuser, no monetary satisfaction from successful lawsuits and no therapeutic assurances can *truly* bring the end to pain that the child longs for. But those who are receptive to the Muses—not only those who have some remarkable talent, but those who suffer and need the consolation of art and imagination—they are the ones who are touched by the Muses. They have the chance somehow to refashion their hurtful histories into future visions.

We have thought that the way to stop the cycle of violence—abused children who become abusive adults who raise abused children—is to provide education and jobs and economic opportunities for young people, to give them dignity and independence, replacing anger and despair. Of course we *must* do this. But what is needed just as desperately, just as deeply, is cultural sanction for art, and a wider appreciation for what constitutes human art forms: not only music, literature, painting, sculpture, but also the amazing poetry of seven-year-olds, old recipes for bread and homemade wine, the crafting of a friendship that lasts a lifetime, slow, patient work that culminates in the stunning beauty of a racehorse coming to the wire, and cultivation of one's garden that brings joy to all who see it.

Art is not just a product; it is an attitude. Artistry is not just skill and training; it is an approach to life. The necessity of art in and for human life is partly demonstrated by its antiquity: we do not know of a time in human existence when there was no art. Witness the prehistoric cave paintings in France, which suggest that from the dawn of humanity activity and art belonged together, simultaneously: pictures of animals made by hunters for whom *the hunt and its portrayal* were practically the same thing. And art certainly does not come only from the sweetly young and innocent, those untouched by tragedy. The greatest art often is born from pain and sorrow, for this is what makes pain and sorrow endurable, and even, sometimes, transformative.

It is important that we learn to remember forwardly as well as remembering what is past. We find this idea, in passing, in one of the great psychological texts of the nineteenth century: in Lewis Carroll's *Wonderland*, where all the laws of time and space are reversed or irrelevant. The White Queen observes that Alice has a terribly linear, and much too limited, notion of memory. Alice, who can only remember what is past, says of her memory, "I'm sure *mine* only works one way. I can't remember things *before* they happen." And the Queen remarks, "It's a poor sort of memory that only works backwards." Though confused, little Alice asks, "What sort of things do *you* remember best?" "Oh, things that happened the week after next," the Queen replied in a careless tone (Carroll 198).

The White Queen is right: it's a poor sort of memory, a poor sort of imaginal memory, that only works backwards. There is an art to remembering forwardly, to anticipating with passion and precision what one can be or do in life. It requires an image, or many images. As the Muses craft history into epic poems, so may a single person craft his or her history—a case history of one's own—into a lived poem, a life full of all kinds of memory images—ugly memories, joyful memories, sorrowful and painful memories, funny and embarrassing and ridiculous memories, sensate memories of how some things felt even when it can't be remembered how it actually was, or if it ever *really* was. In the course of psychic life, literal events by themselves count for relatively little. Look at the paucity of literal events in the life of Emily Dickinson, or Marcel Proust, who spent years in bed engaging in a remembrance of things past. The memory of an experience, the image of the emotions we experience, this is everything, for the image is where the soul resides.

I leave with you a Jewish story: In times past, when the great rabbi, Baal Shem Tov, the Master of the Good Name, had a problem, it was his custom to go to a certain part of the forest. There he would light a fire, say a certain prayer, and find wisdom. A generation later, a son of one of his disciples was in the same position. He went to that same place in the forest and lit the fire, but he could not remember the prayer. But he asked for wisdom and it was sufficient; he found what he needed. A generation after that, his son had a problem like the other. He also went to the forest, but he could not even light the fire. "Lord of the Universe," he prayed, "I could not remember the prayer and I cannot get the fire started. But I am in the forest. That will have to be sufficient." And it was. Now, Rabbi Ben Levi sits in his study in Minneapolis with his head in his hands. "Lord of the Universe," he prays, "look at us now. We have forgotten the prayer. The fire is out. We can't find our way back to the place in the forest. We can only remember that there was a fire, a prayer, a place in the forest. So Lord, now that must be sufficient."

And it is.

BIBLIOGRAPHY

Carroll, Lewis. *Alice in Wonderland*. New York: Vintage Books, 1976.

Hesiod, *Theogonis*. Trans. Dorothea Wender. Harmondsworth, England: Penguin Books, 1973.

Hillman, James and M. Ventura, *We've Had a Hundred Years of Psychotherapy and the World's Getting Worse*. San Francisco: Harper Collins, 1992.

Jung C.G. *Alchemical Studies* from the *Collected Works of C.G. Jung*. Eds. H. Read, M. Fordham, G. Adler, W. McGuire. Trans. R.F.C. Hull. Vol. 13. Bollingen Series XX. Princeton: Princeton University Press, 1967.

Paris, Ginette. *Pagan Grace*. Dallas: Spring, 1990.

20

No One Wins: The Miss America Pageant and Sports Contests As Failed Initiations

MARITA DIGNEY

> Traditional rites of passage were based in the hard knowledge that the sanctity of life and the making of a meaningful death must be struggled for by each person and that the entire drama must be recast for each generation. Participating in "ordeals of finding meaning" was both an inheritance and a requirement that made each child a central figure in his or her own dream and in the life of the tribe.
>
> —Michael Meade, "Rites of Passage at the End of the Millennium," p. 28

Every indicator which can signal trouble is now lighting up and flashing red to warn us that adolescents in our culture are in great danger. This adolescent malaise mirrors a wider, deeper fragmentation of the sense of self in our culture. Adults hide their suffering in various ways; adolescents suffer vividly. Adolescence is likened to a disease, the symptoms being increased drug use, unwanted pregnancy, sexually transmitted disease, depression, violence, and suicide (Foster 55). Nearly half of teens in America are at significant risk of endangering their own lives as a result of high risk behaviors (Carnegie Council Report 10). Many others are negatively impacted upon by the adults around them. In a major Supreme Court decision, Justice William Rehnquist linked statutory rape with what previously had been described simply as teenage pregnancy (*New York Times*, B10). Even before adolescence, children are victims of predators both inside and outside of their homes (U.S. Bureau of the Census Abstract, 217). These painful statistics make clear that for too many teens, "Heroin Chic" is far more than a fashion statement.

From sources as disparate as tribal medicine men to the October 1995 report of the Carnegie Council on Adolescent Development, the causes and cures for this distress are remarkably similar. What is missing in the lives of too many young people are the simple values of a place in community, bonds of affection, and a sense of meaning. The Carnegie Council report states that adolescents are emotionally abandoned by parents during the years of ten to fourteen, just when the children most need guidance, love, and support (12).

Malidoma Somé, a Dagara medicine man from Upper Volta who now lives in the United States, laments the spiritual poverty and lack of community in the United States. He feels we do not carefully initiate the young into adult life. The initiatory rites which he describes provide the young with community, meaning, and an identity. He comments that his initiation gave him a "first medicine," a reference point to which he could return amidst the chaos of life (67).

Failed Initiations

As they are practiced now, adolescent initiatory rites are empty and, for the most part, useless. Adolescents experience psychological, social, physical, and spiritual needs for inclusion, meaning, love, and identity while fast appoaching the demands of adult life. They try in every way possible to meet these needs. In urban areas, gangs with their mystique and blood pacts emerge out of the young people's longing to make sense of their world. In less threatening situations, the club, the clique, the team, pals, the neighborhood, school, or church partially meet these needs. However, peer contact does not suffice. The sad fact is that children cannot welcome other children into adulthood. Only adults can do that for them and adults seem to have forgotten this role and responsibility. Initiation is a step-by-step process in which the ways of childhood are left behind and the responsibilities of adulthood are taken up. The rites recognize a metaphorical death and rebirth. What was, is no more. What is to be is being born. This complex process is not accomplished by simply keeping kids busy, which is often the best we have to offer them. Most of the symptoms of the young today reflect a longing for care: care of body, mind, and spirit.

Instead of authentic child-by-child initiations, our culture offers commercialized, mass events which, though vestiges of former initiatory practices, actually have little value in the moral and psychological development of the individuals involved or those who watch. Examples of these frenetic, empty, mass initiatory practices are beauty pageants and sports rivalries. Evidence that these false initiatory practices are disconnected from reality is found in the fact that they have spread like a virus through the culture to include very young children in beauty pageants and little league sports requiring skill and coordination far beyond their years. Initiation is age-appropriate in adolescence, not early childhood.

The complexities of modern life, including racial and ethnic diversity and mass movements of peoples, have inadvertently conspired to create a society which fails to provide a sufficient bridge between youth and adulthood. Uninitiated teens become unfulfilled adults who are emotionally starved for a sense of purpose and confused as to the value of life.

The Beauty Pageant

A vestige of a once great initiatory practice for girls is the Miss America Pageant. It was a remarkable cultural phenomenon when the American public responded to the invitation to vote by phone on the decision to keep the swim suit contest and the following year to choose the ten semifinalists. The unprecedented response showed us in no uncertain terms that the pageant holds a place in the collective imagination of the American culture, one which borders on obsession. There were a reported three million calls placed in the first fifteen minutes of voting. Clearly the Miss America Pageant evokes a level of the human psyche which is deep and shared, referred to by C. G. Jung as the "collective unconscious." This layer of our psyches is unchanging and seemingly outside of ourselves but one which we recognize as our own when we encounter it. The Miss America Pageant seems to endure because it resonates with something we know to be valuable. This might simply be stated, "Young women are delightful to look at; our species survives in some measure because of their beauty. This is good and right to celebrate."

Though dismissed by many as silly, the Miss America Pageant thrives. Easy to hate as shallow with its raw cruelty and sweet beauty, the audience of millions indicates that this event is compelling. As if the culture were dreaming, the Pageant reflects us. As we change, the Pageant changes. Like all universal phenomena, what happens to us, happens to it. What is of deadly importance is that, just as with movies and superstars, the young are shaped by what they see of this event. Make no mistake, girls are not carefully and lovingly initiated into the joys and sorrows of womanhood by what they watch on their TV screen as it happens to fifty young women in Atlantic City. The power of this phenomenon is not that it initiates the young, but rather that it touches on the unfilled need of the adults in the culture for true initiation. These shallow, obsessive repetitions of long-forgotten rites go nowhere and help no one.

Before the Women's Movement, we were content, even satisfied, to have the great anointing song of the pageant sung by a man. Though elected and crowned, the young woman was not quite Miss America until Bert Parks sang "There She Is, Miss America" as she promenaded for all to see. Frail and infirm, the old king departed and younger, more virile men attempted to take up the task of singing the song. But we had changed, the pageant had changed, and in a few years a woman began singing the initiatory song. This and the inclusion of former Miss Americas in the program suggested that initiated women rather than the old man now had a role in anointing the new queen. In recent years, as if unsure of this bold new step, the pageant planners have returned to the male singer.

A certain shift of awareness is also reflected in the questions which are posed to the five semi-finalists as a way of introducing their personalities to the audience. Previously, the older man teased and flirted with the contestants. He asked inane questions designed to allow the girls to look either clever or confused, but always cute. Now the contestants choose their own topic for discussion. In the recent past the questions were asked by the feminine hostess and her consort. In parallel fashion here too the pageant has retreated to using only the male questioner. The topics covered, however, are more serious and now refer to the culture in general and to women's diverse roles—again this probably unconscious participation with the evolving culture.

These changing choices, to have a man or woman preside, reveal our confusion. These seemingly frivolous details refer to a serious matter. Who, at this time and in this culture, actually initiates the female into womanhood? It is as if we are unsure as to when the girl becomes the woman. Surely menstruation is not the only signifier and we seem to know that. Is it meeting the expectations of a man which makes a girl a woman? Is it with the help of a role model, such as the previous Miss America, that a girl becomes a woman? Is it social approval, the judges' votes or the audience reaction? Is it marriage or childbirth? As the Miss America Pageant slowly evolves, it reflects us as a culture and we are revealed as none too sure.

Ancient Female Initiatory Practices

The Miss America Pageant and all beauty pageants echo ancient feminine initiatory rites. The "coming out" of new debutantes, as well as the high school prom (short for promenade) and the small town cotillion, are further forms of these initiatory practices. They follow deeply familiar patterns (Digney 68). Though only phantoms of the earlier powerful rites, they remain in our culture. Like archeological digs which reveal layer after layer of lost civilizations, so too these practices reveal roots deep in the soil of the wisdom of the ancients. In preliterate cultures, ritual acts served as metaphors which demonstrated the beliefs of the people, just as sacred texts and stories did later (Eliade 3).

Female initiatory practices take many forms. The basic motif consists of removing the young woman, sometimes at the onset of the menses, from her everyday world. In some cases she is taken to the innermost room of her grandmother's home. At other times she is taken to a communal dwelling. She may be joined by age mates. At this time she is instructed in knowledge of the human body, sexuality, and sacred lore, information central to her vital role in the continuing life of her people. She is invited to retreat from everyday reality to dream and to learn, as if incubating her future self.

In the cult of Artemis, in Greece, the young adolescent girl is given to serve the goddess from her twelfth to sixteenth year. During this time she is considered a bear cub and lives by different norms of behavior which allow a certain natural wildness. She is at times swaddled in bear skins, protected and hidden while maturation completes itself. In this way she is sheltered and the issue of sexuality delayed until her personality is developed (von Franz 53). Later, after her personhood is more securely established, she will take on the Aphrodite, or sexual side of her nature. Still later awaits Demeter, the great mother goddess, representing the complex task of mothering, which is available to women. But first, the incubaton of the girl, away from the expected cultural norms, is essential in authentic feminine initiation.

Finally, in culture after culture, the girl emerges as the woman. In delight she is shown off to the village. This ritual display of the returning feminine may take the form of an elaborate communal event where strenuous dances are required of her, or it may consist of a simple walk around the village, visiting each house to receive gifts and praise. Child no longer, she returns to the village to take up her role as woman. The millions who watch the televised pageant or the neighbors who gather on the lawn on prom night unconsciously enact this ritual support of the transformation of the young and the celebration of life renewing itself. Unfortunately the teens too are acting unconsciously and have no sense of the dangers and meaning of what they begin to take up at this time.

In the Mescalero Apache tradition, representative girls are initiated while the male elders sing their people's cosmology and ethno-history in long elaborate songs celebrating the womanhood of the girls. The ceremony is followed by gift-giving and shared meals as well as ceremonious greeting of the girls by all present. So essential were these rites to this culture that when these rituals became illegal in the United States the birthrate of the Mescalero Apaches declined (Farrer 239).

These ancient rites and many others manifest the essential form of the initiation and display of the feminine, one which in our culture has evolved into the beauty pageant. Such rites were originally religious; however, the diluted version we know today has lost its spiritual roots. The pale, profane, commercialized initiations of today do not connect the initiate with her inner resources nor the actual complexity of the role of women. She is not given access to the wisdom in her community or the other world of spirit. The initiatory practices today fail the women who participate in them and therefore add to the deterioration of the level of culture rather than fostering the orderly transition of generations.

Sports Events

The situation for boys is similar; they also participate in residual initiatory activities which act on their psyches and on the culture. In traditional practice, male puberty rites involved taking the boys out of the village with age mates to a sacred space prepared by the elders. Among other experiences in this sacred space, the boys would be subjected to rigorous ordeals which taught them that they were both weaker and yet stronger than they

knew in childhood. These ordeals combined with sacred teaching, information regarding sexuality, and skills training served to birth the boy into
manhood and evoke the hero in him. The initiated was then returned to
the village, warmly received and granted status as a man.

Our culture spends far more energy on masculine initiatory practices
than on those offered to females even since the advent of Title IX, which
was enacted to move the culture toward equal access to sports for girls and
women. Surely some of the tremendous effort which schools and communities have traditionally invested in male sports are a recognition of this ritual, of this necessary ordeal in the process of masculine maturation. Again
we see the culture evolving as sports opportunities for girls begin to
approach those offered to males and more and more girls are using sports
as a vital aspect of their education about life. Yet, as with the girls, the boys
are failed in these rites. Sports activities alone as substitutes for initiatory
ordeals can not create individuals aware of their place in the culture, the
richness of their heritage, and the meaning of life.

Instead of a carefully prepared sacred space in which the elders conduct the activities designed to guide the boy into manhood, we offer the
playing field, as if that were enough. The hype of high school and college
sports offers only limited pseudo-initiations when what is needed are
befriending adults committed to the social, psychological, and educational
development of the young. Young men and women march out on the playing field in good faith, but what is offered to them are empty initiations.
Although each is promised new life when the pageant or game is won, the
promise turns out to be false. One is rarely changed when the game is won
or lost. If there is any change, it is for the few rather than the many. Instead
the young who participate are often injured, psychologically burned out,
disappointed, or exploited to support the need for entertainment in the
adults around them. Perhaps the dedication and determination required of
the athlete for the long hours of practice and training represent the best of
what this system has to offer. Of course there exist coaches, teachers, and
counsellors who protect their students and truly help them to develop on
many levels of awareness. Yet if anything changes as a result of a win or
loss it is more likely the Athletic Department budget or the personnel on
the coaching staff. In this, one is reminded of the early Greek divinity
Chronos, who devoured the young to support his own insatiable, obsessive hunger.

The serious cost to the young of these failed initiations can be seen in
the high risk behavior particularly characteristic of adolescent males in
which they strive to prove themselves. The lack of "secure" ordeals offered
to them by protective elders further put the young in danger. They are left
on their own to meet this need unconsciously, often with disastrous consequences. Getting a driver's license, a true ordeal and rite of passage, provides the young the freedom and lethal means for many self-constructed
challenges.

Homecoming

High school and college homecoming ceremonies are further examples of residual initiatory practices. The queen and her escort, usually a well-known athlete, are crowned at half time of the big game during the Homecoming Weekend festivities. Here we have the preparation and display of the feminine, the ordeal of the masculine, and the triumphant return of both to the community, unconsciously re-enacted year after year, seemingly for the fun of it. Meanwhile, as picturesque as all of this is, very few adults may truly attend to the real developmental issues of the many adolescents who desperately need attention. Again in this residual initiatory rite, no one is changed, no one is helped to become a fuller person. These are frail, fragmentary phantoms of what is needed by adolescents; these are not fully functioning initiatory rites.

The hunger for transformation is a deeply ingrained and legitimate human desire. These activities are repeated obsessively because no one is ever really initiated. This leaves many of us in this culture like hungry people endlessly viewing slides of beautifully prepared food while continuing to starve.

In vital societies, and tight-knit cultural or religious enclaves where the social structure is intact, the puberty rites of initiation serve the vital function of transmitting cultural history and practice from one generation to another. Such cultures are living organisms which attend to the well-being of their members. When these initiatory practices decline, the people, young and old, suffer. We are in such a time.

Despite the vestiges of initiatory practices like pageants and play-offs, few adults consciously initiate the young into adulthood. Gone is the ancestor behind the ritual mask with a knowledge of the past and a hand in the present, guiding the youth across the bridge of experience toward adulthood. The transition from childhood through adolescence to adulthood is on the whole a haphazard and dangerous process in these times. For many this pattern of unintentional cultural neglect is the source of lifelong pain, confusion, and eventual despair.

Without a welcoming into the culture of adults in a meaningful way, members of the society are condemned to a life of perpetual childishness and adolescence. Malidoma Somé writes, "In my village, a person who is not initiated is considered a child, no matter how old that person is. To not be initiated is to be a nonperson" (Somé 68).

Dreams and Initiation

What the outer culture fails to do, the inner world of the psyche takes up and attempts to complete. One dream we commonly experience illustrates this pervasive state of unreadiness. Filled with dread, we are back in the vaguely familiar halls of school. We are urgently searching for a room, running late, trying to finish homework or take a forgotten examination. Or we discover we've missed an essential course and cannot graduate even though in reality we may have taken that very course! At the deepest level, this common dream reveals anxiety born of the lack of completion. The dreamer is wondering, "Am I ready?" "Am I good enough?" "Do I know what I need to know in order to get on with life?" "Do I really know anything or am I just faking it?" Naturally in these dreams the imagination points back to the time when the dreamer most needed to learn what was necessary to prepare for adult responsibilities. In our culture, school provides one opportunity to receive the attention and guidance needed to create a sense of self in the culture. This shared dream experience suggests that many feel they did not master what was, somehow, essential.

Graduation, an attempt to incorporate a ceremonial rite of passage, is often recalled as an empty non-event containing little meaning. It seems to have no connection to the skills acquired or those which are necessary to go on in life. Often the graduates do their best to turn the tiresome event into a battle of wits with the officials to create funny distractions and still get their diplomas. Again, there is a real question as to the purpose: is this ceremony held for the benefit of the adults or to truly serve the need of the young? As the dream of incompletion indicates, for many, the ceremony fails to confer a feeling of confidence on the participants.

A professional man who is a husband and father dreams: *I am back in high school. It is the beginning of my senior year. I decide not to go out for either football or baseball.* In reality he played both sports successfully his senior year and, in fact, entered college on a sports scholarship. This dreamer is a gifted athlete. Perhaps because of his natural talent and personality, he was actually mentored and coached more than most of his age mates. Sports for him provided not only an opportunity for success but also a means to leave home and get into life. Paradoxically, this dream suggests that he did not complete his sports career in high school. He may have been rewarded, coached, mentored, but he remains in some way untouched by these experiences.

This man's quest takes on a new urgency as a life-threatening physical condition has recently been discovered. This startling reality for an otherwise healthy man has added new dimension to his life, activating the unconscious to take up again the unfinished search for personal completeness. What was only partially accomplished in adolescence is, in fact, being approached again. Perhaps living with a life-threatening physical condition is the task now, the true ordeal for completed initiation into manhood. Within each ordeal is the opportunity for the transformation required as the psyche strives for wholeness and individuation.

True initiation begins with any separation from ordinary reality or life as we know it. Therefore any life-changing event—a marriage, death of a loved one, diagnosis, recognition of an addiction, birth of a child, or significant loss of any kind—is an opportunity to be initiated to a higher state of functioning, that is, to be transformed. When the soul is ready and if we are quite attentive, as this man was, we can find opportunities to complete on the inside what we failed to receive from our culture. No life crisis guarantees transformation: we are offered only the opportunity (Digney 8).

Military Initiations

The best example of an initiation in the United States today which is available across gender and subculture is the military initiation of the recruit in basic training. In many respects this is a true initiation. The initiates are taken from their everyday world and immersed in mysteries of military life. The ordeals are rigorous both physically and mentally and directly related to surviving in dangerous situations. Death is an ever-present possibility. A whole new language is learned; a new designation, indicated by rank, is assigned. All that was appears to be no more and what one will become is not yet evident.

This training is an initiation into military life. However, in terms of a true initiation which serves the psychological development of the adolescent, it too is flawed in one way, like every other initiation widely available today. In a true initiation, the personality is re-formed around an encounter with the Divine. This encounter is not a random event, one which may or may not happen. Rather it is carefully built into the process by the elders and usually takes the form of dramatic mythopoetic activities combined with hearing the story of the origin of the group, usually a creation myth of great importance. Enactments of these and other mythological motifs can be included. In short, their religious history is imparted at this time as well as the individual initiate's place in that plan. The new adult personality is formed around the knowledge of the initiate's essential role in this ongoing drama of life.

True Initiation

The true initiate is twice born, once from the mother and once from the culture. The personality is enriched and guided by the experiences of initiation and contact with a greater wisdom which is offered by the elders for the express purpose of helping the young deal with life and ensuring the continuity of community life. By whatever name one chooses—Higher Power, God, Goddess, Source, Supreme Reality, Great Spirit, Divine Other, Isis, Allah, Yahweh, or any one of the thousand names used over the centuries—it is this greater reality which is the missing aspect of the rites of passage which are widely available to the military recruit and in our culture today.

These are spiritually hungry times. In previous ages the wisdom of the ancient practices led initiates to the encounter with the Divine within themselves and within their culture. In our times, most in each generation are thrown back upon themselves without the context to discover what is authentic. Writing in 1959, Jung cautions, "The eternal truths cannot be transmitted mechanically; in every epoch they must be born anew from the human psyche" (Jung, *Civilization* 217). Attention to the transition from adolescence to adulthood which includes the multi-dimensional nature of the individuals involved can support this rebirth. There seems to be a truth which the ancients knew and we have forgotten regarding the sacredness of all life and all activity.

We offer the young fractionated lives where mere survival as an economic unit passes for a full life. We forget that we are more than co-consumers in the supermarket of now. We could offer the richness of a life lived in a culture of meaning. Adults could reflect on what has mattered in their lives and then make vital and imaginative efforts to give this wisdom to the next generation. Most adults live uncomfortably with the knowledge that we have lost much of the meaning of life. Some strive to create the opportunity for the next generation to at least grapple with the question. Some deny that such deep-seated problems exist at all. What is needed is the loving affirmation of the value of the individual in a community of care and concern.

Can parents offer their souls as well as their cell phone number to children who long for contact? Can we as individuals stop merely treating the symptoms of adolescence and get to know the adolescents in our lives? Can people who are child-free help those who have children? Can we humbly walk with the young rather than ahead of or away from them?

In the midst of the social dislocations of contemporary life many wisdom-keepers, those human links to the old ways, have died silent. In the stillness of this silence builds a cacophony we can no longer ignore. We have traded culture for conformity and lost much in the bargain. It is time to make new music and dance together with our young. We can move forward with the complexities and technology of the present yet honoring the wisdom of the past (Meade 27). Health and happiness during the coming millennium depends on our answers to these questions and our attention to these tasks.

BIBLIOGRAPHY

Bly, Robert. *Sibling Society*. Reading, Massachusetts: Addison-Wesley, 1996.

Carnegie Council on Adolescent Development. *Great Transitions: Preparing Adolescents for a New Century*. New York: Carnegie Corporation of New York, 1995.

Commission of Behavioral and Social Sciences and Education. National Research Council. *Losing Generations: Adolescents in High-Risk Settings*. Washington, DC: National Academy Press, 1993.

Digney, Marita. "Ancestors Behind The Masks: Parallel Archetypes in the I Ching and the Bible." Diploma Thesis, C.G. Jung Institute, Zurich, 1990.

Eliade, Mircea. *The Myth of the Eternal Return.* Princeton: Princeton University Press, 1954.

————. *Rites and Symbols of Initiation: Mysteries of Birth and Rebirth.* Trans. Willard R. Trask. Woodstock: Spring, 1994.

Farrer, Claire R. "Singing for Life: The Mescalero Apache Girls' Puberty Ceremony." *Betwixt and Between: Patterns of Masculine and Feminine Initiation.* Eds. L. Mahdi, S. Foster, and M. Little. La Salle: Open Court, 1987.

Ferguson, Sarah. "The Comfort of Being Sad," *Utne Reader* (July/August 1994), 60–62.

Foster, Douglas. "The Disease Is Adolescence," *Rolling Stone* (9 December 1993), 55–57.

Gilligan, Carol. *In A Different Voice.* Cambridge: Harvard University Press, 1982.

Gilligan, Carol, et al. eds. *Making Connections.* Cambridge: Harvard University Press, 1990.

Jung, C.G. *The Collected Works of C.G. Jung.* Eds. H. Read, M. Fordham, G. Adler and W. McGuire. Trans. R.F.C. Hull, Bollingen Series XX. 2nd. ed. *Two Essays on Analytical Psychology.* Vol. VII. Princeton: Princeton University Press, 1953 and 1966.

————. *The Archetypes and the Collective Unconscious.* Vol. IX. Princeton: Princeton University Press, 1959 and 1969.

————. *Civilization In Transition.* Vol. X. Princeton: Princeton University Press, 1964 and 1970.

————. *Psychology And Religion.* Vol. XI. Princeton: Princeton University Press, 1958 and 1969.

Lincoln, Bruce. *Emerging From the Chrysalis.* Cambridge: Harvard University Press, 1981.

Meade, Michael. "Rites of Passage at the End of the Millennium." *Crossroads: The Quest for Contemporary Rites of Passage.* Eds. L. Mahdi, N. Christopher, and M. Meade. Chicago: Open Court, 1996.

Somé, Malidoma. "Rites of Passage." *In Context* (Winter 1993).

U.S. Bureau of The Census. *Statistical Abstract of the United States 1996.* 116th ed. Washington DC, 1996.

Part IV

Peering
Into the
Possible

21
A Psychology for the Age of the Internet

DOLORES E. BRIEN

Once the slogan was a "chicken in every pot," now it is a "computer in every home and school." Ideally and eventually, we are promised, we will be connected to each other and to the world by means of the Internet, basically a system of computers linked to other computers. As restated by Steve Jobs, co-founder of Apple computers and one of the key figures in this computer revolution, it will not be long before there will be an "Internet Browser in every living room."

Meanwhile, the Internet is growing at a phenomenal rate. Not everyone is plugged into it, to be sure, although millions worldwide are, and the numbers are increasing exponentially. One would have to be living in isolation (as many poor are), not to be aware of its existence and the excitement it has generated. For evidence we have only to take note of corporate competition to get control of it and the pronouncements of social policy makers like the Rand Corporation that every citizen should have access to it or the divide in this country between haves and have-nots will only widen.

The Internet links us not only as individuals to other individuals but to a vast collective. This is the fact and power of the "Net," whether we use it, we believe, merely as a tool to give or receive information, or as a way of participating in a self-selected community of shared interests. It is the latest phenomena in our rapidly evolving techno-culture which challenges us with its possibilities. At the same time we find it somewhat frightening because we don't know where we are going with it and what it is doing to us.

The Internet has brought vividly to our consciousness the idea of "interconnectedness." But what is the nature and quality of this interconnectedness? How real is it? How enduring? Is it fully benign in its effects, or is there a downside as well? And, dare we even ask, do we really want to be so connected? Most importantly, is it changing the way we think of ourselves and the way we relate to others? What does it do to our sense of self, where does the "I" fit in? In other words, how can we think about the Internet from a psychological perspective?

The Debate

In an article, "The Electronic Hive: Two Views," published in *Harper's Magazine* in May of 1994, the reader is given two radically opposing and extreme positions about the Internet and all of computer technology. A passionate advocate of the Net, Kevin Kelly is one of the founders of WELL (Whole Earth 'Lectronic Link), the oldest and most successful computer conferencing center on the Internet. He is best-known as Executive Editor of *Wired*, which has been called "the new bible of the techno-culture." Arguing just as passionately against it is Sven Birkerts, a literary critic by profession and author of *The Gutenberg Elegies: The Fate of Reading in an Electronic Age*. Three years later—a long time in the fast-paced world of communications techology—their arguments pro and con remain among the best succinct statements about the problem which is at the heart of our concern.

Kelly says "Embrace It"

According to Kevin Kelly, the Net has replaced the Atom as the dominating icon for the next century. We should embrace it, not only because it is here to stay, but because it signifies an entirely new way of being in the world. For Kelly, the Atom which "whirls alone, the epitome of singleness," has served as a metaphor for individualism as well as for power, knowledge, certainty, simplicity. All that is now done with. The Net is, on the contrary, nothing more than a "bunch of dots connected to other dots." Constantly changing, constantly in motion, "the Net is the archetype displayed to represent all circuits, all intelligence, all interdependence, all things economic and social and ecological, all communications, all democracy, all groups, all large systems." It has no beginning, no end, and no center ("Electronic Hive" 20).

Since there is no center, no one individual or system can control the Net. It has been described as "the largest functioning anarchy in the world," "a shared space of written public conversations" (21). The result is the production of a vast document which is never finished, but always being added to. Unlike the printed word or even a chat around a table, the Net encourages the nondogmatic. Because it tolerates all kinds of ideas, experiences and perspectives it also invites emotional and uninhibited reactions. "Every idea has a backer, and every backer has an idea, while contradiction, paradox, irony and multifaceted truth rise up in a flood" (22).

Kelly describes what the Net has wrought as a kind of "techno-spiritualism" in which human and artificial minds are wired "into one planetary soul." It isn't, he admits, what we were necessarily looking for. "Nobody expected a new culture, a new thrill, or even a new politics to be born when we married calculating circuits with the ordinary telephone, but that's exactly what happened." Kelly identifies the rise of postmodernism with the advance of network computing, which has contributed to creating a world which is paradoxically both "highly connected" and "deeply fragmented" (22).

George Orwell, says Kelly, couldn't have been more wrong about Big Brother and about computers. On the contrary, we now live in a culture where authority has broken down and where uniformity cannot be imposed. "Instead of sucking the soul from human bodies, turning computer users into an army of dull clones, networked computers—by reflecting the networked nature of our own brains—encourage the humanism of their users. Because they have taken on the flexibility, adaptability, and self-connecting governance of organic systems, we become more human, not less so, when we use them" (25).

Birkerts says "Reject It"

While Kelly exults in the advance of technological culture, Sven Birkerts approaches it with fear and loathing. He is dismayed that we have so readily adapted to this technology without thinking through its implications. Because it is there, he says, we assume that it not only must be good, but that we need it. But it is there, he points out, only because the technology is driven by money, for the purpose of making more money. Unlike Kelly, he does not see the Net as autonomous, but rather as the center of a ruthless struggle, through mergers and acquisitions, as to who will get to control it. "The dollar is smart. It is betting that the trend will be a juggernaut, unstoppable; that we are collectively ready to round the corner into a new age." Inevitably, "we are wiring ourselves into a gigantic hive" (17).

The ease with which this has been accomplished is due, Birkerts believes, to our ability to adapt, to accommodate ourselves to change. Furthermore, each adaptation makes us ready for the next. What is different now is the tremendous speed with which these changes occur, and correspondingly we adapt with less and less time or incentive to consider what we are doing, what the consequences of our adaptation may be (17). Nevertheless, "we embrace them because they seem a part of us, an enhancement. They don't seem to challenge our power so much as add to it" (18).

But what worries Birkerts is that we have no interest in debating the deeper significance of these changes. "But why," Birkerts asks, "do we hear so few people asking whether we might not ourselves be changing, and whether the changes are necessarily for the good!" (18).

Kelly is enamored with the idea of "interconnectedness," which he believes the Net is bringing about. Birkerts sees it differently. "In our technological obsession we may be forgetting that circuited interconnectedness and individualism are, at a primary level, inimical notions, warring terms. Being 'on line' and having the subjective experience of depth, of existential coherence, are mutually exclusive situations" (18).

Every time we adapt, Birkerts says, by accepting the technology without question, for its convenience, for its usefulness and efficiency, we begin to distance ourselves from more primary experiences. We think we are improving our lives, not noticing that we are adjusting ourselves to a greater degree of abstraction. And abstraction takes us further away from what is natural, that is, "from our fundamental selves rooted for millennia in an awe of the unknown, a fear and trembling in the face of the outer dark." As a result we react by putting more and more of our trust in our systems until finally, our "solitary self" is given over to the collective, which is ultimately, he believes, what these systems are really about (19).

Birkerts's concern is that we are becoming more and more shallow, lacking in depth or the desire for depth, seeking instead to satisfy ourselves with this lateral, "vast interconnectedness." We have to distinguish, he says, between communication and communion. We have fooled ourselves into believing that the wider we spread our communication networks, the closer we will get to achieving a genuine connection with others. We think our computer technology can do this for us, but it won't. For it creates and operates in "an unreal time which has nothing to do with the deep time in which we thrive: the time of history, tradition, ritual, art, and true communion." Although Birkerts admits to an occasional glimpse of Kelly's vision, he tells us, "From deep in the heart I hear the voice that says, 'Refuse it'"(20).

To oversimplify, Birkerts sees in the Internet a loss of oneness, represented by the individual self, while Kelly sees in it an infinite number of selves connecting to other selves. Here we have a new twist on a problem as old as humankind, that of the One and the Many. In this context the problem is as much psychological as it is philosophic. What is at stake here are not abstractions but human beings whose sense of self and the relationship of the self to others may have to be redefined in the face of the radical changes being brought about by the overwhelming impact of computer technology.

A Psychology for the Age of the Internet

Mainstream psychology does not seem to have much to offer us as we confront the questions raised by the Internet on its way to becoming a pervasive force in our culture. Sherry Turkle in her book *Life on the Screen: Identity in the Age of the Internet* notes that only Jungian psychology and object-relations seem to have developed a theory and language which can help us understand and come to terms with this situation (259). Within Jungian psychology the concept of "the plural psyche," described by Jungian analyst Andrew Samuels is, I believe, the most applicable and original approach that we have at this time. Also relevant is James Hillman's theory of psychological polytheism. Hillman's ideas, however, require more than a superficial acquaintance with Greek classical mythology and deserve to be explored separately.

Originating in Jung's theory of complexes, the psyche, as Samuels describes it, is multiple, many, rather than singular or unitary. If we are venturesome enough, it is possible, using Samuels's "plural psyche" to think of the Internet as a kind of projection, or externalization of the psyche, or as a metaphor for psyche. The psyche and the Internet may be said imaginally to mirror one another. The psyche describes the inner world of the individual. The Internet can be imagined as a manifestation of the outer world of the collective.

The Plural Psyche

Samuels strives, as does Kelly, to be as inclusive as possible. The sense of wanting to embrace it all is palpable. Psychological theory, Samuels writes, "seeks to see how the various conflicts, complexes, attitudes, functions, self-objects, part-selves, sub-personalities, deintegrates, psychic *dramatis personae*, internal objects, areas of the mind, subphases, gods—how all of these relate to the psyche as a whole." To understand what is going on in the psyche, he claims, every source of information has to be accounted for: "innate, biological archetypal facets of personality with environmental and situational factors" (2). Compare it with Kelly's description of the Net as "an archetype displayed to present all circuits, all intelligence, all interdependence, all things economic and social and ecological, all communications, all democracy, all groups, all large systems" ("Electronic Hive" 20). The string can, of course, be extended indefinitely, but you get the point. Nothing is to be left out.

The concept of the plural psyche can be traced back at least to Jung with his theory of complexes and also to William James with his idea of a "pluralistic universe." It belongs to the psychoanalytic tradition of depth psychology which, Samuels claims, is not so much about the individual or things but about how these individuals or things relate to each other and how groups of these relationships again relate to other groups (or "sets" as he calls them.) He himself points out the connection between depth psychology and computer technology. It demonstrates, he says, "cybernetic and systemic features. . . . Impact at one point of the psychic system leads to ripples through the whole apparatus" (9). (Samuels, by the way, doesn't use a computer).

The concept of the plural psyche, as described by Samuels, has striking parallels to Kelly's Net. For Kelly the Net is a "bunch of dots connected to other dots" and is constantly in motion, always changing. Because it has no center it cannot be controlled or dominated by any single individual or system. Lacking a central authority, it is undogmatic and tolerant of every conceivable idea and experience. It does not provide, therefore, "a consensus, a canon and any overriding meaning whatsoever" ("Electronic Hive" 22). Samuel's language, however, is more abstract than Kelly's; he has written for his professional colleagues. To translate it into plain English and run the inevitable risk of oversimplifying his thought, let us imagine the Net as the psyche. How then might Samuels describe his idea of the plural psyche?

First of all, Samuels himself uses the metaphor of the "network" as "an organizing device" for what goes on in the psyche. He further describes the personality as an "imaginal network." "Imaginal," as he uses it here, means archetypal imagery which gives expression to thoughts, emotions, or attitudes which have their source in the unconscious. We experience this imaginal network by its actions, "from our being disturbed by them, and their contribution to our archetypal states of mind" (40). To make his point he culls definitions of the word from political and social science, which are worth quoting here:

> a system of nodes and links;
> a map of lines between points;
> a persisting identity of relationships;
> a "badly knotted fishnet";
> a structure that knows no bounds;
> a non geographic community;
> a support system;
> a lifeline;
> everybody you know;
> everybody you know who. . . swims, collects coins, sings in the church choir,
>   watches the children walk to school, reads Teilhard de Chardin. . . .
>   (Lipnak 2)

Every one of these descriptions which Samuels uses to describe the plural psyche has also been applied to the Net. There are those "dots" or "nodes" or "links" connected to other "dots, "nodes," or "links." We can imagine them as all those "relatively autonomous components" of which Samuels speaks.

In Jungian psychology the psyche contains or is made up of a cast of characters or sub-personalities, each with its own experience, emotion, response and function within the psyche. Whether singly or in combination with other characters, they constitute "a complex" which, to state also in an oversimplified way, is one of the many selves which go to make up our personality. One "dot," one "sub-personality," one complex, or even one cluster of complexes can connect to other dots, sub-personalities, and clusters of complexes in others.

We have each had the experience, at one time or another, if not continuously, that despite my being who "I" am, I am somehow a lot of different "I's," some of them in hot competition with each other. As a child, growing up Catholic, I remember admiring the saints and wishing I could be like them, not so much because they were holy, but because they seemed to be so singularly themselves in every circumstance. Who "I" was seemed to change with who I happened to be with at the time. But there was also a self which recognized, with a vague feeling of guilt, that I was not the same as that self in that particular circumstance but was also many selves. Jung and Samuels in his turn make it clear that this experience of being many selves is natural to the psyche. It *is* the psyche.

This emphasis on the "many" gets us away from thinking of the psyche in predominantly dualistic terms although "the old antinomies and opposites that are really polar and fixed would also have their place." At any one given moment of experience, or of emotion, or of thought, it is likely that more than one aspect of the personality, more than one complex, will come into play, each with its own function, altered and shaped by its connection with still another complex. Applying this to the debate between Kelly and Birkerts, Samuels says that in certain situations, it should not be necessary to choose between these two views. "The Internet is all that they (combined) say it is. Sometimes, we need to accept that the Internet is either one thing or the other, according to our preference. At other times still, there is a mysterious state of affairs in which it is what neither one of them says it is" (letter).

These many selves are foci, "dots," of psychic energy and so constantly moving, changing, transforming, and constantly bumping into one another, "interacting," or linking up with each other. Not every self connects necessarily with all other selves, but does so with at least some, and probably with a great many. But the interconnectedness is forever shifting as some connections are closed off, and others opened. And so the pattern of this Net/psyche changes; it too is never the same. That is why the image of the Web imagined as a spider's web is not appropriate, for the spider's web, unlike the Net, is one of symmetry and regularity.

Another reason why the spider's web is an unsuitable metaphor for the Net is that there, at the center and at the controls, sits the almighty spider. The spider makes the net for its own purpose, as a food supply; it owns the web, and is its "sole authority." Now, as Kelly points out, this Net is not controlled or owned or dominated by any individual or organization. According to Samuels, neither is the psyche governed by any one predominant power. There is no center to the psyche, just as there is no center to the Net. If the psyche has any center, he says, it is to be found in the archetypes, those universal "instincts" of the psyche, around which each of the complexes or many selves cluster. There is no center to an archetype, however, because it is also a cluster of images and ideas. There is no central archetype around which the psyche is organized, Samuels would say, not a self or ego with one archetypal core, but rather, a shifting state among many competing archetypes. In this respect Samuels departs from classical Jungian thought in which the archetypal self is held to be both the center and circumference of the psyche, the totality of the personality. (Note that this "archetypal self" is sometimes capitalized as Self to avoid its being identified with the ego. I use the small "s," however, in accord with Samuels's own usage.)

If the psyche, like the Net, is decentralized, it logically shares with the Net other features which derive from the lack of a central authority. Pluralism in depth psychology, says Samuels, maintains an anti-hierarchical attitude. The objection is not simply to hierarchy itself, but to the presence and influence of what he calls prejudged hierarchies. He contrasts this stance with other psychologies, all of which, he claims, have a hierarchical tendency. That is, they confer a higher rank upon some "good thing" or idea often claimed to be "fundamental" compared to other good things or ideas. He includes, as examples, such ideas as that of the self or the imaginal. A pluralistic psychology, in contrast, avoids methodologies, ideologies, or overriding theories of any kind as having *a priori* importance. (This applies as well, he points out, even to pluralistic psychology.) Instead, it means being receptive to information, from whatever source it comes, to the possibility of many interpretations and even to a resulting ambiguity. Sometimes it means not determining anything at all, but waiting upon the psyche to act of itself (10–11).

The tendency, however, to establish some kind of hierarchy has to do, he believes, with a need for order, for containment, and for structure. Citing Jungian theory, Samuels claims that there is a tendency to single out or even to exploit the idea of the self as being the source of order and of meaning. But this stifles diversity within the psyche and denies to the psyche its power to regulate itself. He is critical of analytical psychology, particularly of the classical school, when it presents a view of the self which is "leaden and static, with its stress on states of integration and its apperception of conflict mainly in terms of its resolution" (11). Not that Samuels denies that at times there is an experience of the self as an "organizing center of the unconscious" or even of "the totality of the individual" (11). But to define the self in this way is to impose on it a hierarchy which is concerned with "structure, pattern, regularity and order at the expense of reversibility, mobility, and interaction" (12). Quoting Rafael Lopez-Pedraza that "the many contains the unity of the one without losing the possibilities of the many" (qtd. in Samuels 12).[1] Samuels believes that the idea of self and the idea of a pluralistic psyche do, in fact, coexist.

Instead of the psyche being dominated by an overriding component or value, Samuels sees the psyche as containing spheres of activity, of experience, of imagery which are relatively autonomous and which compete with one another for predominance at any given time. Referring at another time to these spheres as "styles," Samuels says that "each style is virtually complete in its own right, and in constant, competitive interaction with other styles" (20). The personality of an individual is what emerges from this competition. He then raises questions which mirror those asked in

---

[1] See Lopez-Pedraza in Bibliography.

relation to the Internet. "What kind of access do the various parts of the psyche, the inner interest groups, have to the rest of the psyche? What status and rights does each have? Is there an elite with special privileges?" (2–3). Using the idea of the *puer* (new beginning, revolution, creativity) and the *senex* (balance, steadiness, wisdom, farsightedness) as an example, he believes both characteristics exist inherently in an individual. "Each will monopolize, or colonize, whatever seems to fall into its natural sphere of influence" (2–3). Does each one have access to the power of the psyche as a whole? Probably not at the same time; rather, the *senex* will hold sway at one moment, and the *puer* at another. Samuels's pluralism as a perspective on the psyche wants to hold in tension all claims, whether towards unity or diversity. Not an easy thing to do, he admits, but he asserts depth psychology has always shown itself willing to struggle in the direction of pluralism. A pluralistic psychology recognizes the psyche, as Kelly does the Net, as emergent, and self-governing.

Competition, of course, leads to provocation, which Samuels believes is a good thing and necessary for creativity. He quotes James Hillman approvingly: "the worth of a psychology for another person lies not in the places where he can identify with it because it satisfies his psychic needs, but where it provokes him to work out his own psychology in response" (quoted in Samuels 8–9).[2] Once again, we are reminded that psychology is not as much concerned with things, or people, or experiences, but with what happens between things, people or experiences or between groups of "sets" of them (8–9).

The inner world of the psyche is a world of intense feeling, as Samuels observes. This constant and constantly changing interaction or competition understandably stirs up deep emotional reactions. There is plenty of provocation on the Net as in the psyche, as anyone familiar with the Internet will be aware, from firsthand experience or from reports in the press. The Net, as Kelly sees it, is wide open for all kinds of ideas, experiences, and points of view, evoking emotional, spontaneous, even uninhibited reactions. Here too the Net is a kind of mirror or metaphor for what happens within the plural psyche.

The Plural Psyche and the Self

Many find the notion of the plural psyche unsettling, even distressing, because it seems to deny the presence of a unifying self. They will likely be more in accord with Birkerts, who decries the loss of the individual in this frantic race to become "interconnected." Individuality and interconnectedness, for him, are mutually exclusive. But is this, in fact, the case? Is the interconnectedness we seek via the Net incompatible with holding on to a sense of a unique, personal identity?

---

[2] See Hillman, *Re-Visioning,* in Bibliography.

Kelly sees the Net (and similar metaphors as he explains in more detail in his book *Out of Control*) as a collection of thousands of autonomous units who react according to their own internal rules, who are shaped by their particular environment and who relate to each other as peers. This description seems to be in accord with Samuels's idea of the plural psyche in which the psyche acts autonomously as a self-organizing system. But Samuels argues it is only relatively autonomous because it does not exist in antagonism to other selves but in connection with them, and it is subject to influence by them. Now this autonomous psyche is not represented by the ego, even good Jungians understand that, but neither can it be solely identified with the all-encompassing self.

Can the individual get lost in the Net, in this web of interconnectedness? Using the metaphor of the beehive, Kelly suggests that can certainly happen ("Electronic Hive" 21; Kelly 23). The survival and evolution of the Net does not depend on the individual. It will survive even if the individual perishes. Just as we might say, humankind continues although individuals die. But the Net is not the psyche, but a metaphor for it. You can choose to have nothing to do with it as Birkerts does. You can choose like the neo-Luddites to have nothing to do with any part of communications technology—a nearly impossible feat. But can you have a self without connecting to others and even to things?

In his memoir, *Memories, Dreams, Reflections,* Jung spoke poignantly about those individuals (himself included) who find they have to go it alone, to stand apart from the collective, in order to reach "wider realms." But note the language in which he describes this condition. That individual, he says, will "be his own company."

> He will serve as his own group, consisting of a variety of opinions and tendencies—which need not necessarily be marching in the same direction. In fact, he will be at odds with himself, and he will find great difficulty in uniting his own multiplicity for purposes of common action. Even if he is outwardly protected by the social forms of the intermediary stage, he will have no defense against his inner multiplicity. The disunity within himself may cause him to give up, to lapse into identity with his surroundings. (343)

The individual psyche is neither singular, nor unitary, as described by Jung, but is untidy, conflicted, in tension with itself. So whether it participates in the collective or stands outside of it, the psyche is experienced as multiple.

Even Birkerts in his book *The Gutenberg Elegies* acknowledges unhappily that "the figure ground model, which has always featured a solitary self before a background that is the society of other selves, is romantic in the extreme. It is ever less tenable in the world as it is becoming" (130). He sees private, subjective space dwindling until "one day we will conduct our public and private lives within networks so dense, among so many channels of instantaneous information, that it will make almost no sense to speak of the differentiations of subjective individualism" (131). This may seem like an exaggeration, but we don't know yet whether it is or not.

As we continue to extend the Net wider and wider, will our connections become more and more shallow? It all depends, I suppose, on our expectations and purposes when we sign on to it. Thousands have apparently also been able to form "virtual communities" (nonphysical communities existing in cyberspace) through the Net based on common interests and concerns. As in life off the Net, many, if not most of our relationships will be tentative, superficial, but there will also be closer, more intimate relationships as well. Many of us, like Birkerts, tend to imagine the Net as a vast monolith, rather than a multiplicity made up of thousands of small entities bumping up against one another, sometimes cooperating, sometimes competing, sometimes in conflict.

There are, however, as Birkerts justly points out, serious problems with the Internet and with computer technology as a whole. Among these are its increasing commercialism; the emergence of a new elite class—those that have access to the computer as opposed to those who do not; its openness to social pathology of every description; unresolved problems concerning censorship versus free speech; and the threat of corporate and government control, despite Kelly's sanguine belief, based on the nature of the Internet, that it cannot happen. The computer and the Internet in particular have led to still one more addiction in our heavily addicted society, one which affects children and adolescents as well as adults. Addiction to the computer and to the Internet especially is serious and growing, so much so that it has become, ironically enough, a hot issue for debate on the Internet.

A pluralistic psychology, however, is no panacea for these problems. When Kelly talks about the Net or Samuels about the plural psyche, they are not talking about content, are not talking about "values" (that misused term). The Net is the *carrier* of content, not the content itself, and so I dare say, it is with the psyche. Its contents are to be found in the complexes and the archetypes around which they cluster, or more to the point, in the combining or splitting off of these complexes with one another. And it is here that the inevitable problems, personal or social, must be dealt with. A pluralistic psychology can help us, however, understand the psychological dynamics inherent in each situation. Without that understanding, it will be that much more difficult, perhaps impossible, to come up with workable solutions.

The plural psyche, like the Net which images it, does not offer a comforting, reassuring, stable, secure way in this world. It is not, as Samuels tells it, a way of "wholeness" as a goal of the individual psyche. It offers instead a challenge to rethink what we mean when we use such words as "wholeness," "individuation," or "self," whose meanings tend to become eroded through repetitious and often unreflective usage. Meanwhile, the idea of the plural psyche can be a useful way of coming to grips with this technological culture in which we are increasingly immersed and which is also compelling us to rethink what it means to be a human being, a self in a world of other selves.

BIBLIOGRAPHY

Barlow, John Perry, Sven Birkerts, Kevin Kelly, Mark Slouka. "What Are We Doing On-Line." *Harper's Magazine* (August 1995), 35–45.

Birkerts, Sven. *The Gutenberg Elegies: The Fate of Reading in the Electronic Age.* Boston: Faber and Faber, 1994.

Brockman, John. *Digerati: Encounters with the Cyber Elite.* San Francisco: HardWired, 1996.

Brook, James and Iain A. Boal, eds. *Resisting the Virtual Life: The Culture and Politics of Information.* San Francisco: City Lights, 1995.

Dery, Mark. *Escape Velocity: Cyberculture at the End of the Century.* New York: Grove Press, 1996.

"The Electronic Hive: Two Views." *Harper's Magazine* (May 1994), 17–25.

Henderson, Bill, ed. *Minutes of the Lead Pencil Club: Pulling the Plug on the Electronic Revolution.* Wainscott, New York: Pushcart Press, 1996.

Hillman, James. *Re-Visioning Psychology.* New York: Harper and Row, 1975.

Jung, C.G. *Memories, Dreams, Reflections.* Trans. R. and C. Winston. Rev. ed. New York: Vintage Books, 1989.

Katz, Jon. *Virtuous Reality: How America Surrendered Discussion of Moral Values to Opportunists, Nitwits, and Blockheads like William Bennett.* New York: Random House, 1997.

Kelly, Kevin. *Out of Control: The New Biology of Machines, Social Systems, and the Economic World.* New York: Addison-Wesley, 1994.

Lipnak, J. and J. Stamps. *The Networking Book: People Connecting with People.* London: Routledge, 1986.

Lopez-Pedraza, R. "Comment on Psychology: Monotheistic or Polytheistic?" by J. Hillman. *Spring,* 1971.

Negroponte, Nicholas. *Being Digital.* New York: Vintage Books, 1995.

Rawlins, Gregory J.E., *Moths to the Flame: The Seductions of Computer Technology.* Cambridge: MIT Press, 1996.

Rheingold, Howard. *The Virtual Community: Homesteading on the Electronic Frontier.* New York: Harper Perennial, 1994.

Sale, Kirkpatrick. *Rebels Against the Future: The Luddites and Their War on the Industrial Revolution: Lessons for the Computer Age.* New York: Addison-Wesley, 1995.

Samuels, Andrew. *The Plural Psyche: Personality, Morality, and the Father.* London: Routledge, 1989.

Slouka, Mark. *The War of the Worlds: Cyberspace and the High-Tech Assault on Reality.* New York: Basic Books, 1995.

Stefik, Mark. *Internet Dreams: Archetypes, Myths, and Metaphors.* Cambridge: MIT Press, 1996.

Stoll, Clifford. *Silicon Snake Oil: Second Thoughts on the Information Highway.* New York: Doubleday, 1995.

Tenner, Edward. *Why Things Bite Back: Technology and the Revenge of Unintended Consequences.* New York: Knopf, 1996.

Turkle, Sherry. *Life on the Screen: Identity in the Age of the Internet.* New York: Simon and Schuster, 1995.

22

Its Continuing Mission: *Star Trek's* Machine Mythology and the Quest for Self

ALMIRA F. POUDRIER

> Space. The final frontier. These are the voyages of the Starship *Enterprise*. Its continuing mission: to explore strange new worlds; to seek out new life and new civilizations; to boldly go where no one has gone before.
>
> (Opening lines to the first two *Star Trek* series)

The *Star Trek* series, its Starship *Enterprise*, its captains and crews, have engaged a wide spectrum of popular culture in a wonder-filled journey to different worlds. Having spawned nine major motion pictures and four television series, countless novels, and even a role-playing game, Trekkies are still not satisfied. They flock to *Star Trek* conventions in cities across the nation, playing the roles and donning the costumes of Captains Kirk, Picard, Sisko, and Janeway, or of their favorite aliens, Vulcans, Klingons, and a host of others, even the nastily acquisitive Ferengi. For a few hours, for an evening, they assume the identity of whatever character they have chosen.

Star Trek has entered the soul of popular culture. Its opening lines, quoted above, are repeated at the beginning of every *Star Trek* episode of the original series and the *Next Generation* series. The mission statement of the *Enterprise* has become a part of our modern mythology, resounding in our imaginations, reaching to a deeper sense of meaning and metaphor. *Star Trek* in all its incarnations writes humanity into the future tense, bringing it into contact with new life and new civilizations. Its images are archetypal, its missions those of the hero, like Theseus's journey into the labyrinth in Greek myth. It is in traversing new galaxies, in overcoming the dangers, in discerning and forming alliances with the good, in defeating the evil, in facing the weird and the dark, and in enduring the fear, that the human "enterprise" explores itself and approaches understanding of itself and its necessities.

As travellers through time, *Star Trek* plays with the way things were, the way history could have been; it plays out how things could look from different futures, making us rethink our premises and decisions, making us imagine new ones. Its most interesting aspect, however, involves the constant interaction with the alien, with the "other." C.G. Jung described the human psyche as a phenomenon unique to humans on this planet, something not comparable to anything else. "The possibility of comparison and hence of self-knowledge" he says, "would arise only if [humans] could establish relations with quasi-human mammals inhabiting other stars" (25). *Star Trek* chooses exactly this format. The *Enterprise* explores other worlds, encountering alien beings, recognizing their existence, with all of its conflicts and potential; and if possible, it brings them into relation with the Federation and a peaceful intergalactic world.

A recent television commercial advertising *Deep Space Nine*, the third of the *Star Trek* series, uses a sequence of grotesque masks from different cultures in rapid progression with a pause on the last one, which is the face of the Klingon warrior, Worf. The imagery is accompanied with this commentary: "Every culture has looked into the unknown and seen a face. Ours is no exception." Worf's race is alien, one formerly at war with humans, in fact the race that takes the position as Kirk's arch enemy in the original series. The exploration of Worf's character in *The Next Generation* and *Deep Space Nine* series has revealed in the frightening barbarian warrior the honor, the exaltation of physical superiority, and the fierceness in friendship and in enmity that is not so very different from that which resides in the human psyche. This is the key to the *Star Trek* phenomenon and its continuous popularity. Through *Star Trek* we look ever into the unknown and find ourselves there.

In *Star Trek*'s many years of episodes, a truly impressive array of strange beings and difficult situations have paraded across the screen. Many of these have been enemy races, from the original series's Klingons modelled on Nazi Germany to the torture-loving Cardassians of the *Next Generation*, from the vaguely Mongol-like Kazons of the *Voyager* series to *Deep Space Nine*'s dangerously capable and hopelessly addicted warriors of the Jem'Hadar. Others have varied in intentions: the mischievous Lwaxana Troi, the mysterious Guinan, the ambiguous Q, the macro-snowflake Crystalline Entity, the micro-mechanic nannites, the green dancing slave girls of Orion, the scantily clad inhabitants of Raisa, the genetically superadapted but socially maladjusted Khan, the dimension-hopping Traveller. But the most often repeated and fascinating kind of encounter with the "other" involves technological "beings" and the way they challenge us in our quest to discover what it means to be human.

There are two basic types of machines: non-sentient and sentient. Within the category of non-sentient machines, the basic machine represents physical enhancement in strength, speed, agility, durability, stamina, efficiency, and so on. The thinking machine represents expansion of consciousness to the exclusion of the unconscious and the development of reason to the exclusion of emotion.

The *sentient* machine takes the image one step farther. It represents not only pure consciousness, but self-consciousness. The machine that is self-aware has reached a new plane. The android reaches self-awareness on its own, and thus it gains a potential for danger to humans. The paradox of the machine is that, created for the enhancement or protection of humans, it often turns against them. Humans in contact with machines must therefore either defeat them or humanize them. They must reject the ever-maximizing ratios of power, and use the capabilities of the machine in service of wider human goals.

The machine-other represents yet another voyage into the unknown. Making machines as human as possible is an attempt to recreate self. The sentient machine's quest, one like Data's or the terminator's, is a story of the unknown, of a creature never before seen, and a voyage into self-knowledge. Though it is not always free of the dangerous ambiguity of the machine in the mythology, it plays the part of the hero and stands in for the seeker, and through its journey the audience participates in a quest for self-knowledge.

Techno-History

In machine mythology, the humans are often uneasy about machines, which sets the stage for the theme of antagonism between humans and machines. William Blake Tyrrell writes, "Fear of science dominates popular mentality because we long for freedom from change, for security rather than enlightenment" (288). The Industrial Revolution, for example, brought about great advances in technology. Although improving the quality of life for many people, it violated the wish for "security rather than enlightenment." The rise of the factory lifestyle in the nineteenth century greatly disrupted the traditional lives of the European and American working classes, according to Oscar Handlin, who writes: "The factory regime detached work from nature and from all other aspects of life. . . . From being people who were parts of households, known by a whole community, they had been reduced to being servants of the machine" (160).

Early factories resembled barracks, military camp, or even prison, giving the impression of the constriction of personal liberty by the power of the machine. Nonetheless, people largely accepted and welcomed machines. Creation of machines was ultimately in human hands, and overcoming the resulting difficulties generated a sense of confidence in "the human capacity to master the devices" (Handlin 159). Such ambiguity toward technology has persisted into modern times.

Indeed, it is in our era that humans have the most to fear from machines, since these machines have the greatest capabilities yet seen. Dependency on machines increases almost visibly with the growing omnipresence of e-mail, the Internet, and the World Wide Web. Artificial memory far exceeds the speed and recall capacity of human memory; machines are capable of prolonging life, and just as capable of shortening it. In ironic completion of the Handlin paradigm above, factories have become computerized, putting people out of jobs. Machines now create and run other machines; children's toys teach them to read; assembly-line, computer-driven tools make components for other machines; and cars cannot run without on-board computers that control everything from airbags to brakes. Offices and entire companies shut down when the computers fail; so do whole power, phone, and emergency systems. Modern research would be impossible without the abilities of the computer.

The idea of the machine as sentient entity begins to appear with frequency in literature, art, and the visual media only in the 1960s, after the introduction in the 1950s of the first rudimentary computers. The 1960s television series *Star Trek* opened the way for this new mythology, making technology a force to be reckoned with in many episodes. After that, techno-mythology flourished in a myriad of television series, including modernized variations of *Star Trek* and films such as *Star Wars, Terminator, Blade Runner,* and *2001: A Space Odyssey.*

The Non-Sentient Machine

The techno-mythology of *Star Trek* is profound in its omnipresence. In *Star Trek* and in other science fiction technology appears in some form in every episode. Often this technology is of the non-sentient type. In *Star Trek: The Next Generation,* even if techno-troubles are not the main concern of the episode, in any given plotline, the ship's engineers must give a technological explanation of some trouble and proposed solution. Although this techno-babble means little, since the technology involved does not exist, the repetition of such stock phrases as "warp core," "Dilithium crystals," "tractor beam," "plasma conduit," "warp nacelles," "positronic brain," "tricorder," "transporter lock," "phasers," "photon torpedos," "turbolift," "holodeck," and a host of others, has an almost magical feel: if the correct ones are used at the correct time in the correct order, anything can be accomplished, any disaster averted. There is little ambiguity in any of these scenarios. If it can be fixed, it is; if it cannot, it is summarily bypassed for more reliable equipment.

The *Enterprise* itself is in its entirety a machine. The ship was originally envisioned as run by one giant computer that is undoubtedly a mother-figure; the voice of the computer is female, and the ship contains the crew and protects them from the dangers of the cosmos. Furthermore, in the original series the *Enterprise* is cast as the one great love of the Captain, who is in his turn a father figure, decisive, protective of ship-wife and crew-children, firm with discipline but merciful and kind. The ship is even mourned when destroyed in the third *Star Trek* feature film. This portrayal of the ship does not change in the *Next Generation* series, though the Captain's attachment is more subtle. The *Next Generation* episodes "Elementary, Dear Data" and "Ship in a Bottle" push the ship's computer to the brink of sentience by creating holodeck characters which are conscious of their situations, but the ship itself remains in the category of non-sentient technology.

The Sentient Machine: Antagonist

When a machine begins to think for itself, to reason as humans can instead of simply performing tasks, it becomes a threat to humans, a monster in the labyrinth of the psyche. As Tyrrell states, "[Most] striking is the possibility that the computer may develop a consciousness of its own. The distinction between man and machine becomes blurred" (289). The early sentient machines were all antagonists, calling upon humans to overcome them. The seeker, face to face with the machine, just as with the minotaur, the monster in the labyrinth, actually confronts the dark side of the self.

It is interesting to note that coming into conflict with machines brought humans into contact with creatures of pure consciousness and all the power of reason and logic that they represent. In our age of glorification of the rational, this is an unusual form for the dark side of the self, since reason and logic are usually associated with good and light. Hence the association of Apollo, the rational god, with the sun and all civilizing influences, and Dionysus with the dark, the irrational, the manic, the earth and all things barbarous. Clearly, however, the logic of the machine is not the threat. It is only when reason becomes data, when it is reduced to facts and figures, when it leads them to conclusions dangerous to humans, and when decisions are made devoid of the emotional component which makes them humane, that the dark side triumphs.

In the early myths, then, when the antagonist machines represented the dangerous rationality, the inhumane logic, they were destroyed. Two tactics make destroying the machines possible. First, adherence to logic and rejection of emotion is portrayed as a weakness. The second recurring weakness of the machine is that it is not individualized. As a result of these two factors, the machines cannot adapt to changes in their environment. This is their fatal flaw, and allows humans to destroy them.

In every original series *Star Trek* episode where the *Enterprise* engages dangerously sentient machines, the ambiguity of the plot is resolved in favor of the humans. The humans always prove their human capacity to master the devices. In the episode "I, Mudd," a group of androids plans to take care of humans by controlling them completely, a good example of the theme of logic so pure that it brings a conclusion which threatens humans. The robots use a collective processor and are identical to one another—hence they lack individuality. Kirk and his crew discover that the collective brain of the androids is also unerringly logical and rational. They therefore use irrationality to overload the collective brain and thereby escape enslavement by the androids. The moral is clear, and also Jungian: the lack of irrationality, the inability of emotion to surface, bringing balance from the unconscious, is a dangerous weakness and leads to destruction. The machines rely totally on a collective consciousness, and this is inherently an unworkable situation. Since they have no imagination, they are unable to adapt to the introduction of illogical or totally unforeseen actions.

Another figure in early sentient-machine mythology is HAL, the computer villain of *2001: A Space Odyssey,* released in 1968. The computer, designed to benefit humans and remove the possibility of human error, runs all the mechanics and computer functions on a large ship bound for Jupiter. The ambiguity of the sentient machine is artistically handled by director Stanley Kubrick. In several places the audience sees from the computer's perspective, a ploy to make the audience sympathize with the machine. HAL seems genuinely concerned for the welfare and happiness of the crew in wishing Frank a happy birthday and in showing interest in Dave's drawings. HAL is also obviously proud of its place on the mission in its news interview.

The visual and audial portrayal of the machine, however, makes the audience distrust it; its omnipresent glowing red eye fills the whole screen; its ingratiating, emotionless voice evokes unease. When HAL acts, it acts without emotion or hesitation, methodically disposing of the entire crew. Human capacity to master the devices is again borne out, though, when Dave through his own ingenuity forces his way back onto the ship. HAL's defeat has nothing to do with inability to cope with changes; machines in this film have become sophisticated enough to solve problems. HAL's weakness is its lack of emotion, its ultimate rationality which tells it that the mission would be more successful without the humans. This fact is clear in HAL's final scene, where the machine attempts to rationalize with Dave, who is about to shut it down.

Terminator, which was released in 1984, is an expansion on the idea of the sentient machine. The terminator is a sentient machine from a dark future ruled by machines, sent to dispose of a man by killing his mother before she even conceives him—a perfect example of inhumane logic. There is no internal ambiguity toward the machine in this film; the terminator is visually evil, with glowing red eyes and a leering metal face. In verbal description, too, Reese tells Sarah: "It can't be bargained with, it can't reasoned with. It doesn't feel pity, or remorse, or fear; and it absolutely will not stop, ever, until you are dead."[1]

---

[1] This and all further quotations from television and film were transcribed by the author from the visual media. Information on the relevant television episodes and films is included in the bibliography.

Present here is the paradox of the machine designed to help humans, which subsequently betrays them. The terminator was sent by another sentient machine, Skynet, which was created to protect humans. It decided upon genocide when it became self-aware, and chose to accomplish this goal by setting off the nuclear war it was designed to avoid. Reese says, "They say it got smart. A new order of intelligence. Then it saw all people as a threat, not just the ones on the other side. Decided our fate in a microsecond. . . ." Despite this bleak picture, the humans again prove their capacity to master the devices, both in the future, where John Connor rallies the straggling humans to destroy Skynet, and in the present, where Sarah survives and through the strength of sheer will destroys the terminator. Face to face with the overwhelming capabilities of the machine, it is only human emotion which can overcome it; Sarah's love of Reese and the sheer human fury which she feels at his death gives her such tenacity and desire to live that she can overcome even the physically stronger machine.

The Human-Machine Interface[2]

A second major motif in the mythology of the antagonist machine is that of the human-machine interface. Here, the machine and the human come together—physically and mentally—to create a new type of being.

In every case the human is enhanced by the efficiency, strength, and stability of the machine. But in every case the human also loses something essential to being human. It loses the power to make humane decisions, to be influenced by emotion. It also loses free will. In its antagonist role, the new amalgam of human and machine takes on the same qualities as other sentient machines: it becomes completely rational and loses all emotionality; it loses individuality; it loses the ability to adapt to changes. A shift in the resolution of the plot begins to occur, however. The progressive humanization of the machine is introduced, a theme which becomes integral to the development in the mythology of protagonist machines. This progression indicates a greater acceptance in society of the pragmatic necessity of the machine—it can no longer just be conquered, junked, and forgotten.

The *Next Generation* series repeatedly uses the theme of the human-machine interface. The semi-regular character, Reginald Barclay, creates a neural interface with the ship's computer in the episode "Nth Degree." The joining allows him to save the Argus Array Telescope installation and make great improvements in the physical capabilities of the ship. However, Picard mistrusts the intentions of the Barclay-Computer; Barclay's calm and inquisitive computer voice is distinctly reminiscent of HAL's sinister voice from *2001: A Space Odyssey*.

---

[2] I first heard this term as "man-machine interface" in a seminar run by Ted E. Tollefson on *Star Trek* and mythology, Mythos Institute, Minneapolis (Winter 1995/96).

As in many such stories of the human-machine interface, Barclay loses his humanity in the interface. He tells the captain, "My primary cerebral functions . . . have expanded to such a degree that it would be impossible to be returned to the confines of my human brain." His connection to the computer barely allows him to use his body, a sinister, dangerous, and unnatural division of psyche and soma. In addition, the human part of the interface has lost the emotions of the Barclay character. He no longer has the irrational unconscious; he no longer fantasizes. He has been possessed by the rationality of the machine to the exclusion of all else. The only way to save him is to separate him from the machine, and only then does he regain all that he has lost.

The episode "11001001" involves the Bynars, a race of people doubly other, since they are both alien and machine. They have become so interfaced with their computer that they have conformed their speech, thoughts, even social customs to resemble the machine. The benefits are obvious: everything from their speech to their work with external computers is exceptionally efficient. They have in return given up their individuality. They function in binary pairs and are even physically indistinguishable. The weaknesses are obvious: when the computer is endangered on their home world, they are left helpless, close to death, reliant on the *Enterprise* crew to save them. Their lack of individuality has left them ultimately unable to cope with change, and this threatens their very existence.

The Cyborg

The cyborg, for many perhaps the most profoundly disturbing example of the human-machine interface, has become a pervasive figure in science fiction. The idea of the cyborg is uncomfortably close to reality: the artificial heart, the computer that can be programmed to speak for a disabled person, genotechnology that can control things at the cellular level, the helmet-like headset of the virtual reality game, the tubes and wires that sustain life for people in critical care units who would otherwise die. The concept of such a close, physical, corporeal association with a machine is unsettling. It goes far beyond the type of interface represented in the "11001001" and "Nth Degree" episodes. The body is not discarded; it is invaded—and used—by the machine. The interface involves both psyche and soma. It forces the viewer to ask the question: To what extent have we lost our humanity in merging with the technology of machines?

Perhaps the best known cyborg in the popular media was Darth Vader, the villain of the ever-popular *Star Wars* trilogy, a former Jedi knight who gave up the light for the dark side of "the Force." His repeated warning, "Do not underestimate the dark side," is a key issue in the search for self. The dark side is incorporated into the godlike Force in these films. The light and the dark are both powerful, and the dark demands to be faced and overcome by the hero, young Luke Skywalker. In the progression of the three films the dark side moves closer and closer to Luke as he discovers that Vader is his father and, in a vision, as he sees his own face in the mechanical helmet of his nemesis. Totally evil at the beginning of the *Star Wars* trilogy, Darth Vader even looks like a machine; there is little indication that he has human qualities at all, either physical or mental. That he is enhanced by this mechanization is obvious; he is taller and stronger than a normal human. That he has lost his emotions is also obvious; he is ruthless, but he feels no anger, remorse, joy, or any other emotion.

As Vader is progressively humanized, the audience is introduced slowly to his human component; we see that he has human parts when he bares his head, we learn that he is a father, that he serves his master with loyalty (even though the master is evil), that once he too learned from the Jedi masters that teach Luke, and that he can be provoked to human (albeit dangerous) anger by his colleagues. By the end of *Return of the Jedi*, Darth relearns the value of human life. He makes a decision influenced by emotion when he chooses to save his son, and in choosing emotion he regains the humanness that he has lost. He becomes Annaken Skywalker again: the last we see of him he is no longer cyborg at all, but a whole man once more.

This theme of humanization continues in the most convincing example of a cyborg in the visual media to date: the Borg in recurring episodes of *Star Trek: The Next Generation*. The Borg is really a group of cyborgs which is out to "assimilate" all beings, including humans, so that the whole universe can become one collective mind. The superiority of the Borg is easily seen; it is incapable of being emotionally swayed, its collective mind is very efficient, its determination unstoppable, and its technology highly advanced. The *Enterprise* crew must flee, though they are sure that the Borg will eventually pursue.

In the riveting two-part episode, "Best of Both Worlds," the inevitable occurs—the Borg comes to find and assimilate the humans. Captain Picard is captured and assimilated into the Borg, becoming Locutus of Borg, the mouthpiece for the collective. The physical imagery is chilling; Picard becomes the "other," unable to save himself, unable even to wish for rescue. With his knowledge at their disposal, the Borg proceeds, with Picard at the helm, to destroy the entirety of Starfleet in a single battle at the infamous Wolf 359; it then continues to Earth, where it will proceed with the assimilation of all people—the ultimate devaluation of human life.

The individuality of the man, Picard, is completely overcome by the group mind of the Borg. However, the collective consciousness, which is the core of the Borg's efficiency, is also their weakness. Data, with the recaptured Picard-Locutus as a link, is able to access the collective mind of the Borg and shut it down. Unable to adapt to this sudden change in its programming, the Borg ship self-destructs.

The Borg, however, which so effectively dehumanized Picard in "Best of Both Worlds," is also subject to the theme of humanization. The return of Starfleet's nemesis is heralded by the episode "I, Borg," in which a single Borg unit is captured by the *Enterprise*. In the ensuing period, while the crew tries to decide how best to use it against the collective, this single Borg is individualized to the point that the crew gives it a name, Hugh. It refers to itself as "I" instead of "we." It even begins to make decisions that are apparently influenced by emotion; it pleads the case against assimilation of its new-found friends, since it believes that they would not wish to be part of the collective.

In the last of the Borg episodes, the two-part "Descent," it is discovered that the *Enterprise*'s efforts with Hugh have paid off: some of the Borg, influenced by the growth of individualism spawned in Hugh, have broken away from the collective and banded together. Within that group there is dissension, infighting, and political maneuvering, all human qualities and full of emotion. Hugh, with some of his faction of individualized Borg, joins briefly with the *Enterprise* crew to defeat a common enemy.

The Sentient Machine: Protagonist

The machine as protagonist stands in sharp contrast to the antagonist machine. The creation of the sentient machine is the attempt at creating self, at making machines that look and act like humans. The sentient machine subsequently takes the place of the seeker. Now it faces its own monsters and stands in as the hero of the story. For the audience, it is no longer "other," for although it is still a machine and therefore should still be alien, it now embarks on its own search for self-knowledge; and in witnessing the search, the audience partakes in it. The friendly sentient machine asks a related question: what does being human really mean?

Terminator 2: Judgment Day, sequel to *Terminator*, is a major film in the progressive humanization of the machine. The plot is fairly straightforward. Two terminators have been sent back through time instead of one, and they are at cross-purposes: one is supposed to protect John Connor, who is now a teenager; the other is ordered to kill him. Machines are therefore cast as both antagonist and protagonist, and the protagonist machine is gradually humanized through the course of the film.

The protagonist terminator (model 101) is cast in a human light, while its enemy machine, the prototype T1000, is a techno-monster of even greater proportions. The 101 replaces Kyle Reese, becoming in effect a member of the family. It tells Sarah "Come with me if you want to live," the exact words that Reese, John's father, spoke to her in the first movie. The machine also becomes a father figure to Reese's son. Sarah accepts this:

> Seeing John with the machine, it was suddenly so clear: the terminator would never stop, it would never leave him. It would never hurt him, never shout at him or get drunk and hit him or say it was too busy to spend time with him. It would aways be there, and it would die to protect him. Of all the would-be

fathers who came and went over the years, this thing, this machine, was the only one who measured up.

Through association with young John, the machine learns to act more human; but the 101 must go beyond *acting* (behavior) into *being*. Its enemy, the mimetic poly-alloy liquid metal T1000 terminator, can look like any human it wishes. On a surface level, it can make a more convincing human than the original 101 unit. The T1000 impersonates the police, holds conversations with humans while canvassing to find John, and even replicates the foster mother convincingly enough that the foster father does not notice before it kills him. *Acting* human has become a simple task. But the 101 must make the major step toward *being* human.

The machine learns to understand emotions. It tells John just before it dies, "I understand now why you cry, but I can never do it." This moment illustrates perfectly the point the machine has reached in its progression toward being human. It cannot feel the emotions that the humans do, but it craves them; it cannot self-destruct because that would be irrational, but it has learned to imagine a future free from the dangers of its kind. Sarah Connor delivers the moral of the story: "Because if a machine, a terminator, can learn the value of human life, maybe we can too." Here is the theme realized; in seeking humanity, the machine has become a mirror of self-knowledge and a model for our own attitudes and actions.

The humanity of the machine is also developed in *Blade Runner*, a dark, futuristic film which takes the machine to the next step in its evolution. The main character of the film is Roy Batty, leader of a group of lethal androids known as "replicants." They were created by an industry which engages in the creation of machines in the quest for self-knowledge, since the motto of the company is "more human than human." The original purpose of the replicants was to spare humans from the hazardous work of off-world colonization. The industry, however, now uses them for slave labor and builds in a four-year life span as a fail-safe, because after that time, they begin to develop their own emotional responses. The machine, therefore, has acquired emotions, and can now act irrationally. Rick Deckard is the human who is called in to destroy them.

There is a deep ambiguity in the portrayal of the machine in this film, for although the audience associates with Deckard, the androids are clearly portrayed both as ruthless killers and as emotionally sensitive beings who are wronged and doomed. Roy and his group are near the end of their four-year lives, and they are desperate to extend the time that they have, so much so that they will kill to survive. These androids do not seek emotion and irrationality; they already have it. They seek answers and guidance in their quest to fulfill their lives, to understand their emotional responses. Roy goes to his manufacturer to demand more life and is rejected. He weeps as he kills the man, for as he says "It is a difficult thing to meet one's maker."

Roy's quest, though fruitless, has not yet ended. Roy hunts Deckard almost to death but then saves his life. Deckard comments in his voice-over narration, "I don't know why he saved my life. Maybe in those last moments he loved life more than he ever had before . . . anybody's life . . . my life. All it wanted were the same answers the rest of us want. Who am I? Why am I here? How long have I got?" Deckard's use of both the personal pronoun "he" and the impersonal "it" in reference to the replicant nicely illustrates the ambiguity of the machine throughout the story. The androids are pointedly more human than the people who surround them in this film, feeling more, living more, clinging to life, looking into the darkness in the hope of increasing their self-knowledge. Like the terminator, the replicant teaches humans to respect life. And if it cannot live, it is at least ensouled in the visual imagery, for as it dies, a dove—a symbol for both soul and spirit— flies upward from its hands.

Data's Quest

One of the most startling reflections of the human quest for our full selves is Data, the android Lieutenant Commander of the *Enterprise* in *Star Trek: The Next Generation*. This android is a consummate example of a machine created to be human. Data's creator, Dr. Noonien Soong, has the same face as Data (both characters are played by Brent Spiner), though Soong's face has human coloring and shows aging. Data's avowed quest to act, think, and feel more human occurs as a continuing theme throughout the seven seasons of this series. It is a journey in search of self-knowledge, and the writers deal with many issues, some thorny, such as the morality of Data's classification as the property of Starfleet or his right to propagate his kind. Some are amusing, such as his inability to sneeze, his relationship with his cat, and his difficulty in acquiring a sense of humor. He is even granted an unconscious late in the series, which reveals itself in his experience of dreaming.

Data's importance in *Star Trek* cannot be emphasized enough. The audience feels the emotions that he cannot; they yearn for his humanization with all the desire that is alien to him. They relate to him because he tries so hard to truly understand them. He is other; he is machine; and yet in him they find something of themselves, for in seeking to be human, Data must sort through the light as well as the dark characteristics of humans. His quest through its long progression teaches what it is to be human, including the paradoxes involved in that condition.

In Data's quest, his dark side is embodied in a character called Lore. Lore (also played by Brent Spiner) is the exact replica of Data, in fact, his prototype, his elder twin. Lore is different than Data in that he embodies all the dark human qualities that Data does not. He is ambitious, manipulating, dishonest, and cruel. He was designed with emotional responses; he was given, from his conception, what Data seeks. The two are so similar that Lore is able to take Data's place, a plot line which is used in the episode "Brothers" and also in the episode "Datalore," which by its very title implies the lack of distinction between them.

In the final episode involving Lore, "Descent," Lore seduces Data to leave the *Enterprise* by offering him emotions. It quickly becomes apparent that Lore has given Data only negative emotions such as fear, anger, and greed. The dark side thereby moves closer to Data, becoming a part of him. Once again Data embodies the search for self as he faces his own darkness. He rejects the chance to feel emotions unless he can feel the light as well as the dark ones. He refuses one-sidedness, even when it means giving up emotion, the thing he has desired and worked to achieve. The episode ends with the dilemma unresolved, for Data is still without emotion.

The feature film *Generations*, released in 1996, gives Data emotional responses by means of a chip welded into his positronic brain. This chip cannot be removed, and Data is forced now to deal with both dark and light emotions. He betrays his friends when he first feels fear; he weeps for the first time when he finds his cat alive in the ruins of the destroyed ship. He learns to control fear and to understand humor. His humanization takes a giant step in this film, for in controlling the fear and feeling the joy, he comes closer to self-knowledge and to realizing what it means to be human.

Conclusion

Machine mythology is almost as pervasive in modern media as the machines from which the mythology is spawned. In relating to our own highly mechanized lives, humans find that machines are characters in our reality, and so they become characters in our stories. Roy Batty, Data, HAL, Darth Vader, and Skynet are the future tense, the conceivable descendants, of machines that are real parts of our society—car computers that transport us, life support systems that sustain us, laptops that go everywhere with us, answering machines that substitute for us, and missiles that are called "smart" for their enhanced ability to kill us. Perhaps it is our everyday interaction with these entities of pure logic, of abilities that we cannot match, and of reason so undiluted that it is sometimes frightening, which makes them such potent symbols in our modern mythology.

Techno-mythology brings the viewer into contact with the machine as other. Machine characters, whether they are wholly separate from humans or whether they invade mind and body through an interface with humans, take us on a quest of self-exploration. For as depth psychology shows us, the "other" is also really ourselves. In stories where the machines are enemies, they warn against the dangers of logic which, fortified by the capacities of technology, is so extensive that it excludes irrationality. They illustrate the peril of reasoning without the emotional and relational component, which makes decisions not only human, but humane.

Friendly machines show us our potential to develop fully as human beings, to use our humanity well, and to balance the necessities of inner life and the outside world we live in. They teach that these capacities can come humanely into play only in a universe, inside and out, which includes—and respects—the breadth and depth of human capabilities, that makes a place, a Federation, if you will, for the rational and irrational, the dark and light, the breadth and depth of human soul, the Jungian Self.

Star Trek allows its audience access to that Federation, and in doing so it has found its way into the soul of popular culture. Its archetypal imagery and its heroic missions serve to bring its audience into contact with new life and new civilizations, with creatures outwardly alien but inwardly familiar. Its strange new worlds are the landscapes of self-knowledge. When it goes boldly into those unknown realms, the *Enterprise* seeks always, in its continuing mission, to better understand what it really means to be human.

BIBLIOGRAPHY

Blade Runner. Director Ridley Scott. Harrison Ford, Rutger Hauer, Sean Young. The Ladd Company, 1982.

Blair, Karin. "The Garden in the Machine: The Why of *Star Trek*," *Journal of Popular Culture* 13, 310–319.

Handlin, Oscar. "Science and Technology in Popular Culture," *Daedalus* (1965), 156–170.

Jung, C. G. *The Undiscovered Self.* Princeton: Princeton University Press, 1990.

Nemecek, Larry. *Star Trek: The Next Generation Companion.* New York: Simon and Schuster, 1992.

"Nth Degree," Producer Bob Justman, Director Robert Legato, Executive Producers Gene Roddenberry and Rick Berman. *Star Trek: The Next Generation.* Fox Network (Paramount Pictures), 1991.

Terminator. Director James Cameron. Arnold Schwarzenegger, Linda Hamilton, Michael Biehn. Cinema '84, A Greenberg Brothers Partnership, 1984.

Terminator 2: Judgement Day. Director James Cameron. Arnold Schwarzenegger, Linda Hamilton, Robert Patrick. Carolco Pictures, Inc., 1991.

Tyrrell, William Blake, "*Star Trek*'s Myth of Science," *Journal of American Culture* 2 (1979), 288–296.

23
Star Trek and the Intimate Alien

KEVIN JONES

Popular culture is a fertile realm for deeper inquiry into the human condition. Few examples of popular entertainment provide as much scope for insight and imagination as the multitude of *Star Trek* offerings, from the original *Star Trek* TV series (henceforth abbreviated *ST*) to the later movies and series that have so proliferated over the last ten years or so.

As one of the most successful works of contemporary popular mythopoesis, examination of all the factors pertaining to the appeal of the original series and its spin-offs would require a volume in itself. One pervasive theme that is both of keen interest to those interested in the human condition and a frequent plot device in *Star Trek* is the experience of encounter with the alien. In many of these encounters, the aliens not only walk among but also live among the crew, in intimate proximity. Jungian psychologists have long studied the effects of unnerving contacts with the radically unfamiliar, and I hope to bring something of this knowledge to bear on what the aliens in *Star Trek* have to teach us.

Through movies and television programs over the last several years, we have been all but inundated with highly popular treatments of this theme of encounter with the bizarre, the alien, the uncanny, and the explicitly other worldly—a development that the success of *Star Trek: The Next Generation* (henceforth abbreviated *TNG*) did much to make possible. These offerings range from the frightening and realistic (*Millennium* or *The X-Files*, for example) to the weirdly humorous (*Mars Invades*, *Independence Day* or even *Third Rock From the Sun*). But we needn't stray from the solar system or even the confines of the human beings in this culture for the daily impact of resident aliens to be felt. Whether as illegal immigrants, Heaven's Gate cultists, secessionists from the self-proclaimed Republic of Texas or devotees of David Koresh or Louis Farrakhan, we are increasingly made aware in the daily news that the uniformity of our cultural perspectives, once invisible and all but taken for granted, is now a candidate for the endangered species list. More and more it becomes impossible to hold the view that all right thinking persons understand or believe things in the same ways, or for that matter, could even potentially do so. Surprisingly large gulfs of difference divide our outlooks and understandings, even within this single country at this single time in history.

The resident aliens on the Starship *Enterprise* teach us not so much to see as they do, but more importantly they show us what it is that they might be carrying of our own unwanted and unrecognized qualities. They show us what may seem foreign and unfamiliar to us but for that reason may also hold the key to the ongoing process of self-realization. Notably, these qualities differ from one historical moment to another, as reflected in what each series casts as alien, suggesting that what is seen to be irredeemable in one period may become redeemable in another.

Jung and the Alien

Jung's work is marked by the theoretical and experiential importance he accords to encounters with the intimate alien. There are numerous ways that Jungian approaches to this topic could be discussed, but I would like to briefly summarize four closely interrelated topics—(1) the unconscious, (2) opposites, (3) individuation, and (4) the shadow—which form the core, I believe, of a Jungian approach to this issue.

The Jungian understanding of the unconscious itself offers a broadened and unfamiliar sense of what it is to be human and a new kind of closeness with the radically "other." While agreeing with Freud that humans have an unconscious dimension of mind that differs profoundly from conscious awareness, Jung took issue with the Freudian contention that unconscious contents are the repressed flotsam of the waking ego. Rather he recognized that much of this content is at no point conscious, familiar to, or derived from the ego, but has its own, distinct and non-human character. There are things in my psychological life which I do not create, he would write, but which create themselves and have their own being. His own explorations on this frontier of *inner space* convinced him that these contents are neither reducible to our own personal experiences nor arbitrary and chaotic, but rather exhibit an alien and distinct organization of their own. Further, such mental contents often appear as personified—in the form of persons or as interactions with persons, who likewise cannot be reduced to myself or any other literal human beings of my experience. Such encounters were key in helping Jung to recognize a far richer and more alien unconscious underlying the personal one, including the archetypal realm of the collective unconscious.

As a counterpart to individual consciousness, unconscious experience exemplifies the way that psychic life is always an interplay of opposing elements—ideas and feelings. Jung felt that psychic dynamism arose out of the tension posed by these opposites and that this tension is critical to bringing about the emergence of novel and often synthetic third elements that may reconcile our conflicts and expand our awareness. Out of the kind of oppositions and differences exemplified by the worlds, cultures, and characters in the *Star Trek* mythos can come not only the resolution of conflicts but also the evolving of wholly new understandings and awarenesses.

One keenly felt opposition that Jung specifically addressed is the opposition between ego and shadow. The process of building an ego involves living life and making choices, and what is not chosen (or perhaps more significantly, what is chosen against) becomes part of the shadow. We generally have strong antipathetical feelings about the shadowy possibilities we have chosen against, making their integration into our awareness a difficult enterprise. It is far easier to see them in (or project them into) other people, and to thus have someone else carry these conflictual possibilities for us. A great deal of the hatred and fear which characterize our relationships with different, alien-seeming others (including our inclinations toward stereotyping, stigmatizing, and prejudice) may be traced to our struggles with bearing our own shadows, and owning our own possibilities for darkness.

This work to own shadow and integrate opposites is a key part of the great work of self-realization that Jung called "individuation." Our goal, Jung felt, should not be the pursuit of narrow perfection that excludes our weaknesses, shortcomings, shadows, and idiosyncrasies. Rather than seeking to be perfect we should seek to be whole, to find a place for all of the elements which make us up. Not unlike the ideal of the Federation itself, the ideal is an inclusive valuing of the different in a polycentric constellation of diverse elements.

The Resident Aliens

The resident aliens of *Star Trek* exemplify many of the Jungian concerns discussed above. Many surprise and shock human sensibility, broadening our awarenesses about the kinds of sentience that do not arise in us or operate in the way human sentience does. These aliens will often, in fact, reveal us to ourselves in ways we would otherwise never see, making more apparent what we are by virtue of what we are not. Even more interesting, we may come to perform this service for the alien also, allowing, by the fact of our being each other's opposite, a new awareness to rise synthetically between us. This will not occur easily: the alien carries not merely incomprehensible but often terrifying possibilities, including those against which we have defined ourselves by passionate opposition. But if our goal is the realization of our deeper integrative possibilities, our "continuing mission" must be to persist in the pursuit of new and more comprehensive wholenesses, broadening our sense of who "we" are to encompass ever more divergent possibilities.

First Officer Spock: Half Human

No character of the original *ST* series allows us to so profoundly explore this theme of the resident alien as does First Officer Spock. The cast of the original *Enterprise* crew was assembled as an act of including the alien, the unrepresented, and the adversarial by crossing the exclusionary lines which so characterized television and U.S. society as a whole in the middle 1960s. Made members of the crew and even brought onto the bridge as part of the command structure were: an Asian (Lieutenant Sulu), a black female (Lieutenant Uhuru), and a Russian (Lieutenant Chekov)—not an uncontroversial move at the height of the Cold War. But it is with the inclusion of Spock, this half-Vulcan Science Officer, that the bounds of the human species itself are crossed—or expanded—for Spock (as will all our aliens) serves to reveal more deeply the familiar in what is strange and the strange in what is familiar. He broadens our understanding of what we find "human," and allows us an intimate relation with profound differentness. As a crew member he is a part of the "band" who (as in all quests and adventures) must be "as one," trusting each other with their lives and the success of the venture. There must necessarily be trust, familiarity, and intimacy, and Spock is accorded this membership. Yet the essentially unfamiliar and indeed unknown character of the alien is maintained with him as well. Spock becomes known, trusted, admired, and eventually held in awe by his fellows, without becoming any less alien, or even less aloof. In his person he holds together the paradox of both standing with us while still standing apart.

It is worth looking in detail at some of our projections concerning the alien features which Spock carries, for these can tell us something of what is still alien and awaiting fuller inclusion among us. On the most immediate level, there are those ears! More than just acting different, he *looks* different, and as every "different-looking" child on a playground has ever discovered, this can be the most basic ground of alienation. We think at first that we can never forget, in just looking at him, that he is different from us, not human. And yet to our surprise, we (and the crew) discover that we *can* forget, or almost can, as we become not only used to but indeed fond of his alien physiognomy. They (and we) become surprisingly adept at reading the "inscrutable" character of his expression, anticipating his actions and reactions in coming to know him better.

More able, but not wholly so. As knowledge of Spock deepens, so does awareness of what is perhaps also the chief aspect of his alienness—his emotionality or (perhaps) his lack thereof. As their own culturally definitive act, the Vulcan people, at a point almost mythically distant in their history, created a relationship between thought and emotion subordinating the latter, particularly the disruptive and conflictual passions, to Logic—a complex amalgam of abstract reason, esthetic values, and analytic self-examination. Though not wholly Vulcan, Spock embraces this philosophy with the zeal of the orthodox among unbelievers, taking it up to preserve and indeed even deepen his outsider status. Spock does not yearn for intimate inclusion and membership among us: what emotional reactions he has might best be seen as an overtaxed tolerance covering a deeper disdain for human indulgences. Thus in Spock we find an alien eye which looks coolly at our human emotional follies and takes a refuge in distance, refusing our efforts to warmly take him in.

The relationship of Spock to Logic also qualifies him to embody for us the perspective of another culture both intimate and alien within our own: that of science itself. It is no coincidence that Spock is Science Officer on the *Enterprise*. *ST* is prototypically a story of the beautiful, progressive, and even utopian possibilities within our relation to science and technology, about their capacities to extend and deepen our humanity. But there is, of course, another side to the story. Spock admirably personifies the inhuman, dispassionate, and impersonal character which science is seen to have, and carries with it a Promethean or even Satanic character (again, those ears!) that science and technology can wear for us. From Dr. Frankenstein to Dr. Edward Teller, the frightening, potentially evil, "mad" scientist is a figure of fascination and horror, seemingly alienated from the feelings, ethics, and personal involvements that so define our "normal" human life. Such figures are, as we suggest here, deeply ambiguous for us: we are unsure whether to consider them subhuman, inhuman, or superhuman. They, with Spock, seem uncomprehending of the most common grounds of daily human contact, of basic emotional parlance or even humor. And yet, by their powers they may see deep and hidden things in us or in the world, things we often feel humans were not meant to know.

In many of our greatest stories, alien figures often exhibit skills, gifts, or powers which show us not only the shape but the limitations of the human. Spock's mental and spiritual depths are shown by many of these features, from the Vulcan Nerve grip to the *pon farr*, the "Amok Time" of the Vulcan mating cycles. But it is perhaps in the Vulcan Mind Meld we most clearly glimpse an awe-inspiring sense of this giftedness. The technique's strangeness reveals something of alien culture's mastery of things still profoundly mysterious to human culture, even some three hundred years in the future. More importantly however, it displays again the mystery that it is the alien, Spock, who can touch us in ways that are beyond the reach of our own kind, overcoming the isolation that we (now) realize is so much our human lot.

Spock's inhuman character and gifts often render him incomprehensible and even frightening to those humans in close contact with him, perhaps because he represents a rejected element in our own makeup. Here we come to see Spock as carrier of our own internal divisions, the homeless and forever uprooted part of ourselves that may tell us that there is no place where we truly belong. For Spock is also of divided origins and can belong fully nowhere. He is only half Vulcan, and while he has his share of both human and Vulcan characteristics, he is shown to be genuinely accepted by neither culture. Dr. McCoy, whose intensely emotional character (and, presumptively, his Southern and racist antipathy for the different) makes him a natural foil to Spock, becomes here a spokesman for our inclination to fear, disparage, and demonize that which carries an alien half. Spock thus stands between worlds—Earth and Vulcan, humanity and science, the *Enterprise* crew and the alien lives that they encounter—and his greatest gift perhaps is to be able to move and mediate among them. This capacity gains recognition in *TNG* where he has grown into the role of ambassador, exemplifying his capacity to bring peace and conciliation between alienated cultures.

Beyond Homo Sapiens: *Data, the Borg, Worf*

In *TNG*, the role of the resident alien is substantially broadened. More and different human races and genders are dealt with. Giordi LaForge, the blind Chief Engineer reveals to us a whole new range of seeing. Deanna Troi, the Betazoid empath, and Beverly Crusher, the human physician and mother, broaden the female presence and make contributions to a richer sense of the healing arts. But, in roles analogous to Spock's, two new representatives split the task of expanding the sense of what we find "human" beyond *Homo sapiens*. Such diversification perhaps reduces some of the chronic displacement and exclusion under which Spock labored alone, but Data and Worf also represent wholly different elements of the alien and very different kinds of challenges to our sense of who we are.

Data. Data, an artificial life form constructed to resemble a human being, assumes Spock's ongoing inquiry into what it means to be human, and inherits many of the characteristics and burdens under which Spock operated in *ST*. Like Spock, he shows the mix of sub-, super-, and inhuman traits that mark the truly alien. Data possesses extraordinary strength and a virtually unlimited lifespan; his memory is compendious and the superhuman speed at which he can operate is completely beyond that of humans for most activities.

Despite these capabilities he recurrently stumbles over the subtleties of human language, custom, and feeling. He is unable to use contractions in his speech or grasp the nature of humor—a word appropriately sharing the etymological roots with both of "human" and "humus," the earth itself. Data's thoroughly dispassionate, logical, and curious mind also sets him apart from the human crew, as Spock's did, and occasionally also rouses the fear and prejudices of his human crew members. But unlike with Spock, the threat is not simply the confrontation with an intelligent but alien lifeform. Rather it is a culminating confrontation with the work of our own hands, in the centuries-old promise of the replication (or replacement) of human function by machines, including the creation of an artificial intelligence. While machinelike in his dispassion, Spock more closely represents the scientist than the scientist's creation. With Data we are confronted less by Frankenstein than by his monster.

Two things most fundamentally make Data's circumstances different than Spock's and, surprisingly, render him more a part of the crew. The first involves his goals and aspirations. In the pilot episode of *TNG*, Data reveals that while there are several ways in which Data is superior to humans, he would nonetheless give many of them up to *be* human, upon which an incredulous Commander Riker aptly christens him "Pinocchio." Perhaps more than anything else it is this desire to be human, or at least to understand them more deeply, that undercuts the fear he might otherwise inspire among his biological companions. Unlike Spock, who often held humans in overt disdain, Data admires human culture and psychology, seeks coaching from humans to emulate them better, and works diligently at such human tasks as painting, drama, intimate relationships, and even dreaming.

The second point of difference has to do with culture. Spock stands between two cultures, with a foot in each, but Data has no such cultural ground at all. On one level, Spock's belonging is always also a renunciation, an awareness that he both belongs and does not on either of his worlds, while Data's entry into the Federation or Starfleet costs him no membership elsewhere. Quite the contrary, it constitutes the ground of possibility for such membership. Spock is a cultural being, albeit one at sea as to which culture he may belong to. Data by contrast is acultural, without any intrinsic social ties. Had he been created by the Klingons, say, or the Romulans, his functioning and adaptation to their cultures might have been equally smooth.

In that sense, we may view Data as generally representing the positive side of the prospect of the fusion of humans with their technology, of the emergence of a humanity from within the machine. As we have seen with Spock, there is also a dark, shadow side: Data as Frankenstein's (or in this case, Noonien Soong's) monster, an unholy amalgam of the biological and the mechanical that may turn on and threaten its creators from a position of superior power. While Data is without kindred creatures or culture in which to seek membership, he does have one "relative." A dark side of science and of the draw of kinship appears when Data's disassembled "brother" android, Lore, is discovered. Lore understands and masters those very elements which Data cannot—humor, human emotions, and indeed the dark human conditions of jealousy and duplicity. But Lore's understanding also incorporates an attitude of essential hostility toward his biological creators. Data is powerfully motivated by fellowship with Lore, and tempted by the promise of his more human understanding, but the hostility ultimately leads Data to oppose him. He must then find his own more solitary road to an enhanced humanity.

The Borg. This dark, monstrous side finds a far more compelling representation in the Borg, a race of beings who, having fused the biological and mechanical into a single novel life form, relentlessly pursue their centralized directive to assimilate all other cultures they encounter to their own use. In the words of a character who knows them well, they are the ultimate users, seeking with dispassionate efficiency to convert the raw materials of other beings and their technology into something they can utilize. What appear to be individual members of the Borg collective are biological individuals adapted to be profoundly interconnected working parts. Whether they are born aboard Borg ships or assimilated from other cultures, their personal identities become subsumed to the service of the whole as thoroughly as component parts to a larger mechanism. The Borg qualify for inclusion here as "resident aliens" not only because of their (temporary) assimilation of the *Enterprise* captain, Picard, and subsequent episodes in which individual Borg are brought aboard to become better known, but also because of what they represent, for the Federation and ourselves.

In the description above, it is not too much of a stretch to see the Borg as an Anti-Federation. Where the Federation's outward exploratory urge to "seek out new life and new civilizations" is constrained by the Prime Directive, which curbs such appetites in the interest of the autonomous evolution of individual cultures, the Borg present the shadowy alternative. In terms of our own time, they may be seen as representation of our own far less constrained consumer culture. In contrast to our proclaimed goals and values, we are also "consumer units," "ultimate users" within an inhuman assimilating world order which views the earth itself and all the beings and cultures on it as mere raw material for its own relentless purposes. No more than the individual Borg are we genuinely able to step outside the culture into which we are increasingly wired, or seriously consider checking its primary assumptions or operating principles. No more than they do we tend to question the ends which this relentless assimilative process is supposed to serve—even when the victims of this process are not only the diversity and identity of other peoples, but our own as well. Is it any wonder that the Borg have risen, within the *Star Trek* mythos to the status of arch-villains? In the words of a Pogo cartoon (Walt Kelly) from the 1950s, "We have met the enemy and he is us."

The Klingons and Worf. The enemy that is most fully and successfully met from the original series are the Klingons, and they thus stand as the most notable example in *TNG* of an interaction with the alien which changes but does not destroy the culture so encountered, or even diminish their own essentially alien character. *TNG* begins in a period when the Federation and Klingons, the direst of enemies in *ST*, have reached an accord and signed a treaty ending hostilities between the two cultures. Cultural exchanges and a degree of mutual appreciation are beginning to emerge. But each still carries much that is abhorrently shadowy for the other. Federation culture seems weak, soft, decadent, dangerously unrealistic, and essentially lacking in savor or spice to most Klingons, while the warlike Klingons remind us of our own propensities to violence and cruelty, our historic thirst for glory and conquest. It is only through our aquaintence with Worf, the first Klingon to serve in Starfleet, that we can begin to see this alien, feared culture from within.

Like Spock, Worf stands between worlds, less than fully a member in either and seen as alien by both sides, but for that reason, he is able to mediate between and synthesize the two. He esteems (though critically) his incompletely known birth culture, and carries its savagery and martial character overtly. Nonetheless, he is the one entrusted with the role of Chief Security Officer aboard the *Enterprise*. There is a wisdom Jungians would recognize in this appointment: that there is more security in finding a place and a role for what one fears than in efforts to repress or exclude it. As with Spock, Worf does not fit seamlessly into human culture either. He does not fully understand the social or emotional realities of his shipmates, their tastes or their humor, and takes a degree of pride in his capacity to stand apart from them. But where with Spock we see reflected our culture's fantasies of the alien character and esoteric disciplines of science and the mind, with Worf we see the equally alien character and esoteric diciplines of the warrior—a similarly familiar, yet alien character. Under his starfleet uniform we feel his (and by extension, our own) struggle to maintain the standards of conduct within a culture that has set some unsettlingly alien restrictions on our wildness and through him feel the pull of the blood against the rational elements of our cultural identity.

Worf's life is an ongoing pursuit of a difficult, dynamic balance, perpetuated by an allegience to a fundamental discipline. What maintains the balance for Spock is Logic, a language we understand—but would not use like *that*! For Worf it is Honor, again a language we speak, though not as relentlessly he does. Spock and Worf show us the frightening, unhuman depths that such seemingly common and definitely human standards may have, and in so doing they show us how much we define our humanity not *by* but *in contrast to* such standards. The measure of the human seems, in this light, to be a hard-to-formalize mix of rigor and principled slovenliness in regard to such principles as logic and honor. And yet Spock and Worf and Data too, also show us the possibilities for an expanded sense of humanity that we may gain by understanding how these aliens manage to reside among us and be (in part) understood.

Alien Experience for Our Times

The developing *Star Trek* mythos beyond *TNG* offers us some tantalizing glimpses of alien elements now among us. In the setting for the later *Star Trek* series, both *Star Trek: Deep Space 9* (henceforth *DS9*) and *Star Trek: Voyager* (*STV*) we do not find ourselves exploring the alien unknown or patrolling the frontier with the the distrusted "other" but, in these times of deep change, living in the aliens' place, on *their* turf. With *DS9* we are no longer roving the galaxy on a cutting-edge starship but occupying someone else's recycled space station, beyond the edge of the Federation itself but near the only known stable "wormhole"—a fixed but unpredictable portal to unknown and unexplored parts of the galaxy. Now, we need not go journeying in search of the alien: *we* are the aliens residing among *them* and, as we cross into the new millennium, the yet-more-unknown lies just beyond the threshold, and may come barreling down on us unexpectedly. In *DS9*, the Federation, paralleling the American geopolitical realities in the late 1990s, no longer finds itself playing Cold-War-style brinksmanship with an Evil Empire (Klingons or Romulans, as in *ST* or *TNG*), but rather, facing a far more balkanized and polycentric galaxy. Fundamentally unsure of its role, its place, or its interests, it stands between the receding Cardassian occupiers and the world of Bajor, attempting to be the guarantor of peace, commercial prosperity, and open access to the wormhole. It is a long, long way from home. In *STV*, the *Voyager* is even further from home, completely lost in the realm of the alien, where indeed no one (human) has gone before. Rather than seeking new frontiers, all its efforts are bent on returning to familiar ones, finding a way home—though no one necessarily expects to make it back within his or her lifetime. In both cases the setting itself is the most fundamentally alien element and suggests how much more alienated we are from a sense of home or our more familiar roles than was true in the earlier series.

The end of our own Cold War and the presumed triumph of the Western democracies has given us a new world order, whose dubious glories include a sanctification of capitalism unprecedented since the robber barons of the late nineteenth century. In a cultural milieu of free market, free-fire zones, where no target of opportunity goes unexploited for long and where merchant princes like Donald Trump, Ted Turner, and Ivan Boesky emerge as the nobility, it is perhaps inevitable that the Ferengi would be created. A race whose culture *is* "the art of the deal," the Ferengi first appeared in *TNG*, but it was only with *DS9* and the appearance of Quark that a personal relationship with an individual Ferengi occurred, allowing us (as Worf allowed us with the Klingons) to lift the veil a bit and see both culture and individual as familiarly alien.

Part of Quark's appeal is the lifting of a repression around what is the most conflicted, erotically charged, and taboo element of contemporary American life: not sex—but money! What startles us about Quark's pursuit of profits is that it is carried out without a trace of the lingering guilt or need to justify that marks our own economic activities. Quite the contrary, the Ferengi Rules of Acquisition constitute an all but biblical sanctification of the profit motive and the virtues of stealthy dealings. As we watch him wheel and deal, a trickster figure in touch with the underworld, running a legalized gambling establishment and a less visible black market, we not only see more clearly all our own ambivalent hedging about money and greed. And we also become a bit more aware of the archetypal and hence inescapable nature of such. Though the Federation may have transcended the threat of poverty which still drives most humans to work, it does not get us beyond those still playing the game of Mammon, that greedy pursuit of wealth.

It seems apt to close by examining the character of Odo, the security chief aboard *DS9's* space station. With Spock we see the alien presence within science, logic, and the mind's depths. With Data, we see the alien possibilities of artificial life and intelligence. With Worf it is the shadow of the warrior, with Quark, the shadow of capitalism and with the Borg, the shadow of the culture of consumption. But with Odo we find ourselves facing the daunting prospect of the formless, that which may take any form at all and which in its native state has no form of its own. Our other aliens show us the possibility of losing the original form of our life or nature as we live among people who have different forms or natures. The character of Odo causes us to confront the possibility that we may have no original, genuine form, that we may be as shifting and protean as polystyrene—not an insignificant concern for us as inhabitants of an increasingly rootless, shapeless, and ahistorical postmodern culture.

Similarly, Odo also occupies an extreme position in terms of being cultureless. Spock and Worf fall between two cultures, as does Quark, though to a lesser extent. The Borg remake all cultures into their own and are thus always on familiar ground. Even Data has a notion about his creator and his sibling. But Odo begins the series without any awareness of whether he even *has* a culture; he may be some unique singularity. Again, for those of us increasingly exposed to the ambiguity of cultural or subcultural membership and of where, if anywhere, we belong, Odo seems a potent symbol of a profound loss of a sense of belonging.

As with our other aliens, Odo survives this double loss of grounding by making a cultural home through an extreme and even fundamentalistic allegiance to a discipline which can give his life an enduring shape or structure, in his case, justice and the law. As with Worf, he is that alien presence to whom security is entrusted, and he becomes ironically the most trusted being on the station, the most ruthless seeker of the truth and opposer of lawlessness (which, naturally, puts him in constant conflict with Quark's capitalistic eye for profits). The irony deepens as the series continues, for Odo comes to find his native shape-shifting race and to find that they pose the greatest threat to the security and well-being of his adopted home. Ultimately he turns against this long-sought reunion with his native people to cast his lot with those for whom he has so long been the most alien of aliens.

If there is a consolation for our own Odo-esque loss of cultural ground and personal form it may be in just this—that the once foreign ground of our alienation may yet become a new home. As countless generations of immigrants know, while you can't really go home again, you can make your home in the strangest places—*if* you can harness the ability to find a kinship with those strange folks next door.

24
Holy Madness at Heaven's Gate

MARITA DIGNEY

> *In the threatening situation of the world today, when people are beginning to
> see that everything is at stake, the projection-creating fantasy soars beyond the
> realm of earthly organizations and powers into the heavens, into interstellar
> space, where the rulers of human fate, the gods, once had their abode in the
> planets."*
>
> —*C.G. Jung,* Civilization

One of the most overused words in the popular culture is "archetype."
All manner of ordinary human experience has suddenly become "archetypal," the current version of the eternally sought elixir of life. Everything
from a workshop on drumming to a simple camping trip has become an
"archetypal experience." Books on the soul and the gods and goddesses
within abound. Such works can suggest to the naive that one can somehow contact archetypal energies and then live a fuller, happier life. Presto!
Along with this preoccupation with the archetypal realm comes an overvaluing of the "unconscious," although both are often vaguely defined.
Those who know realize that the experience of touching archetypal energies is always life-changing and, not infrequently, life-threatening. The religiously motivated suicide by the members of the Heaven's Gate
community during Holy Week 1997 provided an illustration of the mesmerizing power of an archetype that came to possess a small community
of Americans. Their obsession is not new. It has stirred the soul of our
species for millennia.

All archetypes pull to consciousness feelings best described as "numinous"; they inspire awe, a sense of the holy. This proliferation of the use
of the word "archetype" stems from a misunderstanding of the work of the
Swiss psychiatrist C. G. Jung. The work of Jung is presently in vogue with
a culture starved for inner experience because this is what provides meaning in life. Our culture and our lives are saturated with sensory overload
in the form of images impinging on us from the outside. Most of these

315

images arrive at our sensory receptors via technology. This abundance can both inhibit and enrich the capacity to relate to the images that speak to us in some vital way. There is a mysterious connection between experiencing the sensory world and our ability to apprehend the richness of symbolic images. Direct experience, including human interaction, is essential to a full encounter with the symbolic. Consider the difference between watching a child being hugged, even on the big screen, and hugging a child. Imagine the difference between an encounter with an angel in a TV program compared to an inspiring personal event like receiving an unexpected call from a friend when you are in a moment of despair.

Jung included the spiritual dimension as a legitimate aspect of the psyche when most psychologies labeled any religious feeling a "crutch" or a neurotic symptom. He spoke thoughtfully about the multidimensionality of the human personality. Devoting his entire professional life to helping people reconnect with vital, ancestral images and deepen their own experience of life, he dismissed the modern prejudice that we are different from our ancestors. He insisted that as humans we are a part of our species's history and not newly formed with each birth.

Jung had the courage to take the soul seriously and to value the imaginative, myth-making aspect of the mind as a legitimate resource of the person to make sense of the world. He included in his structure of the psyche an ego complex, the center of waking consciousness, or more simply, the part of us which does business with the world. The ego answers to our name and has a sense of continuity in life. In Jungian psychology, often called Analytical Psychology, the ego does not imply egotism; rather it is a very good thing indeed to have developed a healthy, well-functioning ego. The ego represents our sense of capacity and is related to the "-able" words: capable, reliable, and knowledgeable.

The everyday ego consciousness does not explain the totality of our capacities as human beings. Another aspect of mental life is apparent in human behavior. Part of us dreams, part of us forgets and remembers in unexpected patterns, and part of us creates. These qualities do not seem to be under the control of the ego. Rather, the ego either cooperates with or resists them. They come from a source unknown, in Jungian terms, from the aspect of the psyche called "the unconscious." Jung saw the unconscious as profoundly meaningful. Valuable life energies can be trapped away, out of contact with ego consciousness, and cause mental dysfunction. Ego consciousness that is too strong or rigid defends against the deeper meaning of life, in both its positive and negative aspects, and prevents the personality from living in a way that is truly full.

Like Jung, students preparing to be analysts still study world mythologies, religion, art history, and ethnology as well as psychology, psychiatry, and psychopathology. Dreams and the imaginative life of contemporary men and women continue to speak in ancient symbols, in a language that we have forgotten on a conscious level. This symbolic language is rooted in patterns of human existence which are present wherever humans live and form community. Jung called these patterns "archetypes," borrowing the word from Plato. He describes archetypes as shared impersonal and enormously powerful archaic impulses in the psyche around which human behavior forms. "From the unconscious there emanates determining influences which, independently of tradition, guarantee in every single individual a similarity and even a sameness of experience, and also of the way it is represented imaginatively. One of the main proofs of this is the almost universal parallelism between mythological motifs, which, on account of their quality as primordial images, I have called *archetypes*" (*Archetypes*, par. 118). Typical archetypal patterns are mother, father, hero, and child. Large archetypal patterns gather around the concept of masculine and feminine. All archetypes have positive and negative, spiritual and mundane polarities.

To be seized by an archetype, that is, to have the ego taken over by these archetypal energies, can both heighten and severely limit the range of human experience. The energy released is beyond the realm of the everyday. Hitler was seized by the negative aspect of an archetype, as was his nation. Joan of Arc was seized by an archetype as are all saints and mystics, both East and West. Olympus, the realm of the gods and goddesses of ancient Greece, was created through the imagination of the human psyche to reflect the power of the archetypes. To be visited by a god or goddess was to have ordinary human experience shift to an archetypal, extra-mundane level. In more everyday terms, the woman who must mother every person and thing which enters her life is trapped in the archetype. So is the man who works, even slaves, to provide for his family and neglects his own emotional and social development. For both, one trapped in the mother and one in the father, there is a terrible comedown when the archetypal task is completed and they are left as psychological shells, rather than fully developed persons.

For many of us the adventure of falling madly in love is the nearest we come to a deeply archetypal experience. The kind of love where the other is so important to our existence that we somehow only truly live in their presence represents a projection of the archetype of the masculine or feminine onto the beloved. Another powerfully archetypal experience is generally described as religious conversion. In religious conversion, it is the archetype of the Self that touches or at times overwhelms the ego. Of this experience, Jung writes, "The Self as an archetype represents a numinous wholeness which can only be expressed by symbols. . . . The realization of the self is nearly always connected with the feeling of timelessness, 'eternity' or immortality" (*Symbolic Life*, par. 1567). In the East, someone who has had this experience is described as a "God intoxicant"; a similar Christian term is "a fool for Christ." The archetype of the Self is a concept identified by Jung which indicates the true center of our being, including both the conscious and unconscious.

Once Jung used the metaphor of a circle, describing the Self as both the center and the circumference. At times, he defined the Self as simply the God within. Encounter with the Self moves the ego from concerns primarily with the everyday world into a love and desire to care for the universal. Personal tasks give way to soul work. Sometimes, this concern for the transcendent can undervalue the ego and the physical body. Saint Francis often called his body "Brother Ass" and subjected himself to extreme physical mortification. Later in his life he saw self-negation as a mistake. Well into this century, until contemporary reforms became effective, some Catholic religious orders encouraged self-flagellation.

Religion has traditionally helped us understand, even experience, an encounter with the Divine from which all else in life flows. The speech which religions have used to express the language of the soul has been primarily symbolic. A startling example of ancient religious impulses finding expression in new symbols was vividly demonstrated in the Holy Week mass suicide carried out by the Heaven's Gate cult members. *In all forms of religious fanaticism, the symbolic is mistaken for the literal.* Put another way, truths expressed poetically and metaphorically are taken as objective reality. The religious urge is, to be sure, real. We are, however, as a culture, in a dramatic shift of symbolic consciousness.

Theologians currently speak of a "post-Auschwitz New Age" of questioning religious authority and of understanding religious symbolism. The capacity of Christianity to contain the archetypal projections of the believers has dramatically lessened. And a battle rages between scholars who call for inclusion of recent biblical discoveries necessary for a revival of authentic Christianity and the orthodox, who cling to their unquestioned beliefs. Meanwhile, phenomena like the Heaven's Gate suicide and the upsurge of new cults and religious communities are born to contain the unfilled religious needs of many. During much of the media coverage of the Heaven's Gate story, the group was vilified as an example of a dangerous religious cult. The real question is far more complex. Is the behavior of this group the result of a dangerous cult or of a dangerous cultural situation in which we find ourselves?

There was nothing new in much of the religious behavior of the Heaven's Gate cult, which was nonetheless widely labeled as "bizarre" by the media. We know religiously motivated suicide through the actions of the Jews at Masada and the Druids at Anglesea fleeing Roman domination. Some scholars question the motivation of martyrs who sought a better life in the next world as a release from this one. In Hinduism, *Sati*, the suicide of the widow on the pyre of the husband, was expected for centuries. In Stone Age religions like the one practiced by the Celts, voluntarily offering oneself for human sacrifice through a system of choosing lots has been documented. Buddhism like Christianity condemns suicide, but there are examples of self-immolation based on religious principles performed by

Buddhist monks. The Zen Buddhist tradition regards *hara-kiri*, or self-disembowelment, a form of honorable death.[1]

Several of the men in the Heaven's Gate group had been castrated. That, too, is an old religious practice belonging to the category of ritual mutilation. Ancient priesthood often required castration; sporadic cases of priestly castration have been reported in Brahmanic India and in Nepal and Tibet. Doctrines of sexual abstinence are strong in the Christian tradition and according to some writers, the Greek father Origen and other ecclesiastic authorities castrated themselves in order to extinguish definitively any desire for sexual intercourse (Eliade 111). So widespread was the practice in early Christianity that it was condemned by the Council of Nicaea (325 A.D.) and in a bull of Pope Leo I (395 A.D.) (Eliade 111).

The rejection of the world was also obvious in the shaven heads, communal living, and simple dress of the Heaven's Gate members. These marks have been the sign of the renunciant since humans have formed religions. Druid priests wore white. Druid priestesses wore black. Saffron robes, the dress of the Buddhist monk, are recognized around the world. Franciscan friars and nuns still wear the dress of their founder, a beggar's cloak fastened by a piece of rope. Renunciation has often been the object of ridicule by the materially minded and the reaction to the Heaven's Gate choices illustrates that our times are no exception.

In theological language, the Heaven's Gate cult was an apocalyptic community. Many of the early Christian communities were apocalyptic, although Jesus, of course, was not. The most well-known example of apocalyptic literature is the Book of Revelation, which was composed about one hundred years after the death of Jesus and is the final book in the biblical cannon. The author of the Book of Revelation and the members of the Heaven's Gate cult expected an imminent end of the world. It is speculated that this religious belief emerges out of a rejection of the injustices and confusion in this world and a desire for a more peaceful and heavenly existence.

Psychologically, apocalyptic thinking may represent a projection of the phenomenon known religiously as "death of ego." In other words, the individual feels his or her own ego attitudes and desires slipping away as the Self and its universal consciousness predominates in their psychology. The person then projects this experience outward onto the whole world. Therefore, what is a legitimate religious experience for the individual becomes concretized and is seen as an outward rather than an inward experience. Truly, for "God Intoxicants," life as they have known it is ending. Also, the power of the experience of the Self does transform the personality and insight sharpens regarding the foibles of the prevailing ethos,

---

[1] However, the often-cited Jonestown cult suicide has been documented by survivors as, in reality, a forced suicide and massacre of those who did not conform; it is not really an example of religiously motivated suicide, as is often thought.

which is always in radical flux. This does not, however, constitute verifiable proof of the end of life on this planet. In this situation, the literal version of the belief is ridiculous. However, parallel realities exist here. On the one hand is the individual psychological experience and on the other hand the outer world. Apocalyptic communities, at least up to the present, have been mistaken about the world ending; and they have been correct about the power of religious experience on the psychology of participants.

What has produced the most widespread ridicule of the Heaven's Gate cult members is their stated belief that a flying saucer was hiding behind the Hale-Bopp comet. This extraterrestrial vessel represented another level of soul evolution which was coming for them. Suicide was their commitment to join this otherworldly higher consciousness expressed in the form of the flying saucer. They died in homemade uniforms with the slogan "Away Team" embroidered on their shirts and Nikes on their feet. Perhaps they allowed Nike, the ancient Greek goddess of Victory, to proclaim their suicide as triumph. Interesting, their choice of Nike, as she was the daughter of Styx, and thus associated with the river in the Underworld, the abode of the deceased.

It is not an exaggeration to say that the image of the flying saucer had become for them a religious symbol. Like their belief in the end of the world, they made this symbol of an inner reality literal. Again the paradox of the parallel reality, since as individuals and as a community they had accessed an attitude and a freedom which was higher than ego consciousness. Yet the symbol of this "higher state" was not physically coming to this planet for them. Their mistake, if there was one, was to believe in the literal interpretation of a perfectly good metaphor. Their identification with their own souls, one might say with the Christ within, was so complete that they were living out in an ultimate concretization the mysteries of Holy Week. They literalized the resurrection and bet their lives on their belief.

Many traditional religions foster this kind of literalism. The interpretation of the virgin birth as literal truth is one such example. As a metaphor hinting at the relationship of the soul to the Divine, this concept has exquisite accuracy. To the spiritually blind ego, the archeytpal energies of the psyche can be experienced as the visitation of the Divine Other. However, this is an issue of parallel realities as it is difficult to believe in the virgin birth on a physical level. Such dogmatic statements that concretize the metaphoric reduce religious truth to the level of shared delusions and belie the profound wisdom preserved in the sacred texts. As a system of thought and inspiration, for instance, the folksy metaphors and "Good News" of Jesus Christ actually speak of the universality of access of humans to the Divine.

For years the literary genre of science fiction has idealized space and space travel. Much of human longing for a better world has been projected onto the heavens and the emerging ability to actually navigate space. The archetype of the hero has shifted from earthly war to Star Wars. The Starship *Enterprise* in the widely popular *Star Trek* series sailed in the service of an ethically superior egalitarian culture, the Federation. Luke Skywalker carries the image of the Christ. He redeemed his culture and his father, who in this new myth, was a Satanlike figure. The unmistakably religious themes of many of the blockbuster science fiction movies cry out the spiritual needs of the era. Like psalmists, Roddenberry, Spielberg, and Lucas speak of the unfilled messianic needs of lonely people. ET may turn out to be the prophet of our age, announcing the alien as savior, recognized best by children and delivered by technology. The "post Auschwitz" religions, both traditional and contemporary, have lost their ability to contain the archetypal projections of the human psyche, but for millions, space adventure has "beamed them up." That is to say that many have become captivated by the possibility of a higher consciousness primarily through these films. If science as savior has become the myth of our era, science fiction is the sacred text.

Writing in 1958, C.G. Jung suggested that the worldwide phenomenon of flying saucer reports indicated that a projection of the Self, the central organizing principle of the psyche, was being experienced in these sightings. Of the UFO phenomenon he writes, "they have become a living myth. We have here a golden opportunity of seeing how a legend is formed, and how in a difficult and dark time for humanity a miraculous tale grows up of an attempted intervention by extra-terrestrial 'heavenly' powers" (*Civilization*, par. 614). Further, the roundness of these objects in the sky caused Jung to relate them to other symbols of God and the totality of existence, which have been created in many epochs. He likened the UFOs to mandalas, the sacred circles of Hinduism, and the Tibetan Buddhist intricate drawings, which represent the totality of the physical, cosmic, and psychological planes. Other healing mandalalike forms are found in Native American sand paintings, the rose windows of medieval cathedrals, the roundness of the monstrance and the host of Catholicism, and the spirals prevalent at Celtic religious cites. Jung had observed in the dreams of his patients for over forty years that dreams produced mandalic round objects to help unify the personality during periods of outer confusion and stress.

Likewise, he viewed the widespread sightings of UFOs as indicators of the cultural, political, and environmental stresses of our times. He saw them as spontaneous attempts by the psyche to heal the psychic split in the rational world view that had consistently created significant disasters in the twentieth century. Jung would have seen the Heaven's Gate cosmology as further proof of his theories. Indeed his speculations of the 1940s and 1950s are eerily reflected in their concretizing of the newly emerging religious symbols of the UFO and space travel.

Jung wrote that the consciousness of our age had been split by political, social, philosophical, and religious conflicts of unprecedented proportions. When such tremendous opposites split apart, he said,

> we may expect with certainty that the need for a savior will make itself felt. . . . Between the opposites there arises spontaneously a symbol of unity and wholeness, no matter whether it reaches consciousness or not. Should something extraordinary or impressive then occur in the outside world, be it a human personality, a thing, or an idea, the unconscious content can project itself upon it, thereby investing the projection carrier with numinous and mythical powers. The impetus for the manifestation of the latent psychic contents was given by the UFO. (*Civilization,* par. 784)

The members of the Heaven's Gate religious community were seized by an archetype. Through their considerable religious practices, which included celibacy, ritual mutilation, itinerancy, begging, fasting, studying, communal living, shared resources, and meditation, they heightened their identification with their souls and appear to have subdued the ego. In fact, they identified so strongly with their souls that they negated their own bodies. In a Gnostic split of body and soul they saw their bodies as simply "containers" to be discarded rather than valuing the body as an active participant in transformation. In the process, they became overwhelmed with archetypal images of the Self. They found no religious home in the wider culture to mediate their experiences, therefore they created their own religion, cosmology, and eschatology. There was no fault in their belief that they were truly spiritual beings and that the potential for divinity dwelled in each of them. Most world religions teach the same. In addition, their use of popular metaphors is a hallmark of the spiritual seeker attempting to describe the ineffable in terms of the mundane.

The Judeo-Christian scripture uses the poetic images of the rock, the shepherd, the water of life, the light of the world, as well as the father as images of the Divine. Paul of Tarsus used images like the Body of Christ as an image of the Christian community and athletic races as an image of life. Jesus, a great metaphorical thinker, used the ordinary experiences of a peasant culture in his sayings and parables to tell the mysteries of the realm of God. The Heaven's Gate people used the images of space travel, space aliens, and science fiction to express their beliefs, and we have   not heard the last of them. They reflect an archetypal wound in contemporary culture, one which is so deep and so profound that it cannot go unexpressed.

The obvious need for new religions, which the Heaven's Gate group represents, indicates a crisis in our culture that is both spiritual and psychological. Like the canary in the mine, they are a warning to traditional and New Age religion. Although they may initially have been attached to their given names and pre-cult identities and desires, their greatest psychological wound was too little ego, not too much. Their religious experience became, metaphorically, completely ungrounded and they were swept away by the more powerful archetypal energies available to the human personality. With a more developed ego, it is possible they could have held the tension between the natural and the supernatural potentialities in the human personality. They split themselves up into pieces, which were then unconsciously projected out onto aliens, space-ships, and comets. The challenge is rather to hold these psychic contents within and bear the pain and the ecstasy of being human.

Instead, they succumbed to the fateful belief, common in religious thinking, that all good is outside of me. They projected their very soul onto the UFO and died for the need of it. They represent a logical expression of unpsychological fundamentalist religious thinking which vilifies human-ity as possessors of original sin until saved by a God who is other. They went mad for their desire to know their own goodness, and to know it as humans. They, and many in contemporary expressions of religion, betrayed the God within for the God in the sky.

BIBLIOGRAPHY

Adler, Jerry. "Far From Home." *Newsweek* (7 April 1997), 37.

Borg, Marcus, ed. *The Lost Gospel Q*. Berkeley: Ulysses Press, 1996.

Cahill, Thomas. *How The Irish Saved Civilization*. New York: Doubleday, 1995.

Caprio, Betsy. *Star Trek: Good News In Modern Images*. Mission, Kansas: Andrews and McNeel, 1978.

Crossan, John. *The Essential Jesus*. San Francisco: Harper San Francisco, 1994.

Eliade, Mircea, ed. *The Encylopedia of Religion*. New York: MacMillan, 1987.

Funk, Robert. *Honest To Jesus*. San Francisco: Harper San Franscisco, 1996.

Goode, Erica. "The Eternal Quest For A New Age." *U. S. News and World Report* (7 April 1997), 32.

Hedges, Stephen. "www. Masssuicide.com." *U.S. News and World Report* (7 April 1997), 26.

Hastings, James, ed. *Encyclopedia of Religion and Ethics*. New York: Charles Scribner's Sons, 1950.

James, David, ed. *Celtic Connections*. London: Cassell, 1996.

Jung, Carl. *The Collected Works of C.G. Jung*. Eds. H. Read, M. Fordham, G. Adler, W. McGuire. Trans. R.C.F. Hull. London: Routledge, 1953–1979.

———. *The Archetypes and The Collective Unconscious*. Vol. 9i. 2nd ed. London: Routledge, 1959.

———. *Civilization In Transition*. Vol 10. 2nd ed. London: Routledge, 1964.

———. *The Symbolic Life*. Vol. 18. London: Routledge, 1976.

Stolen, Tim. "The Most Horrible Night of My Life." *Newsweek* (7 April 1997), 44.

Underhill, Evelyn. *Practical Mysticism*. Columbus: Ariel Press, 1914.

Woodward, Kenneth. "Christ and Comets." *Newsweek* (7 April 1997), 40.

Index

psychoanalysis, beginning of,
220–21
Psychologists for Social
Responsibility, 244
Pulp Fiction, 4, 8, 11, 154–57,
158–66
and alchemical processes, 158,
162
cynical characters in, 155, 156,
159, 163
as Genesis story, 157
good and evil in, 160, 164, 165
individuation in, 160–61, 162
mythical elements in, 158,
159–60, 166
the numinous in, 161
opposites in, 158, 164–65, 166
on patriarchal forms, 157
political symbolism in, 155–56
post-heroic perspective of, 156
redemption in, 158, 160, 162,
165
religious/spiritual experience
in, 154–55, 159, 161
as satire of violence, 155
shadow elements in, 158–59,
160, 162, 163, 164
Pygmalion, 112, 115

Q

Queen Elizabeth I, 144
Quetzalcoatl, 32, 44

R

Rambo, 97
Rand Corporation, 277
Reagan, President Ronald, 155
Rehnquist, Justice William, 263
religious practice and symbolism,
318–19
Rembrandt, 259
Return of the Jedi, 298
Rhames, Ving, 156

Rhea, 118–19, 121
Rice, Anne
The Witching Hour, 171–72,
177, 178–79
Risky Business, 112, 115
Robotech, 81
Rocky Horror Picture Show, 107
Roddenberry, Gene, 321
Rogers, Buck, 7
Romanyshyn, Robert, 166
Roosevelt, Franklin, 242
The Rose, 46
Rosencreutz
Chymical Wedding, 163
Rosie the Riveter, 7

S

sacrificial victim, sacrifice, 19, 43
(*see also* Presley: as sacri-
ficial victim)
prerequisites for, 25, 26–30
in stylized form, 33
Sacrificial Victim Conditions Scale,
26–29, 30
applicability of, 34–35
Sailor Moon, 79
Saint Francis, 318
Sakai, Stan, 81
saman, 46
Samuels, Andrew, 2, 13
on the plural psyche, 280–86,
287
Sandman, 82
Saturday Night Fever, 156
Schaef, Ann Wilson, 237
Co-Dependence:
Misunderstood—
Mistreated, 232
Scheherazade, 129
science, and myth, 183
science fiction, spiritual longing
in, 320–21
Second World War, 242, 243
Sexton, Anne, 45

shadow energy (*see also* Jung: on
    the shadow; the vampire:
    as shadow figure)
    cultural, 174, 175
Shakespeare, William, 117, 150,
    257
Shelley, Mary, 186–87
    Frankenstein, 183, 185, 186–88,
    190–91
Shelley, Percy, 186–87
    Prometheus Unbound, 186
Shepard, Sam, 200
shin jinrui, 74
The Silence of the Lambs, 4, 8, 9,
    51–66 (*see also* Lecter,
    Hannibal; Starling,
    Clarice)
    on American society, 59–60
    feminine principle in, 59, 63
    male symbolism in, 52–53
    and the masculine/feminine
    schism, 64, 66
    patriarchal motifs in, 55–56,
    62–63
    and prejudice against the femi-
    nine, 53, 60
    on women's experience, 53
"The Simpson Case," archetypal
    symbols in, 85–86
Simpson, Nicole Brown, 84, 92
Simpson, Orenthal James (O. J.),
    6, 9
    and Hercules, similarities
    between, 85, 86–92
    news coverage of the trial, 84,
    85
Skywalker, Luke, 7, 54, 62, 297–98
    as Christ figure, 321
Snow White, 107
Somé, Malidoma, 264
Sontag, Susan, 195
Spielberg, Steven, 321
Spiner, Brent, 301
Springsteen, Bruce
    Streets of Philadelphia, 195

Stanton, Elizabeth Cady, 60, 61
*Star Blazers (Space Cruiser
    Yamato),* 72, 75–76, 81
Star Trek, 14, 96, 290–303,
    304–14
    the Borg in, 298–99, 310–11
    and the Cold War, 307, 313
    cyborgs in, 298–99
    Data in, 301–2, 309–10
    human-machine interface in,
    296–97
    humanization of machine in,
    301–2
    and interaction with the alien
    "other," 291, 304–14
    Klingons in, 311–12
    as modern myth, 290, 293,
    304
    Odo in, 314
    Quark in, 313–14
    sentient machines in, 294,
    301–2
    Spock in, 307–9
    techno-mythology in, 293–94
Star Wars, 65, 107, 293, 297
Starling, Clarice, 8, 9
    emotionality of, 52, 59, 61
    feminine ethics of, 52–53, 55,
    61–62, 65–66
    heroine's journey of, 61, 65
    interaction of, with Hannibal
    Lecter¨ 56–58¨ 61–66
    inward movement of, 61, 65
    as a new female heroine, 52,
    54, 57, 61, 63, 64, 66
    self-development of, 61
    and submersion, 58, 64
    self-development of, 61
    working with the demonic, 57,
    58, 61–62, 65, 66
Steffens, Lincoln
    *The Autobiography of Lincoln
    Steffens,* 247
Stoker, Bram, 174
Stone, Sharon, 111

storytelling among Cree Indians
131 (*see also* Keillor,
Garrison: storytelling of)
Sullivan, Barbara Stevens, 54, 59
*Psychotherapy Grounded in the
Feminine Principle,* 54–55
Superman, 68
Superman II, 69
Sykes, Charles
A Nation of Victims, 102

T

Tally, Ted, 51, 56
Tannen, Deborah, 99
Tarantino, Quentin, 154, 156, 157,
158, 164
Taxi Driver, 154
Teasdale, Sara, 45
Terminator, 293, 295
Terminator 2: Judgment Day,
299–300
Thelma and Louise, 4, 113–15,
116, 121
Theseus, 290
Third Rock from the Sun, 304
Thurman, Uma, 156
the Titans, 119, 122
Travolta, John, 154, 156
Triton, 119
Trump, Donald, 313
Tsati, 153
Turkle, Sherry
*Life on the Screen: Identity in
the Age of the Internet,*
280
Turner, Ted, 313
2001: A Space Odyssey, 293, 295,
296
Tyrrell, William Blake, 292, 294

U

the unconscious, 4–5
collective, 2, 85, 108, 265
cultural, 5, 108

personal, 108
and rationality, 5
Upstairs Downstairs, 117

V

Vader, Darth, 297–98, 302
the vampire, 6, 11 (*see also*
Dracula)
and addictions, comparison
between, 172
as archetypal, 168, 169, 176,
177
and consumerism and materialism, 169, 172
and economic vampirism, 171,
176
and eroticism, 170, 172, 173,
174
and fusion, 174, 175, 177
female versions of, 173
and gender-role stereotypes,
173
and incest, 177
and intrapsychical conflict, acting out of, 176
motifs of, 173
as oral/infantile stage of development, 173–74
and the "other,"
fear of, 174, 175, 176
as object, 169
and passive submission, 172,
174
and power
abuse of, 171, 173, 176, 177
national, 169, 170, 171, 175,
176
and predator/victim roles, 168,
169–70, 171, 172, 175, 176
and primitive consciousness,
175
and redemption, 169
and "return of the repressed,"
170